Baseball
in the
Bay State

Baseball in the Bay State

KEVIN LARKIN

Baseball in the Bay State

Cover Design and Book Design by Cory Freeman

Printed in the United States of America
The Troy Book Makers • Troy, New York • thetroybookmakers.com

To order additional copies of this title, contact your favorite local bookstore or visit www.tbmbooks.com

ISBN: 978-1-61468-2233

Contents

Thank You

....

I know if I try to write something about every person that has helped me along the way I will leave someone out and hurt their feelings. So that being said there are a few people here that I do want to thank because they have had such a positive influence on me I would be remiss if I did not tell them how I feel about them.

First I would like to thank Doreen Hutchinson who is the vice president of Fairview Hospital. I had asked her to proof read a project for me whenever she had the time. She said she would. She kept apologizing to me as she could not seem to get to my project because she was so busy. I assured her it was ok and to not worry, that whenever she had the time it would be appreciated. After a bit she called me into her office and she took time out of her day to give me the guidance I needed. As I was retyping her suggestions I realized that I needed to put that project on the back burner and to turn to this project which is the book you are all reading now. Without her guidance and thoughtfulness I would never have been able to do this, so thanks a million Doreen you are the best.

Next there are two people who I am proud to call my friends. Both ladies are coworkers and the first one I have known for longer than either of us care to remember. It seems that every day I am bugging her about issues with my computer and how to set this project up and she has been the best person I could ask as she never says no. Dee Dee Rintoul you will always have a special place in my heart and I hope you know how much I think of you, I hope we stay friends for a very long time. The second is also a nurse and I have only known her for a short time however she is right at the top of the list when it comes to friends. She and I have had many discussions on baseball and she is a true fan, but she is an even better friend who I care for dearly. So Rita Tassenari you were a tremendous help to me and I really appreciate that and also you are the best nurse supervisor I know.

These next two gentlemen define the word class. Dr. Daniel Patel and Ira Zimbler were a tremendous influence on my life and I owe them so much for getting me thru a particularly tough time in my life. These two men helped me physically and psychologically and I am forever indebted to them.

I had a friend in high school named Julie Blanchard and after we graduated our lives took us in different directions and we just lost touch. Thru the miracle of Facebook and emails Julie and I were able to reconnect which turned out to be very important. Turns out we both ended up in the same profession but took different routes to get there. I had retired and Julie is still working. As we talked and began to catch up on what had gone on in both our lives I told Julie of the personal hell I had been going thru. Considerately and thoughtfully she listened and encouraged me to not keep things buried and to talk to someone. I did and after Julie and I talked, I really felt better about myself and where my life was headed. I promised myself that I would find a way to repay her for her making me realize the grass is really greener on the other side of the hill. Julie B Patton you were and still are one of my closest friends. Thank you for everything.

I would be remiss if I did not thank the people who helped me with putting this book together. My friend Eric Wilska who owns a local store called the Book Loft needs a big thank you as he is the one who first gave me the idea to write this book. Jack Passetto who has been my friend for over 40 years did the editing for me and it was he who I wanted to stump with the trivia challenge in the front of the book so it is him you are to blame. Also before going any further I will admit now to everybody that I did not get the call wrong with you at second base Jack you were out by just a bit sorry, but I cannot tell a lie. Next Derek Gentile who wrote the introduction to this book, Derek I have known you for a while and I am proud to call you a friend. You truly are a first class person and a great newspaper man who I always could trust. Finally my friend Tom Warner who did the cover design for this book, you Tom are a true artist and friend and thanks for doing such a great job. Of course this book would not look like it does without the help of my cousin Tom Roy who was a tremendous help with all the computer work. So I thank you so much "cuz" you are a fantastic talent.

The final two people are my best friends in the world and they are my heroes. Steven and Ashley Larkin whether you know it or not you are the best children and the two best friends anyone could ever want. I am so proud of you both and I hope that someday that like me you two can realize and achieve your dreams.

Preface

....

I guess it may be the fantasy of every boy growing up in America to be a baseball player. I, like everybody else, wanted to win the seventh game of the World Series as a pitcher or hit the walk off home run to win that seventh game. To pitch like Tom Seaver, to hit like Hank Aaron, or to catch like Johnny Bench was all I ever wanted to do growing up in the Berkshires. However, it became quite evident that my fastball could not break a pane of glass, I couldn't hit a curve ball and I could not stand the thought of having to squat for three hours behind home plate, so the history of the game of baseball and its players became my passion.

I started out by studying the backs of the baseball cards I would buy at Harmon's Store or Ted's Smoke Shop. I would memorize the statistics and factoids on the backs of the cards and would set up fantasy games or meet up with friends and flip cards for hours upon hours. As I got older I began to read any magazine article or book on baseball and I can still remember the first time I ever saw "Pride of the Yankees" with Gary Cooper and Teresa Wright. I will admit to you all, that yes, I did cry the first time I saw the movie and still tear up while watching it. Lou Gehrig became my favorite baseball player and I became a baseball junkie, a disease for which there is no cure.

Great Barrington, Massachusetts where I grew up was and still is a great place to live. As a youngster growing up the baseball I knew was "The Impossible Dream Red Sox" of 1967, "The Big Red Machine" Cincinnati Reds of the early to mid-1970's and "The Bronx Zoo" Yankees of the mid 1970's. The more I would read about baseball the more I became fascinated with the game and its early history. Besides Gehrig and Ruth of the Yankees, I loved to read about Ty Cobb, Honus Wagner and Walter Johnson, as these men became my heroes. The older I got, the more I read and of course, school got in the way, so I had to finish that up and get it over with. But as much as I complain about it, my high school years were some of the best years of my life, and I sometimes wish I could go back to those days when all that mattered was the game of baseball. I was not the greatest student in the world, but I always tried to maintain a relationship with my teachers, and to this day I still consider them to be some of my best friends.

The Negro Leagues and its history became my passion and when I started to read of the exploits of players like Satchel Paige and Josh Gibson it made me want to read further into the history to learn about men like Cool Papa Bell, Willie Wells, Oscar Charleston and Joe Rogan. The trials and tribulations that these men went through to play the game of baseball is a story I never get tired of hearing or reading about. After high school I kind of hung around town and did not do a lot of anything other than work and go out on the weekend with my friends. I became a policeman in the town of Great Barrington (Which is a book in itself) got married, and had two wonderful children. The marriage did not work out, and I guess I needed something to keep myself busy when I was not with my children or working. So my old friend baseball started to hang around and I read more and more about the game I am so passionate about. I retired from the police department, then worked at a golf course and the local hospital with baseball at my side. After awhile, I began to think that I wish that there was something that I could give back to baseball after baseball had given me such joy over the years. I began to think back to my high school days and while I wasn't the greatest student I always was fascinated with history and that's when it hit me that I wanted to write a book about baseball. But that presented another dilemma as what would I write about and what could I write that had not already been written about someone like Ruth or Gehrig. I was fortunate that the internet craze was just happening and that opened up a whole new array of baseball stories for me.

I ended up deciding that my book on baseball would be about the history of the sport in Berkshire County where I grew up and knew of players like Mark Belanger, Jack Chesbro and Jeff Reardon, but did not know of players like Frank Grant and others you will read about later in this book. I searched on line and found out there are well over 10,000 books published on baseball. I began to collect those books and as of today have a collection of a little over 400 baseball books on a wide variety of subjects related to the sport I love. I began researching and writing and just when I thought I was finished, I would find another piece of information and it would be back to the drawing board. The more I wrote the more it became apparent that I would need to write this book about baseball as a whole in Massachusetts, so that is what I did. I hope that this book takes you on an enjoyable journey because not for one minute while I was doing this did I ever feel as though it was work. It was the most fun I have had and I thank all of you for deciding to take a ride into Baseball in the Bay State. In fact, I can close by saying I know what my hero Lou Gehrig was feeling when in his speech he said that he "Felt like the luckiest man on the face of the earth," because I feel very lucky to have done this book. Again, thank you all very much.

Introduction

The contributions by Massachusetts to the sport of baseball are well-known. But until now, they haven't really been cataloged in one volume. Kevin Larkin's "Baseball in the Bay State" fixes that.

The book is well-researched, a little playful and more than a little interesting. Larkin has clearly put in a lot of work here, and it shows. (The chapter listing Massachusetts ballplayers town-by-town is worth the price of the book.)

Larkin, a Berkshire County native, gives his home county a few more props, but it's not just gratuitous. When one considers that possibly the first municipal ordinance concerning baseball was drafted here in 1791. the first college baseball game took place here and Wahconah Park, one of the oldest ballparks in the nation was built here, it's easy to see why "Baseball in the Bay State" is enjoyable and a good read, which is the best of both worlds.

Derek Gentile

(Derek Gentile, a reporter and columnist for The Berkshire Eagle, is also the author of nine books about baseball.)

BASEBALL QUIZ

....

1. The timeline with regards to baseball roots says it could be possible that stick and ball game were played as early as 2000 BC. True/False

2. The designated hitter rule was proposed as far back as 1928 in an effort to speed up the game. True/False

3. What two events happened in baseball history on April 23, 1923?

4. In the early years of baseball the batter could tell the pitcher where to throw the ball. True/False

5. What was the name of the first team to play at Wahconah Park in 1894?

6. Name the two Berkshire County born baseball players that are enshrined in the Baseball Hall of Fame in Cooperstown, New York.

7. Mark Belanger held the career scoring record for basketball at Pittsfield High School for almost 50 years. True/False

8. Name the only player enshrined in the Baseball Hall of Fame who played on a team that was based at Wahconah Park in Pittsfield.

9. Name the pitchers who played for a team based out of Wahconah Park who went on to the major leagues and pitched a perfect game and a no hitter.

10. Massachusetts ranks in the bottom 25 states with regards to the number of major league baseball players born in the state. True/False

11. Name the six baseball parks in Boston that have hosted a major league baseball team.

12. Name the other baseball park in Pittsfield to host minor league baseball.

13. The first ever perfect game in the history of major league baseball was pitched in Worcester, Massachusetts at the Driving Park at the Fairgrounds on June 12, 1880. Who was the pitcher who threw that ballgame?

14. All of the following Hall of Fame enshrines were born in the state of Massachusetts except whom? A). Wilbert Robinson B). Tommy McCarthy C). Mickey Cochrane D). Carlton Fisk E). John Clarkson

15. Who was the first player to play in the Cape Cod League to be inducted into the Baseball Hall of Fame?

16. Name the 3 pitchers born in Massachusetts who later went on to win 300 games in the major leagues.

17. Name the only pitcher for a Pittsfield based team who went on to win 300 games in the major leagues.

18. Name the career hit leader for the state of Massachusetts.

19. Name the 14 baseball players born in Massachusetts who are enshrined in the Baseball Hall of Fame.

20. The first ever intercollegiate baseball game was played in the state of Massachusetts. What two teams played, where did they play and what was the final score of the ballgame?

BASEBALL TIMELINE

....

2000 BC — History tells of very primitive stick and ball games that were played for a variety of reasons such as recreation, fertility rites and different religious rituals.

1500 BC — There were findings in the royal tombs of ancient Egypt of wall inscriptions that show people of that era playing games with bats and balls.

900 AD — In Chichen Itzu Mexico there were ceremonial courts that were used by the Mayan Indians to play games with sticks and balls.

1621 — On Christmas Day in 1621 Governor Bradford of the Plymouth Plantation in Massachusetts wrote in his memoirs that he found the men of the planation out in the street pitching a ball and playing a stool like or shurch like sport.

1744 — John Newberry published a book in England which was called "A Pretty Little Pocket Book." In the book there is a wood cut illustration that shows boys playing a game with a rhymed description that goes like this: " the ball once struck off/ Away flies the ball/ to the next desired post/ then home with joy."

1778 — The diary of a soldier who served at Valley Forge was found and in it the soldier refers to the game of base which was played by the troops.

1791 — The city of Pittsfield, Massachusetts enacts a ban on a game played within a specific distance of a meeting house or church. The ban specifically names baseball.

1796 — A German by the name of Johann Mathias Guts publishes a book in which the rules of the English Base Ball Game appear. In the book he tells the number of bases varied as well as the number of players and one out would end up retiring the entire side.

1818 — Jane Austen in her book "Northanger Abbey" writes the following verse: "Catherine who had by nature nothing heroic about her should prefer cricket, baseball, riding on horseback and running about the country at the age of 14, to books or at least books of information."

1834 — **"The Book of Sports" by Robin Carver has besides a wood carved picture of boys playing baseball in Boston a printed set of rules for the game.**

1839 — Supposedly Abner Doubleday invented baseball at the New York village of Cooperstown. Supposedly because at the time Doubleday was alleged to have been in Cooperstown, he was actually a cadet at the United States Military Academy at West Point, New York. There is nothing to show he ever visited Cooperstown that year, nor did he have anything to do with the making of the game of baseball. Even in his diary, he makes no mention or claim with regards to inventing the game of baseball.

1845 — Alexander Cartwright gives us the first twenty rules of baseball.

1858 — The first ball game with paid admission is played in Newton, Long Island with spectators paying $.50 to see a game played between a team from New York and a team from Brooklyn.

1859 — **The first intercollegiate baseball game is played when Williams College is defeated by Amherst College 73 to 23 at a field at the corner of North Street and Maplewood in Pittsfield, Massachusetts.**

1869 — On September 18 the Pythians of Philadelphia an all black team defeated the City Items an all- white team in what is believed to be the first recorded game between an all- white team and an all- Negro team.

1879 — The controversial "reserve clause" in baseball begins with players bound to one team only. The move was made by the owners to keep salaries under control.

1884 — Moses Fleetwood Walker catches for the Toledo Blue

Stockings when they pay the Louisville Eclipse in AA ball. Walker becomes the first Negro to play in the major leagues.

1888 — Ernest L Thayer's "Casey at the Bat" debuts at the Wallack Theater in New York City.

1892 — Wahconah Park in Pittsfield opens up.

1901 — The American League declares itself a Major League.

1903 — American and National Leagues agree on separate and equal schedules culminating in a World Series.

1909 — League Park in Cincinnati hosts the Cincinnati Elks and a team from Newport Kentucky in the first night game played in baseball. **The idea for night baseball was thought of by George Cahill of Holyoke, Massachusetts.**

1910 — President William Howard Taft is the first US President to throw out the ceremonial first pitch to open a baseball season. This was a game between the Philadelphia Athletics and the Washington Senators on April 14.

1912 — Fenway Park opens up in Boston.

1913 — The Federal League announces plans to compete against the established major leagues starting in 1914.

1914 — Federal League debuts on April 15, 1914.

1916 — Federal League disbands.

1919 — On September 9 the fixing of the World Series between the Cincinnati Reds and the Chicago White Sox is planned in a room at the Buckminster Hotel in Boston.

1920 — Carl Mays of the New York Yankees hits Ray Chapman of the Cleveland Indians with a pitch; Chapman dies the next day of the injuries he sustained.

Eight members of the Chicago White Sox re-indicted on charges of conspiring to fix the 1919 World Series. Besides those eight, former major leaguer Hal Chase is indicted as well.

1921 — Judge Kennesaw Mountain Landis is named the first commissioner of baseball replacing the three -man National Commission.

1923 — Yankee Stadium opens up in the Bronx.

1927 — Babe Ruth hits 60 home runs to lead the New York Yankees to the American League pennant. The Yankees then swept the World Series, beating the Pittsburgh Pirates in four straight games.

1928 — National League president John Heydler proposes a tenth player or "designated hitter" to bat for the pitcher to help speed up the games. The National League votes yes and the American League votes no and nine players remain the status quo.

1929 — The New York Yankees become the first team in major league baseball to permanently add numbers to the backs of the uniform jerseys. Numbers corresponded to the players place in the batting order; hence, Babe Ruth 3 and Lou Gehrig 4 etc.

1933 — Major League baseball's first All Star game is played at Comiskey Park in Chicago.

1939 — Baseball Hall of Fame opens in Cooperstown, New York.

Lou Gehrig ends his consecutive game streak at 2,130 games.

1941 — Lou Gehrig passes away just before his 38th birthday of amyotrophic lateral sclerosis or what is later known as "Lou Gehrig's disease."

Joe DiMaggio of the Yankees hits in 56 straight ballgames and Ted Williams becomes the last major leaguer to hit .400 when he goes 6 for 8 in a double header and ends up with a batting average of .406. It is one of baseball's finest seasons.

1947 — Jackie Robinson breaks down the color barrier in baseball as he debuts for the Brooklyn Dodgers. Robinson later becomes a spokesman and a pioneer in the civil rights movement.

Larry Doby becomes the first Negro to play in the American League when he debuts for the Cleveland Indians.

1948 — Babe Ruth passes away after a two year battle with throat cancer.

1951 — Bobby Thomson of the New York Giants hits the "Shot Heard Round The World, a three run homer that helps the Giants defeat the Dodgers for the National League pennant.

1955 — The Brooklyn Dodgers defeat the New York Yankees in a thrilling 7 game World Series to win Brooklyn's only World Series title.

1956 — Don Larsen of the New York Yankees pitches the only perfect game in the history of the World Series as the Yankees defeat the Dodgers 2-0.

1957 — The Brooklyn Dodgers announce that they are moving to Los Angeles and the New York Giants announce they are moving to San Francisco.

1961 — Roger Maris hits his 61st home run to break the record of 60 hit by Babe Ruth in 1927.

1965 — The Houston Astrodome opens up as the first indoor ballpark in baseball.

1966 — Marvin Miller is named as the executive director of the Major League Baseball Players Association.

1967 — Carl Yastrzemski wins the American League Triple Crown and leads the Boston Red Sox to the American League pennant.

1968 — Denny McLain becomes the last pitcher to win 30 ballgames in a season as he wins 31 for the Detroit Tigers.

1970 — Curt Flood challenges the "Reserve Clause" in baseball.

1972 — Jackie Robinson dies of complications of diabetes at the age of 53.

1973 — The designated hitter rule is adopted by the American League only. Ron Blomberg of the Yankees is the first man credited with an at bat as a designated hitter.

1974 — Hank Aaron, a former player in the Negro Leagues, breaks Babe Ruth's career home run record of 714 when he hits number 715 off of Al Downing of the Los Angeles Dodgers.

1975 — Baseball's free agency is again challenged; this time by pitchers Andy Messersmith and Dave McNally.

1976 — Owners lock the players out of spring training following the absence of a basic labor agreement.

1978 — Locker rooms become coed after a New York District Court judge rules that women reporters cannot be banned from locker rooms.

1980 — Major league baseball players threaten to strike in May if a new basic agreement is not reached.

1981 — Players set a May 29th strike deadline if the free agent compensation issue is not resolved: the strike deadline is later extended to either June 4, 1981 or June 1, 1982.

1985 — Pete Rose breaks Ty Cobb's record for career hits as he hits a single off of San Diego Padre pitcher Eric Show for his 4,192nd hit.

1986 — Player's Association files a grievance charging the club owners with collusion in regards to free agents and their salaries.

1988 — Wrigley Field becomes that last ball park in the major leagues to install lights.

1989 — Pete Rose meets with former baseball commissioner Peter Ueberroth and his successor A. Bart Giamatti, and Rose is questioned about allegations he bet on baseball games.

8/24/89 — Pete Rose is permanently banned for betting on baseball games.

9/1/89 — A Bart Giamatti dies at age 51 on Martha's Vineyard.

10/17/89 — an earthquake measuring 6.9 on the Richter scale forces Postponement of Game 3 of the World Series

1990 — Owners threaten to lock players out of training camp unless a new agreement is reached.

2/15/90 — players locked out of training camp

3/18/90 — lockout is resolved

1993 — A bill is introduced in the US Senate to end baseball's anti-trust exemption.

1994 — Player's Association sets August 12, 1994 as date for a strike due to the lack of a basic bargaining agreement.

8/12/94 — Players go on strike.

9/14/94 — Season cancelled as player's strike goes on.

1995 — On April 2, 1995 after 234 days the baseball player's strike is over; the season will begin on April 26, 1995

1997 — The first interleague games in the major leagues are played on June 12, 1997 as the San Francisco Giants defeat the Texas Rangers 4-3, as Willie Mays and Nolan Ryan throw out the ceremonial first pitches.

1998 — Mark McGwire and Sammy Sosa spend the year battling in a thrilling race for the home run title, McGwire ends the season with 70 home runs and Sosa ends with 66 as both break Roger Maris' record of 61 home runs set in 1961.

1999 — Ceremonies held to commemorate the first 100 years of baseball.

Baseball Rules Changes Over The Years

1857- Game changed to nine innings with the winner being the team that scores the most runs

1858- Called strikes are introduced- Batter is called out on a ball fair or foul that is caught on the fly or after one bounce

1863- Bat size regulated- Pitcher's box now 12 feet by 4 feet-Pitcher cannot take a step forward during delivery and both feet have to be on the ground at the same time

1864- Each base runner must touch all four bases in order to make a run

1867- Pitching box is now a six foot square and the pitcher can now move while inside the box- Batter can call for a pitch high or low

1872- Ball size and weight changed to the present dimensions

1877- Fifteen inch square canvas bases used-Home plate is placed by the angle formed by the intersection of the first and third base lines-Hitter not charged with an at bat if he is walked

1879- Reserve clause in contract-Pitcher must face batter before pitching-Nine balls for a walk

1880- Base on balls reduced from nine balls to eight balls-Base runner out if hit by batted ball-Catcher must catch third strike for out to be recorded

1883- Pitcher can throw the ball from above the waist

1884- Base on balls reduced from eight balls to six balls

1885- A portion of the bat can be flat

1887- Calling for high or low pitches stopped-Five balls for a base on balls instead of six-Batter awarded first base when hit by pitch

1888- Base on balls exemption from a time at bat restored-The reserve clause was written into minor league contracts

1889-Four balls become a walk

1893-Pitching distance increased from 50 feet to 60 feet 6 inches-Pitcher must have back foot on rubber

1894-Foul bunts classified as strikes

1895-Infield fly rule adopted-A held foul tip is a strike

1903-Foul strike rule adopted by the American League

1908-Pitchers were prohibited from soiling a new ball-Sacrifice fly rule adopted

1910-Cork center was added to the official baseball

1920-All freak deliveries including the spitball were outlawed; however, if the pitcher was already throwing the spitball he was grandfathered

1925-minimum home run distance set at 250 feet-Pitchers allowed to use rosin bag

1959-Regulations set up for minimum boundaries for all new parks left and right fields to be 325 feet at least and centerfield 400 feet at least

1969-Pitcher's mound dropped five inches-Strike zone shrunk from armpit to top of knees

1971-All major league players ordered to wear protective helmets

1973-American League began to use the designated hitter for pitchers on an experimental basis

1975-Three day suspension mandatory if batter hits a fair ball with a doctored, filled or flat surfaced bat

2008-Major league baseball adds limited instant replay (whether home runs are fair or foul) to be in effect for all games starting on August 29

Baseball State by State

Listed below are the States along with the number of major leaguers that call that state home:

California 2,016

Pennsylvania 1,362

New York 1,103

Illinois 1,018

Ohio 993

Texas 817

MASSACHUSETTS 649

Missouri 587

Florida 426

Michigan 418

New Jersey 409

North Carolina 386

Indiana 357

Georgia 319

Alabama 307	Maine/Rhode Island 73
Tennessee 277	New Hampshire 51
Maryland 276	Delaware 50
Kentucky 272	Utah/Vermont 38
Virginia 269	Hawaii 37
Oklahoma 238	South Dakota 36
Wisconsin 237	Nevada 29
Louisiana 234	Idaho 27
Iowa 215	New Mexico 25
Kansas 210	Montana 21
Mississippi 193	North Dakota 15
Washington 182	Wyoming 13
Connecticut 178	Alaska 11
South Carolina 170	
Minnesota 159	
Arkansas 150	
Oregon 124	
West Virginia 119	
Nebraska 109	
Washington D.C. 91	
Arizona 90	
Colorado 85	

Baseball in the Bay State
Different Variations

....

STOOLBALL

Dating back to the 15th century, stoolball is a sport that has its origins in the southern part of England in Sussex. It resembles the game of cricket, baseball and rounders. The tradition of the sport is that it was played by English milkmaids who used their milking stools as wickets.

According to Alice Gomme, who was a pioneer is the study of children's games, early references refer to the game as stobball or stoball. In a dictionary by Samuel Johnson, he defines stoolball as a game where the players drive a ball from one stool to another.

The Christian holiday of Easter also has a strong association with stoolball as it may be that the game is a Christian adaptation of some pagan games which use a ball and have to do with the rites of fertility. Early readings say that stoolball is also associated with romance and courtship and is also in the comedy written by Shakespeare and Fletcher called "The Two Noble Kinsmen," where the term stoolball is used as a euphemism for sexual behavior.

Stoolball may also be known as stowball, stobball or stumpball. Stumpball is closely related to cricket as it can be a manner of dismissing the batter, part of the wicket or the end of day play. Stobball and stowball mean stump in some dialects and were regional games similar to stoolball. In earlier versions of stoolball the object of the game was to defend the stool by the bare hand. Later on in the evolution of the game some type of bat would be used. A point was scored for each pitch until the stool was hit.

PRISONER'S BASE

Prisoner's base is a game of tag that has been around for ages and ages. Different people play the game different ways and there have been changes in the game throughout the years. A game closely related to Prisoner's base was played back in the time of William Shakespeare and the writer even included it in one of his plays.

It has also been called children's bars, bars game or base prison. It is played by having one team of players try to tag and put in prison players on the other team who venture away from their base or home territory. In France the game is called barres and is mentioned in the writings of the 14th century. It was one of the more popular games in medieval times in Europe, and is still played in this day and age but not as often as it was.

The game of Prisoner's base and other related games may have been descendants of the border warfare. There is mention in Parliamentary proceedings early in the reign of Edward III which says, "Where in Prisoner's base is prohibited in the avenues of the palace at Westminster during the sessions of Parliament because of the interruption it occasioned to the members and other passing to and fro." At that time it was played by the adults of the times.

ROUNDERS

Rounders is a game that has its origins in the Tudor times in England. It is like baseball in that there is a fielding team and a batting team and the players score runs by running around four bases on the field. The earliest reference to the game was in 1744 in "A Little Pretty Pocket Book" when they referred to it as **base-ball.** The book was written by John Newberry and then in 1828 in London a book by William Clarke called "The Boys Own Book" was published which contained the first description of a bat and ball game with base running that was in English.

After formalizing the rules of the game of rounders in Ireland, there were associations or clubs that were formed in Liverpool and Scotland by 1889. The defunct Massachusetts game version and the New York game of baseball share the historical roots of rounders which is linked to British baseball. Rounders is an older game than baseball and in the early references to **base-ball** in England the term **base-ball** is used instead of rounders.

As for the rules the pitcher, who is called either the "bowler" or the "feeder," bowls the ball underhanded to the batter. The ball is good if the ball is in reach between the batter's knees and the top of his head. If not, the ball is said to be bad and the batter does not have to hit the "bad" ball if he does not want to. After the batter hits, he may run from post to post but cannot be declared out if he is standing at a post or a base. A rounder is scored if the batting team completes what is called a circuit without being out.

TOWNBALL

Townball is described as being played with a bat and ball and is similar to rounders. The game of Townball was also known as "base," "roundball," "baseball," or just plain "ball." Later on the term Townball was used to describe games that were similar to baseball.

The rules of the game may vary, but below are listed three aspects of the game that are fairly common among the variations.

The number of players is more than nine.

There is no foul territory; everything hit was in play.

The base runner could be put out by hitting them with the ball which was known as soaking or plugging.

Henry Chadwick who was born in England wrote in the 1903 edition of "Spaulding's Official Baseball Guide" that the New York game was an improved version of Townball and that would mean that

Townball was an improved version of the English game of rounders.

OLD CAT AND ITS VARIATIONS

Old cat which is also known as ol cat or catball games were bat and ball games from the 19th century. The number of bases varied as the number of players increased or decreased.

One old cat is a very basic version of the game with a pitcher who is sometimes called a giver and a batter or a striker. There is a catcher and at times in the game there may be a fielder or two. If the batter was able to hit the ball he would run to a base and back. The fielder's job was to try to retrieve the ball and sting or hit the batter with the ball when the batter was not on a base. Each base touched would be a point for that batter and his team.

In the game two old cat, two batters would be opposite each other and they would run to the opposite base after the ball was hit. Sometimes, according to John Montgomery Ward, the players would also call out numbers that would correspond to a position, one for the batter, two for the pitcher and so forth. If the batter was to make an out then he would go to the highest numbered position.

For three old cat the bases would be laid out in a triangular pattern for the three strikers (batters) and in four old cat the bases were laid out in a square pattern for the four batters. Albert Spaulding has made the suggestion that four old cat was a precursor of townball which is where baseball evolved from.

LAPTA

Lapta is a game that is played with a bat and a ball and it also was a sport that originated in the 14th century in Russia. The game has been mentioned in medieval manuscripts and during the process of the excavation of Novgorod, bats and balls were found and were dated back to the 14th century. It is a game similar to cricket, rounders, and of course, baseball.

The object of the game is to hit a ball as far as possible, then to run to the kon line which is across the field, and if possible the runner may run back to the gorod line. The runner must try to avoid getting hit by a thrown ball. If a run is successful, then points are scored. To win the game a team must either get more points within the time frame or have all their players' complete runs.

Alexander Kuprin has described the game as being a very useful tool and that it required fast running and confidence that you cannot lose the game. Little Light and Izvestia which are Russian magazines had said that baseball has its roots and was developed from the game of lapta which was played in the 1700's by Russian Americans.

OINA

Another sport that has some similarities to baseball is the Romanian sport called oina, which was first mentioned during the rule of Vlaicu Voda in 1364. The game spread across Wallachia. Different theories have the game being played either by shepherds or being played during a war. There are two teams in the game and each team has 11 players. One side attacks or bats and the other team is the defending or "at catch" side. The game is played in halves and at the end of the half the teams switch positions. Each team has a captain or "baci" and midfielder two is usually that person because he is able to throw the ball at an attacking player for any of the positions in the game.

To score a player must hit a runner with the ball which is worth two points, unless the ball touches either the palm or the back of one's palm. The ball is made of leather and is filled with horse, pig or bovine hair and is similar in weight to that of a baseball.

PESOPALLO

Pesopallo is referred to as a Finnish baseball. It is a quick- paced sport and very often it is called the national sport of Finland. Also it is played in Germany, Sweden, Switzerland, Australia and Northern Ontario in Canada. It is a bit like rounders, baseball and lapta.

The game is a combination of traditional batting games and North American baseball. It was developed in the 1920's by Lauri "Tahko" Pikahla and is now informally known as pesis.

The rules of the game are hard to understand, but the idea of the game is really quite simple. One team hits and runs the bases and the other team has to catch the ball and get the runner out. The most important part of the game and the major difference between peso-pallo and baseball is the ball is pitched or tossed vertically.

Though this game was invented eighty to one hundred and twenty years after baseball was developed, it is fairly easy to see the similarities between the two sports.

BRANBOLL

Branboll or slaball (hit ball in Norway) and rundbold (roundball in Denmark) is a game similar to rounders, baseball, lapta and pesopallo. The name of the game is derived from the act of catching a player between bases at the end of a batting round, which is referred to as burning them (or branna) which is the equivalent of being out in baseball.

One of the major differences between branboll and baseball and cricket is that in branboll there is no pitcher. The batter throws or bounces the ball to himself and then hits it with his bat. There is a selection of bats available ranging from metal to wood and also a paddle like bat similar to the one used in cricket that is called a tjejtra which means girl-bat. That type of bat is used by for a player who is less experienced.

CRICKET

Cricket is the second most popular sport in the world behind soccer. It is a game played with a bat and a ball between two teams of
eleven players each. The field on which the game is played is oval
shaped with a twenty two yard long pitch which is in the shape of a
rectangle. One team bats and tries to score as many runs as possible
and the other team bowls (pitches) and fields while trying to keep
the team at bat from scoring. A run is scored by the striking batsman
who hits the ball and then runs to the opposite end of the pitch and
touches the crease there without being dismissed (put out).

In the early history of the game of cricket, it was described as a club
hitting the ball, which is kind of like the ancient games of clubball,
stoolball, trapball and stobball.

Different Major Leagues

Some of the ball clubs and players in this book are referred to as major leagues or major leaguers. The same can be also said for the Negro Leagues although the records for the Negro Leagues are much scarcer. So what follows here is a very brief narrative history of the major leagues where Massachusetts teams played. The website www.projectballpark.org was extremely informative and I offer my congratulations on a job well done. It was a truly enjoyable journey back in time and it made me realize how rich in tradition baseball was and is in Massachusetts. The list is in chronological order and the leagues that are talked about all had at least one team playing in the state of Massachusetts.

As of 2012 Major League baseball consists of both the National and American Leagues. The two leagues merged in 2000 under the banner of Major League baseball an organization led by one commissioner. For the previous 100 years they were two separate and legal entities. Now Major League baseball has 29 teams in the United States and 1 in Canada.

1869 has been used as the year Major League baseball was founded because that was the first year that a professional team (Cincinnati Red Stockings) was in existence. Right now the Atlanta Braves and the Chicago Cubs can trace their histories back to the National Association of Professional Baseball Player which had its start in the early 1870's.

As stated earlier, there is the National League which was started in 1876 and the American League which began in 1901. There were several other leagues that were thought to be major leagues and the records that were made and the statistics from these leagues are included in a player's major league records. They include the Union Association, the American Association, the Players League and the Federal League. There was also, in the later part of the 1950's an attempt made to form a third major league which would have been called the Continental League but there was not even one single game played.

The National Association was considered a major league and it existed from 1871 until 1875. The standards that the league set for memberships were not very strict. All a team had to do was to pay a fee of $10.00 and play every other team in the league five times. Each of the leagues teams was allowed to make its own schedule. The league did not have a central governing body and the umpiring as well as the prices of the tickets was not consistent. Some teams would not even show up for scheduled games. A player could also jump from team to team. What happened next was that some of the stronger teams that made up the National Association got together and formed the National League.

The Boston Red Stockings who played their home games at the South End Grounds were the lone team from Massachusetts that played in the National Association as they were in the league for the entire four years that the league was in existence.

In 1876 William Hulbert led a group of owners in the National Association to form what us now known as the National League. Hulbert was sick of dealing with the association's lack of organization and integrity. Hulbert was president of the National League from 1877 until he passed away in 1882. The owners of the new league wanted the power back from the players and they wanted the league to be stronger. The National League was a very well organized venture as they had a board of directors, secretary/treasurer and of course a president. The league had each team pay a fee of $100 to join. The league showed its power when the New York and Philadelphia teams did not make the final road trip because the teams had lost enough money already, so the league proceeded to kick both teams out of the league. The one thing that the league did that had a lasting effect on how baseball was run was that they guaranteed that the player could play for one team and one team only. This was the beginning of the reserve clause that was felt throughout the baseball world for over 75 years.

As for Massachusetts teams, the National League Boston Braves were a charter member of the league and played from 1876 until 1914 at the South End Grounds. In 1914 and 1915 the Braves would play at Fenway Park and from 1915 until 1953 when they moved to Milwaukee they played their home games at Braves Field.

The American Association was classified as a major league and was in existence from 1882 until 1891.It was formed by two men who owned baseball teams, Chris Von der Ahe who owned the ST Louis Browns and H.D. McKnight who owned the Pittsburgh Alleghenies. The league was formed so the players could play for whoever they wanted to which was obviously the opposite direction to the National League and its reserve clause which had been formed five years earlier. The American Association also only charged a $.25 admission fee instead of the $.50 that the National League charged. The American Association also sold liquor and the ballgames and played baseball on Sunday. The league ended up weakening because of a few things. Some of the teams jumped to the National League because the National League was in a better financial position and was better suited to survive the hard times. Also some of the owners of the American Association teams owned teams in the National League. But the final nail in the coffin of the American Association was in 1890 when a third major league was formed called the Player's League which took away some of the American Association talent and of course gate receipts.

Massachusetts was represented by the Boston Reds who played for only the 1891 season and who played their home games at the Congress Street Grounds.

Next in the chronological timeline of different major leagues is the Union Association which lasted for only the 1884 season. The league was thought by many people to be a joke. Henry Lucas was a millionaire who owned the St Louis Maroons in the Union Association and Lucas was one of the Union Association founders. Lucas's team was much better than any of the other teams in the league. The Union Association started with 12 teams and finished the season with five teams. The association had no set number of games a team had to play. The only reason that it was even considered to be a major league was because they played baseball in major league cities.

The lone Massachusetts entrant in the Union Association was the Boston Reds who played their home games at Dartmouth Grounds.

Now we go forward to 1890 and the formation of the Player's League whose actual name was The Player's National League of Professional Base Ball Clubs. The first ever player's union in baseball was called the Brotherhood of Professional Base-Ball Players. It was this union that led to the formation of the Player's league as it included some of the best baseball players including John Montgomery Ward who was a shortstop and pitcher as well as a lawyer. Ward and the other players left the National League and formed the Player's League because the players felt that there was a lopsided player-management relationship in the National League. The league's games were well attended, however, severely underfunded and the owners did not have the confidence to try another season so the league folded.

The championship of the Player's league was won by the Boston Reds who played their home games at the Congress Street Grounds.

The American League is one of the two leagues that presently make up Major League Baseball. Its origins go back to the Western League which was a minor league based in the area of the Great Lakes and was being led by Byron Bancroft "Ban" Johnson. It developed into a major league after the American Association disbanded. The league is sometimes called the junior circuit because it was formed 25 years after the "Senior Circuit" or National League.

The Boston Americans were a charter member of the American League in 1903 and won the first ever World Series which was a series of games played between the winners of the American and National League pennants. The Americans in 1908 became the Boston Red Sox who are still a team in the American League. From 1901 thru 1911 the Americans/Red Sox played their home games at the Huntington Avenue Grounds. From 1912 and every season beyond, the Red Sox have played their home games at venerable old Fenway Park.

Massachusetts did not have a team in the Federal League which was a major league for the 1914 and 1915 seasons, but the Federal League was an important part of baseball's history so it would only be right to give the Federal League a short mention here. It started in 1914 and was supposed to be in direct competition with both the American and National Leagues. They had the same number of games as the other leagues and it was very well planned out and organized. Players in both leagues rejoiced at the creation of the third league as its formation caused player's salaries to jump to a more respectable level. The Federal League built state of the art ball parks, including Wrigley Field, which was first named Weeghman Stadium after the owner of the Chicago Federal League team Charles Weeghman. Unfortunately there was a lawsuit brought and the owners of the Federal League could not pay the bills, so the owners sold their teams and assets and the league folded.

The state of Massachusetts did not have an entrant into the Negro National League which existed from 1920 until 1931. It also did not have a team in the Eastern Colored League which ran from 1923 until 1928. Nor did it have a team in the American Negro League which ran in 1929. The Negro East-West League was in existence for only the 1932 season and that league did not have a Massachusetts entry in it. The second incarnation of the Negro National League ran from 1933 until 1948 and no Massachusetts based team played in that league either. Finally from 1937 until 1954 the Negro American League was in existence without a Massachusetts based team.

In conjunction with reading about each city and town and the teams and players from them it is important to know about the leagues that some of these teams played in. Some were easy to find out about and some took a little more time and effort. What follows is just some basic knowledge about these leagues that were so important to the development of baseball and its players. It is also important to remember that back when a lot of these leagues started, baseball was all people had to keep them entertained. There was no internet, no Facebook, no video games and no shopping malls so the townspeople would meet at these ballgames and catch up with their neighbors about the goings on. Baseball was all these people had for entertainment and it really did not cost a lot of money to go to a ball game. There were some great ball players and some great baseball teams in the state of Massachusetts. These minor leagues gave the players the time to hone their talents and made them into the great professionals that they became.

EASTERN LEAGUE - There has been four different Eastern Leagues in minor league baseball. The first came into existence in the early part of the 19th century. The second in 1884 and the third started in 1916 and ran successfully until 1932. The league that was in existence from 1916 to 1932 was a successor to the New England League, although not affiliated with the Eastern League that started in 1938. The league that started in 1916 was classified as a Class B league until 1919 when it was given Class A status. During the league's existence there were a total of eight teams. This edition (Eastern League 3) collapsed during the peak of the Great Depression in 1932 as did many other teams and leagues

As for the fourth edition of the Eastern League it was originally started in 1923 and for the first 15 years that it was around it would be known as the New York -Pennsylvania League. The league has had a total of 52 different cities that have hosted a team. These cities come from 13 different states and two of the provinces of Canada. The following is just a partial list of some of the people who played for an Eastern League team at some point in their careers. Also all of the following names have one other thing in common. They are all enshrined in the Baseball Hall of Fame in Cooperstown. Here we go with the list: Andre Dawson, Nolan Ryan, Juan Marichal, Mike Schmidt, Whitey Ford, Early Wynn, Warren Spahn, Richie Ashburn, Johnny Mize, Bob Lemon, Carlton Fisk, Gary Carter, Ralph Kiner, Jim Palmer, Lefty Gomez, Heinie Manush, Travis Jackson, Tony Lazzeri, and Rabbit Maranville. Also a player by the name of Leon Day from the Negro Leagues had a connection to the Eastern League. Not all of these players were based on teams in Massachusetts, but at some point may have played minor league baseball in the Bay State.

The CAN AM LEAGUE - The Can Am League was a class C circuit that operated from 1936 thru 1951 except for a three year break during the course of World War 2. The only teams from Massachusetts in this league were the Pittsfield Electrics 1941-42, 1946-48, the Pittsfield Indians 1949-50 and the Pittsfield Phillies of 1951.

EASTERN ASSOCIATION - Another of the minor leagues that were around was the Eastern Association which like the Eastern League had four different versions. The first or Eastern Association 1 was in 1882, Eastern Association 2 ran in 1891 and Eastern Association 3 ran in 1909 only. Finally Eastern Association 4 ran for 1913 and 1914 and was a class B league.

HUDSON RIVER LEAGUE - There was also the Hudson River League which is mentioned because it did have a team in Massachusetts, but the league itself was basically comprised of New York State teams. The one season that Massachusetts had a team in the Hudson River League was 1905 and the team was the Pittsfield Hillies. Originally the team was based in Saugerties, New York and moved to Pittsfield on July 4, 1905; the team lasted only until July 25, 1905 and then disbanded. The Hudson River League was a class D minor league when it was formed in 1903 and by 1904 was upgraded to class C. It continued as a class C league until 1907 when the league collapsed.

CONNECTICUT STATE LEAGUE - Obviously the Connecticut State League was a minor league that was based in the state of Connecticut. It began in 1902 and was also known as the Connecticut League. It was a class D league that had eight teams in eight cities. It became a class B league in 1905 and lasted until 1913 when it became the Eastern Association when several teams from outside the state of Connecticut joined up. The league ended up folding after the 1914 season. The Massachusetts teams that played in the league were the Springfield Ponies from 1902 to 1914, the 1904 Worcester Norwich Reds, the 1903 to 1911 Holyoke Paperweights/Papermakers, the Northampton Meadowlarks from 1908 to 1911 and the Pittsfield Electrics in 1913 and 1914.

NORTH ATLANTIC LEAGUE - The North Atlantic League was actually the name of two different leagues. The first operated from 1946 until 1950 and was a class D league. There were no teams with a Massachusetts base. The second coming of the North Atlantic League ran in 1995 and 1996 as an independent league. Three of the teams that were in the North Atlantic League joined up in the Northeast League after the North Atlantic League folded following the conclusion of the 1996 season and the only team from Massachusetts was the Massachusetts Mad Dogs who were based out of the Lynn -Nahant area in Massachusetts.

LEAGUE ALLIANCE - Al Spalding proposed a League Alliance in 1877 and the league only lasted for that season although a different version was tried in 1882. The only teams from Massachusetts in the 1877 league were teams from Fall River and Lynn, Massachusetts.

NATIONAL ASSOCIATION - The National Association was around in 1879 and in 1880 and it is not to be confused with the National Association that was a major league of the same name. Holyoke, Springfield and Worcester all had teams in the league for the 1879 season.

INTERNATIONAL ASSOCIATION - Actually the International Association was called the International Association of Professional Base Ball Players. The name was used on two occasions from 1877 until 1880 and from 1888 until 1890 and it was for two different Canadian American baseball leagues. The 1877 version of the league consisted of the London Tecumschs, the Pittsburgh Alleghenies, the Rochesters, the Manchesters, the Columbus Buckeyes, the Guelph Maple Leafs and the Lynn Massachusetts Live Oaks. It cost each team $10.00 to join the league and if the team wanted to play for the championship it would cost an additional fee of $15.00. In 1878 while playing for the Lynn Live Oaks, Bud Fowler became the first African American player to play in organized baseball. Back in the late 19th century it was very common for both teams and players to jump alliances and this over a period of time affected the International Association. In 1879 the Buffalo team and the Syracuse team switched to the National League and the International Association also lost the London Tecumschs. The league came back for a three season period from 1888 until 1890, but there were no Massachusetts teams involved.

INTERNATIONAL LEAGUE - In 1896 Farnhum, Quebec, Hull, Massachusetts, Malone, New York, Plattsburgh ,New York, St Albans, Vermont and St Hyacenthe, Canada joined together to form the International League. Very little is known about the league which appears to have only lasted one season. There was another version of the International League formed from the merger of the following three leagues: the 1884 Eastern League, the New York State League and the Ontario League which were both formed in 1885. What had happened was the New York and Ontario Leagues had formed the International League in 1886, and then in 1887 the Eastern League was absorbed making the International League a 10 team league. The league ended up folding because the teams from the north said it was too difficult to travel to the south. The North teams formed the International Association and over the years the league itself changed. After the American Association disbanded the International League absorbed three teams and then reorganized.

EASTERN NEW ENGLAND LEAGUE - During its inaugural season of 1885 the Eastern New England League had five teams in it, four of which were from Massachusetts and the fifth team was from the state of Maine. The four teams from Massachusetts were Brockton, Haverhill, Lawrence and Newburyport and the Maine team was from Portland. Each team played each other a total of 20 times for a total of 80 games. The season ended in controversy over forfeited games, teams playing more than the 80 scheduled games and players jumping contracts. Sadly the Eastern New England League only lasted for the 1885 season.

ATLANTIC ASSOCIATION - the Atlantic Association ran for the

1889 and 1890 seasons. In 1889 the teams from Massachusetts were from Lowell and Worcester and for 1890 Massachusetts would be represented by the Worcester Grays. Then in 1908 the league would try again to resurrect and the only team from Massachusetts was a combination from the cities of Attleboro and Taunton.

SOUTHERN NEW ENGLAND LEAGUE - this was a seven team league that lasted for only the 1885 season. The seven teams in the league were from Bridgeport, Hartford, Meridian, New Britain, New Haven, and Waterbury, Connecticut, while the lone Massachusetts entry was from Springfield.

COLONIAL LEAGUE- 1914 and 1915 were the only two years for the Colonial League. In 1914 the league was classified as a class C league and was independent for the 1915 season. Brockton played in the league for both seasons as did the Fall River Spindles and the New Bedford Whalers. The Springfield Tips and the Taunton Herrings played for just the 1915 season.

NORTHEAST LEAGUE - Another of the independent minor leagues was the Northeast League which operated from 1995 until 1998 and for 2003 and 2004.From 1999 until 2002 the Northeast League merged with the Northern League and then in 2005 the Canadian American Association of Professional Baseball absorbed the teams that were in the Northeast League. For the 1995 season there were six teams in the league that were based in Southern or Central New York State. They were the Albany Diamond Dogs, the Adirondack Lumberjacks, Yonkers Hoot Owls, Newburgh Nighthawks, Mohawk Valley Land Sharks and the Sullivan Mountain Lions. The Sullivan Mountain team was sold and moved to the North Atlantic League where it was renamed the Catskill Cougars. Mohawk Valley moved to West Warwick, Rhode Island and became the Rhode Island Tiger Sharks. Elmira, New York was granted a franchise as the team that was in

Elmira moved to Lowell ,Massachusetts. The Yonkers team folded and was replaced by the Bangor, Maine Blue Ox.

The league grew to eight teams in 1997, as Newburgh and Rhode Island folded their teams. After 1996, the North Atlantic League disbanded and the Catskill team rejoined the Northeast League. Also the Lynn, Massachusetts based Massachusetts Mad Dogs joined the Northeast League. The league also added the Waterbury, Connecticut Spirit and the Allentown, Pennsylvania Ambassadors. For the 1999 season the Albany New York team was renamed the Albany -Colonie Diamond Dogs. After the Bangor, Maine team folded they were replaced by the New Jersey Jackals, who ended up winning the league title in their rookie season. The league then merged with the Northern League in 2000 and the Catskill, New York team folded again. After the period from 1999 to 2002 the league returned to a separate entity and the Northern League Brockton Rox won the Northeast title in 2003 and then in the league's last season the New Jersey Jackals captured the league title.

CANADIAN AMERICAN ASSOCIATION OF PROFESSIONAL BASEBALL - This is an independent league based out of Durham, North Carolina. The cities which have teams do not have either another major or minor league team based out of that particular city. The level of play is about on par with a Class A league. This league may sometimes be referred to as the Can Am League which was also the name of a league that operated between 1936 and 1951. This current league was formed in 2005 after the reorganization of the Northeast League.

After the Allentown Ambassadors folded before the start of the 2004 season , the Northeast League was able to field a travelling team called the Aces. The reason this was done was because it would give the league an even number of teams. In 2005 the league gained a new team called the Worcester Tornados who became that eighth team. Three weeks before the start of the season the Bangor Lumberjacks

folded necessitating the formation of a new travelling team called
the Grays. In 2009 the Nashua team transferred to Pittsfield, Mas-
sachusetts to play as the Pittsfield Colonials. . Those teams are the
Adirondack Lumberjacks, Albany Colonie Diamond Dogs, Allentown
Ambassadors, Berkshire Black Bears, Brockton Rox, Catskill Cougars,
Elmira Pioneers, Massachusetts Mad Dogs, New Jersey Jackals, Les
Capitiales de Quebec and the Waterbury Spirit.

NEW YORK PENN LEAGUE - operates in the northeastern part of
the United States and was originally known as the Pennsylvania-
Ontario-New York League when it was founded in 1939. The original
teams in the league included the Batavia Clippers, Bradford Bees,
Hamilton Red Wings, Jamestown Jaguars, Niagara Falls Rainbows
and the Olean Oilers. After the Hamilton Red Wings folded in early
1956 there were no teams in Canada so the league adopted the
name of the New York Penn League. Twenty nine years later the St
Catherine's Blue Jays entered the league followed by the Hamilton
Redbirds in 1987 and the Welland Pirates in 1989. By the year 2000 all
three of these clubs moved back into the United States. The current
teams in the league now are: the Aberdeen Ironbirds (Orioles),
Brooklyn Cyclones (Mets), Hudson Valley Renegades (Rays), Staten
Island (Yankees), Auburn Doubledays (Nationals), Batavia Muckdogs
(Marlins), Jamestown Jammers (Pirates), Mahonig Valley Scrappers(
Indians), State College Spikes(Cardinals), Williamsport Crosscutters
(Phillies,) Connecticut (Tigers), Lowell Spinners(Red Sox), Tri City
Valley Cats (Astros) and the Vermont Lake Monsters (Athletics).

NEW ENGLAND LEAGUE - was a minor league that played off and
on in every New England State with the exception of Vermont from
1886 until 1949. For a period after 1901 it was kind of like a little
brother to the Boston Braves and Boston Red Sox, the region's two
major league teams. Unfortunately the difficulties the area was having with the economy as well as other factors eventually caused the
league to cease operating after the 1949 season. The first game in the

New England League was in 1886 and was played between a team from Maine and a team from Massachusetts. There was not any activity in the league with any regularity until 1892 although there were seasons in which teams played under different classifications but still under the New England League banner. The New England went through a period where they played from1891 until 1915 although the news of what happened is hard to obtain as the league was going through team changes and such so that while the league played those years it is hard to have any continuity due to the changes.

When the Federal League challenged the major leagues in 1914 and 1915, there were long reaching effects that came to the minor leagues because the Federal League caused salaries to escalate and the players were really not forced to take what the owners of the ball teams offered them. The New England League then tried a rebirth in 1919, but ended up shutting down in August of that year. Seven years later in 1926 the league returned with eight teams. The league based the teams around the cities that had manufacturing mills in them as that was where the most people were employed and those were the people who would hopefully be coming to the baseball games. When the Great Depression hit the United States, the New England League like all other businesses, suffered greatly and was ultimately forced to shut down on June 22, 1930. The league attempted a comeback in 1933 and then in 1934 changed its name to the Northeastern League for the 1934 season.

Throughout World War Two the league really did not have a consistency, but after the war ended, the true Golden Age of baseball began. The New England League was back to eight teams and it is important to note that after the war it was only a matter of time before integration came to major league baseball. With that being said one of the most notable teams to play in the New England League was the Nashua, New Hampshire Dodgers which was a farm team of the Brooklyn Dodgers. It would be with the Nashua Dodgers that Dodger greats Don Newcombe and Roy Campanella made their professional debuts. The 1947 season would also see the team from Lawrence, Massachusetts cancel a home game and in the end that team switched both the town they played in and the name they went by. That team became the Lowell Stars for the rest of the 1947 season. At the end of the season the team moved again, this time to Springfield, Massachusetts where they became the Springfield Cubs which was a farm team of the Chicago Cubs. This was the only New England team to survive the 1949 season and it became one of the two Cubs AAA franchises for the 1950 through 1953 seasons. That Nashua team would win the New England League championship in 1946, 1947 and 1948. The league started the 1949 season with eight teams, but the Providence team dropped out in June and the Manchester team suspended operations, the teams in Lynn and Fall River suspended operations on July 20, 1949, and the four remaining teams would finish out the league season with the Portland Pilots winning the final New England League championship.

It probably isn't the correct thing in writing to do but now I think is the time to promote one of the books that can give so much information on the subject. If you the reader is really interested in minor league baseball and its history I would highly recommend reading the book "The New England League" by Charles Bevis. It is one of the best baseball books I have ever read and it is amazing to have learned so much about a league that to be real honest, that I did not know even existed. Thank you, Mr. Bevis, your book was fantastic, a real classic.

MASSACHUSETTS STATE ASSOCIATION - this league lasted

for just the 1884 season. There were seven teams in the league: the Boston Reserves and teams from Holyoke, Lawrence, Lynn, Salem, Springfield and Worcester. The Lawrence team and the Springfield team were the only teams that survived the 1884 season as the Lawrence team played in the Eastern New England League in 1885 and the Springfield team played in the Southern New England League.

To keep from getting confused when reading about the different minor leagues and the classifications named, what follows is a brief explanation of the different minor league classifications by centuries;

19TH CENTURY

Class A- protection for contract and reservation

Class B- protection but a player can be drafted for a set price

Class C -contract only protection

Class D -contract, however a higher class can draft a player for a set price

Class E-lowest fee, it was used by the solid leagues who didn't need help getting or protecting players

....

20TH CENTURY

AAA- highest classification one step below the major leagues, started in 1946

AA- established in 1908 second highest classification

A1 just a little above class A effective 1945-1946

A-lowest classification

B- second highest was in effect until 1963 and then all class B teams became class A teams

C-third to the highest 1902-1907

D- lowest classification 1902-1972, moved to class A in 1963

E- only good for one year and was used only in the Midwest

Major League Teams In Massachusetts

No discussion about baseball in Massachusetts would be complete without talking about major league baseball in the Bay State. First and foremost when one thinks of baseball in Massachusetts the Boston Red Sox come to mind. The Red Sox have been members of the American League since 1901 yet from 1901 to 1907 they were known as the Boston Americans. It would be after 1907 that the team became known as the Red Sox. From 1901 until 1911 the Americans/Red Sox played their home games at the Huntington Avenue Grounds and starting in 1912 they began to play at majestic Fenway Park.

The Red Sox have won 13 pennants 1903, 04, 12, 15, 16, 18, 46, 67, 75, 86, 2004, 2007 and 2013.

They have also won eight World Series titles (1903, 12, 15,16,18,2004,2007 and 2013). Boston was dominating during the early years of the American League winning five world titles in the first 18 years of the league. John Taylor the team's owner in 1907 chose the name Red Sox after the red in the team's uniform. As a side note the name Red Sox had also been used as the name of a Negro League team in Norfolk Virginia.

But to go back to the beginning, in 1901 the Western League which was a minor league had declared itself a major league and began to compete against the more established National League after changing its name from the Western League to the American League. The team known as the Americans competed in and won the first ever World Series in 1903 beating the Pittsburgh Pirates. In 1904 the Americans beat the Highlanders (Yankees) after the Highlanders pitcher Jack Chesbro uncorked a wild pitch which allowed the winning run to score for the Boston nine.

Starting in 1909 after Tris Speaker became an outfielder for the Sox their dominance came into play. The outfield would consist of Speaker, Harry Hooper and Duffy Lewis. The pitching staff had Smokey Joe Wood, Ernie Shore and a crafty left hander by the name of Babe Ruth who turned out to be a pretty good hitter.

After Ruth was sold to the Yankees in December of 1919 Boston began a steady downhill slide with an absence of World Series titles that spanned 86 years. It is a shame because there were some very good players that played on Boston teams during those years and they were denied that elusive World Series ring. There were men like Johnny Pesky, the great Ted Williams, Bobby Doerr and Mel Parnell during the 1940's and 1950's. Then during the 1960's and into 1970 there were players like Carl Yastrzemski, Jim Longborg, the "Boomer" George Scott during the 60's then into the 70's it was players like Fred Lynn, Jim Rice, Dwight Evans, Carlton Fisk and Luis Tiant.

The man known as "Yaz" carried the Red Sox to the American League pennant in 1967 practically by himself winning the American League batting Triple Crown in the process. It was this 1967 team that became known as "the Impossible Dream". Then into the 1970's and 1980's heartbreak again came to Boston when the Sox could not clinch the deal in 1975 after Carlton Fisk hit his memorable game six home run to carry the Sox to a game seven showdown with the Cincinnati Reds. In 1978 Bucky Dent hit a three run home run that helped the New York Yankees defeat the Sox in a one game playoff to get to the American League championship. Then perhaps the most heartbreaking loss in Sox history occurred in 1986 when the Red Sox were ahead in the World Series over the New York Mets three games to two and the Mets were down to their last out and chance when Mookie Wilson hit that ground ball which eluded the grasp of Sox first baseman Bill Buckner. Just as the Sox began to play good and compete in 2003 Aaron Boone of the Yankees dashed the hopes of Sox fans everywhere when he hit a walk off 11th inning home run off of Tim Wakefield that propelled the Yankees into the 2003 World Series.

It seemed that the Sox had found more ways to lose than to win, but in 2004 that all changed when they mounted the greatest comeback in sports when after being down three games to none against the New York Yankees they came back to beat their hated rivals in a thrilling seven game series. But the party was not over as then the Sox moved into the 2004 World Series against the St Louis Cardinals whom they swept in four games to bring Boston its first world title in 86 years. The Sox then went on to win the series in 2007 as well as in 2013 and Boston fans were rejoicing.

The Sox also have had some notable records and accomplishments by their players and some of them are as follows:

Pedro Martinez 1.74 ERA in 2000

Nomar Garciaparra hits a club record .372 for a right hander

David Ortiz franchise best 54 home runs in 2006

Overall club winning % since 1901 .516

September 1, 2007 Clay Bucholtz throws no hitter in 2nd major league start, 1st rookie and 17th Red Sox pitcher to throw a no hitter

September 8, 2008 Red Sox set Major League Baseball record with 456th consecutive home game sellout.

The following is a list of players now in the Hall of Fame who at one time or another wore the uniform of the Boston Red Sox / Americans, if the name is in capitals then the player went into the Hall wearing a Red Sox baseball cap.

Luis Aparicio, WADE BOGGS, Lou Boudreau, Jesse Burkett, Orlando Cepeda, Jack Chesbro, JIMMY COLLINS, JOE CRONIN, BOBBY DOERR, Dennis Eckersly, RICK FERRELL, CARTON FISK, JIMMY FOXX, LEFTY GROVE, Rickey Henderson, HARRY HOOPER, Waite Hoyt, Ferguson Jenkins, George Kell, Heinie Manush, Juan Marichal, Herb Pennock, Tony Perez, JIM RICE, Red Ruffing, Babe Ruth, Tom Seaver, Al Simmons, Tris Speaker, Dick Williams, TED WILLIAMS, CARL YASTRZEMSKI and Cy Young.

So here we have a very brief history on the Boston Red Sox. Like them or not the Sox are one of baseball's historic and iconic teams and the loyalty of the fans to them is amazing. There have been hundreds or books written and magazines articles written on this franchise and it would be impossible in only a few pages so this is just an overview of the Boston nine.

But the Red Sox were not the only major league team in the state of Massachusetts. From 1876 until 1882 the Boston Red Stockings played as members of the National League. They played at the South End Grounds I and during their time in baseball they had a record of 299 wins and 226 losses. The Red Stockings won 2 pennants during that time frame. Then from 1893 until 1906 the Boston Beaneaters played in the National League as well. The Beaneaters played in South End Grounds I, II and III as well as the Congress Street Grounds and ended up with a record of 1,742 wins and 1,465 losses they won a total of six National League pennants. After the Beaneaters from 1907 until 1910 the team was known as the Boston Doves. They finished with a career mark of 219 wins and 389 losses playing their home games at South End Grounds III. Still in the National League the 1911 Boston team would be known as the Rustlers and for that season they played at South End Grounds III finishing with a record of 44 wins and 107 losses.

The team switched names again in 1912 and from then until 1935 they were known as the Boston Braves. From 1936 to 1940 they would be called the Boston Bees and then it was back to the Braves until the team moved to Milwaukee for the start of the 1953 season. They stayed in Milwaukee until 1965 and then moved to Atlanta were they still play today. From 1912 until the team moved to Milwaukee in 1953 the team won one World Series and two National League pennants. Their record for those years was 2,814 wins and 3,411 losses. The one championship that the Braves won was in 1914 and that was when the Braves upset the heavily favored Philadelphia Athletics in a four game sweep. That Boston team was known as the "Miracle Braves" they were such underdogs in that series. For the Braves that year they started off with a record of four wins and eighteen losses and it seemed like they were headed for a last place finish. On July 4, 1914 the Braves lost a double header and fell into last place, 15 games behind the New York Giants. After that they went on a winning streak and from Jul 6th until September 5th the Braves won 41 games while losing only 12 overtaking the first place team and catapulting themselves into the World Series. In fact that was the first ever four game sweep by a team since the World Series had started in 1903. After 1914 the Braves finished 2nd and then 3rd. After that they were in a prolonged slump until they won the National League pennant in 1948. After the pennant in 1948 the Braves finished 4th three times and 7th once before moving to Milwaukee.

Listed next are the players who at one time in their career played for the Boston Braves and then went on to glory by becoming elected to the Baseball Hall of Fame. Just like with the Red Sox if the entire name is capitalized then that player went into the Hall of Fame as a Boston Brave. Earl Averill, Dave Bancroft, Dan Brouthers, JOHN CLARKSON, Jimmy Collins, HUGH DUFFY, Johnny Evers, Burleigh Grimes, Billy Hamilton, Billy Herman, Rogers Hornsby, Joe Kelly, King Kelly, Ernie Lombardi, RABBIT MARANVILLE, Rube Marquard, TOMMY MC-CARTHY, Bill McKechnie, Joe Medwick, KID NICHOLS, Jim O'Rourke, Charley Radbourn, Babe Ruth, FRANK SELEE, Al Simmons, George Sisler, Casey Stengel, Ed Walsh, Lloyd Waner, Paul Waner, Deacon White, VIC WILLIS, George Wright, Harry Wright and Cy Young.

There were two other teams that called Boston home during their times as major league baseball clubs. The first was the Boston Reds who played in the only year of the Union Association which was 1884. That year the Reds finished with a record of 58 wins and 51 losses 34 games behind the St Louis Maroons who finished with a record of 94 wins and only 19 losses. The team played its home games at Dartmouth Grounds which was also known as Union Park. Future Hall of Famer Tommy McCarthy played on that team during the 1884 season as an outfielder and as a pitcher.

The other team was also called the Boston Reds and they played for two seasons. In 1890 they played as members of the Players' League and in 1891 they were members of the American Association. The 1890 team won the pennant of the Players' League over the New York Giants and in 1891 the won the American Association pennant over the St Louis Browns (Cardinals). That Reds team was one of two teams to win pennants in two consecutive years. The other team was the Brooklyn Dodgers who beat out all the other teams for the American Association pennant in 1889 and then beat out every team in the National League to win that pennant as well. Those Reds teams played their home games at the Congress Street Grounds before abandoning that park which lay dormant until 1894 when it went into use again after the South Ends Grounds Park was being rebuilt after a fire had destroyed the park. Congress Street Grounds was also the site of a baseball first when Bobby Lowe hit four home runs in one game the first major league player to do so.

There is one other team found to have played in the major leagues and had its home base in the state of Massachusetts and that was the Worcester Worcesters. The Worcesters in 1879 played baseball in the National Association which was a minor league at the time. The people in charge of the National League at the time thought that the Worcester franchise could replace the team from Syracuse known as the Stars. The Worcesters joined the National League on 1880 and on June 12 of 1880 pitcher Lee Raymond threw the first ever perfect game in major league history when he put zeros across the board against the Cleveland Blues. Also on August 20, 1880 the Worcesters again made history when they were the first team in major league history to be no hit in their own ballpark. The pitcher who turned that trick was Hall of Famer Pud Galvin who was pitching and playing for the Buffalo Bisons at the time. There was one other way that the Worcester team had an impact on baseball that year and that was when Worcester had the Cincinnati Reds thrown out of the National League because they (Reds) had violated league policy by selling beer at the ballpark.

The team played its home games at the Worcester Driving Park Grounds at the Worcester Agricultural Fairgrounds in Worcester. The team was also called the Brown Stockings or the Ruby Legs and they had as players at one time the aforementioned Lee Raymond, a player by the name of

Lip Pike who was the first ever player to lead the league in home runs for four years. They also had John Clarkson on the team who was later elected to the Baseball Hall of Fame in Cooperstown.

In conclusion it is very easy to see that the state of Massachusetts had a very prominent role in the early days of baseball and especially in the major leagues. Both the Red Sox and the Braves (even though they are in Atlanta now) have very strong and storied roots in the state and it is something that the state should be proud of. Of course there are also many other stories about these major league teams and their players but time nor space permits anything other than a very brief history into this part of baseball's history.

Minor League Baseball In Massachusetts

In baseball's infancy minor leagues and minor league teams abounded in many of the small towns across the United States, and Massachusetts was not any different. The sport was a pleasant diversion from the hard work that many endured to make ends meet and the games that were played had a holiday type atmosphere about them. Then as money entered the equation players found that it was not so bad to get paid for playing a game. Proportionately the wages were ok, but certainly not like they are in today's game. In fact most of the players had second jobs to make ends meet during the off season.

What follows next are stories about different towns and the baseball teams that played representing those towns. Also what the reader will find is if there was a particular player that made an impact in the game of baseball whether it is the minor or major leagues, I debated for a very long time as to whether or not to include any mention of semi pro teams. Finally in the end I decided that it would be near impossible to research the entire list semi - pro teams and players as a part of the book. What I did find out was that in my area of Massachusetts in Berkshire County there was an exhibition game played in the village of West Stockbridge between the Troy's Garage team and the Philadelphia Athletics led by Connie Mack. This certainly was an event that people in the area must have talked about. In fact a number of years ago the local paper (Berkshire Eagle) had a front page story about this game that was an absolute fascinating read. But the reason that I did not make more of a mention of it here was because I just did not feel that it fit with the flow of the book as I was hoping it would go. However, please feel free to contact me if it is something that anyone would be interested in reading about as I know where there are some people who are a wealth of knowledge when it comes to this game.

Minor league baseball will always be small town America's way of bringing the national pastime into someone's back yard, so anytime the chance arises to go to a minor league game, you may see history in the making in your back yard.

ATTLEORO - In 1908 the class D Atlantic Association had 6 teams in the league, a team from Lewiston Maine, Newport Rhode Island, Pawtucket Rhode Island, Portland Maine, Taunton/Attleboro Massachusetts and Woonsocket, Rhode Island. The Taunton/Attleboro team was called the Angels and it was managed by a man named McDermott.

In 1928 the class B New England League was comprised of the Attleboro Burros and four other teams from Massachusetts. The Attleboro team won the pennant under the management of Patsy Donovan and Bill Hunnefield.

1933 would see the towns of Attleboro/Lawrence/Woonsocket co-hosting a team which was in the class B New England League, a team that was an affiliate of the New York Giants. That team finished the year in first[t] place well ahead of the other five Massachusetts teams which were the Lowell Lauriers, New Bedford Whalers, Quincy Shipbuilders/Nashua Millionaires/Brockton Shoemakers, Taunton Blues and Worcester Chiefs.

CAMBRIDGE - The Cambridge Orphans/Lowell Orphans were a class F minor league team who played in the New England League in 1899. The team was managed by a man named Spalding and finished the 1899 in second place behind the Brockton Shoemakers.

Going forward to 1934, the Cambridge Cantabs/Wayland Birds were a member of the Class B Northeastern League. They were managed by Bill Morrell, Mack Hills and Dick Phelan. They finished the season in last place with a record of 19 wins and 42 losses.

HAVERHILL - Baseball in Haverhill began on the minor league level in 1885 when the team from Haverhill played in the Eastern New England League. That year Haverhill was one of five teams in the league along with Brockton, Lawrence, Newburyport/Biddeford and Portland. The team was managed by George Brackett.There were two players on that team who ended up playing a very big part in the early history of baseball. The first was Tommy McCarthy, who is profiled under Massachusetts born players. Over a 13 year major league career McCarthy played with the Boston Reds, Boston Beaneaters, Philadelphia Quakers, St Louis Browns and the Brooklyn Bridegrooms. He is credited by many with bringing the hit and run play into baseball as well as other innovations. He was elected to the Baseball Hall of Fame by the Old-Timer's Committee in 1946.

The name John K. Tener may not mean much to the novice baseball fan, but Tener was an outfielder and a pitcher in the major leagues. As a pitcher he had a record of 25 wins and 31 losses as well as an ERA of 4.30. His batting statistics had him appearing in 73 games where he had 62 hits including 5 doubles, 2 triples and 3 home runs. But it is not his batting or his pitching which makes him an important part of baseball. After Tener's playing career ended, he served from 1911 until 1915 as the 25th Governor of Pennsylvania. Before that he was a member of the House of Representatives and after his term as governor ended, the lure of baseball beckoned him back to the sport where he became the president of the National League.

In 1886 the New England Baseball League was where the Haverhill team played and Frank Selee, John Irwin and Fred Doe combined to manage the squad. 1887 would have the team from Haverhill join forces with the Boston Blues and play in the New England League. The team was managed by Arthur Williams and Fred Doe before the merger with the Blues and then Walter Burnham after the merger. There is no manager listed for the 1894 Haverhill team that was a member of the classs B New England League. However one of the players on the squad deserves mention and that player was John "Buck" Freeman, who was a right fielder and first baseman during his career. Freeman was one of the early power hitters in baseball and held the seasonal record for home runs with 25 which he hit in 1899. He held that record until a man by the name of Babe Ruth broke his record by hitting 29 home runs in 1919.

The 1895 Haverhill team also was a member of the New England Association along with teams from Fitchburg, Lawrence, Lowell, Nashua New Hampshire and Salem Massachusetts. The Haverhill team was managed by Frank Leonard and William Laverty.

From 1901 until 1912 and the again in 1914 the team was known as the Haverhill Hustlers. The Hustlers played in the New England League which was a class B minor league. In 1901 Frank Selee was the manager long with Arthur Williams and Fred Doe. Billy Hamilton would manage the club in 1902, 1903, 1904 and 1905. For the 1906 season James Sayer would be in the manager's seat and then it would be back to Hamilton for the 1907 and 1908 seasons. One of the players that Hamilton managed on the 1908 squad was John "Stuffy" McInnis who would later go on to fame in the major leagues as part of the $100,000 infield with Jack Barry, Eddie Collins and Frank "Home Run" Baker for Connie Mack and the Philadelphia Athletics.

1909 would have Frank Connaughton as the Haverhill manager, 1910 would be Tom Flemming and 1911 Tom Bannon would be at the helm for Haverhill. No record for a manger could be found for 1912 and in 1913 Haverhill did not have a team. However in 1914 the Hustlers would be back and Christy Wilson and Daniel Noonan shared the duties of manager. It would be five years later when Haverhill's team in the New England League would be known as the Haverhill Climbers. The manager of the team was Jesse Burkett. Burkett was a left fielder who played in the major leagues for the New York Giants, Cleveland Spiders, St Louis Cardinals, St Louis Browns and Boston Americans. As a major league player Burkett put up some impressive numbers. He was a three time National League batting champ in 1895 by hitting .405, 1896 by hitting .410 and 1901 when he hit .376. Burkett at various times also led the league in runs scored, hits and at bats. He was elected to the Baseball Hall of Fame in 1946.

Seven years later the Haverhill Hillies returned to action in the New England League for the 1926 season when Jack Kiernan managed the squad. Kiernan also managed the team in 1927 and shared the duties in 1928 with Jack Ryan. Haverhill along with Fitchburg and Gloucester combined to field a team in the New England League for the 1929 season as well.

LOWELL - The city of Lowell has a rich history with regards to baseball in the Bay State as the city has had a team in minor league baseball off and on since 1877 until the present time. Starting in 1877 the Lowell team played in the League Alliance under the managerial reigns of a man named White. Also Lowell fielded a team called the Ladies Men in the New England League for a part of the 1877 season as well. In 1878 the Lowell tem was managed by Josiah Butler and was a part of the International Association.

Nine years later in 1887 the Lowell Magicians were a member of the New England League and had Bill McGunnigle as the team's manager. One of McGunnigle's players was Hugh Duffy, who later went on to a Hall of Fame career in the Major Leagues as he played for the Chicago White Stockings, Chicago Pirates, Boston Reds, Boston Beaneaters, Milwaukee Brewers and Philadelphia Phillies. Duffy led the league in runs scored in 1890, in hits (1890/1894), home runs (1894/1897) and batting (1894) when he hit .440. Duffy was elected to Cooperstown in 1945.

Jim Cudworth managed the Lowell Chippies in 1888 when they were a member of the New England League. Then in 1889 the Lowell team was managed by Nate Kellogg, John Cosgrove and D Sullivan when they played in the Atlantic Association. In 1891 the Lowell Lowells were managed by Dick Conway as they went back to playing in the New England League where they stayed for the 1892 season and were managed by Jim Cudworth and Art Whitney.

Lowell, Massachusetts, Manchester, New Hampshire and Boston, Massachusetts were all under one team banner in 1893 in the New England League as Bill McGunnigle was the team's manager; after a one year hiatus baseball was back in Lowell as in 1895 Lowell was a part of the New England Association, with Michael Mahoney and William Meade as the team's managers. In 1899 the Lowell/Cambridge team was managed by a man named G. Spalding as they completed in the class F New England League.

For 1901 the Lowell team would be known as the Tigers. They would also be known as the Tigers from 1902 through 1904 when they were managed by Fred Lake. In 1905 Lowell and Taunton would combine forces in the New England League and be managed by both George Grant and William Conners. In 1906 Fred Lake would be back in the manager's seat for Lowell, and then in 1907 and 1908 the Lowell Tigers would be managed by Alexander Winn.

The team would still be known as the Tigers for the 1909 season and Tom Flemming, Tom Bannon and Phenomenal Smith would be the managerial trio. For the 1910 season it would be Fred Teney at the helm and for 1911 the team would go through a manager change and a name change as Jim Gray took over as skipper and the team switched names to the Grays. Jim Gray would stay on to manage the team through the 1914 season and in 1915 it would be Cuke Burrows and Pop Kelcher managing the Lowell nine. The Lowell Grays would be members of the Eastern League for the 1916 season and would be managed by the trio of Pat Kilhullen, Jesse Burkett and Harry Lord.

Lowell and Lewiston/Auburn Maine played in the New England League in 1919 and had as their manager Charles Hayden. In 1926 the Lowell Highwaymen/Salem Witches would be managed by Tom Whelan. The partnership for the 1929 season was between the Lowell Millers and the Nashua Millionaires. Lowell changed their name to the Lauriers for the 1933 season and was led by Rusty Yarnell and Jesse Burkett. Another year, another name change, and another league change as in the 1934 season the team would be known as the Honeys/Hustlers under the leadership of Bill Hunnefield in the Northeastern League. Thirteen years later in 1947, Lowell and Lawrence partnered up to be known as the Millionaires/Orphans under manager George Kissell.

Forty nine years later in 1996 minor league baseball returned to Lowell as Billy Gardner was the manager of the Lowell Spinners. The team would stay the Spinners through the 2012 season and the roster of managers was as follows: Dick Berardino in 1997 and 1998, Luis Arguayo in 1999, Arnie Beyeler in 2000 and 2001, Mike Boulanger in 2002, Lynn Jones and John Deeble in 2003, Luis Aliciea in 2004 and 2005, Bruce Crabbe in 2006, Gary Disarcina in 2007, 2008 and 2009, a return by Bruce Crabbe in 2010, Carlos Febles in 2011 and then back to Bruce Crabbe again in 2012. From 1996 on the roster of players that have played for the Lowell squad is quite impressive as David Eckstein, Brent Saberhagen, Kevin Youklis, Hensley Raimierz, Jonathan Papelbon, Jacoby Ellsbury and Clay Buchholtz are some of the players who have worn the Lowell uniform.

NEWBURYPORT - Newburyport had two minor league teams; one in 1885 was called the Newburyport Clamdiggers. That team also was in partners with the town of Biddeford, Maine in the Eastern New England League. The second team was the Lynn/Newburyport Clamdiggers and they were a part of the New England League in 1886 under the managerial trio of Dan Shannon, Ed Flanagan and Fred Doe.

SALEM - While Salem is more famous for witch trials, the Massachusetts city has a history with minor league baseball as well even though it is a brief one. Starting in 1884, the Salem team was part of the Massachusetts State Association League and had for their manager a man by the name of F. Doyle. Salem had two teams in 1887; the first was a combination team with the city of Lawrence and that team played in the New England League and was managed by Pat Pette and Harry Putnam. The second team played in the New England League as well

and was called the Salem Fairies and was managed by Wally Fessenden and Ed Flanagan. The 1888 Salem Witches were part of the New
England League as well and were managed by Wally Fessenden.

Salem had an entry in the 1891 and 1892 New England League season and while no record was found for 1891, the manager of the 1892
team was Louis Bacon. In 1895 the Salem team was part of the New
England Association and was managed by Frank Leonard. Thirty one
years later the Lowell Highway men and Salem Witches partnered
up in the New England League under the leadership of Tom Whelan.
In 1927 Thomas DeNoville managed the Witches in the New England
League and in 1928 former major leaguer Stuffy McInnis would manage the Salem nine. As for the 1929 season the Salem Witches would
be managed by Sam Post.

WATERTOWN - The lone Watertown, Massachusetts team featured
here is the 1934 Watertown Townies, who played in 1934 as part of
the Northeastern League with Bill Barrett as the manager.

FALLRIVER - Fall River started its baseball journey in 1877 with an
entrant in the New England League called the Fall River Cascades
who were managed by Jim Mutrie. One of the players on the Cascades that year was Edward "Ned" Hanlon who played in the major
leagues for 13 years with the Cleveland Blues, Detroit Wolverines,
Pittsburgh Alleghenies, Pittsburgh Burghers and the Baltimore
Orioles. Hanlon later went on to a career where he won three pennants consecutively with the Baltimore Orioles in 1894, 1895 and
1896. He then won two more pennants with the Brooklyn Superbas
in 1899 and 1900. Hanlon was elected to the Baseball Hall of Fame by
the Veteran's Committee in 1996.

In 1878 the Fall River team was independent and not affiliated
with any other league. It would be 1893 when baseball returned to
Fall River when the Fall River Indians played in the New England
League under Mike McDermott's managing. For 1894 they would

still be known as the Indians and in 1895 the team would be led by a
man named A. McDermott.

Charles Marston would manage the 1896 Fall River Indians in the
New England League. One of the players on the team that year
was Napoleon Lajoie.Lajoie had a twenty year career in the major
leagues with the Philadelphia Phillies, Philadelphia Athletics and the
Cleveland Naps, who later became the Cleveland Indians. He led the
league in runs batted in with 127 in 1894, 125 runs batted in in 1901
and 102 runs batted in in 1904. He led the league in hit four times
(1901, 1904, 1906 and 1910). He was the league batting champion in
1901, 1902, 1903, 1904 and 1910. He won the batting Triple Crown
in 1901. In the 21 seasons that Lajoie played he batted over .300 17
times and hit over .400 once. His .338 career batting average is good
enough for 20th place on the all-time list and his 3,242 hits ranks him
14th. He was elected to the Hall of Fame in Cooperstown in 1937 and
was a part of the inaugural class in 1939.

The 1897 version of the Fall River Indians played in the New England League and was managed by Charles Marston, who managed
the team in 1898 as well. One of the players on that 1898 team deserves mention. His name was Joe Delahanty and he was one of five
brothers to play in the major leagues, including brother Ed who was
elected to the Baseball Hall of Fame in 1945. One of the other players
on this squad was Roger Conner who was a star during baseball's
early years in the 19th century. He ended his career with 138 home
runs which does not seem a lot but that figure of 138 led major
league baseball until Babe Ruth broke the record in 1921. Conner was
elected to the halls of Cooperstown in 1976.

From 1902 until 1906 with the Fall River team still being called the
Indians they continued play in the New England League. The 1907
through 1911 squad was known as the Brienes and still was a mem-
ber of the New England League under leadership skills of John O
Brien. Still playing in the New England League in 1912 were the Fall
River Brienies. In 1913 the team changed its name to the Fall River

Adopted Sons, which was Fall River's final year in the New England League for a while.

For the 1914 and 1915 seasons the team would be known as the Spindles and would play in the Colonial League. Thirty-one years later the Fall River Indians were back and played in the New England League with Jack Burns as the manager. John Holden managed the Fall River Indians in 1947, while in 1948 Frank Zubik and Luke Urban took over the helm. Fall River played in 1949 under the New England League banner with Dick Porter as the manager.

HOLYOKE - In 1879 a team from Holyoke, Massachusetts played for managers Jack Chapman and Fergy Malone under the National Association banner. There were two pitchers on that team who went on to bigger and better things in the major leagues. The first was Larry Corcoran who played in the major leagues for eight years. In his first five years in the league Corcoran won 43 games the first year, 31 wins the second, 27 the third, 34 wins in the fourth year and 35 wins in the fourth year. He led the league in wins in 1881 when he won 31 games and ERA once with 1.95 in 1882. Corcoran had a winning percentage of .665 which is good enough for 8th best of all time. He spent his career in the major leagues with the Chicago White Stockings, New York Giants, Washington Senators and Indianapolis Hoosiers.

Mickey Welch was the second pitcher of note on that Holyoke team and Welch's career lasted 13 seasons as he played with the Troy Trojans and the New York Giants. In 9 out of his 13 big league seasons Welch won 20 or more games, including 4 seasons where he won 30 or more and one season where he won 44 games. Welch won a total of 307 games in the major leagues during his career and he was rewarded when in 1973 the Veterans' Committee elected him to the hallowed halls of Cooperstown.

Dan O'Neil and Horace Rescott managed Holyoke when the team was in the Massachusetts Association in 1884. From 1903 until 1913 the Holyoke Paperweights would play in the Connecticut State

League, and during that time Peter Woodruff and Daniel O'Neil managed the squad in 1903, 1904 would have Frank Fitzpatrick, P. Pridniville and W. Winkler in charge, and in 1905 it would be Jesse Frysinger. The 1906 Paperweights had M. Prindiville, Tom Flemming and Tommy Dowd as managers. Tommy Dowd managed the team for the 1907 season and in 1908 it would be Fred Winkler. For the 1909 season it would be Kid McCormack, Pop Foster in 1910, and Daniel O'Neil in 1912. The manager of the Holyoke Papermakers in the first season in the Eastern Association would be James Gary.

Sixty four years later in 1977 minor league baseball returned to Holyoke when Matt Galante managed the squad that was a farm team of the Milwaukee Brewers. In 1978 and 1979 the squad would be managed by George Farson. The Holyoke team was called the Millers and in 1980 they were managed by Lee Sigman, for the 1981 season it would be Jim Saul in charge of the squad, and then in 1982 it would be Jack Hiatt who managed the Holyoke nine.

LYNN - In 1877 the Lynn Live Oaks were members of the New England League and they were also a part of the International Association as well for the 1877 season. During the time they spent in the International Association they were managed by George Adams, James Gorman, Candy Cummings and George Smith. Cummings is the man that most people credit with developing the curveball and Cummings became a member of the Hall of Fame in 1939 when he was elected as a pioneer. In 1878 the Live Oaks paired up with the team from Worcester to form a team in the International Association with George Brackett as their manager.

The Massachusetts Association was the league that the Lynn team played in in 1884 and the managers for that team were Edward Chamberlain and Wally Fessendon. 1886 would see Lynn and Newburyport team up with Dan Shannon, Ed Flanagan and Fred Doe as the team's managers. George Bracket and Henry Murphy managed the Lynn Lions for the 1887 season and Brackett came back in 1888 to manage the Lynn team who were then known as the Shoemakers at this time. The 1891 season would come around, and the Lynn squad would play in the New England League under the leadership of Harry Putnam.

Ten years alter in 1901 the Lynn Live Oaks were in the New England League pennant race. For the 1905 season the name of the team would change back to the Shoemakers where Frank Leonard and Fred Lake were managers of the team. In fact Leonard managed the team by himself until 1908 except for the 1905 season when he shared the duties with Fred Lake.

For the 1909 and 1910 season the Lynn Shoemakers had as their manager "Sliding" Billy Hamilton, who is ranked third on the all-time list for career stolen bases in the major leagues with 912 stolen bases. Hamilton was elected to Cooperstown in 1961 by the Veterans' Committee. The Lynn team was known as the Leonardites for both 1911 and 1912 as they were managed by Frank Leonard. For the 1913 season it would be the Lynn Shoemakers, and for 1914 it would be the Fighters and both of those years the team's manager was Patsy Flaherty. The 1915 Lynn team was known as the Pirates and was managed by Louis Pieper. In 1916 Lynn switched from the New England League to the Eastern League and also switched names as they would be known as the Pipers with Louis Peiper still managing the team. There was a pitcher on the Lynn team that year who would go on to win 237 major league games pitching for the New York Giants, Boston Red Sox, New York Yankees, Detroit Tigers, Philadelphia Athletics, the Brooklyn Dodgers and the Pittsburgh Pirates. He was a three time World Champion and was also a broadcaster for the Cincinnati Reds for 24 years. He was elected to the Hall of Fame in Cooperstown in 1969 and his name was Waite Hoyt.

1926 would be another year and another name change as the team would now be known as the Lynn Papooses which was a name that would stay with the team through the 1930 season. For those years 1926 through 1930 the Papooses were managed by King Bader and

Tom Whelan. Baseball returned to Lynn after a 16 year absence and in 1946 the team would be called the Lynn Red Sox with Lawrence Kennedy as the manager. Mike Ryba managed the team in 1947 and in 1948 the manager was Eddie Popowski. One of the players on that 1948 team was Dale Long, who went to the major leagues and at one time held the record for consecutive games with a home run at 8 games. This record was later tied by Don Mattingly and Ken Griffey Jr. Onto the 1949 season and the Lynn Tigers would be managed by Thomas Kennedy and Charles Webb.

Thirty years later the Lynn Sailors would play in the Eastern League under Booby Floyd. Floyd would manage the team in 1980 and 1981 and then he gave way to Allen Bowers who managed the team in 1982. For the 1983 season Tommy Sandt would skipper the Sailor's ball club. Twenty years later in 2003 the Lynn team would be called the North Shore Spirit and would be members of the Independent Northeast League where John Kennedy would manage the club for 2003, 2004, 2005 and 2006. The Spirit did switch leagues as for 2005 and 2006 they were members of the Canadian American League. In 2007 Vic Davilla would manage the Spirit squad and kept them atop the league standings as Kennedy had the year before.

NORTHAMPTON - Northampton's minor league history consisted of three years, 1909, 1910 and 1911. The team was called the Meadowlarks and would be members of the Connecticut State League for those 3 years. In 1909 the team was managed by Gil Edwards and in 1910 by William Luby. On the 1910 Northampton team was a player who would become famous or infamous depending on how you looked at it and who you believed. George Daniel "Buck" Weaver was on that 1910 Northampton squad. He was not a great ballplayer, just very steady. He always maintained his innocence during the course of the trial of the 1919 Chicago White Sox players who were accused of throwing the World Series. Weaver always proclaimed his innocence and denied he was ever at any of the meetings in which the fix was discussed. Unfortunately, he was banned from baseball for life paying the ultimate price. The Meadowlarks also played in the 1911 season, but no manager is listed.

SPRINGFIELD - In addition to being the birthplace of basketball, Springfield, Massachusetts has a rich history of minor league baseball which began in 1878 as Springfield had a team in the International Association with Billy Arnold as the manager. In 1879 Springfield's baseball team was a member of the National Association and had as its managers George Fayerweather, Lip Pike and Bob Ferguson. Five years later in 1884 Springfield would play under the banner of the Massachusetts State Association with Charlie Shaw as their manager. In 1885 Springfield would play in the Southern New England League as Charlie Hackett, M. Kennefick and Henry McDonald would share the managerial duties.

During the 1887 season the Springfield team would be known as the Horsemen and would have Charles Shaw as their manager for the Eastern League season. The Springfield Ponies would play under the Eastern League banner for the 1893 season and would have as their manager Tom Burns, who also managed the team in 1894 when they were known as the Ponies and the Maroons. The Springfield team was also known as the Maroons for the 1895 season as they were still playing under the banner of the Eastern League. One of the players on that team was Jack Chesbro of Adams Massachusetts who later went on to a Hall of Fame career that was detailed in the chapter on Berkshire County baseball players.

Tom Burns also was the manager of the 1896 Springfield team when they were known as the Ponies and still playing in the Eastern League. One of the players on that year's team was Dan Brouthers who had a 19 year career in the major leagues with the Troy Trojans, Buffalo Bisons, Detroit Wolverines, Boston Beaneaters, Boston Reds, Brooklyn Grooms, Baltimore Orioles, Louisville Colonels, Philadelphia Phillies and finally the New York Giants. When Brouthers retired from baseball he had a lifetime batting average of .342 which is still good enough for ninth best all time. He also was a five time league batting champion and led the league in total hits three times. He led the league in home runs twice and was voted into the Baseball Hall of Fame in 1945 by the Old Timer's Committee.

The 1897 Springfield Ponies/Maroons would be managed by Tom Burns and then in 1898 the duties of manager would be split between Bill Barnie, Jim Rogers and Billy Lush. In 1899 Tom Brown was the manager of the team as they played in the Eastern League that year. In 1900 after they had stayed with the name of the Ponies they switched back to the name Maroons during the season. Tom Brown was the manager that year as well.

The team switched leagues for the 1902 season and kept the name Ponies while paying under the banner of the Connecticut State League. Roger Conner was the manager of the 1902 as well as the 1903 team and one of the members of the 1902 team was James Henry "Orator Jim" O'Rourke who had previously played in the major leagues for the Middletown Mansfields, Boston Red Stockings, Providence Grays, Boston Red Caps, Buffalo Bisons, New York Giants and the Washington Senators in a career that lasted 23 years. He had the nickname "Orator Jim" because he had obtained a law degree from Yale Law School. He was an outfielder, catcher and first baseman who led the league in runs in 1877 with 68, and hits in 1884 with 162. He was elected to the Hall of Fame in 1945. It should be noted that when O'Rourke played with the Springfield team, he was 52 years old.

Dan O'Neil managed the Springfield team from 1904 through 1908 as they remained in the Connecticut State League. In 1909 J. Zeller took over as Springfield manager and he held that post through the 1912 season. In 1913 and 1914 the Springfield Ponies would play under the Eastern Association banner under the leadership of Frank Corridon in 1913 and Simon McDonald and Billy Hamilton in 1914. The team in Springfield in 1915 was called the Tips and that team was part of the Colonial League. Another year in Springfield for 1916 and it was another league and name change as the team went back to the

Eastern League and the name Ponies for the 1916 season. In 1917 the team would be known as the Green Sox with the team reverting back to the name Ponies for the 1918 season. Freddie Parent managed the 1918 team and in 1919 Ed Holly would be the manager.

In 1920 and 1921 the team would be known as the Hampdens still playing under the Eastern League banner. For the 1922 season it would be back to the Ponies with John Hummel as manager. In 1923 it would be Patsy Donovan, and from 1924 through the 1926 season Gene McCann would be in charge of the Springfield club. Joe Benes took over as manager for the 1927 and 1928 seasons while in 1929 it would be George Burns in charge of the Springfield nine. The manager for the 1930 Eastern League Springfield Ponies would be William J "Kid" Gleason who may be better remembered as the manager of the ill-fated 1919 Chicago Black Sox team that was involved in the fixing of the World Series that year. Gleason was a fine manager and not a bad ballplayer either, as he spent 22 years in the major leagues as a pitcher and second baseman.

Bill Stewart managed the Ponies in 1931 and for the 1932 season the team changed its name and would be known as the Springfield Rifles with Bill Meyer as the manager. One of the players on Meyer's team that year was Spurgeon Chandler who was better known as "Spud." Chandler was a four time American League All Star as well as a member of three World Series winning New York Yankees teams. He was a pitcher who holds the single season New York Yankee record for earned run average in a season which is 1.64, a mark he set during the 1943 season. 1943 was a good year for Chandler as he was also selected as the American League's Most Valuable Player, the only pitcher from the New York Yankees to be selected for that honor. It would be seven years before baseball returned to Springfield and when it did, the team would be known as the Springfield Nationals who were a farm team of the Washington Senators. Spencer Abbott was the manager of the team that year and on the roster of that team was Mickey Vernon. Vernon was a seven time All Star selection, a two time American League batting champion and a fine defensive first baseman who finished his career with a fielding percentage of .990. He also holds the record for participating in 2,044 double plays. Spencer Abbott was also the manager of the 1940 Springfield team as well.

For the 1941 season Springfield native and future Hall of Famer Rabbit Maranville would manage his hometown team. However, Maranville was not the only future Hall of Famer on that team as one of the pitchers on that team was Early Wynn. Wynn played for the Washington Senators, Cleveland Indians and Chicago White Sox during the course of his 23 year major league career. He was an 8 time selection at All Star a 5 time winner of 20 or more games in a season who finished his career with exactly 300 wins. He won the Cy Young Award for best pitcher and was elected to Cooperstown in 1972. He was a hardnosed player who once said in the right situation he would knock his mother down if she were batting against him.

One of Wynn's teammates on that 1941 team was Jim Konstanty, who had a 12 year career in the major leagues as a pitcher with the Cincinnati Reds, Boston Braves, Philadelphia Phillies, New York Yankees and St Louis Cardinals. He was primarily a relief pitcher before the role became as glamorous as it is now. He was a member of the 1950 National League All Star team and won the 1950 National League Most Valuable Player award as a member of the Phillies squad.

In 1942 the Springfield team was called the Rifles and had Les Bell as their manager. In 1943 the Rifles played in the Eastern League as an affiliate of the New York Giants with Spencer Abbott as the manager. It would be five years before baseball returned to Springfield and when it did, it would be as an affiliate of the Chicago Cubs. The team was known as the Springfield Cubs and had Robert Peterson as the man in charge while they played in the Class B New England League. One of the players on that squad was Jim Brosnan who later went on to pitch for nine years in the major leagues. Brosnan achieved some notoriety as the author of a book called the "Long Season," where he wrote a diary of the 1959 major league season. He later went on to write more books and become a sportscaster. Peterson also was chosen to manage the 1950 Springfield squad as well.

From 1950 until 1953 the Springfield Cubs would be a part of the
AAA International League. In 1950 the manager would be former
major leaguer Stan Hack, while in 1951 and 1952 Bill Kelly would
be the manager. The 1953 squad would have as managers Jack
Sheehan, Bruce Edwards and Tom Sheehan. After a three year break
Springfield was back in a different league with a different affiliation.
Springfield was a member of the Eastern League and was affiliated
with the New York Giants. In that first year Mike McCormick and
Ray Murray were the managers, and one of the players on that team
was Felipe Alou, who was one of the three Alou brothers to play in
the major leagues (along with Jesus and Matty). Felipe went on to a
career in the majors and had some success as a manager on the big
leagues. He is the father of Moises Alou, who also had a pretty good
major league career like his father.

In 1958 Andy Gilbert began his career as a manager for the Springfield squad. He managed the team from 1958 through the 1962
season. During his five years as a manager Gilbert had many future
major league ball players on the roster but there are three that will
be mentioned here. The first is Matty Alou, who is the brother of
Felipe Alou. Matty was a two time All Star, the 1966 National League
batting champ and a member of the 1972 World Champion Oakland
Athletics. The second player is Manny Mota. Mota was an All Star selection in 1973. Mota at the time held the record for career pinch hits
and has been a coach with the Los Angeles Dodgers for 33 years. The
third and final player to be mentioned is one of the greatest if not the
greatest pitcher to hail from the Dominican Republic, Juan Marichal.
Nicknamed the "Dominican Dandy," he had a 16 year career in the
major leagues with the San Francisco Giants, Boston Red Sox and
Los Angeles Dodgers. He was a 10 time All Star selection, the 1965
All Star Game Most Valuable Player and he also threw a no hitter on
June 15, 1963 and he had his number 27 retired by the San Francisco
Giants. He was ranked 71st on the Sporting News 100 Greatest Play-
ers List and was a finalist for the All-Century team. He finished his

career with 243 wins, a 2.98 earned run average and 2,303 strikeouts. He was noted for his high leg kick and was not afraid to throw close to batters. He was voted into Cooperstown's hallowed halls in 1983.

The 1963 Springfield club was managed by Buddy Kerr, and then, Andy Gilbert came back for the 1964 and 1965 seasons, which were the last 2 years for minor league baseball in Springfield.

WAYLAND - In 1934 the Cambridge Cantabs/Wayland Birds were members of the Northeastern League. The team was managed by the trio of Bill Morrell, Mack Hillis and Dick Phelan.

BOSTON - Now is the time for discussing the history of baseball in Boston, the capital of Massachusetts. Obviously most of the history of baseball in Boston has to do with the Red Sox and to some extent the Braves, but in the beginning there were other major league teams in the Boston area, and there were other teams in some of the different leagues that sprang up that helped shape the history of baseball in Massachusetts. The history of baseball in Massachusetts began in 1871 and is still going strong today.

It was 1871 and there was major league baseball in Boston and it was played at the South End Grounds and the Union Grounds. It was not the Boston Braves and it was not the Boston Red Sox, but it was the Boston Red Stockings who played in the National Association which was considered a major league for that period of time. The team had a record of 20 wins and 10 losses. It scored 401 runs in the 30 games that were played which meant that the Red Stockings were averaging a little over 13 runs per game. The team was managed by Harry Wright, who over the course of a 23 year managerial career won 1,255 games and 6 pennants all with the Red Stockings. Wright, who was born in Sheffield, England in 1835 was regarded as the "Father of Professional Baseball" during baseball's early years. He was a pitcher who used off speed pitches instead of just rearing back and throwing the ball as many of the pitchers did during that part of baseball's early years. After Wright would pitch he would bring in a fastball pitcher to offset what he (Wright) had been throwing which threw off the batter's timing. This was the first instance of the term "relief pitching" in baseball. Wright also emphasized the necessity of fair play and high ethics which he hoped would advance the evolution of the game. He was also one of the first people to adhere to the theory of "spring training" in baseball as he took his teams south to get a head start on the competition. Other teams saw what Wright did and began to follow suit. Wright died in 1895 and 58 years later, he was elected to the Baseball Hall of Fame joining his brother George who had been elected in 1937.

Harry Wright was again the manager of the Red Stockings in 1872 and this time the team finished first in the National Association with a record of 39 wins and 8 losses. In 1873 it would be another pennant for the Red Stockings and Wright, and as a bonus there were four future Hall of Fame inductees on the team that year. It would be the brothers combination of George and Harry Wright, Jim "Orator" O' Rourke and Albert Spalding. The team would play its home games at South End Grounds, Hamden Park Race Track and the 23rd Street Park. Wright's managerial genius was still working as he led the 1874 Red Stockings to the National Association pennant as the team played its home games at both the South End Grounds and the Worcester Driving Park.

The 1875 season would produce another National Association pennant as this time the Red Stockings would finish first with a record of 71 wins and only 8 losses. They would play their home games at South End Grounds, Hampden Race Track Park and the Adelaide Avenue Grounds. Boston's national League team would end up playing at the South End Grounds until 1914 as they played the World Series that year at Fenway Park and defeated the Philadelphia Athletics in a four game sweep. The Braves would play at Fenway for the 1915 season too and then move to Braves Field in Boston where they would remain until they moved to Milwaukee after the 1952 season ended. The team would be known as the Red Stockings until 1883 when they were renamed the Beaneaters until 1907 when they would become the Boston Doves. They would remain the Doves until 1911 when they would be known as the Rustlers. They would be known as the Boston Braves from 1912 until 1935, from 1936 to 1940 they would be the Boston Bees and then it would be back to the Braves.

There would be a number of great ball player and Hall of Famers who played for the Boston teams while they were in the National League. They had a trio of 300 game winners in Charles "Old Hoss" Radbourne, John Clarkson and Charles Augustus "Kid" Nichols. There was Rogers Hornsby, probably the greatest right handed hitter of all time. Of course Babe Ruth came back to Boston after playing with the Yankees but he was just a shell of the great slugger he once was. There was also Ernie Lombardi, a Hall of Fame catcher who played for the Braves and was elected to the Hall of Fame in 1986. Of course the National League Boston team had another 300 game winner in the later part of their existence, Warren Spahn, who may have been the greatest left handed pitcher in baseball and who was elected to the Hall of Fame in 1973. But the Hall of Famers did not end with just the players. Boston had Hall of Fame managers as well. There was Dave Bancroft who managed the Braves from 1924 through 1927 and was elected to the Hall in 1971 by the Veterans' Committee. Bill McKechnie managed the Braves from 1930 through 1937 and was elected to Cooperstown in 1962. Then of course there was a man who managed the Braves and later on went on to manage the New York Yankees in the glory days of the late 40's and the 50's, Charles Dillion "Casey" Stengel who was elected to Cooperstown in 1966.

In 1884 Boston had a team in the Massachusetts State Association called the Boston Reserves. Little is known of this team other than they were managed by a man named S.R. Brown and that on the roster were Bill Annis, Marty Barrett, Peter Duffy, Mike Hines and others. Also in 1884 Boston had a team in the Union Association that was managed by Tim Murnane and included on the roster future Hall of Fame player Tommy McCarthy.

1886 would have the Boston Blues playing in the New England League under the leadership of managers Walter Burnham and Tim Murnane. Murnane was a sportswriter for the Boston Globe for over 30 years. He organized and helped to govern minor league baseball. He served as president of both the New England League and the Eastern League, and in 1978 he was awarded the J.G. Taylor Spink award for excellence in baseball journalism.

The 1887 Boston Blues/Haverhill team was a member of the New England League and had as its manager Walter Burnham. Also in 1887 Negro League baseball made an appearance in Boston as the Boston Resolutes began to play. What needs to be noted is that a lot of times the city that was in front of the teams name was used because there was a high population of blacks within its boundaries. Also what needs to be known about this league is that two of the eight teams, the Cincinnati Browns and the Washington Capitol Cities, did not play a game. The Pittsburgh Keystones played seven games, Baltimore Lord Baltimores played six games, the Philadelphia Pythians played five games, the New York Gothams played four games and the Louisville Fall City team played three games. The Boston team had played one game and the league ended up folding after two weeks.

The 1890 season would be one that challenged the way baseball was run as the National League was up against the Player's League. The Player's League was a league started due to issues between the players and management. Boston had a team in the league and it was called the Boston Reds and they were managed by Mike "King" Kelly, who later on was inducted into Cooperstown in 1945 by the Old Timer's Committee. Kelly managed Boston to a first place finish in the Player's League with a record of 81 wins and 48 losses. Hall of Famer Dan Brouthers was Kelly's teammate on this squad. In 1893 Bill McGunnigle would lead the Lowell/Manchester/Boston Reds under the banner of the New England League.

The 1901 season would bring significant changes to the baseball landscape in America as there was another major league forming that would play alongside the National League. 1901 would be the year that the American League was founded by Ban Johnson. One of the charter members of the league was the Boston Americans. The Americans would play until 1908 when they were renamed the Red Sox. No history of baseball in Massachusetts would be complete without a brief history of the Boston Americans/Red Sox. There have been volumes and volumes of books written on the Red Sox, and the bad luck that seemingly followed the team after the trading of Babe Ruth to the Yankees. What people need to remember is that in the early history of the Red Sox, which coincides with the history of the American League, that the Red Sox were a very good team with some all-time great players. Boston has had a history rich with baseball talent and the names that follow are all connected to the Red Sox in one way or another. They are also all members of the Baseball Hall of Fame in Cooperstown. They are as follows: Wade Boggs, Dennis Eckersley, Carlton Fisk, Jim Rice, Eddie Collins, Jimmy Collins, Joe Cronin, Bobby Doerr, Jimmy Foxx, Left Grove, Harry Hooper, Rick Ferrell, Babe Ruth, Tris Speaker, Ted Williams, Carl Yastrzemski, Tom Yawkey and Cy Young. That is definitely not a lineup any major league team would like to face, and it does not take into account players like Fred Lynn, Johnny Pesky and Mel Parnell among others. The Boston Red Sox are one of the most beloved franchises in sports, and Fenway Park where the Red Sox play is one of the nicest ballparks to watch a game from and hopefully it will be around for another 100 years.

1942 was a tumultuous year on both the foreign and domestic front. With World War II in full swing all Americans were looking for a way to just forget for a while. All sports, baseball included, were beginning to feel the pressure to allow the Negro athlete to compete on the same playing fields and at the same times as his Caucasian counterparts. This would be especially true as war holds no prejudice and soldiers of all colors and nationalities were getting hurt or killed on the battlefields. In 1942 a team called the Boston Royal Giants was an independent Negro League baseball club that would also be known as the Boston Giants, Quaker Giants, Philadelphia

Giants and the Boston Colored Giants. While Boston never really
had a Negro League team based in the city, the name of the city was
taken due to the high Negro population.

It should be noted however that baseball for the Negros started in
Boston in the early 1870's. The teams associated with Boston were not
as well-known as teams like the Pittsburgh Crawfords, Detroit Stars or
Homested Grays but black baseball was alive and well in the capital of
Massachusetts. The Negro League teams played at smaller venues like
Playstead Park in Cambridge or Lincoln Park in Boston, but in certain
cases Braves Field, which is now Boston University's Nickerson Field,
or Fenway Park were rented out for the Negro baseball games. In 1946
during the time just before Jackie Robinson integrated major league
baseball, Branch Rickey began steps to develop a third major league
to compete against the other two major leagues. This would give the
Negro male a chance to compete. Unfortunately this league never got
off the ground and the team associated with Boston nor any other
team ever played a league game.

Baseball after the 1940's was and is still being played in Boston on
the major league level, and there is nothing more I can add here that
will add to what people already know so while what was written
here does go into details deeply the purpose is to show the history
of baseball in Massachusetts and the effect some of the players and
teams have had on the game and its history. With that being said, it
is time to move to a different city and see that history as well as the
history of more towns/cities in this great state.

FITCHBURG - In 1895 Fitchburg, Massachusetts had a team that was
in the New England Association and the team was managed by Larry
Thyne. It was an independent league with no classification and no affiliation. 1899 would have Fitchburg and the city of Lawrence in a partnership in the New England League with Ed Norton as the manager.
There would be a 15 year gap before minor league baseball returned
to Fitchburg. Still playing in the New England League they would be

known as the Burghers, and would partner with the city of Manchester, New Hampshire, which had a team called the Textiles. This two town team would be managed by Fred Lake during the 1914 season. In 1915 the Fitchburg Burghers were managed by Hugh McCune.

For 1919 the Fitchburg team would be called the Foxes and would be managed by the trio of Bill Phoenix, John Quinn and William Page. 1922 would have the Fitchburg/Worcester Boosters playing in the Eastern League with Jack Mack and John Flynn as the team's managers. One of the players on this team reached glory on the football fields of America and in the track and field arenas of Europe. He was given the title of "The Greatest Athlete Who Ever Lived" by King Gustav after winning gold medals in the pentathlon and decathlon, two of the toughest tests of endurance around. He also played professional football an as elected to the Pro Football Hall of Fame in Canton, Ohio in 1963 and the College Football Hall of Fame in South Bend, Indiana in 1951, and his name was Jim Thorpe.

As for 1929, which was the last season that a minor league team played in Fitchburg, it would be the Fitchburg Wanderers, Haverhill Hillies and Gloucester Hillies playing in the Class B New England League.

HULL - Little is known about the team from Hull that played in the International League in 1896 other than they played with a team from Farnham, Quebec, Malone New York, Montreal, Quebec, and Plattsburgh, New York as well as teams from St Albans, Vermont and St Hyacinth, Quebec.

TAUNTON- The history of minor league baseball in Taunton began in 1897 when the Taunton Herrings played in the New England League under the manager ship of John Irwin. The Herrings also played in 1898 as well as 1899 in the New England League when their manager was Con Murphy. One of the players on Murphy's squad later went on to a spectacular major league career as a pitcher. The man spent 16 years in the major leagues where he won 373 ballgames which is tied for third best of all time. His 2.13 earned run average is good enough for 8th best all time and he also completed 435 of the 552 games he started. He twice won the National League pitching Triple Crown and also threw two no hitters. He was a member of the Baseball All-Century team and was ranked at number 7 on the 100 Greatest Players list put out by the Sporting News. During the 1905 World Series he threw three complete game shutouts within a six day period that led the Giants to their first World Series title. Along with Babe Ruth, Ty Cobb, Walter Johnson and Honus Wagner, he was a member of the first class elected to the Baseball Hall of Fame in 1936. His name was Christy Mathewson.

In 1905 the Lowell/Taunton Tigers partnered up in the New England League with George Grant and William Conners as the managers. The 1908 New England League would see a joint effort between Taunton and Attleboro as the Taunton/Attleboro Angels played with the team being led by manager M. McDermott. In 1914 the Taunton Herrings were managed by Thomas Gilroy and Ambrose Kane and then Thomas Gilroy took over Taunton for the 1915 season. Both the 1914 and 1915 teams would be members of the Colonial League. Then finally in 1933, the Taunton Blues would play in the class B New England League with Kenneth Black as their manager.

WORCESTER - Worcester, Massachusetts is another Massachusetts city with a rich baseball tradition and it was the only other city in Massachusetts to host a major league team. In 1878 the International Association had a team called the Lynn Live Oaks/Worcester that was managed by a man named George Brackett.

In 1880 the Worcester Ruby Legs were a team in the National League that was managed by Frank Bancroft, and which played its home games at the Agricultural County Fair Grounds. The Ruby Legs finished 5th that year with a record of 40 wins and 43 losses. In 1881 the Ruby Legs would finish 8th in the National League standings with a record of 32 wins and 50 losses with Mike Dorgan and Harry Stovey as managers. The final year for major league baseball in Worcester was 1882 and again the Ruby Legs finished 8th with a record of 18 wins and 66 losses. The managers were Freeman Brown, Tommy Bond and Jack Chapman. One of the players on the Ruby Legs that year was John Clarkson who finished the year with a record of one win and two losses. It would be of no matter, however, as Clarkson later went on to win 327 more games as a major league pitcher, good enough for 12th best of all time.

The 1884 Worcester team was part of the Massachusetts State Association and had as its managers Matthew Barry and David McGarvey. The Worcester Grays were members for the New England League in 1888 and were managed by Walter Burnham. One of the members of that team that year was Billy Hamilton, who was later elected to the Baseball Hall of Fame. Burnham again managed the Worcester squad in 1889. However, the team was now part of the Atlantic Association and would be for the 1890 season as well, only with Jim Cudworth as the manager instead of Burnham. In 1891 Worcester would play in the New England League as did the 1894 Worcester team under the leadership of Mike Slattery and Pat Murphy.

In 1898 the New Bedford Whalers/ Worcester team was an entrant in the New England League with Charles Rice and Fred Doe leading the squad. The Worcester Farmers were members of the 1899 Eastern League and were managed by Frank Leonard. In 1900 Malachi Kitteridge would manage Worcester while they were still in the Eastern League. One of the players on the 1900 Farmers team was Jim Delehanty, who was one of five brothers to play in the major leagues. The 1901 team would be known as the Quakers and were managed by Zeke Wrigley. The 1902 team were called the Worcester Hustlers and were part of the Eastern League which was managed by Frank Leonard, and on this team Leonard had another Delehanty brother (Joseph). In 1903 the Montreal Royals/ Worcester Riddlers would play in the Eastern League under the direction of Gene DeMontreville and Zeke Wrigley.

It would be another name change for the Worcester team in 1906

as they would be known as the Worcester Busters and they would
be playing in the New England League with Jesse Burkett as their
manager. In fact Burkett would manage the squad every year up
until 1915 with the exception of 1912, when John O Donnell took
over for a while. The team would keep the name Busters and pay
the 1916 season in the Eastern League for manager Billy Hamilton.
The 1917 edition of the Busters would be managed by a man named
M. McMahon as would the 1918 and 1919 squads when they were
known as the Boosters. McMahon must have been doing something
right as he stayed on to manage the Boosters in 1920 and 1921 too.
Gabby Hartnett, who later went on to a major league career with the
Chicago Cubs and New York Giants, was a member of the 1921 team.
He was considered by many to be one of the best catchers in baseball.
He was a six time All Star and was voted Most Valuable Player in the
National League in 1935. The Woonsocket, Rhode Island native was
voted into the Hall of Fame in Cooperstown in 1955.

For the 1922 Eastern League season Jack Mack and John Flynn would
be managers of the team, which also had as one of its members Jim
Thorpe, the football great. The 1923 Worcester Panthers would be
managed by Jesse Burkett, who also managed the 1924 Worcester
team. 1925 would see the Worcester Panthers managed by Eddie
Eayrs, and a man who go on to become one of the greatest major
league managers of all-time Charles Dillon "Casey" Stengel. Stengel
would have a relatively unspectacular career as a manager for the
Brooklyn Dodgers from 1934 through 1936 and the Boston Bees/
Braves from 1938 until 1943. It would be six years before Stengel
managed in the major leagues again, and when he did he became
manager of the New York Yankees. From 1949 through the 1960
season, the Yankees would win 10 American League pennants and
7 World Series titles. Stengel ended his managerial career with the
New York Mets with a total of 1,905 wins which was good enough
for 11th on the all-time list for managers. He was elected to the Halls
of Cooperstown in 1966 by the Veterans' Committee.

1933 would have the Worcester Chiefs as members of the New

England League and in 1934 the Waltham/Worcester Rosebuds would play in the Northeastern League under the direction of Freddie Maguire. It would then be 75 years before minor league baseball returned to the "Heart of the Commonwealth," and it would be in 2005 when the Worcester Tornados would join the Canadian American League with former Red Sox catcher Rich Gedman managing the team until 2011 when it was managed by Ed Riley. For the 2012 season the Worcester manager would be Chip Plante.

BROCKTON - Baseball in the city of Brockton began in 1885 when the team from Brockton was part of the Eastern New England League along with teams from Haverhill, Lawrence, Newburyport and Portland, Maine. The Brockton team was managed by Bill McGunnigle. McGunnigle also split the managing duties in 1886 with Jim Cudworth. The team had as one of its player's future Hall of Fame outfielder and native of Boston Tommy McCarthy. Jim Cudworth was the manager of the 1892 Brockton team, which was now called the Shoemakers and then Fred Doe would take over the manager's seat for the 1893 season and he in turn was replaced by William Allen and C Wilson for the 1894 season. The 1895 season would see the Brockton team, still known as the Shoemakers, in the New England League being managed by R. Perrin. Then from 1896 through the 1899 season the team would be managed by Walter Burnham.

For the 1901 season the Syracuse Stars/Brockton B's would play in the Eastern League under the direction of Frank Leonard and in the later part of the 1901 season the B's would switch back to the New England League. Fred Doe would be the manager of the Brockton/New Bedford Whalers in the New England League, and then it would be four years before a Brockton team returned to the New England League with a new name and a new manager. The new name was to be the Brockton Tigers and the new manager was Stephen Flanagan. Things would stay that way for the next two years with Brockton still competing in the New England League and Flanagan remaining as the team's manager.

1910 would see Flanagan still in charge of the Brockton nine and they would be now known as the Shoemakers. Ed McLane would manage the team in 1912 and in 1913 the Shoemakers would have as their manager Nick Rufiagne. Brockton would move to the Colonial League for the 1914 season and have Burt Weeden and William Reardon as their managers. For the 1915 season the name of the team would change to the Pilgrims and would still be played under the Colonial League banner.

After 13 years without a team, the Brockton Shoemakers returned in 1928 to begin play in the New England League with Lewis Courtney as their manager. Arthur Ryan became the skipper in 1929. It would then be 1933 when the Quincy Shipbuilders/Nashua Millionaires/ Brockton Shoemakers would play for manager Hal Weafer in the New England League. The team had an affiliation with the American League's Detroit Tigers.

Sixty nine years later in the 2002 Northern League East the Brockton Rox would begin play with Ed Nottie as their manager. Nottie continued to manage in 2003 and 2004 with the Rox now playing in the Northeast League. The Rox would play in the Canadian American Association for the 2005 season with Nottie still at the helm. One of the players on the Rox that year was former Boston Red Sox pitcher Dennis "Oil Can" Boyd, who was attempting a baseball comeback after being out of the game since 1997. From 2006 through 2008 the Rox would be managed by Chris Miyake and for the 2009 and 2010 seasons the Rox' manager would be Chris Carminucci. There was another former Red Sox pitcher on the Rox staff that year, Bill "Spaceman" Lee. Then for the 2011 season the Rox brought back Bill Buckner to manage the team. Buckner had been vilified after he was made the scapegoat for the 1986 World Series, but the Red Sox Nation welcomed him back with open arms. What is important to remember about Buckner is that during the course of his 22 year career he had over 2,700 hits, was a member of the 1981 National League All Star team and won the 1980 National League batting crown.

GLOUCESTER - Gloucester, Massachusetts had one entry in minor league baseball and that was a combined effort in 1929 between the Gloucester Hillies, the Haverhill Hillies and the Fitchburg Wanderers.

LAWRENCE - Minor league baseball came to Lawrence, Massachusetts in 1884 as Lawrence fielded a team in the Massachusetts State Association. There were five men who managed the squad that year and they were Matthew Barry, L. Dow, Frank Selee, Charles Freleigh and Harry Clark. For 1885 Lawrence was a member of the Eastern New England League and would be managed by Walter Burnham. Lawrence was a New England League member in 1886 and was managed by Frank Cox. In 1887 Lawrence and Salem came together to form a team as a part of the New England League with Pat Pettee and Harry Putnam sharing the manager's duties . In 1892 the Manchester Gazettes/Lawrence team would be managed by Jim Cudworth and W. Freeman. In 1899 Fitchburg/Lawrence would play under the banner of the New England League with Ed Norton as the team's skipper.

The team would take on a new name for the 1902 season as they would be now known as the Lawrence Colts with Frank Cox, George Keefe and William Parsons as the team's managers. The 1903 version of the Colts would be managed solely by William Parsons, and they still would be members of the New England League. The 1904 Colts would have Stephen Flanagan as the manager and the 1905 Manchester/Lawrence Colts would be led by Win Clark for the New England League season. James Rolley, Albert Weddige and Phenomenal Smith would be the trio of men chosen to lead the Colts for the 1906 season. James Rolley would fly solo for the 1907 season, and would then turn over his manager's cap to Mal Eason for 1908 and Eason would stay on to manage for the 1909 season as well. Then in 1910 Jimmy Bannon would manage Lawrence, and in 1911 Louis Pieper would take over for Bannon as the manager of the Lawrence team who would now be known as the Lawrence Barristers. Pieper would stay to manage Lawrence for the 1912, 1913 and 1914 seasons as well. Alex Pearson took over the Lawrence team in 1915. The 1916 season would have Lawrence playing in the Eastern League under the leadership of Jesse Burkett and Lawrence Mahoney. Lawrence would have two managers for the 1917 season as Ned O'Donnell and John Flynn led the team in the Eastern League that season.

The Lawrence team would go back to the New England League for the 1919 season and the manager would be William Page. It would be 1926 before minor league baseball returned to Lawrence as the team returned to play in the New England League under the direction of Lefty Tyler and that version of the Lawrence team would be known as the Merry Macks. Fredy Parent would be in charge of the Lawrence team for the 1927 season. Six years later the three cities of Attleboro, Lawrence and Woonsocket, Rhode Island would enter play in the New England League, affiliates of the New York Giants. Thirteen years later the Lawrence Millionaires would play in the New England League with manager George Kissell in charge. Kissell was also the manager in 1947 when the Lawrence Millionaires and the Lowell Orphans teamed up in the New England League.

NEW BEDFORD - New Bedford/New Haven and Hartford would join together in 1878 during the International Association season to form a team with Frank Bancroft and Benjamin Douglas as the managers. On the squad would be two future Hall of Famers, Candy Cummings and Roger Conner. Seventeen years later in 1895 The New Bedford Whalers would begin play in the New England League with Frank Bancroft and Fred Doe as the managers. For 1896 Doe would be the sole manager and the name of the team would be the New Bedford Whalers/Browns. For the 1897 season the Whalers/Browns would have Con Murphy and Mike McDermott at the helm. In 1898 New Bedford and Worcester would play as one under the New England banner with Charles Rice and Fred Doe as skippers. As for the 1903 season The New Bedford Whalers/Brockton team would compete in the New England League with Fred Doe still the manager, a post he would stay at in 1904, as well as 1905.

After the 1906 season Jack Coveney started as the Whalers manager for the 1907 season. Tommy Cocoram took over in 1908 and Tommy Dowd was in the manager's chair for the 1909 season and 1910 season as well. James Sullivan would take over the reins for the 1911 season with a young player by the name of Walter Maranville on the squad. This would be the same person who would later be known as Rabbit and be enshrined in Cooperstown's hallowed halls. Sullivan stayed on to manage in 1912, and then in 1913 Frank Connaughton and John O'Briend would head the Whalers nine. O'Brien stayed to manage the team in1914 as they pursued the Colonial League pennant, a chase they would continue into the 1915 season.

After 14 years, baseball returned to New Bedford as the team then known as the Millmen played for the 1929 New England League crown under the watch of manager Jack Ryan.. The year was now 1933 and the name of the team had changed back to the Whalers with Freddie Macguire in charge. Then in 1934 Jean Dubuc would manage the team in the Northeastern League. One of the players Dubuc would coach was Birdie Tibbetts, who some baseball people regarded as one of the league's best catchers in the late 40's and early 50's Tibbetts played with the Detroit Tigers, Boston Red Sox and Cleveland Indians. He was a four time All Star, and when he retired he stayed in baseball as a manager. He was rewarded by being named 1956 National League Manager of the Year as the pilot of the Cincinnati Reds.

QUINCY - The Detroit Tigers had an affiliate for the 1933 season that was a combination of two Massachusetts cities and one city in the state of New Hampshire. The team was the Quincy Shipbuilders/Nashua Millionaires/Brockton Shoemakers and it would be managed by Hal Weafer.

WALTHAM - Freddie Macguire was the manager for the 1934 Waltham/Worcester Rosebuds, who played the 1934 season as members of the Northeastern League.

While conducting research for this project I came across a city by the name of Berkshire. I found out that the team played in 1976 as the Berkshire Brewers in the Eastern League and as the Berkshire Black Bears in 2002 in the Northern League East and 2003 in the Northeast League. Those teams played out of Wahconah Park and were discussed in the book's chapter on Wahconah Park, its teams and players.

There was also a period of four years from 1996 through 1999 where a team called the Massachusetts Mad Dogs played. The Mad Dogs acquired their name when students from the Lynn and Nahant schools entered a contest to choose the name of a team to represent Lynn in the North Atlantic League in 1996 and the name Mad Dogs was chosen. The Mad Dogs went on to play the 1997, 1998 and 1999 seasons. The team ceased operations after 1999 because of what they said were issues with the team's home field in Lynn which was Fraser Field. The team resumed operations three years later and was resurrected as the Berkshire Black Bears who played at Wahconah Park.

Negro League Baseball In Massachusetts

....

Massachusetts never hosted a major Negro League ball club, which is especially puzzling given the number of African Americans residing in and around Boston and the surrounding areas during the time when the Negro Leagues were flourishing. Although again, this is not surprising because what has to be remembered is the Boston Red Sox were the last major league baseball team to sign a Negro ballplayer when they inked Pumpsie Green to a contract in 1959, 12 years after Jackie Robinson broke the color barrier in baseball. But the greater Boston area has a history that is rich in touring Negro clubs, so it is on to that subject now.

There were a number of different leagues that the black baseball player could play in, and of course, there were teams in the area as well. The role of the Negro in baseball in Massachusetts began in April of 1878 when Bud Fowler played on a team from Chelsea, Massachusetts as a pitcher. Towards the end of the month of April, Fowler also played for the Lynn Live Oaks and then managed to finish out the year with a team from Worcester, Massachusetts. In 1879 Fowler played with a team that was based out of Malden, Massachusetts and after that he played with teams out of the Midwestern part of the United States, but he would end up encountering prejudice at every stop. It is a shame because Fowler, Frank Grant and another player in the Negro Leagues by the name of George Stovey were very good players and were more than adequately equipped to play major league baseball. In fact Bud Fowler had played more games in league play than any other Negro Leaguer, including Jackie Robinson. In fact Fowler had played in more league games with white competition until Robinson finally passed him after his 11th season in the major leagues. Of course a lot of Fowler's playing time was marred by prejudice, which is truly a shame because baseball is supposed to be America's game.

In 1887 there was an initial attempt to start an all Negro team league. This was very significant as it would be over 30 years before the Negro National League was started by Andrew "Rube" Foster. This 1887 league was called the National Colored Baseball League, and the president of the league was Walter Brown, who was also the manager of the Pittsburgh franchise in the league. There were a total of eight teams in the league and they were the Pittsburgh Keystones, Baltimore Lord Baltimores, the Boson Resolutes, Cincinnati Browns, Louisville Fall City, New York Gorhams, Philadelphia Pythiens and the Washington Capitol Citys. Unfortunately, the league lasted only two weeks and then disbanded. Even though the league was not a success, it would start out to be the beginning of Negro League baseball as Americans would come to know it.

There was also a club in the area called the Boston Colored Giants, and it was run by a man named A.A. "Bob" Russell during the early 1920's and into the early part of the 1930's. Boston was in the midst of the Great Depression and the blacks from the south were migrating to the northeastern area in search of jobs. These teams would compete against teams from factories, semi pro teams and town teams made up of mostly white ballplayers.

The team was very well organized and the stars of the team were Moses Sisco and Billy Burke, who were a pair of speedy outfielders. They along with outfielder Spike Cohen and first baseman Oscar Moore made up the strong nucleus of the team. In fact, Moore later went to the college ranks to coach baseball at Florida A&M. A lot of the players on the Boston Colored Giants were good ballplayers who were products of the athletic program at Cambridge Ridge and Latin High School. Obviously these were not the only players on the team as they also had Joel Lewis, who pitched and hailed from Allston, Massachusetts. While in high school, Lewis hooked up with Danny MacFayden, who later went on to a career in the major leagues. Apparently this game went into extra innings and was considered a classic example of good baseball.

Russell was a whiz as a promoter and at one of the meetings of the Negro Leagues, Russell proposed that his team be added to the league. However, some of the other owners who were present felt that the fan base for a Negro League team in the area was lacking and Russell and his team were denied entry into the league.

In 1923 there was a team called the Quaker Giants that was organized into a team that was based out of Boston. The team was renamed the Philadelphia Giants for the purposes of better marketing and the team was led by veteran Negro League player Danny McClellan. What happened here was what had happened to other teams. The sports teams would name themselves after cities that were heavily populated by Negros. That is why the Harlem Globetrotters were named as they were, even though they were founded in Chicago Illinois by a man named Abe Saperstein. Anyway, the Giants were a team that was very talented and the leader of the group was a long tall drink of water that threw the ball sidearm and went by the name of "Cannonball" Jackman. Jackman's catcher on that Giants team was a man by the name of Burlin White.

During the 1920's teammates came and went and the name of the team changed to the Boston Colored Giants and the Boston Royal Giants, but the duo of Jackman and White were a constant. John McGraw, the legendary manager of the New York Giants, thought Jackman would be an asset to any team and that the only thing holding him and others like him back was the color of their skin. Bill Young played in the Negro Leagues during that time and later went on to scout for the New York Yankees. Young said that Jackman was the greatest all around baseball player he had ever seen. Jackman and White often would play for other teams like the Newark Eagles, Watertown Arsenal and a team from East Douglas, Massachusetts that had the legendary Detroit Tiger slugger Hank Greenberg on it. Jackman also played with the Santop Broncos and the Washington Quake Giants. The Royal Giants played all over the Northeast from the Cape Briten League in Canada to leagues and teams in Maine, Vermont and New Hampshire. Jackman and White were both approaching 50 years of age and still playing with the Royal Giants in the Park League and they were still tough to beat. In fact, one of the people who batted against Jackman said that Jackman was a harder pitcher to hit against than future Hall of Fame pitcher Robin Roberts.

However, the Royal Giants were not the only team to play in the area. There was a semi-pro team that played in the Boston area in the 1930's called the Boston ABC's. The team's promoter was a man by the name of Clem Mack and the team's president was a lady by the name of Clare Muree Jones and she would not let the team play on Sundays because it was sacrilegious. One time the ABC's played the Homestead Grays two games and lost which was not really that bad as the Grays were considered the elite team in the Negro Leagues. The ABC's outstanding players were Leroy Powell, who also played with the Washington Black Sox, Speedball Syms and Jimmy Rhem who both played with the Schenectady Mohawk Giants and the Edgewater Giants.

There was another team in the area called the Boston Blues. The Blues were part of the United States Baseball League which was founded by Branch Rickey in 1945. According to Rickey, the league was founded to give the Negro League ballplayer a place to play. What has to be remembered at this point is that while there was never anything written or said it would seem as though major league baseball was under some type of "order" which prevented the black ballplayer from playing in the major leagues. Even though Rickey founded the league, he was roundly criticized because people felt that he was in fact promoting segregation and was out for his own personal gains. The fact of the matter is this through the United States Baseball League allowed Mr. Rickey to scout the Negro Leagues and its players for the players who would best fit into Rickey's future plans for the Brooklyn Dodgers. In 1945 the United States Baseball League consisted of the Atlanta Black Crackers, Chicago Brown Bombers, Detroit Motor City Giants, Philadelphia Daisies, Brooklyn Brown Dodgers, Pittsburgh Crawfords and the St Louis Stars. In 1946 there were only four teams in the league and they were the Boston Blues, Cleveland Clippers, Pittsburgh Crawfords and a team from Milwaukee, Wisconsin. Unfortunately, the league folded because of scheduling issues.

Another problem that teams like the Colored Giants and the Royal Giants and the ABC's had was the games were most of the time played in smaller public parks like Playstead Park in Cambridge or Lincoln Park in Boston. Braves Field in Boston, which is now home to Northeastern University's Nickerson Stadium, finally was rented to African American teams beginning in 1938. Fenway Park, home of the Red Sox was heavily used after the 1945 season as well. There were protests and boycotts that would try to get the Boston teams to integrate and for reasons unknown the Boston Red Sox were the last team in the major leagues to integrate and that came a full 12 years after Jackie Robinson in 1947. The first Negro ballplayer or the Boston Red Sox was Elijah "Pumpsie" Green.

No mention of baseball in the state of Massachusetts would be complete without mentioning the Cape Cod Baseball League. It is a league for college age players and it also uses the wooden bat which is a rarity in college level baseball in this day and age. The skill level for the players in the Cape Cod League is about that of a high level of Class A ball in the minor leagues.

Baseball on the Cape dates back to 1865 when sea captain Edward Nichols invited a baseball team to play on his field which was located on School Street in the town of Sandwich, Massachusetts. The team was named the Nichols Club in his honor and it is believed that the team was the first organized team on the Cape and that it surely would have included soldiers from the Civil War as they had brought the game home after learning it on the battlefield. Officially, however, the league started around 1885 or about the time that Chester Arthur was succeeded as President of the United States by Grover Cleveland.

The ten teams which were in the league at this time were: the Bourne Braves, Cotuit Kettlers, Falmouth Commodores, Hyannis Harbor Hawks, Wareham Gatesmen, Brewster White Caps, Chatham Anglers, Harwich Mariners, Orleans Firebirds and the Yarmouth-Dennis Red Sox.

Cape Cod's baseball history is that of a league that was started back in the 1880's and one of the teams that have been in the league the longest has been the team from Bourne, which is now known as the

Braves. When baseball started in Bourne in the 1860's, Bourne was still part of the town of Sandwich. It was in 1933 when a team from Bourne joined the Cape Cod League. The league was reformed in 1946 and Bourne was represented by the Sagamore Cloutiers and the Bourne Canalmen. The team would cease to operate in 1973 after ten years of not making the playoffs. It wouldn't be until 1988 when the Bourne team was reformed and joined the Cape Cod League along with the Brewster White Caps. After making numerous appearances in the playoffs, the Bourne Braves were able to climb to the top of the sand dune in 2009 when they beat the Cotuit Kettlers for the Braves first ever Cape League Championship.

When the team played as the Canalmen they would play at Keith Field, which was located under the Sagamore Bridge. Also when the team played based out of the town of Sagamore, they were very successful they won the league championship in 1951, 1954, 1956, 1959 and in 1965. Some of the players who have played for the Bourne team over the years were Chris Capuano, Jeremy Giambi, Bill Mueller and Kevin Youklis. The team plays its home games at Upper Cape Cod Regional Technical High School's Doran Park.

A team from Falmouth has been a member of the Cape Cod League since the early part of the 20th century. In fact one of the early Falmouth teams had as their shortstop Harold "Pie" Traynor, who later became the first player from a Falmouth team to be elected to the Baseball Hall of Fame when he entered Cooperstown's hallowed halls in 1948.

Falmouth has fielded a team in the league for every year of the league's existence. The Central Grounds in Falmouth Heights was the site of the club's ballgames for the first 63 years they played there. It was a very picturesque place for a baseball field as the spectators would either sit on a grassy knoll which overlooked the field, or they would sit in their cars along the first base line. The only problem that the field had was that it had a very short right field. It was so short that some of the balls hit over the fence would sometimes strike a house on Ventral Park Avenue and would then be scored as doubles. At one time the team was named The Cottage Club because of the fact that there were so many cottages in and around the area. In fact the players would often stay there during their time on the Cape.

The old Cape Cod League which played from 1923 to 1939 had four teams in it when it was formed and they were the teams from Falmouth, Hyannis, Osterville and Chatham. There were other teams that joined the league and the high water mark for that was in 1930 when the league had seven teams which represented six towns. The first championship that the team from Falmouth won was in 1929 and that almost did not happen because of a managerial change and a threatened walkout over the release of a player. The first night game in the Cape League was played on July 19, 1939 between the Falmouth team and a team from Barnstable.

Sadly, 1939 was the last year of the old Cape League as the owners of the Falmouth, Bourne, Barnstable and Harwich teams did not appropriate money to have their teams continue. The league was revived in 1946 after the end of World War II. In 1950 the Falmouth Falcons were a team that played games against other teams that did not count in the standings.

There was another reorganization of the Cape League in 1963, which was also the last year the team played its home games at the Falmouth Heights Field. They were then allowed to use Guv Fuller Field starting in 1964. Falmouth turned around its baseball luck in 1965 after hiring Bill Livesy as the manager as the team won five league championships including four in a row from 1968 to 1971. In 1975 the league toyed with the possibility of using aluminum bats for the next ten years. The team now plays its home games at the Arnie Allen Diamond at Guv Fuller Field. The field is named in honor of Arnie Allen who was the Falmouth team batboy for 46 years. Some of the alumni of the Falmouth team who later went on to play in the major leagues included Tino Martinez, Jacoby Ellsbury, Mark Loretta and David Aardsma.

The Orleans Firebirds are another team that makes up the Cape Cod League. From 1946 until 2008 they were known as the Orleans Cardinals. Fifteen years prior to the beginning of the modern era of the Cape League the team won seven championships including back to back titles in 1949-1950 and 1952-1953. They won a title in 1957 and then went almost 30 years before winning another title with that one coming in 1986. The Orleans team was known as the Cardinals until the end of the 2009 season when they changed the name of the team to the Firebirds. The name change was because of an agreement between the Cape League and Major League baseball which said if a team shared its name with a major league ball club then the uniforms would have to be purchased through a vendor licensed by major league baseball. The Firebirds have been playing their home games at Eldredge Park at the Nauset Middle School. As for the alumni of the Firebirds that played in the major leagues, the list includes Aaron Boone, Nomar Garciaparra, J.T. Snow, Mark Teixeira and Matt Wieters.

The towns of Yarmouth and Dennis have had teams in the Cape League since the League's early days. The Yarmouth Indians won the league title in 1958 and again in 1960. Of course this was before the modern era of the Cape League which started in 1963. It would be 10 years in the modern era before Yarmouth would make an appearance in the championship series. The 1973 season would have the Yarmouth team beating the Chatham Athletics before falling to the Cotuit Kettlers in the five game championship series finals. The team was now known as the Yarmouth-Dennis Red Sox. They again lost the league championship to Cotuit in 1977 and would not return to the championship round until 1987. It would be four straight years in the playoffs which culminated in 1989 when the Yarmouth team won the league championship by defeating the Hyannis Mets. They would win the title again in 1990 when they beat the Wareham Gatemen in the championship finale.

The 21st century has been good to Yarmouth-Dennis as they won the league title in 2004, 2006 and in 2007. Their home games are played at the Red Wilson Field on the campus of Dennis –Yarmouth Regional High School. Some of the Yarmouth Dennis alumni include Craig Biggio, Buster Posey, David Robertson, JJ Putz and Gordon Beckham.

Chatham had a team in the early 1900's in the old Cape Cod Twilight League. That team was one of the dominant teams of the era as between 1933 and 1939 they won seven consecutive league titles. The Chatham team has been playing at Veteran's Field since 1923. That field is in an optimum location as it sits in a natural bowl which actually forms a stadium around the stadium because of the additional seating that it provides in addition to the seating already there. The field sits in Chatham between Depot Road and Main Street.

The success of the Chatham team has carried over into the modern era as they have won five league titles in that era. The late great Yankee catcher Thurman Munson led the Chatham team to a league record 30 wins and nine losses and four ties when they won the title in 1967. During the 1970's the team changed its name to the Chatham Athletics and reached the series championship round four more times before finally reclaiming the title in 1982. The Athletics were one of the more successful franchises during the 1990' as they won the league titles in 1992, 1996 and 1998.

The team changed its name from the Athletics to the Anglers in 2009 and besides Thurman Munson, some of the alumni who played in Chatham were Bobby Valentine, Jeff Bagwell, Ryan Braun and Evan Longoria.

Harwich has been a member of the Cape Cod League since 1930. Since the beginning of the modern era of the league Harwich has been in the playoffs 10 different times. They made the finals in 1968, 1978 and 1979 and lost, but were finally able to claim the title in 1983. In 1987 Harwich again won the title when they beat Yarmouth-Dennis and would wear the crown of the champion in 2008 and 2011. The team, which is known as the Mariners, plays their home games at Harwich High School at Whitehouse Field. Mariner players who have gone on to play in the major leagues include Tim Lincecum, Kevin Millar, Todd Stottlemyre and Carlos Pena.

Wareham has been a member of the Cape Cod Baseball League since 1963.Known as the Gatemen they would win the league title in 1976 by beating the Chatham Athletics in a thrilling five game series. That title was Wareham's first ever league crown. After a 12 year stretch they came back to win their second title in 1988. They then went through a period where they made the playoffs for 13 years which is still a Cape Cod League record. They played in the championship round seven times and ended up winning four titles. The team plays its home games at Clem Spilane Field which is at Wareham High School. Alumni of the Mariners include Lance Berkman, Chuck Knoblauch, Ben Sheets, Nick Swisher, Mo Vaughn and Barry Zito.

The Brewster White Caps are one of the newer teams in the Cape Cod League as 1988 was their first season and it was also the first season for the Bourne Braves. The Brewster team would make the playoffs in 1989, but lose in the first round to the team from Yarmouth-Dennis. The first championship round appearance came in 1994 after they beat Orleans in the first playoff round, but they lost in the finals to Wareham that year.

In the 2000 playoffs Brewster would beat Chatham two games to one and would advance to the championship round where they would win their first and as of yet only league championship by beating the team from Hyannis. It is unfortunate that regular season success does not breed success in the playoffs as Brewster has lost in the first round of the playoffs three out of five times to the team that has eventually gone on to win the league title. The team played its home games at Cape Cod Regional Technical High School until 2006 when the Stony Brook Field opened. Some of the alumni that have gone on to play in the major leagues from Brewster include Sean Casey, Chase Utley, Ryan Braun and Troy Tulowitzki.

The Cotuit Kettlers is also a team in the Cape Cod League. According to local legend around 300 years ago the English settlers were bartering with the local Indian tribes for the land where the towns of Santuit and Cotuit are now. One of the terms of the sale was that a brass kettle and a hoe would be included in the deal. The Cotuit Kettlers' name was derived from that part of the real estate transaction and the former sports editor of the Cape Cod Standard Times Ed Semprini who is the man who came up with the name Kettlers.

The Cotuit Athletic Association began sponsoring the team in 1947 and Cotuit won the last two league titles in the pre-Modern era of 1961 and 1962. The Kettlers were fortunate enough to win the first two titles in the modern era of 1963 and 1964 giving them a run of four straight league crowns. In fact during the 1963 regular season Cotuit had a record of 28 wins and 4 losses and defeated the team from Orleans in the finals in two straight games. 1964 was even better as Cotuit had a record of 31 wins and 3 losses and then defeated the Chatham Athletics three games to one to again win the title.

The years 1969 through 1987 would show that Cotuit was a very consistent team as they made the playoffs 18 out of 19 years. They won eight league titles including a string of four straight from 1972 through 1975.After the 19 year run ended, it would take the Kettlers five years to make the playoffs, and it would be 10 years before they would win another league title.

The Kettlers have the league record as they have won 13 titles and also have the most playoff appearances with 28. Their home games are played at Lowell Park and some of the players that have gone on to play in the major leagues include John Franco, Joe Girardi, Scott Spezio and Greg Vaughn.

The Bourne Canalmen were eliminated in the first round of the playoffs in the modern era in 1963 and then would not make the playoffs for the next 10 years and would cease operating after the 1973 season. In 1976, with the assistance of former state senator Jack Aylmer, the Hyannis Harbor Hawks were formed. In 1978 after only two years in the league, the Hyannis team finished with a record of 31 wins and 11 losses, which was the best record in the league. In the playoffs they beat the Orleans Cardinals in a hard fought five game series. They then played the Harwich Mariners who they defeated three games to one to win their first league title. Hyannis repeated as champions in 1979 after they set a Cape Cod League record by winning 33 games and that record still stands. They would again defeat the Harwich Mariners for

the title and would become the first team since the 1975 Cotuit Ket-
ters to defend a championship. Hyannis was in the playoffs five times
during the 1980's, but it would be 1991 before they would again win a
league title, which as of now, is their last. Albert Belle, Buck Showalter,
Jason Varitek and Robin Ventura are some of the major league players
that played for the Harbor Hawks at one time or another.

Cape Cod League Champions

Orleans—1949, 1950, 1952, 1953, 1955, 1957, 1986, 1993, 2003, 2005

Sagamore—1951, 1954, 1956, 1959, 1965

Yarmouth—1958, 1960

Yarmouth-Dennis—1989, 1990, 2004, 2006, 2007

Cotuit—1961, 1962, 1963,1964,1972,1973,1974,1975,1977,1981,1984, 1985 ,1995, 1999, 2010

Falmouth—1966, 1968, 1969, 1970, 1971, 1980

Wareham—1976, 1988, 1994, 1997, 2001, 2002

Chatham—1967, 1982, 1992, 1996, 1998

Hyannis—1978, 1979, 1991

Harwich—1983, 1987, 2008, 2011

Brewster—2000

Bourne—2009

Massachusetts Ballparks by Cities/Towns

....

ATTLEBORO - In the town of Attleboro, Brady Field played host to the 1908 Attleboro Angels of the Atlantic Association. There are now houses were the ballpark once stood.

Also the Attleboro Burros and the Attleboro team that played in 1933 called Hayward Field their home. Both of these teams played in the now defunct New England League. Hayward opened in 1921 and baseball is still being played there today.

....

HAVERHILL - Riverside Park in Haverhill was a recreational venue for many years. The baseball field was first laid out in 1916. In 1931 the WPA (Works Progress Administration) made funds available so that a wall and a grandstand could be built. There was another grandstand at the park that was built in 1921 and used for baseball, but it was demolished in 1991. Babe Ruth and Lou Gehrig both played exhibition baseball there and in a bit of football trivia the Boston (now New England) Patriots held their first ever scrimmage at Riverside Park.

There was also a place in Haverhill called Recreation Park which hosted the minor league Haverhill Blues. The park was located in the center of Haverhill and besides baseball other outdoor activities such as hiking and lawn tennis were also played. It is now the site of a Pentucket Bank

Athletic Park in Haverhill hosted the 1895 Haverhill Duffers as well as the Hustlers, Orphans and Hillies. In 1904 the New England League pennant was played there. It is now the site of a vacant lot.

Also located in Haverhill is Tener Park which was named after John Tener who was the president of the National League at the time. His wife came from the area and today it is still in use, just not for baseball.

BOSTON - The Boston Braves called South End Grounds home from 1876 until 1914 as did the Boston Red Stockings who called South End home from 1871 until 1875. The grounds actually opened for business on May 16, 1871 and closed for good on August 14, 1914. It was also known as Walpole Street Grounds, the Grand Pavilion and the Boston Base-ball Grounds. South End Grounds was across the street from the Huntington Avenue Grounds and was one of three structures that once stood on this property. In 1894 the stadium burned down during the course of a baseball game and the fire was known as the Great Roxbury Fire of 1894. The fire started in the right field bleachers and then spread. Now Ruggles Station stands there as a public transportation (MBTA) station for the Orange Line T, and there is also a parking garage there as well.

It would be impossible to write a history of baseball in Massachusetts without mentioning Fenway Park which is the oldest still in use ballpark in the major leagues. It was opened for business on April 20, 1912 at a cost of around $650,000. It is the place where Babe Ruth made his major league debut, Lefty Grove got his 300th win there in 1941 and Carl Yastrzemski got his 3000th hit there in September of 1979. It is a true treasure of baseball and a very important part of the history of baseball in Massachusetts.

On April 18, 1915 Braves Field opened in Boston. It hosted major league baseball from April 18, 1915 until September 21, 1952. The 1915 and 1916 World Champion Boston Red Sox played there because Braves Field sat more people than Fenway Park. The park opened in 1915, but it was not until 1925 when the first ball was hit over the fence for a home run. From 1915 until 1928 Braves Field had the largest outfield in the major leagues. It was 402 feet to left field, 550 feet to center field and 402 feet to right field. In that 13 year period there were only 7 balls hit over the fence for home runs, but an astonishing 209 inside the park home runs were hit there. It was purchased by Boston University when the Braves moved from Boston to Milwaukee and the University renamed it Nickerson Field and it is still in use by Boston University today.

Dartmouth Grounds played host to the 1884 Boston Reds of the Union Association as well as the 1886 Boston Blues of the New England League. Dartmouth Grounds was also known as Union Park and was located in the Back Bay section of Boston in Copley Square. There was a bicycle track around the park and the baseball field was below street level.

The Congress Street Grounds were host to the 1890 Boston Reds of the Player's League and also the 1891 Boston Reds of the American Association. The Boston Reds also played there in the New England League in 1893 and the Congress Street Grounds was their home field as well. The Boston Braves played there in 1894 after fire destroyed the South End Grounds. To enter the ball park a person had to walk through two 75 foot towers that flanked the entrance and the towers contained stairs to allow people onto the second deck of the pavilion. Office space now occupies where the ballpark once was.

Huntington Avenue Grounds opened on May 8, 1901 and closed on October 7, 1911. It was located across the street from the South End Grounds. It had the deepest center field in baseball as it measured an astounding 635 feet to dead center field. It played host to the very first World Series in 1903 and it was the site of Cy Young's 300th win on July 12, 1901, Young's perfect game on May 5, 1904, and finally his 400th win on September 20, 1904. It was built on a circus lot and there was also a tool shed that was deemed in play during a baseball game. In 1993 where the pitcher's mound once was, there now stands a statue of Cy Young commemorating him leading the Red Sox to their first ever World Championship.

BROCKTON - Brockton Grounds had a grandstand that was 100 feet long and 28 feet deep which sat 1,500 customers. There also were 1000 free seats and everything to do with the grounds was made with the thought of comfort and convenience for the public. There are now houses located on the property.

Highland Park was located in Acton, Massachusetts and was owned by the Brockton Street Railway Company. It opened for business on August 11, 1892. It was quite the showcase with regard to ballparks of the day. It had a large dancing pavilion and places for a permanent orchestra as well as a dancing hall, merry go round and a bandstand. The grounds had handsome walkways and drives and also had rustic bridges and rockeries all over the park. Tennis courts were built and gardens were laid out to beautify the entire seven acres. Houses now sit where the ball field once did. It also played host to the 1897 and 1898 New England League Champions.

In 1894 and 1895 Centre Street Grounds or Walkover Park played host to the Brockton Shoemakers. There is a more modern ballpark there now seemingly fit for Little League or Babe Ruth/high school ball. The field also hosted the Brockton Shoemakers from 1907 to 1912.

May 31, 2002 was the opening day for Campeanelli Stadium in Brockton, Massachusetts. It plays host to the Brockton Rox of the CanAm League and has a seating capacity for 6,000 people. It has hosted the 2003 Northeast League Champions as well as the 2005 CanAm League All Star Game.

CAMBRIDGE - Charles River Park in Cambridge, Massachusetts was home to the Cambridge team in the 1899 New England League. There is a large office building at the street intersections where Charles River Park once stood.

The Locust Street Grounds Park also hosted the Cambridge team in the 1899 New England League and on the land where the ballpark stood are now all kinds of industrial type buildings.

In 1934 the Cambridge Cantabs played at what is known as Russell Field. There is now a football field there on the Russell Field property.

FALL RIVER - From 1893 until 1898 the Fall River Indians of the

New England League played their home games at the Bedford Street Grounds. It has also played host to the Brinies, the Adopted Sons and the Spindles. One of the other names that the park was known as was simply Athletic Park. This is the ballfield that on May 1, 1896 future Hall of Famer Napoleon "Nap" Lajoie began his professional baseball career. Now the Thomas Chew Boys and Girls Club is located on the property.

Fall River Stadium was the home ball field for the Fall River Indians from 1946 until 1949. It was also called Mark Stadium after Sam Mark who owned two of Fall River's more popular night spots, the Highway Casino and the Piccadilly.

FITCHBURG - The Fitchburg Driving Park was the home ball field for the Fitchburg Trilbys in 1895, the Fitchburg entry in the New England League in 1899, the Fitchburg Burghers in 1914 and 1915, the Fitchburg Foxes in 1919, the 1922 Fitchburg entry in the Eastern League and the 1929 Fitchburg Wanderers who played in the New England League. It also went by the name of Summer Street Park. After the park was built for the 1914 season, there was a fence put up on the property and it was painted green. Fred Lake, who was the player/manager of the team, left a blank spot in center void of any ads as an aid for the batter to be better able to see a pitch. As of 2008 there is still a baseball field on the property.

GLOUCESTER - Centennial Avenue Park in Gloucester was home to the 1929 Gloucester Hillies. There is still an athletic complex located on the property.

HOLYOKE - Falco Field played host to the Holyoke Papermakers in the Eastern Association from 1903 to 1913. Later on the field was renamed MacKenzie Stadium where the Holyoke Millers played as members of the Eastern League from 1977 to 1987. It has also been known as Elmwood Park and Beech Street Grounds at various times. It has hosted the 1903, 1905 and 1907 Connecticut League (Eastern Association) pennant winners and the 1980 Eastern League Champions. In 1884 then Holyoke mayor James E Dalaney proposed in his inaugural address to the city that Holyoke start up a park system. It was 1895 when Elmwood Park (Falco Field) was built. It has been used for all kinds of outdoor activities since. The Charles Ranlet estate was purchased for $9,000 in 1908 and that purchase added 14 acres to Elmwood Park. After the park was enlarged it made for tremendous centralized sporting grounds as it was in close proximity to Holyoke High School, Trade School and Sacred Heart Schools. They first put portable bleachers there in 1937 and then in 1938 with a Works Progress Administration Grant they installed permanent cement bleachers. The first time night baseball was played there would be 1949 and while that was under temporary lights, permanent lights were installed by Holyoke Gas and Electric in 1959. It was renamed MacKenzie Field after John S. MacKenzie who was awarded the Congressional Medal Of Honor when he saved 80 of his shipmates when a depth charge came untied during a storm. MacKenzie held onto the depth charge until the ship reached calmer waters and the depth charge could be retied.

LAWRENCE - From 1885 until 1887 and then in 1892 the Lawrence entry in the New England League played their home games at Association Grounds. The team used the grounds until 1887 when the Union Street Bridge burned down forcing the team to move to Nashua as the ball field became isolated and hard to get to. The property now has a factory building on it.

Glen Forest was located just over the Lawrence city line in the town of Methuen. The Lawrence Indians in 1895 and the Lawrence team in 1899 as well as the Lawrence Colts from 1902 until 1910 played here. It was the site of the New England Association pennant in 1895. It was located at the end of an electric trolley line and was later carved up into housing lots.

Riverside Park was the home field for the Lawrence Barrister from 1911 until 1917. From 1911 until 1915 the barristers played in the New England League and after that the team was a member of the Eastern League. In 1919 Riverside Park was renamed O'Sullivan Park and it was home to the 1919 Lawrence team that played in the New England League. The Lawrence MerryMacks played there in 1926 and 1927, the Lawrence Weavers in 1933, the Lawrence Millionaires in 1946 and the Lawrence Orphans in 1947. From 1919 until 1947 the Lawrence teams that played there were members of the New England League. The 1912 and 1914 New England League pennants were won there and now the Lawrence Boys and Girls Club sits on the property.

LOWELL - In 11887 the Lowell Browns played their home games at Fairgrounds Park as a member of the New England League and the 1889 Lowell Browns played there as a member of the American Association and they also played at Fairgrounds Park in 1891, 1892 and 1893 when they were back in as members of the New England League. The 1895 Lowell Indians played there as members of the New England Association as did the Lowell Tigers in 1901. Fairgrounds Park was owned by a man named Lennon who also owned a harness track with a grandstand, which he rented out to the Lowell baseball club. The problem he had was the fans who had a season pass to the harness track could watch a baseball game without paying to get in, so Lennon tried to raise the rent. The Lowell team countered by renting another piece of the fairgrounds land and then built the ballpark themselves. The owners did not want to play there as there was a limited amount of public transportation because the track was located so far from downtown Lowell. The land now has residential properties on it.

On May 5, 1887 the River Street Grounds opened as home to the Lowell Browns. It was a very small field that had a river running behind it in left field and it really was not very far from home plate. In fact the team put up a fence to keep balls from going in the river. During the 1887 season there were 88 home runs hit at the River

Street Grounds, a surprisingly high number given the Deadball Era where home runs were a rarity. The owners who then purchased the Browns moved because the field was so tough even for the home team's pitchers. There is now an industrial park on the property.

In 1895 because the Lowell Indians wanted to avoid Fairgrounds Park because sewer work there made access to the park limited. So the team played their games at the Dracut Oval which was located in a town adjacent to Lowell. Trolley access was worse there and the team went back to Fairgrounds Park. The Dracut Oval was primarily used for cricket but now has residential homes on the property.

Mountain Rock Park in Tyngsborough played host to the Lowell Tigers when baseball returned to Lowell in 1901. Sometimes there were bicycle races at Fairgrounds Park so the Tigers played some of their home games in Tyngsborough. There are now apartment houses on the property where the ball field once stood.

From 1902 until 1916 the Lowell Tigers, then the Lowell Grays played their home games at Spalding Field. After 1916 it was renamed Alumni Field with the official name being the Stanley Stoklosa Alumni Field. The Lowell Grays played there in 1919 as did the Lowell Highwaymen in 1926, then the Lowell Millers in 1929, the Lowell Orphans in1947 and the Lowell Spinners in 1996 and 1997. It was the site of the 1903, 1911, 1913 and 1919 New England League pennants. In the latter part of 1901 owner Fred Lake was able to get some land at the Atherton Grounds in Tewksbury (which was later annexed into part of Lowell in 1905). Lake built a ball field and named it Spalding Park after A.G. Spalding, who at the time was one of the most powerful men in baseball as he owned a large sporting goods company. Spalding had played for Lowell and for both the Boston Red Sox and the Chicago White Sox. After he retired, he built his sporting goods empire. It was not a perfect ballpark and it was hard to get to, so the Tigers moved closer to the downtown area of Lowell. Andrew Rock and James Kennedy bought the team in 1911 and moved it back to Spalding Park but the field was in dire needs of repair due to a fire that had occurred.

The Lowell Grays went out of business in 1916 and high school games were played there as the city of Lowell had taken control of the facilities. In 1996 the owner of the Elmira Pioneers, Clyde Smoll moved the team from Elmira to Lowell as he was promised a new ballpark. Over $600,000 was spent and for two years the Lowell Spinners played there waiting for a new field to be built. Alumni Field is still being used today in a college wooden bat league.

From 1906 to 1909 Washington Park was the home field for the Lowell Grays of the New England League. Al Winn had bought the team and right away built a ball park close to downtown Lowell. The park was so small that many of the balls that were hit off of the right field fence ended up as singles. The drainage system in the field was very good for its time as it could rain right up until the time of the game and the players would still be able to play. 1,500 of the seats had backs (opera style) and were covered by a roof. Winn was forced to sell the team in 1909 and when the new owners found out they would have to pay a $50.00 rental fee on the Washington Park property they found it to be less expensive to move the team back to Spalding Park which is what they did and the park in still in use today as a multi-purpose facility.

Laurier Park was the home field for the Lowell Lauriers in 1933 and 1934. In 1933 the team was part of the New England League and in 1934 they were part of the Northeastern League. The team was the co-champion of the New England League in 1933 and the Northeastern League champion in 1934. The park was built by the president of the Laurier Social Club Valerie "Vic" Lecourt. It was conveniently located so the average working man could stop in. The ballpark was small when built, but expanded in 1934. The expansion though was for naught as the Northeastern League folded after the 1934 season because the league president was convicted of embezzling funds. The team folded and the park was torn down. The grounds went from an auto junkyard to a supermarket. The University of Massachusetts at Lowell took the property over and made it into a research center.

LaLacheur Park was built in 1998 and has been the home to the Lowell Spinners of the New York Penn League. It cost $13 million dollars to build and it is located next to the University of Massachusetts at Lowell which is in the revitalized and cleaned up warehouse district. The Merrimack River is visible over the left field wall and the rustic looking Aiken Street Bridge is visible over the right field fence

LYNN - The West Lynn Grounds was home to the Lynn Lions in 1886 and 1887. It is still in use today as a baseball field and appears as though it is in a residential area of the city.

The Lynn Lions in 1887 and 1888 and the Lynn team in the New England League in 1891 and 1901 played at Glenmere Park. The park was built on 13 acres of land when the owner of the Lynn Live Oaks Charles Gay laid out a bicycle track. He later built a baseball field inside the track. The park was late sold after being assessed at $20,000 dollars so it could be broken up into housing lots which there are no on the property.

From 1905 to 1915 Ocean Park was home to the Lynn team of the New England League. It was aptly named as the park sat right on the ocean. Unfortunately that resulted in a lot of fog which would occasionally necessitate the need to cancel ballgames. There are now apartment complexes on the property.

The Lynn Papooses of the New England League played their home games at Lynn Stadium which was also known as Municipal Stadium. The main purpose of the stadium was to host football games for high schools, but it also hosted baseball and other sporting events. It had played host to concerts including one by Aerosmith and the Rolling Stones. It was torn down in 2005 to make way for a smaller and more modern facility.

GEAA Park was officially known as General Electric Athletic Association Park and it was one of the home fields for the Lynn Papooses of the New England League. The president of the New England

League Claude Davidson was hoping to improve attendance at league games, because the Sunday "Blue Laws" prevented Sunday baseball from being played. Most of the games were played when people were working so attendance was low. Davidson worked with the engineers at General Electric so that a ballgame could be played under an artificial lighting system. There was a game scheduled on June 23, 1929 which was a day that the New York Yankees would be leaving Boston after playing the Boston Red Sox. The game had a lot of hype to it because Babe Ruth would be there. The game ended up being postponed because of rain, so on the next day the Lynn Papooses played the Salem Witches in what was the "first organized night baseball game."

Curtain Field in Lynn, Massachusetts played host to the Lynn Papooses for a brief period in 1929. The ball field had uncovered grandstands and bleachers on both the third and first base lines. The fences in left and left center field were very short. The field was officially known as John H. Curtain Field but was also known as Lynn Gas and Athletic Field. It appears as though there are a number of industries on the property now.

Fraser Field in Lynn, Massachusetts has played host to the following ball clubs in its history: From 1946 to 1948 it was the Lynn Red Sox of the class B New England League, 1949 it was the Lynn Tigers also of the New England League, 1980 to 1982 it would be the Lynn Sailors of the AA Eastern League that would call Fraser Field their home. 1983 would have the Lynn Pirates there and then from 1996 to 1999 it would be the Massachusetts Mad Dogs who played in the North Atlantic League, the Northeast League and the Northern League. 2003 thru 2007 it would be the North Shore Spirit playing there first as part of the North East League then as part of the Can AM League. Then from 2008 until the present time it is home to the North Shore Navigators of the New England Collegiate Baseball League. It opened for business in June of 1940 at a cost of $210,000 and it was later upgraded at a cost of $3,000,000. It has hosted the 1946-48 New England League pennant winners the 1982 Eastern League North

Division pennant winners, the North Atlantic pennant winners of 1996, the Northeast League North Division pennant winners in 2004 and 2007 Can Am League pennant winners for the second half of the season. It was built as a WPA project and was named after Eugene Fraser who was a city Councilor that was the biggest booster of the Semi Pro Lynn All Stars. In fact the first game at Fraser Field was between the All Stars and the Pittsburgh Pirates. It is also the ball field where Roy Campanella hit his first professional home run.

New Bedford- Olympic Field in New Bedford, Massachusetts was the home field for the New Bedford Whalers of the New England League from 1895 until 1898. There is a Domino's Pizza there as well as other small businesses.

Sargent Athletic Field in New Bedford was the home field for the New Bedford Whalers from 1903 until 1915, and then again in 1934. From 1903 until 1913 the team was a member of the New England League, in 1914 and 1915 the team was in the Colonial League and in 1934 they were in the Northeastern League. The Athletic Field had a capacity of 3,500, and is also known as the Paul Walsh Athletic Field. It is currently now in use by both high school and college teams.

The New Bedford Millmen of the New England League in 1929 and the New Bedford Whalers of the New England League in 1933 played their home games at Battery Park. It was Memorial Day May 30, 1924 when the town of New Bedford opened Battery: D" Square Park. It was a monument to the soldiers who were killed during World War I. The soldiers were members of the 102nd Field Artillery in the Yankee Division of the New England National Guard. During the 1930 season there were only two teams from Massachusetts in the New England League and they were from Salem and Lynn. All of the other teams were from either New Hampshire or Maine and Massachusetts was the only place where Sunday baseball was legal. Battery Park was used as a neutral site between teams who were not playing either Lynn or Salem.

NEWBURYPORT - In 1885 and 1886 the Newburyport Clamdiggers played their home baseball games at the Newburyport Base Ball Grounds. It appears now that there is a parking lot where the ball park once was.

Also in 1885 the Clamdiggers played baseball at Salisbury Beach. There is a boardwalk there now with small shops and eateries on the property.

NORTHAMPTON - The Northampton Meadowlarks of the Eastern Association played at the Driving Park for the 1901, 1910 and 1911 seasons. The park was located in the city of Northampton. In 1891 there was an enclosed baseball park that was built at the city's Driving Park which was designed for horse racing. It took until 1909 until affiliated baseball came to Northampton. The owner of the Lyric Club was Gil Edwards and along with Goldie Bowler, a former player who pitched for the Springfield Ponies, bought the team from Meriden, Connecticut and moved them to Northampton. Driving Park was reworked and home plate was moved nearer the grandstand. It was hard for baseball in Massachusetts to survive because of the laws that prohibited baseball on Sundays which in turn caused a myriad of money difficulties for a lot of the Massachusetts based teams. The Meadowlarks were one of them and they along with the team from Holyoke, Massachusetts were tossed out of the league because they failed to pay their debts. There is still a horse racing track on the site.

PITTSFIELD - For the part about Wahconah Park see that chapter.

In Pittsfield the first ballpark for baseball was called the Berkshire Pleasure Park. It was purchased by five men who wanted to build a place for flowers and grape vines. It would be a place with large and beautiful grounds that would also have Ornamental Gardens and Fountains along with artificial ponds which would turn the area into a replica of Central Park in New York City. The grounds were easily accessible for a walker or a rider or a driver and filled the needs of the growing Berkshire County city of Pittsfield. The first baseball team to play there was the Pittsfield Hillies and there is now a series of high tension electrical power lines that run through the property.

QUINCY - The Quincy Shipbuilders played in the New England League and in 1933 their home ball field was the Fore River Field. The unique part of this park was that it did not have a fence to prevent people from coming into the ballpark to watch baseball. The team did not charge admission, but they passed the hat to help with expenses. There is still a baseball field on the property now.

SALEM - The Bridge Street Grounds in Salem, Massachusetts hosted baseball for a team that played in the New England League in 1885. In 1887 and 1888 the New England League Salem Witches played there as well. Fast forwarding a bit to1891 and 1892 there was another entry in the New England League from Salem that played at Bridge Street. The Salem team in 1895 played at Bridge Street. However, they were a part of the New England Association. It was also known as Donovan's Field as it was owned by a man named Frank Donovan. The Salem Witches played there from 1926 through 1928 and again in 1930 all as part of the New England League. There are now electrical high tension wires that run through the property where the ball field once was.

SPRINGFIELD - Minor league baseball in Springfield has been around since 1872 when the Middletown Mansfields of the National Association played at Hampden Park. The Boston Red Stockings also of the National Association played there in 1873 for one game and in 1875 for one game as well. It was Hampden Park and League Park from 1872 until the early 1940's. During that time frame it had as some of its highlights, the 1895 International League Pennant, 1908 and 1911 Eastern Association pennants, the 1927 Eastern League champions and the 1932 Eastern League pennant. The land was bought by the Hampden Agricultural Society for meetings of the National Trotting Organization. In 1863 the 46th Infantry Regiment

mustered there for the Civil War. There was then a horse racing
track built on the site and early on in the park's life there were horse
racing and bicycle races there. In 1875 the famed Yale -Harvard
football game was played there as well. In 1895 the Boston and
Maine Railroad owned the property and a corner in the northwest
part of the property was used as a dump. In 1911 William Carrey and
John Zeeller bought the Springfield baseball team and proceeded to
build a grandstand on the dump site. The new place called League
Park opened in 1922. Now in the early part of the 1940's the park
was renovated and a steel grandstand was put up. It was renamed
Pynchon Park after William Pynchon who helped found the city
of Springfield. Unfortunately on September 11, 1966 Pynchon Park
burned to the ground. Besides the teams named above the following
teams also played their home games at this field:

Springfield Ponies 1893-1900 International League, Springfield
Ponies 1902-1914 Eastern Association, Springfield Tips 1915 Co-
lonial League, Springfield Rifles 1916, 1918, 1932 Eastern League,
Springfield Green Sox 1917 Eastern League, Springfield Hampdens
1919 through 1922 and 1931 Eastern League, Springfield Ponies
1934 Northeastern League, Springfield Nats 1939 thru 1941 Eastern
League, Springfield Rifles 1942 and 1943 Eastern League, Springfield
Cubs 1948 and 1949 New England League, Springfield Cubs 1950
through 1953 International League, 1957 through 1965 Eastern
League. There is now a restaurant and other industrial/business
buildings on the property.

TAUNTON - The Taunton Fairgrounds hosted the Taunton Herrings
of the New England League when the Herrings played there from
1897 until 1899. The Fairgrounds also hosted the Taunton team in
1905 when it was a New England League franchise and in 1908
when the Taunton team was in the Atlantic Association.. It hosted a
Taunton team in 1914 and 1915 when that team was in the Colonial
League as well. The Sproat Farm was purchased in 1859 by the
Bristol County Fair Board of Directors as the fair was growing and

more land was needed. It took some time, but eventually there was an exhibition hall, some bandstands, a racetrack as well as a baseball field that were built on the property. There are now apartment complexes on the property.

Baseball in Taunton during the 1933 season was played at Hopewell Park. The Taunton team was called the Blues. There is a multisport complex on the property now with soccer, football and baseball fields present.

WATERTOWN - The Watertown Townies of the 1934 Northeastern League played their home games at Victory Field in Watertown. It was designed by Curtis W. Bixby and built with a capacity of 1,100 people. It cost $75,000 and was dedicated to the Veterans of World War I. It has a baseball field as well as a football field. Even though part of the football field extends into the outfield of the baseball diamond, because of the "L" shape of the entire park, neither the football field nor the baseball field is compromised.

WAYLAND - The Wayland Birds played their home games at Rosebud Gardens in Wayland. Rosebud Gardens was actually the name of a bar that was situated near the ball field. The owner of the bar owned and sponsored the baseball team and it led to the downfall of the bar owner as he began to use money to finance the team that he should not have. This in turn caused both the bar and the baseball team to fold. Now there is a quiet residential neighborhood that runs through the property.

WORCESTER - The Driving Park at the Agricultural Fair Grounds in Worcester, Massachusetts is a very historical site when it comes to the history of major league baseball. Yes, major league baseball because it was at the Driving Park site on June 12, 1880 that Lee Raymond of the Worcester team pitched the first ever perfect baseball game in the major leagues against the Cleveland club of the National League. In fact there is a plaque on the site that commemorates the historic event. The park was open for business on May 1, 1880 and closed its doors on September 29, 1882. It would appear as though the field was closed down due to an attendance issue when only 18 fans showed up for a game on September 29, 1882, there were 25 fans there on September 28th annd54 fans there on May 15th 1882. Coincidentally all three of the games were against the Troy Trojans. Now Becker College sits on the property where the ball field once did.

Worcester had a number of teams that played at a ball field called the Grove Street Grounds. A list of the teams that played there includes the 1888 Worcester Colts of the New England League, the 1889-1890 Worcester team of the Atlantic Association, the 1891 Worcester team of the New England League, the 1933 Worcester Chiefs of the New England League and the 1934 Worcester Rosebuds of the Northeastern League.. The ballpark hosted the 1899 Atlantic Association pennant game the 1891 New England League pennant game and the 1934 Northeastern League pennant game. It also was known as League Park. When the park was built it had a very short backstop and fence. It was also in a densely populated area which meant the baseballs flew out of the park frequently and were striking neighbor's houses. In 1934 one neighbor was so upset that he asked for and received a court injunction against the home team. The injunction was not to prevent the team from playing baseball at the field. The injunction was to keep the team from hitting baseballs out of the park. The team asked the city for permission to heighten the fences and the city would not allow it, so the team moved. There now sits a number of industrial buildings on the site.

The following teams played at "The Oval" in Worcester for their home games: 1894 team in the New England League, 1898 team in the New England League, The Worcester Farmers who played in the International League in 1899 and 1900, the Worcester Quakers in 1901 who were part of the International League, the 1902 Worcester Hustlers who were part of the International League, the Worcester Riddles of the 1903 International League and the 1904 Worcester entry in the Eastern Association. The Oval was built in 1892 and was originally meant for track and field events. In fact from 1893 to 1907 the New England Intercollegiate Games were held there. There was also bicycle racing as well as Gaelic football. The first team to use the Oval for baseball was the 1904 Worcester entry in the Connecticut League which ended up being transferred to Norwich, Connecticut. Currently there are no signs or anything to note that a ball park once stood there. In fact St George's Cathedral now sits on the property.

Boulevard Park was in Worcester and was the home ball field or the Worcester Boosters of the New England League from 1906 until 1915, and the Eastern League version of the Wooster Boosters from 1916 to 1922. The Worcester Panthers played there as part of the Eastern League from 1923 until 1925. It was also known as Cristofo Columbo Park when it opened in 1906 with a seating capacity of 3,500. Unfortunately the park burned in 1926, and there are now a group of stores sitting on the property.

Whittall Field was the home to the Worcester Rosebuds for part of the 1934 season when they played in the Northeastern League. The field opened for business on July 4, 1934 and played host to the 1934 Northeastern League Pennant. There are now apartment buildings on the site.

Fitton Field is located in Worcester Massachusetts and it is also known as Hanover Insurance Park at Fitton Field. The original opening date was in 1905. It is named for Father Fitton who in 1840 purchased the land for the Catholic Church as he founded the Mount St James Seminary. In 1843 Father Fitton deeded the land to Bishop Benedict Joseph Fenwick who founded the College of Holy Cross in 1843. Holy Cross had begun to play baseball in 1876, and they did not start using Fitton Field until 1905. The field was renovated 100 years later and in addition to the Holy Cross Crusaders playing there, the Worcester Tornados of the Can Am League play there as well.

There are two other ballparks to mention here even though professional baseball was not played there. There may in fact be more parks, but the research has led to information about the parks named in this chapter. If there are any other parks that professional baseball was played. I would be more than happy to share the information with others.

The first park is in Clinton, Massachusetts and is called Fuller Field. It has been hosting baseball continuously since 1878. At first A.J. Bastracache who researched the field found that at one time Hall of Famer Tim Keefe played there as a third baseman for the Clinton Baseball Club in 1878. Bastracache found the field was simply referred to as grounds and the site could not be found until Bastracache found an oil cloth survey map in a closet that showed the ball field being located in the northern part of Clinton along the Nashua River. If baseball has been played there since 1878 then it would make Fuller Field the oldest park in continuous use for baseball. Labatt Park in Canada has disputed this claim by saying they opened in 1877. However, supposedly home plate had been moved making that an entirely different ball park and making Fuller Field the oldest park to host baseball year after year.

The second ballpark to be mentioned is Nantasket Bay in Hull, Massachusetts and yes it does play a significant part in baseball's history. It was there that on September 2, 1880 the first ever baseball game under lights was played. The game was sponsored by the city of Boston's Northern Electric Light Company. Thomas Edison had invented the light bulb only a year before and the electric company wanted to show people what it could do. The field had a total of 3 light towers and each tower had 12 of the light bulbs on it. Teams from Jordan Marsh and R.H. White 2 of Boston's Department stores played to a 16-16 tie. There were 300 spectators there, but no one seemed to care about the game, as it was the lights that attracted people. The park was located behind Nantasket's Sea Foam House which at this point has been gone a very long time.

Pittsfield's 1791 Baseball Bylaw

....

Pittsfield, Massachusetts received some very nice publicity from all over the United States in 2004 because of a discovery made of a document written in 1791, which is now one of the earliest references to baseball as we know it in the United States. This document predates the common notion or idea that baseball was invented by Abner Doubleday in Cooperstown, New York almost 50 years after baseball by name was mentioned in this Pittsfield Bylaw. Below is a copy of the bylaw:

At a legal meeting of the inhabitants of the town of Pittsfield qualified to vote in Town Meetings held on Monday the fifth day of Sept 1791 Voted

The following bylaw for the preservation of the Windows in the New Meeting House in said Town_____v12

Be it ordained by said Inhabitants that no person, an inhabitant of said Town, shall be permitted to play at any Game called Wicket, Cricket, Baseball, Batball, Football, Cat, Fives or any other Game or Games with Balls with the Distance of Eighty Yards from said Meeting House_____ and every such Person who shall play at any of the said Games or other Games with Balls within Distance aforesaid, shall for any Instance there of forfeit the sum of five shillings (about one dollar at today's exchange rate) to be received by the Action of Debt brought before any Justice of the Peace to the Use of the Person who shall sue and prosecute therefore_____

And be it further ordained that in every Instance where any Minor shall be Guilty of a Breach of this Law, his parent ,Master ,Mistress or Guardian shall forfeit the like Sum to be recovered in Manner and to Use the afore said_____

Woodbridge Little was the first lawyer in Pittsfield and a longtime selectman. He also was the author of the above document which was written in 1791. The document was voted on at the town meeting in Pittsfield on September 5, 1791 and its purpose was to protect the windows of the soon to be built meeting house (It was in fact the Congregational Church which was designed by architect Charles Bulfinch in 1789 and construction was completed in 1793). The original document was still as of this date in possession of the City Clerk in Pittsfield. The city of Pittsfield is a small New England city, and in May of 2004 officials in the city along with former New York Yankee pitcher and Berkshire County resident Jim Bouton made the startling discovery of this document. Bouton was contacted by John Thorn the baseball historian who authored the book "Baseball in the Garden of Eden" who read about this document while doing the research for his book. Thorn learned of the possible existence of the document while reading "The History of Pittsfield from 1734 to 1800," which was written by J.E.A.Smith. The document found is the earliest of its kind which documents the known existence of baseball in North America. According to Thorn's research, people felt strongly enough about the damage the game of baseball could do to a meeting house, that a by-law was drafted to protect that property. The question I wonder about is, where could the sport of baseball actually come from?

In Thorn's book, he brings up and asks some very good questions especially when it comes to the relationship between baseball and the city of Pittsfield. Thorn wonders what the game looked like in 1791 because there are no actual written accounts of the game. Even though the bylaw specifically names baseball is the game that was played in 1791 close to the game that is played today? There are also other games that are mentioned in the bylaw that are loosely related to baseball such as the game of "fives," which is a form of handball and the game of cricket, which is the national sport in England. Other variations of the game will be briefly talked about later in this book, and it will be easy to see that someone did not just wake up one morning and decide to invent a game and call it baseball.

Also mentioned in "Baseball in the Garden of Eden" is the town of Upton, Massachusetts which is there because a man by the name of Henry Sargen sent a message to the Mills Commission, that a man by the name of George Stoddard played the game of roundball in the 1850's with the Upton Excelsiors. Stoddard's grandfather and great grandfather had played the game of roundball right after the end of the Revolutionary War and long before that when Upton became a village which was in 1735.

Before going any farther the Mills Commission was a commission that was headed by Abraham Mills for the purpose of finding out the roots of baseball. Along with Mills (who was the fourth president of the National League of Professional Base Ball Clubs), there was Morgan Buckley the National League's first president, Arthur P Gorman who was a former player and ex-president of the Washington Base Ball Club, Nicholas E Young who was the league's first secretary and the man who replaced Mills as president, Alfred J. Reach and George Wright, who were two of the more famous players during the day as well as being two of the leading sporting goods representatives, and James E. Sullivan, who was the president of the Amateur Athletic Union. What the commission did was to request that any American who may know how baseball came to pass, contact the commission. A mining engineer from Colorado named Abner Graves sent a response to the commission stating that Abner Doubleday was responsible for improving a version of Town Ball that was being played by students at the Ostego Academy and Green's Select School in Cooperstown. Graves in his letter said he was a personal witness to the formation of the game which Double-day termed Base Ball. The commission believed Graves and accepted the story as fact. However, it would appear that this was not to be as Doubleday was not even in Cooperstown when this was alleged to have taken place, and in the end Mills even said that he had doubts and that there was not any evidence to suggest that Graves' claim of Doubleday inventing baseball was true.

Thorn also brings up the point in his book about baseball being banned in Pittsfield, that the sport of baseball did not just materialize in Pittsfield and that it would have had to been played before and not just in Berkshire County. Also asked in the book is the question why was the sport of baseball banned and not roundball. What also has to be remembered is that the border between the states of New York and Massachusetts had only been agreed upon four years before in 1787, and to the people who were playing the game in 1791, it did not matter where the boundary line was; the game would be played no matter what it was or would be called by other people.

I also agree with Mr. Thorn when he says that it is entirely possible that baseball was not thought of in either Pittsfield or Cooperstown because there is evidence to suggest that bat and ball games had been around 4,500 years earlier when a game called seker-hemat or "batting the ball" was played. In the shrine of Hathor, the goddess of love and joy in Hatshepsut's temple at Deir-el-Bahari, Thutmose III is seen holding a bat in one hand and a ball in the other and in the hieroglyph that accompanies the art reads "Striking the ball for Hathor who is foremost in Thebes." There is also another inscription that reads "Catching it for him by the servants of the gods." The date on that was 1460 BC, but there is also evidence that 1,000 years before, bat and ball games were played in Egypt.

Wahconah Park

....

City owned and located on Wahconah Street in Pittsfield, Massachusetts, Wahconah Park is one of the last ballparks in the United States
with a wooden grandstand. Baseball has been played at the present
location since 1892.

Obviously the park was built before the advent of night baseball, so
no one thought about the effect the setting sun would have on batters.
The park is famous for having delays as the sun sets, and finally in
1989, management put up a screen to assist with blocking the setting
sun. However, even with that, the ballpark still has had delays for the
setting sun.

The wooden grandstands were built in 1919 and at the time sat 4,500
people to watch a ballgame. Also in 1919 the owners of the park do-
nated it to the city of Pittsfield. Eight years after in 1927, the severely
deteriorated grandstand was replaced and a dike was built to keep the
nearby Housatonic River from flooding. During the Great Depression
in 1931 1,300 men were put to work fixing the field at a cost of $25,000.

Still the old ballpark would need work and in the fall of 1949, major
renovations would be taking place. Soggy soil necessitated the use of
heavy pilings as a firm base for the foundation of the new grandstands.
It has been alleged that the ballpark was built on the site of an old city
dump, but there has been no evidence to support that claim. All of this
renovation work on Wahconah Park started in 1946 when night time
baseball came to Pittsfield. There were eight eighty foot light towers
that were sent from the city of Boston to light up the field. Also one of
the concessionaires at the park, Sport Services Corporation, put up a
brand new scoreboard at a cost of $1,800. Still on the subject of the late
1940's, renovated Wahconah Park also got new lockers, toilets, fences
and new areas for the concessions. The field was also regarded, and
the total cost for all of these renovations was $114,000. Speeding the

calendar up to 1976 the Federal Government provided $700,000 in funds for more renovations to the ball field with the emphasis to be placed on the continuing flooding issue caused by the Housatonic River.

Now let's look at the baseball teams that have called Wahconah Park their home ball field. In 1894 two years after Wahconah Park opened, the Pittsfield Colts played there as a member of the New York State League. This short lived experiment lasted one month. That team was managed by George Roberts and Edward Cain. Some of the players on the roster were Ira Davis of Philadelphia, Pennsylvania, Mike Hickey of Chicopee, Massachusetts, Frank McParthen of Hoosick Falls, New York John Papalar of Albany, New York and Pussy Tebeau of Worcester, Massachusetts. The Colts along with the Albany Senators disbanded on July 3, 1894.

In 1905 the team from Saugerties, New York moved to the city of Pittsfield, took on the name of the Pittsfield Hillies and began play in the Hudson River League. The two men that managed the team that year were D.J. Schulmar and Daniel Cassidy as the team moved to Pittsfield on July 1, 1905, sporting a record of 8 wins and 34 losses. On July 25, 1905 with a record of 13 wins and 49 losses, this team disbanded leaving the city of Pittsfield without a team to call their own.

In 1913 and 1914 the Pittsfield Electrics would call Wahconah Park home as members of the Eastern Association. The manager of the team was John Zeller and pitcher W.T. Smith of the Electrics led the league with 175 strikeouts as Pittsfield finished the season with a record of 62 wins and 73 losses. Also during the season of 1913 on August 6 W.T. Smith threw a no hitter against the Waterbury Contenders winning by a score of 3-0. Under Zeller's management in 1914, the Electrics finished with a record of 60 wins and 65 losses and Pittsfield pitcher Bob Troy led the Eastern Association with 212 strikeouts.

From 1919 through 1930 the Pittsfield Hillies of the Eastern League would play their home games at Wahconah Park. In 1919 Joe Birmingham would be the manager as the Hillies finished in first place in the Eastern league by two and a half games over the Worcester Boosters. The Hillies record was 64 wins and 44 losses and Hillies pitcher Gary

Fortune led the league in wins with 24 and strikeouts with 182. In 1920 the Hillies had a record of 69 wins and 69 losses which left them in 6th place in the league standings.

It was back to first place in the standings in 1921 as the Hillies won 92 games and lost 59. Walter Hammond of the Hillies led the league with a .351 batting average and pitcher Colonel Hammond won 25 games while Al Pierotti won 22 games and lost only 7 for a league leading winning percentage of .759. Pierotti also threw a no hitter on July 23 leading the Hillies to a 2-0 victory over the Albany Senators. Gus Gardella managed the Pittsfield team in 1922 and they finished in fourth place with a record of 77 wins and 74 losses. Catcher Charlie Hargraves made the All Star team that year and Adelbert Capers scored 105 runs to tie for the league lead with Walter Shay of the New Haven Indians.

In 1923 Art Wilson led the Hillies to a dismal seventh place finish in the league standings. Things were looking up in 1924 as Billy Gilbert, Bud Stapleton and Andy Coakley led the Pittsfield squad to a 5th place finish in the standings with a record of 70 wins and 81 losses.

It was back down to last place in 1925 as Pittsfield struggled thru the season to a record of 54 wins and 98 losses leaving the Pittsfield squad 33 games behind the pennant winning Waterbury Braves. W.D. McPhee split time between Waterbury and Pittsfield and compiled a record of 19 wins and 3 losses for a league leading winning percentage of .864. The Hillies remained in the cellar for 1926 as they finished with a record of 50 wins and 102 losses, which left them 47 games behind Rube Marquard and the Providence Rubes.

Bill Whitman managed Pittsfield to a third place finish in 1927 as Pittsfield ended up with a record of 84 wins and 67 losses. Dennis Lothern of the Hillies led the league with 117 runs scored. The Hillies record in 1928 was 87 wins and 65 losses and they also placed third baseman Eugene Sheridan, outfielder George Loeppard and pitcher Joey Cascarella on the All Star team. Then in 1929 no one from Pittsfield made the All Star team and the Hillies ended up in 4th place in the final league standings with a record of 77 wins and 75 losses.

The year was 1930 and it would be the Hillies last year in Pittsfield. They withdrew from the league on June 30, 1930. Pittsfield was followed by the Hartford Senators, who withdrew from the league as well as the Providence Grays and the New Haven Profs, as there would be only four teams that would finish that season as everybody was feeling the effects of the Great Depression with minor league baseball being especially hard hit.

Baseball had to wait until 1941 to return to Pittsfield and it would be the Pittsfield Electrics that would call Wahconah Park home as members of the Canadian American League. The Electrics finished the season in 4th place with a record of 62 wins and 59 losses. That was good enough to get the Pittsfield team into the playoffs where they defeated the Amsterdam Ragmakers in the first round of the playoffs before falling to the Oneota Indians in the championship round four games to two. Art Funk managed the team that year and also was selected to the All Star team ass a shortstop where he was joined by teammates Lloyd Moore at second base and Arthur Duda as a pitcher. Art Wilson of the Electrics threw a 7 inning no hitter that year against the Trois Rivieres team beating them by a score of 15-0.

Pittsfield was still a part of the Canadian American League in 1942, and the Electrics finished with a record of 53 wins and 62 losses as Shano Collins, Rabbit Moore and Lloyd Moore guided the squad to a fifth place finish in the league standings. Lloyd Moore led the league in runs scored with 106, while Costic Narocki led the league in hits with 173 and runs batted in with 104. Ernest Thomasson of the Electrics was the league leader in ERA with a 2.62 average.

The Canadian American League lay dormant from 1942 to 1946 because of World War II and then in 1946, Pittsfield would finish second in the league standings with a record of 69 wins and 47 losses. The only team ahead of Pittsfield was the team from Trois Rivieres. The Electrics beat the Oneota Red Sox four games to three in the semifinals to advance to the championship series against Trois Rivieres who beat Pittsfield four games to one. Pittsfield's Al Rosen led the league in home runs with 15 and runs batted in with 86. Pittsfield pitcher Louis Palmisiano had a league leading 2.67 earned run average.

1947 would see Pittsfield fall to 5th place in the league standings with a record of 71 wins and 69 losses. In 1948 Pittsfield would finish 4th in the league standings with a record of 69 wins and 67 losses under first baseman/manager Gene Hasson, who was selected as the manager of the All Star team that year. Hasson won the league's batting Triple Crown by topping the circuit with 27 home runs, 106 runs batted in and a batting average of .368. Hasson was also the Most Valuable Player and pitcher Louis Palmisiano joined Hasson on the All Star team that year. Hasson was still managing the team in 1949 when the Pittsfield team was known as the Indians. Again Pittsfield finished the season in 4th place recording 74 wins and 65 losses. Outfielder Charles Hewer was selected as a member of the All Star team and on July 4, John Masuga pitched a no hitter against the Schenectady Blue Jays winning by a score of 8-0.

Lloyd Moore managed Pittsfield in 1950 and they finished in seventh place in the league standings and then for 1951 the team from Pittsfield would be known as the Phillies. Maybe it brought luck to the team as the finished the season in second place, but then all good things must come to an end as Pittsfield was defeated in the first round of the playoffs by the Gloversville/Johnstown Glovers. Phillies pitcher George McPhail led the league with 24 wins and made the All Star team where he was joined by teammates pitcher Lakey Leech and Charles Ruddock who played shortstop. Robert Jeffries of the Phillies led the league with 140 strikeouts during the 1951 season. Jumping all the way forward to 1965 the renamed Pittsfield Red Sox were led by manager Eddie Popowski and finished the season with a record of 85 wins and 55 losses. George "The Boomer" Scott had a fantastic season as he would win the batting Triple Crown when he led the league with a .319 batting average, 94 runs batted in and 25 home runs. Scott also led the league with 167 hits. Fellow Red Sox Chris Coletta led the league with 92 runs scored and pitcher Bill MacLeod finished the season with a record of 18 wins and 0 losses. Pittsfield placed third baseman George Scott, outfielder Chris Coletta, catcher Owen Johnson, and pitcher Bill MacLeod on the All Star squad, which was managed by the Red Sox manager Eddie Popowski. As a sidenote, Pittsfield native Mark Belanger was selected as the shortstop of the All Star team that year.

Popowski managed Pittsfield in 1966 and they finished the regular season in 3rd place with a record of 68 wins and 71 losses. Tony Torchia of the Pittsfield squad led the league with 83 runs batted in and made the All Star team as a first baseman, catcher Jerry Moses joined Torchia on the All Star team and pitcher Jerry Hudgins led the league with 15 wins. The Eastern League switched to an East/West division format for the 1967 season and the Sox ended up the season with a record of 75 wins and 62 losses. Outfielder Bill Schlesinger, catcher Gerald Moses and pitcher Ken Brett were members of the All Star team that year. Bobby Mitchell of the Sox led the league with 74 and tied Schlesinger for the league lead in hits with 141. Schlesinger also led the league with 81 runs batted in and 21 home runs. The Red Sox pitchers threw two no hitters that year within a five day period as Bob Guindon pitched a seven inning no hitter against York and then five days later Bill Farmer pitched another seven inning no hitter against the team from Elmira.

The 1968 AA Eastern League season ran from April 20, 1968 until September 2, 1968 and Bill Gardner led the Sox to a record of 84 wins and 55 losses which had the Sox finishing the season in 1st place in the league standings. Pittsfield beat Elmira in the first round of the playoffs two games to none and then fell to the team from Reading in the finals three games to one. Third baseman Carmen Fanzone, shortstop Luis Alvarado, outfielder Tony Torchia and pitcher Dick Baney joined manager Bill Gardner on the All Star team. Fanzone won the league's Most Valuable Player Award as he led the league with 71 runs scored, 98 runs batted in and 17 home runs. Torchia led the league with a .294 batting average and Luis Alvarado had 175 hits which led the league. Dick Baney tied for the league lead with 14 wins as a pitcher.

For the year of 1969, Pittsfield would finish in fourth place in the league standings. In the playoffs Pittsfield was leading the series one game to none against the New York Pirates when all of the games were cancelled because of poor attendance and bad weather. That year only one member of the Pittsfield squad made the All Star team and it was future Hall of Famer and native New Englander Carlton "Pudge" Fisk, who made the All Star team as a catcher. Pitcher Gary Washington of Pittsfield threw a no hitter against the Manchester Yankees, but suffered the loss in the game as Manchester won 3-0.

In 1970 the team from Pittsfield became known as the Senators and the newly renamed team finished the season in 3rd place in the league standings after winning 72 games and losing 66. There were not any playoffs that year and as for the All Star team, shortstop Toby Harrah, catcher Rich Stelmaszek and pitcher Bill Gogolewski represented the Pittsfield team. Gogolewski led the league with 14 wins and a .737 winning percentage and pitcher Mike Whitson threw a no hitter for the Senators against the Waterbury Pirates on May 29 winning the game 4-0.

The AA Eastern League split into a National and American division in 1971 and Pittsfield finished second in the American Division with a record of 68 wins and 69 losses. Bill Fahey at catcher and Joe Lovitto at second base were the lone representatives on the All Star team. Richard Guarneria led the league with 132 hits and Al Thompson led the league with 92 runs batted in and 27 home runs. 1972 did not go well for Pittsfield as they finished the season 17 and ½ games back of the West Haven Yankees in the American Division. No Pittsfield player made the All Star team, but again Al Thompson led the league in runs batted in with 110 and home runs with 31.

The fortunes would change for Pittsfield in 1973 as they again went through a name change as they would now be known as the Rangers. Pittsfield finished in 1st place in the American division with a record of 75 wins and 61 losses. Unfortunately come playoff time, the Rangers lost to the Reading Phillies three games to one in the playoffs which certainly put a damper on the season. On the good side, however, first baseman Tom Kolson led the league in runs scored with 81, runs batted in with 126 and home runs with 38. He made the All Star team that year along with second baseman Mike Cubbage. Kolson also won the Most Valuable Player Award as well.

The Rangers did not have anyone who led the league in any major pitching or hitting categories in 1974, but shortstop Roy Smalley made the All Star team. The Rangers finished the 1974 season with a record of 69 wins and 70 losses. They made it to the league finals that year, but lost to the Thetford Mine Pirates two games to none. Jackie Moore and Orlando Martinez managed the 1975 Pittsfield squad to a record of 59 wins and 73 losses which placed them 22 and ½ games behind the Reading Phillies in the league standings. Bump Wills (son of former major leaguer Maury Wills) led the league with 140 hits and made the All Star team as a utility player, which was probably the only bright spot for the Pittsfield Rangers that year.

Pittsfield underwent another name change in 1976 as they would now be known as the Berkshire Brewers. Brewers third baseman Jim Gantner made the All Star team and fellow Brewer Danny Thomas was voted the league's Most Valuable Player after he led the league with 83 runs batted in, 29 home runs and a .325 batting average, which netted him the Triple Crown that year.

Baseball would return to Pittsfield in 1985 as the team would be known as the Pittsfield Cubs. The Cubs finished with a record of 59 wins and 79 losses as they finished the year in 7th place 22 and ½ games behind the Albany- Colonie Yankees. Shortstop Mike Brumley was the lone Cub representative on the All Star team that year and pitcher Gary Parmenter threw a no hitter on June 8th and Johnny Abrigo threw a no hitter on August 8th that year for the only Cub's bright spots.

The Cubs would rise to a third place finish in 1986 as they won 76 games and lost only 64 for manager Tom Spencer. Pittsfield was beaten by the Vermont Reds in the first round of the playoffs three games to two. All Star representatives for the Cubs that year were Phil Stephenson at first base, Paul Noce at shortstop and outfielder Rafael Palmeiro. Palmeiro led the league with 156 hits, 95 runs batted in and he also won the Most Valuable Player Award as well. Paul Noce led the league with 87 runs scored which capped off a pretty good season for him as well.

Jim Essian took over the managerial reins in 1987 as the Cubs finished the season in 1st place with a record of 87 wins and 51 losses. However, the Vermont Reds beat the Cubs in the first round of the playoffs to end Pittsfield's season on a sour note. Dwight Smith made the All Star team that year as did Mark Grace, who won the league's MVP award. It was the second year in a row that a player from the Cubs had won with Rafael Palmeiro winning the award in 1986. Grace led the league with 101 runs batted in and Smith scored a league leading 111 runs. Cubs' pitcher Dave Masters had the best winning percentage in the league with a .813 average after he won 13 games and lost only 3.

The Cubs finished the 1988 season with a record of 75 wins and 63 losses, good enough for 3rd place in their division. The season for Pittsfield ended however when the Vermont Mariners beat the Cubs in the first round of the playoffs. Outfielder Jerome Walton and pitcher Dean Wilkins were All Star selections. Walton led the league with a .331 batting average, and pitcher Mike Harkey led the league with a .813 winning percentage as he won 9 games and lost only 2. Cub pitcher Kris Roter threw a no hitter versus the Harrisburg Senators on July 8th winning the game 3-0.

The New York Penn League was single A ball at the time and for the 1989 season that is where the newly named Pittsfield Mets would play. Again Pittsfield finished the season in first place only to lose in the first round of the playoffs for the straight straight year. John Johnstone led the league with 11 wins and was the sole All Star representative from Pittsfield that year. In 1990 the Pittsfield Mets had a record of 43 wins and 34 losses as they finished in 3rd place that year. There were not any All Star selections, but pitcher Edgardo Vasquez tied for the league lead in wins with 10.

Jim Thrift was the Mets manager in 1991 and Pittsfield finished the season with a McNamara West division best of 51 wins and 26 losses.

Pittsfield won the first round of the playoffs against Elmira Pioneers, but lost in the finals to the Jamestown Expos. Again there were no All Star selections from Pittsfield that year, but the Mets Randy Curtis led the league with 72 runs scored and pitcher Chris Shanahan tied for the league lead with 10 wins.

In 1992 the Mets were a .500 ball club as they finished the season with a record of 37 wins and 37 losses which was good enough for 2nd place in their division. Bill Rulscher, a pitcher for the Mets, made the All Star team, as did shortstop Edgardo Alonzo, who also led the league in batting with a .356 average as well as leading the league in hits with 106 were the Pittsfield representatives that year. The Mets would finish the 1993 season in 1st place in the McNamara division when they went with a record of 40 wins and 35 losses. Pittsfield beat the Watertown Indians in the first round of the playoffs, but fell in the championship finals to the Niagara Falls Rapids in two straight games. That year Mets pitcher Jason Isringhausen led the league in strikeouts with 104.

The Mets finished the 1994 season with a record of 37 wins and 38 losses and were represented on the All Star team by outfielder Jay Payton, utility player Todd Whitehurst and pitcher Steve Aifa. Payton was selected as Rookie of the Year and he also led the league with a.365 batting average. Unfortunately, 1995 would have the Mets finishing the year at the bottom of the league standings with a record of 34 wins and 42 losses. Outfielder Fletcher Bates was the lone All Star selection and Russ Daly led the league with 60 runs batted in.

The Mets managed to turn it around in 1996 as they finished the season with a record of 46 wins and 29 losses good enough for 2nd place under manager Doug Davies. The only All Star selection that year was outfielder Danny Ramirez. In 1997 the Mets finished with a record of 42 wins and 32 losses which placed them atop the McNamara division. The Mets beat the Erie Seawolves in two straight games to put them in the league finals against the Batavia Clippers. Pittsfield beat Batavia to claim the New York Penn League title for the 1997 season. Scott Comer led the league in strikeouts and also made the All Star team that year.

Roger Lafrancies managed the Mets in 1998 to a record of 35 wins and 41 losses and a 3rd place finish in the standings. Tony Tyerina was the Mets manager for the 1999 season, and he was able to steer the club to a record of 41 wins and 35 losses which placed them 4th. In the year 2000 the Mets finished with a record of 38 wins and 37 losses. Infielder Chris Basak, outfielder Ronald Acuna and designated hitter John Wilson made the All Star team. Basak led the league with a .349 batting average. For the 2001 season the team would undergo another name change and would now be known as the Astros. They finished the season with a record of 45 wins and 35 losses, which netted them a 3rd place finish in the standings. Outfielder Todd Self and pitcher Brian Radaway were the Astros's All Star representatives and Self tied Kevin Youklis of the Lowell Spinners with 52 runs scored for the season.

In 2002 the team would be known as the Berkshire Black Bears and would be managed by former Pittsfield and Boston Red Sox star George "Boomer" Scott. The team finished the year 27 and ½ game behind the Adirondack Lumberjacks. In 2003 the Black Bears had a record of 41 wins and 51 losses and the only bright spot was the pitching of Eddie Aucoin, who led the league with an ERA of 1.46. After that season Pittsfield and Wahconah Park would play host to the Dukes and the American Defenders, who were members of the New England College Baseball League. The Pittsfield Colonials would play at Wahconah Park as well as members of the Canadian American Association. As for the 2012 season Wahconah Park would be home to the Pittsfield Suns of the Futures Collegiate Baseball League.

Pittsfield Players
who played in the Majors

....

Lew Wendell played for the Pittsfield Electrics during the 1913 season. Wendell then played two years with the New York Giants and three years with the Philadelphia Phillies. He was a catcher who appeared in 62 games. He had 18 hits, had 10 runs batted in and a career batting average of .180.

Pat Parker was a right fielder who played with the Pittsfield Electrics during the 1914 season. His major league career consisted of three games with the St Louis Browns in 1915. He had one hit in six at bats for a career batting average of .167.

Otto Rettig spent the 1914 season with the Pittsfield Electrics. He had a four game career with the Philadelphia Athletics in 1922 as a pitcher. His record was one win and two losses and had a career ERA of 4.91.

Cliff Brady played in 1919 and 1920 for the Pittsfield Hillies as a second baseman. He played in 53 games for the Boston Red Sox in 1920. He had 41 hits in his career and 12 runs batted in as well as a .228 batting average.

Paddy Smith was a member of the 1920 Pittsfield Hillie team. He appeared in two games as a pinch hitter and a catcher for the Boston Red Sox in 1920.

Charlie Hargreaves played with the Pittsfield Hillies in 1921 and 1922 and then went on to play in the major leagues with the Brooklyn Robins from 1923 to 1928 and the Pittsburgh Pirates from 1928 to 1930. He was a catcher and he appeared in 432 games during his career. He had a batting average of .270 and had 321 hits, 139 runs batted in and four home runs.

Bob Barrett was a member of the Pittsfield Hillies in 1923. His major league career was spent with the Chicago Cubs from 1923 to 1925, the Brooklyn Robins in 1925 and 1927, as well as the Boston Red Sox in 1929. He was a utility infielder who appeared in 269 games and had 169 hits. He also hit 10 home runs and had 86 runs batted in. His career batting average was .260.

Joe Batchelder was a Pittsfield Hillie in 1923 and 1926 and in between those appearances he spent 11 games with the Boston Braves between 1923 and 1925. He was a pitcher and had a record of one win and no losses as well as a 5.66 ERA.

Si Rosenthal was an outfielder and a pinch hitter in the major leagues who played with the Boston Red Sox between 1925 and 1926. He was in 123 games and had 95 hits, four home runs 42 runs batted in and a career batting average of .266. He was also a member of the Pittsfield Hillies in 1923.

Ed Taylor was a member of the Pittsfield Hillies in 1923. In his career as a third baseman and shortstop he had 73 hits in 92 games. He also had 33 runs batted in and a batting average of .268.

Clay Van Alstyne played with the Hillies team in 1923 and 1924. He spent his major league career with the Washington Senators between 1927 and 1928. He appeared in six games as a pitcher and did not have a win or a loss, but he did have a career ERA of 5.18.

Earl Webb was a right fielder who played with the Pittsfield Hillies in 1923 and 1924. He played in the major leagues with the New York Giants in 1925, the Chicago Cubs in 1927 and 1928, the Boston Red Sox from 1930 to 1932, the Detroit Tigers from 1932 until 1933 and he finished out his career with the Chicago White Sox in 1933. In the 650 games he played in, he had 661 hits, 333 runs batted in and 56 home runs. He ended his career with a batting average of .306.

Chick Autry was a catcher who played with the Hillies during the 1924 season. In the major leagues he played with the 1924 New York Yankees and was a member of the Cleveland Indians from 1926 to

1928 and the Chicago White Sox in 1929 and 1930. He had 68 hits, 2 home runs, and 33 runs batted in for his 124 game career and he also had a career batting average of .245.

One of the pitchers for the Hillies in 1924 was Hal Goldsmith. In the major leagues he played with the Pittsburgh Pirates and the Boston Braves as well as the St Louis Cardinals. He had a record of six wins and 10 losses and a career ERA of 4.04.

Mule Haas was a Pittsfield Hillie in 1924. He then played with the Pittsburgh Pirates in 1925. From 1928 through 1932 Haas played with the Philadelphia Athletics and was a member of the team that played in three consecutive World Series. That team won the championship in 1929 and 1930 and some baseball people feel that team is one of the greatest teams of all time. Haas was a centerfielder and first baseman that played in 1,168 games. He had 1,257 hits, 43 home runs and a .292 batting average.

Ike Kamp played with the Boston Braves in 1924 and 1925 and also played with the Hillies in 1924. His major league career was 25 games long and he had two wins and five losses to go with his ERA of 5.10.

Hunter Lane appeared in seven games for the Boston Braves in 1924 as a third baseman and a pinch hitter. He had one hit in 15 at bats for a .067 batting average. He too was a member of the 1924 Pittsfield Hillies team.

Art Mills played with the Pittsfield Hillies from 1924 to 1926. He was a pitcher and in the majors he appeared in a total of 19 games for the Boston Braves between 1927 and 1928. He did not have a win and was saddled with one loss as well as a 5.36 ERA.

Joe Benes played second base, third base and shortstop in a brief major league career that was 10 games long for the St Louis Cardinals in 1931. He had two hits in 12 at bats for a .167 batting average. Before that he played for the Pittsfield Hillies in 1925.

Bill Cronin was a member of the 1926 Pittsfield team and in his major league career as a catcher he appeared in 126 games between 1928 and 1931 for the Boston Braves. He had 68 hits including 15 doubles and also had 27 runs batted in. His career batting average was .230.

Paul Richards was a member of the 1926 Pittsfield Hillies. In the majors he was a catcher for the Brooklyn Dodgers, New York Giants, Philadelphia Athletics, and the Detroit Tigers. His career lasted from 1932 until 1946. He played in 532 games and had 321 hits including 15 home runs. He had 155 runs batted in and his batting average was .227. He was also a member of the 1945 World Champion Detroit Tigers.

Charlie Bates was a Hillie in 1927. He was a catcher in the majors for nine games with the Philadelphia Athletics and had nine hits including two doubles, two triples and a .237 batting average.

Joe Cascarella played for the Pittsfield Hillies for the 1927 and 1928 seasons. In the majors he played with the Philadelphia Athletics and the Boston Red Sox as well as the Washington Senators and the Cincinnati Reds in a career that lasted from 1934 until 1938. He was a pitcher who appeared in 143 games and had a record of 27 wins and 48 losses as well as a 4.84 earned run average.

Augie Walsh was a 1927 member of the Pittsfield Hillies and as a pitcher in the major leagues he appeared in 39 games for the Philadelphia Phillies in 1927 and 1928. He recorded four wins and 10 losses and his earned run average was 6.05.

Jack Burns played in Pittsfield for the Hillies in 1928 His major league career began in 1930 and ended in 1936. He played with both the St Louis Browns and the Detroit Tigers. He was a first baseman and in 890 games he had 980 hits including 44 home runs to go along with his .299 batting average.

Ed Connolly played with Pittsfield in 1928 and 1929. He was a catcher for his major league career which began in 1929 and ended in 1932, all with the Boston Red Sox. He had eight doubles, four triples and a total of 68 hits in 149 games as well as a .178 batting average.

George Loepp was a Pittsfield Hillie for 1928. Also in 1928 he played in the major leagues for the Boston Red Sox and then played in 1930 for the Washington Senators. He was an outfielder who appeared in 65 games. Of his 46 hits, 10 were doubles and one was a triple. Loepp finished with a batting average of .249.

John Shea was a member of both the 1928 and 1929 Pittsfield Hillie teams. He played his only game in the major leagues in 1928 and his pitching record showed him with a career ERA of 18.00.

Joe Cicero played for Pittsfield in 1929. He also played for the Boston Red Sox in 1929 and 1930 and then there was a gap of 15 years when he played his next major league game for the Philadelphia Athletics in 1945. He was an outfielder as well as a third baseman and a pinch hitter. In 40 games he had 18 hits including three doubles and one triple. He finished his career with a batting average of .222.

Ed Dunham played with the Hillies in 1929. He spent from 1929 to 1932 with the Boston Red Sox and then spent 1933 with the Chicago White Sox. He was a pitcher and he appeared in 143 games and had an earned run average of 4.45 to go with his record of 29 wins and 45 losses.

Frank Mulroney was a Hillie in 1929 and his two game major league career was spent with the Boston Red Sox in 1930. He had no wins and one loss in his career and his ERA was 3.00.

Owen Kahn was a Pittsfield Hillie in 1930. He played one game in the major leagues with the Boston Braves in 1930. He was a pinch runner and scored a run in his only appearance on a big league diamond.

Jorge Comellas played with the Pittsfield Electrics in 1945. He had a seven game major league career with the Chicago Cubs in 1945. He went 0-2 and had an ERA of 4.50.

Walt Linden was a member of the Pittsfield Electrics in 1941. In 1950 as a member of the Boston Braves he appeared in three games as a catcher and a pinch runner. He had a single and a double and a batting average of .400.

John O'Neil spent 1942 with the Pittsfield Electrics. In 46 games as a shortstop with the Philadelphia Phillies in 1946 he had 25 hits including three doubles and a batting average of .266 to go with his nine runs batted in.

Al Rosen played for the Pittsfield Electrics in 1946. He played with the Cleveland Indians in the major leagues as a first and third baseman from 1947 to 1956. He was pretty good with the bat and had acquired the nickname of "The Hebrew Hammer." He appeared in 1,044 games and had 1,063 hits including 192 home runs. He finished his career with a batting average of .285. He was a four time American League All Star and the 1953 American League Most Valuable Player. He was a member of the 1948 World Champion Cleveland Indians. After retiring he became involved with stocks and 20 years after his playing career had ended he became the President and Chief Operating Officer of the New York Yankees in 1978 and 1979. He had the same position with the Houston Astros from 1980 until 1985 and then went on to become the president and general manager of the San Francisco Giants from 1985 to 1992.

Hal Naragon played the 1947 season with the Pittsfield Electrics. He played with the Cleveland Indians in 1951 and from 1954 through 1959. He also played for the Washington Senators in 1959 and 1960 and the Minnesota Twins in 1961 and 1962. He was a catcher and pinch hitter who appeared in 424 games. He had 262 hits including 27 doubles, 11 triples and six home runs to go with his .266 batting average.

Jim Lemon was a member of the Pittsfield Electrics from 1948 thru 1950. He played with the Cleveland Indians in 1953, the Washington Senators from 1954 through 1959, the Minnesota Twins from 1961 through part of 1963 and the rest of 1963 was spent with both the Phillies and the White Sox. He was in a total of 1,010 games as an outfielder and he got 901 hits including 164 home runs to go with his batting average of .262.

Don Minnnick was a member of the 1949 Pittsfield Indians. He was a pitcher in his two game major league career and he showed a record of no wins and one loss as well as an ERA of 4.82.

Brooks Lawrence played in Pittsfield for the Indians in 1950. From 1954 to 1955 he played with the St Louis Cardinals. He was with the Cincinnati Reds from 1956 to 1960. He was a pitcher who appeared in 275 games. He had 69 wins and 62 losses and a career ERA of 4.25.

Stan Pawolski also was a member of the Pittsfield Indians in 1950. His career in major league baseball lasted two games with the Cleveland Indians as a second baseman where he had one hit and a career batting average of .125.

Dick Tomanek played as a member of the Pittsfield Indians in 1950. He was also a part of the Cleveland Indians organization for parts of the 1953, 1954, 1957 and 1958 seasons. He also played for the Kansas City Athletics for part of 1958 and 1959. He appeared in 106 games as a pitcher and had a record of 10 wins and 10 losses and an earned run average of 4.95.

Chris Coletta played with the Pittsfield Red Sox from 1965 to 1969. In the major leagues he was in 14 games for the California Angels as a left fielder and a pinch hitter. He had nine hits and a batting average of .300.

Pete Magrini was a 1965 member of the Pittsfield Red Sox who had a three game career in the major leagues with the Boston Red Sox in 1966 as a pitcher. He did not record a win and had one recorded loss in his career to go with his earned run average of 9.82.

Al Montreuil was with the Pittsfield Red Sox from 1965 to 1968. As a second baseman for the Chicago Cubs he played in five games during the 1972 season. He had one hit and a batting average of .091.

Jerry Moses's career with the Pittsfield Red Sox was from 1965 until 1967. In the major leagues he played with the Boston Red Sox from 1968 to 1970, the California Angels in 1971, the Cleveland Indians in 1972, the New York Yankees for 1973, the Detroit Tigers in 1974 and both the San Diego Padres and the Chicago White Sox in 1975. As a catcher he appeared in 386 games. He had 269 hits of which 25 were home runs. He also had a career batting average of .251 and he was a member of the 1970 American League All Star team.

George Scott aka "The Boomer" was a member of the 1965 Pittsfield Red Sox team. Scott then played with the Boston Red Sox from 1966 until 1971. 1972 through 1976 was spent with the Milwaukee Brewers, then back to the Red Sox for 1977 and 1978 and part of the 1979 season. He also spent 1979 with the Kansas City Royals and the New York Yankees. He was a first and third baseman who was in a total of 2,034 games. He had 1,992 hits and 271 runs batted in. His career batting average was .268 and he was the league leader in home runs with 36 and runs batted in with 109 in 1975. He was chosen for the All Star team in 1966, 1967 and 1977. He also won the Gold Glove Award in 1967,1968,1971,1972,1973,1974,1975 and 1976. Scott then came back to Pittsfield to manage the Berkshire Black Bears in 2002.

Reggie Smith played on the 1965 Pittsfield Red Sox with George Scott. They were also teammates as well on the Boston Red Sox as Smith played there from 1966 through 1973.He then went on to play with the St Louis Cardinals from 1974 thru 1976, the Los Angeles Dodgers from 1976 through 1981 and the San Francisco Giants in 1982. Reggie was a first baseman and an outfielder who took part in 1987 games. He had 2,020 hits which included 314 home runs and 1,092 runs batted in to go with a batting average of .287. He led the league in total bases in 1971 with 301 and doubles in 1968 with 37 and 1971 with 33. He was a member of the 1981 World Champion Los Angeles Dodgers and was an All Star selection in 1969, 1972, 1974, 1975, 1977, 1978 and 1980.

Gary Waslewski pitched for the Pittsfield Red Sox during the 1965 season. He then went on to pitch in the major leagues for the Boston Red Sox in 1967 and 1968, the St Louis Cardinals in 1969, the Montreal Expos in 1969 and 1970, the New York Yankees in 1971 and 1972 and the Oakland Athletics for part of 1972 as well. In the 152 games that he appeared in he had a record of 11 wins and 26 losses to go with his 3.44 earned run average.

Fred Wenz was another member of the 1965 Pittsfield Red Sox team and he was a pitcher. In the major leagues he spent 1968 and 1969 with the

Boston Red Sox and 1970 with the Philadelphia Phillies. His 31 game career showed him with a record of 3-0 with a 4.68 earned run average.

Billy Conigliaro played with Pittsfield in 1966 and 1968. In the majors he played with the Boston Red Sox from 1969 to 1971, the Milwaukee Brewers in 1972 and the Oakland Athletics in 1973 where he was a member of the World Series winning Athletics of 1973. In the outfield he appeared in 347 games and had 289 hits including 40 home runs and 128 runs batted in. For his career he batted .256. He is the younger brother of former Red Sox star Tony Conigliaro.

Carmen Fanzone was a Pittsfield Red Sox for 1966 to 1968. He started his major league career with the Boston Red Sox in 1970 and then played with the Chicago Cubs from 1971 to 1974. He was a utility infielder playing first, second, and third base in his 237 game career. He had 66 hits, of which 20 were home runs and he had a batting average of .224.

Gerry Janeski was a member of the Pittsfield squad in 1966 and again in 1968. He was with the Chicago White Sox in 19790 the Washington Senators in 1971 and the Texas Rangers in 1972 He was a pitcher and in 62 games his record was 11 wins 23 losses and a 4.73 earned run average.

Albert "Sparky" Lyle played at Wahconah Park as a member of the Pittsfield Red Sox in 2966. From 1967 to 1971 he played with the Boston Red Sox and from 1972 to 1978 with the New York Yankees. He then went on to play with the Texas Rangers in 1979 and 1980 and the Philadelphia Phillies from 1980 through part of the 1982 season. He finished up the 1982 season and his career with the Chicago White Sox. Lyle was a relief pitcher who appeared in 899 games. He had 99 wins and 76 losses and his career earned run average was 2.88. He had 238 saves in his career and led the league twice in saves, first in 1972 with 35 and then in 1976 with 23. He won the American League Cy Young Award in 1977 and was a member of the World Champion New York Yankees in 1977 and 1978. He was an American League All Star in 1973, 1976 and 1977. When he entered the game as a reliever at Yankee Stadium the song over the loudspeaker was "Pomp and Circumstance." He also wrote a book about life with the New York Yankees during the early years of George Steinbrenner which was aptly named "The Bronx Zoo."

Bobby Mitchell played with the Pittsfield Red Sox in 1966 and again in 1967. His career in the majors was spent as a designated hitter and an outfielder. He played with the New York Yankees in 1970 and the Milwaukee Brewers from 1971 to 1975. He was in 273 games and had 143 hits including 21 home runs. He finished his career with a batting average of .235.

Bob Montgomery was a member of the Pittsfield Red Sox in 1966 and then went on to play in the major leagues with the Boston Red Sox from 1970 to 1979. He was a catcher and he appeared in 387 games in which he had 306 hits including 23 home runs and a .258 lifetime batting average.

Ken Wright played at Wahconah Park from 1966 to 1968. He pitched for the Kansas City Royals from 1970 to 1973 and then the New York Yankees for 1974. In 113 major league ballgames he had 11 wins and 15 losses and a career earned run average of 4.54.

During part of 1967 **Ken Brett** played with the Pittsfield Red Sox. In his major league career he pitched for the Boston Red Sox in 1967 and from 1969 to 1971, 1972 was with the Milwaukee Brewers, 1973 the Philadelphia Phillies, 1974 to 1975 was spent with the Pittsburgh Pirates, part of 1976 was with the New York Yankees, and the rest of 1976 and part of 1977 was with the Chicago White Sox. The rest of 1977 and part of 1978 was with the California Angels, part of 1979 was with the Minnesota Twins and the Los Angeles Dodgers, and he then went to the Kansas City Royals for the 1980 and 1981 seasons. He appeared in 349 games and had 83 wins and 85 losses. He completed 70 of his starts and finished his career with an ERA of 3.93. He was a member of the 1974 All Star team and is the older brother of Hall of Fame third baseman George Brett.

Ross Gibson was a catcher with the Pittsfield Red Sox in 1967 and then went on to play in the major leagues with the Boston Red Sox from 1967 to 1969 and the San Francisco Giants from 1970 to 1972. He was in 264 games and had 188 hits, 8 home runs and a batting average of .228.

Ron Klimkowski was with the Pittsfield Red Sox in 1967. From 1969 to 1970 he was with the New York Yankees, and then the Oakland Athletics in 1971, and then back to the Yankees in 1972. In the 90 games that he appeared in as a pitcher he had a record of eight wins and 12 losses and an earned run average of 2.90 for his career.

Ed Phillips was a member of the 1967 Pittsfield Red Sox. In his one major league season which was 1970, he appeared in 18 games as a pitcher for the Boston Red Sox. He went 0-2 with an ERA f of 5.32.

Ken Paulson was a Pittsfield Red Sox for the 1967 season. He also played for the Boston Red Sox in 1967 in a career that lasted five games. He was a third baseman, shortstop and pinch hitter and in his career he had one hit and a .200 batting average.

Luis Alvarado in 1968 was a member of the Pittsfield Red Sox. He played second base, shortstop and third base in a career that started in Boston with the Red Sox in 1968 to 1970. He then played with the Chicago White Sox from 1971 to 1974, the St Louis Cardinals in 1974, and the Cleveland Indians in 1974, back to the Cardinals for 1976, and finally he spent 1977 with both the Mets and the Tigers. He played in 463 games and had 248 hits, five of which were home runs. He also had a career batting average of .214.

Dick Baney was a Pittsfield Red Sox in 1968. In 1969 he played with the expansion Seattle Pilots and then from 1973 to 1974 he played with the Cincinnati Reds. He was a pitcher and he appeared in 42 games and had a record of 4-1 as well as a 4.28 earned run average for his career.

Mark Schaeffer played with the Pittsfield Red Sox in 1968 and then went to San Diego in 1972 to pitch for the Padres. In 42 games he had a record of two wins and no losses and an earned run average of 4.62.

Carlton Fisk was a member of the 1969 Boston Red Sox. He then went on to a Hall of Fame career with the Boston Red Sox from 1969 to 1980 and then the Chicago White Sox from 1981 to 1993. He was a catcher and he appeared in 2,496 games. He had 2,356 hits including 376 home runs. He also had 1,330 runs batted in. He was voted American League Rookie of the Year in 1972 and was an All Star in 1972, 73, 74, 76, 77, 78, 80, 81, 82, 85 and 1991. He won a Gold Glove at the catching position in 1972 and the Silver Slugger Award in 1981, 1985 and 1988. He also hit one of the most dramatic home runs in baseball history when during the bottom of the 12th[h] inning in game 6 of the 1975 World Series he hit a game winning home run. The image of Fisk waving the ball to be fair remains in the mind of many sports fans and it showed to them and all fans that baseball truly is a game played by kids in an adult body.

Buddy Hunter was a member of the 1969 Pittsfield Red Sox. He played with the Boston Red Sox for part of 1971, 1973 and 1975. He was a second baseman who appeared in 22 games and had five hits and a batting average of .294.

Bill Lee also played with the 1969 Pittsfield Red Sox. He was a member of the Boston Red Sox from 1969 to 1978 and the Montreal Expos from 1979 to 1982. He appeared in 416 major league games as a pitcher and had a record of 119 wins and 90 losses. He also had 72 complete games and an earned run average of 3.62. He was a member of the 1973 American League All Star team. He may be better known as "The Spaceman" for his propensity to speak his mind on any and all subjects.

Rick Miller was a teammate of Bill Lee on the 1969 Pittsfield Red Sox squad. He also played with Lee from 1971 to 1977 on the Boston Red Sox. Miller then went on to play for the California Angels from 1978 to 1980, and then back to the Red Sox from 1981 to 1985. Miller was an outfielder who appeared in 1,482 games. He had 1,046 hits that included 28 home runs and a batting average of .268. He also won a Gold Glove for fielding in 1978.

Dick Mills was on the Pittsfield Red Sox in 1969. His major league career was two games long and he did not have a decision in either game, but he did have a 2.45 earned run average.

Larry Biittner was a member of the Pittsfield Senators for the 1970 season. From 1970 to 1971, he was a member of the Washington Senators, the Texas Rangers from 1972 to 1973, 1974 to 1976 was spent with the Montreal Expos and then the rest of 1976 as well as 1977 through 1980 he was with the Chicago Cubs. In 1981 and 1982 he was with the Cincinnati Reds and he spent 1983 which was his final season as a member of the Texas Rangers, Biittner played the outfield and first base as well as pinch hitting and in 1,217 games he had 861 hits, 29 home runs and 354 run batted in. His career batting average was .273.

Dan Castle was a Pittsfield Senator in 1970 and had a four game stay in the major leagues with the Texas Rangers in 1973 as a designated hitter. In those four games he had four hits and a batting average of .308.

Dave Moates spent 1970 to 1972 with the Pittsfield Senators. His major league career was from 1974 to 1976 and he played with the Texas Rangers as a center fielder. He was in 140 games and had 81 hits including 16 doubles one triple and three home runs. He had 31 runs batted in and a career batting average of .260.

Rich Stelmaszek was a Pittsfield Senator in 1970 and played in the major leagues for the Washington Senators in 1971, the Texas Rangers in 1973, the California Angels in 1973 and the Chicago Cubs in 1974. He was a catcher who appeared in 60 games and had one home run amongst his 15 hits and 10 runs batted in. He also had a career batting average of .170.

John Wockenfuss spent from 1970 to 1972 with the Pittsfield team. From 1974 to 1983 he was a member of the Detroit Tigers and from 1984 to 1985 he was a member of the Philadelphia Phillies. He played catcher, first base and the outfield appearing in 795 games. He had 543 hits including 86 home runs and 310 runs batted in as well as a .262 batting average.

Steve Foucault pitched for the Pittsfield Senators in 1970, and then went on to pitch in the major leagues with the Texas Rangers from 1973 to 1976, the Detroit Tigers for 1977 and part of 1978 and with the Kansas City Royals for the rest of 1978. He is credited with appearing in 277 games. He had a record of 35 wins and 36 losses and a 3.21 earned run average.

Bill Gogolewski was a pitcher on the 1970 Pittsfield Senators team. He spent from 1970 to 1971 with the Washington Senators, 1972 to 1973 with the Texas Rangers, 1974 with the Cleveland Indians and 1975 with the Chicago White Sox. He pitched in 144 games and had 15 wins, 24 losses and a 4.02 ERA.

Rick Henniger was a pitcher with the Pittsfield Senators in 1970 and 1971. His major league career consisted of six games with the Texas Rangers in 1973. He had one win and no losses and a 2.74 ERA in those 6 games.

Jeff Terpko in 1970 and 1971 was a pitcher with the Pittsfield Senators. He also pitched for the Pittsfield Rangers in 1974. As for his major league career he was with the Texas Rangers in 1974 and 1976 and the Montreal Expos in 1977. In 48 games he went 3-4 with a 3.14 earned run average.

Mike Thompson was a member of the Pittsfield Senators for 1970. He then went on to play in the major leagues with the Washington Senators in 1971, the St Louis Cardinals in 1973 and part of 1974. He then finished out 1974 with the Atlanta Braves and played his final season in baseball in 1975 with the Braves. He also was a pitcher and had a record of one win against 15 losses and a 4.86 earned run average.

Bill Fahey was a member of the 1971 Pittsfield Rangers; He also played with the Washington Senators in 1971 and with the Texas Rangers from 1972 to 1977, the San Diego Padres in 1979 and 1980 and the Detroit Tigers from 1981 to 1983. He was a catcher who appeared in 383 games and had 225 hits, seven of which were home runs. He also had 83 runs batted in and a batting average of .241.

Jim Kremmel was a Pittsfield Ranger in 1971 and 1972. He was with the Texas Rangers in 1973 and the Chicago Cubs in 1974. He had no wins and four losses and a 6.08 ERA.

Joe Lovitto was a Pittsfield Ranger in 1971. He then played with the Texas Rangers in the major leagues as a centerfielder and a 3d baseman appearing in 306 games. He had 165 hits, four home runs and 53 runs batted in as well as a .216 batting average.

Bill Madlock was with the Pittsfield Rangers in 1971 and 1972. He started his major league career with the Texas Rangers in 1973 and then went to the Chicago Cubs from 1974 to 1976. From 1977 to part of 1979 he was with the San Francisco Giants, he finished out 1979 with the Pittsburgh Pirates and stayed in Pittsburgh until 1985 when he went to the Los Angeles Dodgers where he stayed until 1987 when he finished out his career with the Detroit Tigers. He was a second and third baseman who appeared in 1,806 games. He had 2,008 hits including 163 home runs and 860 runs batted in. His career batting average was .305 and he led the league in batting in 1975, 1976, 1981 and 1983. He was a member of the 1979 World Champion Pittsburgh Pirates and also was an All Star in 1975, 1981 and 1983. He was selected as the All Star game Most Valuable Player in 1975.

Lew Beasley was with the Pittsfield Rangers from 1972 to 1975. He was in the major leagues in 1977with the Texas Rangers where he appeared in 25 games. He had seven hits, three runs batted in and a batting average of .219.

Roy Howell was a member of the 1972 to 1973 Pittsfield Rangers. In the major leagues he was a third baseman and played with the Texas Rangers from 1974 to 1977, the Toronto Blue Jays from 1977 to 1980 and the Milwaukee Brewers from 1981 to 1984. He appeared in 1,112 games and had 991 hits including 80 home runs. He also had 454 runs batted in and a .261 batting average.

Pete Mackanin was on the 1972 Pittsfield Rangers squad. From 1973 to 1974 he played with the Texas Rangers, from 1975 to 1977 the

Montreal Expos, and 1978 and 1979 were spent with the Philadelphia Phillies. He ended his major league career with the Minnesota Twins playing with them for the 1980 and 1981 season. He played second base, third base and shortstop in a career that lasted 548 games. He had 355 hits including 30 home runs and he also batted in 141 runs. His career batting average was .226.

Greg Pryor played for the Pittsfield Rangers in 1972 and again in 1974 He was with the Texas Rangers in 1976, then the Chicago White Sox from 1977 to1981 and finally the Kansas City Royals from 1982 to 1986. He was a utility infielder and played second and third base as well as shortstop as he appeared in 789 games. He had 146 runs batted in, and 471 hits that included a total of 14 home runs. He also had a career batting average of .250.

Tom Robson played at Wahconah Park in 1972 and 1973 as a member of the Pittsfield Rangers. He spent two years in the major leagues with the Texas Rangers in 1974 and 1975. He was a designated hitter, first baseman and a pinch hitter who appeared in 23 games where he had 10 hits four runs batted in and a batting average of .208.

Dave Criscione was with the Pittsfield Rangers in 1973. During his seven game major league career with the Baltimore Orioles he had three hits including a home run as well as a run batted in and a .333 batting average. He played the position of catcher.

Mike Cubbage played the 1973 season for the Pittsfield Rangers. In the major leagues he played first, second and third base while appearing in 703 games. Of his 503 hits, 34 were home runs and he had 250 runs batted in to go with his .258 batting average.

Ken Pape from 1973 to 1974 played with the Pittsfield Rangers at Wahconah Park. His only season in the major leagues was 1976 when as a member of the Texas Rangers, he appeared in 21 games as a pinch runner, shortstop and third baseman. He had five hits, one home run and four runs batted in, and his batting average was .217.

Jim Sundberg was a Pittsfield Ranger for the 1973 season. He then went on to play for the Texas Rangers from 1974 to 1983, the Kansas City Royals in 1985 and 1986, 1987 and 1988 with the Chicago Cubs and then back to the Texas Rangers for 1988 and 1989. He was a catcher and he appeared in 1,962 games. He had a total of 1,493 hits including 95 home runs and 624 runs batted in. His career batting average was .248. He also was selected for the All Star team in 1974, 1978 and 1984 and was a member of the World Champion Kansas City Royals in 1985. He was a good defensive catcher too as he won the Gold Glove for fielding in 1976, 77, 78, 79, 80 and 1981 and his career fielding percentage is .993 is good enough for 32nd all time.

Stan Thomas was a Pittsfield Ranger in 1973 and played in the major leagues for the Texas Rangers in 1974 and 1975, the Cleveland Indians in 1976 and both the Seattle Mariners and New York Yankees in 1977. He was a pitcher who threw in 111 games and had a record of 11 wins and 14 losses to go with his 3.70 earned run average.

Doug Ault's 1974 and 1975 season were spent in Pittsfield as a member of the Pittsfield Rangers. In 1976 he played in the major leagues for the Texas Rangers, and then went to the Toronto Blue Jays from 1977 to 1980. He was a first baseman and leftfielder who in 256 games had 168 hits including 17 home runs and a career batting average of .236.

Brian Doyle played for the Pittsfield Rangers at Wahconah Park in 1974. Doyle then went on to play for the New York Yankees from 1977 to 1980 and the Oakland Athletics in 1981. He was a utility infielder who played second and third base as well as shortstop during his career. In 110 games he had 32 hits including a home run and a batting average of .161. He was a member of the 1978 World Champion New York Yankees where he had seven hits in six games and had a batting average for the World Series of .438.

Ron Pruitt, in 1974 played for the Pittsfield Rangers. In the major leagues he played with the Texas Rangers for 1975, the Cleveland Indians from 1976 to 1980, and the Chicago White Sox in 1980 as well, and then he went back to the Indians for 1981 and for the 1982 and 1983 season he was with the San Francisco Giants. He was an outfielder, catcher and pinch hitter who appeared in 341 games where he had 214 hits, 12 home runs and 92 runs batted in. His lifetime batting average was .269.

Jim Umbarger spent the 1974 season with the Pittsfield Rangers. He was a pitcher in the major leagues who played for the Texas Rangers from 1975 to 1976, the Oakland Athletics for part of 1977 and then back to the Rangers for the rest of 1977 and all of 1978. He pitched in 133 games and had a record of 25 wins, 33 losses and a 4.14 earned run average.

Len Barker was with Pittsfield in 1975. He started his major league career with the Texas Rangers in 1976 and stayed there until 1978. From 1978 to 1983 he was with the Cleveland Indians, from 1983 to 1985 the Atlanta Braves and he ended his career with the Milwaukee Brewers in 1987. He pitched in 248 games and had a record of 74 wins and 76 losses as well as an ERA of 4.34. He completed 35 of the games he started and led the league in strikeouts in 1980 and 1981. He was selected to the American League All Star team in 1981 and on May 5th of that year he threw a perfect game against the Toronto Blue Jays. He never had a count of three balls on any batter and it was the first perfect game thrown during the designated hitter era in the American League.

Tommy Boggs was a Pittsfield Ranger in 1975 He played in the major leagues with the Texas Rangers from 1976 to 1977 then the Atlanta Braves from 1978 to 1983 and back to the Rangers for his final season which was 1985. He pitched in 114 games and had 20 wins against 44 losses with an earned run average of 4.22.

Dan Duran played for the Pittsfield Rangers in 1975 and with the Texas Rangers in 1981. He was a leftfielder, first baseman and pinch hitter who appeared in 13 games getting four hits, good enough for a .250 batting average.

Greg Mahlberg in 1975 was a member of the Pittsfield Rangers. He had an eight game major league career with the Texas Rangers in 1978 and 1979. He had two hits in his eight game career and one of those hits was a home run.

John Poloni played with the Pittsfield Rangers in 1975. In the major leagues he played in two games for the Texas Rangers in 1977 He was a pitcher who had a record of 1-0 and had a 6.43 earned run average.

Keith Smith played at Wahconah Park in 1975 for the Pittsfield Rangers. He was called up to the major leagues in 1977 by the Texas Rangers where he played during the 1977 season. He also played with the St Louis Cardinals from 1979 to 1980. He was a left fielder and a pinch hitter who appeared in 53 games. He had 23 hits including two home runs and he also had 8 runs batted in to go with a .207 batting average.

John Sutten was a member of the 1975 Pittsfield Rangers. He was a pitcher and had a two year career. 1977 was spent with the St Louis Cardinals and 1978 was with the Minnesota Twins. In 31 games he had two wins and one loss and a career earned run average of 3.15.

Bump Wills was a Pittsfield Ranger in 1975. As a second baseman in the major leagues he played with the Texas Rangers from 1977 to 1981 and the Chicago Cubs in 1982. He played in a total of 831 games and had 807 hits, 36 home runs and 502 runs batted in. He also had a career batting average of .266. He is the son of former major league star Maury Wills.

Dick Davis was a Pittsfield Brewer in 1976. From 1977 to 1980 he was with the Milwaukee Brewers and from 1981 through part of the 1982 season he was with the Philadelphia Phillies. For the remainder of the 1982 season he split time with the Toronto Blue Jays and the Pittsburgh Pirates. He was an outfielder and a designated hitter that appeared in 403 games. He had 323 hits, 27 home runs and 141 runs batted in. he also had a career batting average of .265.

Greg Eradi was with the 1976 Pittsfield Brewers and in the majors he played with the Texas Rangers in 1979. He was in five games as a pitcher and had a record of 0-1 to go with his 6.00 earned run average.

Gary Holle was on the Pittsfield Brewers roster for the 1976 season. In the major leagues he appeared in five games as a pinch hitter and a first baseman for the Texas Rangers where he had one hit in six at bats for a batting average of .167.

Dan Thomas in 1976 was a member of the Pittsfield Brewers. He was a left fielder in the major leagues that played for the Milwaukee Brewers in 1976 and 1977. He got into 54 games, had 48 hits, including six home runs and also had 26 runs batted in to go with a .274 batting average.

Gary Beare was also a member of the Pittsfield Brewers in 1976. He pitched for the Milwaukee Brewers for 1976 and 1977 appearing in 23 games. He had a record of five wins and six losses and an earned run average of 5.15.

Barry Cort played for the Pittsfield Brewers in 1976. He played in the major leagues for the 1977 season with the Milwaukee Brewers and as a pitcher appeared in seven games. He had a record of one win and one loss and an ERA of 3.33.

Sam Hinds played at Wahconah Park in 1976 as a member of the Pittsfield Brewers. He was a pitcher who appeared in 29 games for the Milwaukee Brewers in 1977. He had a record of no wins and three losses and a 4.73 earned run average.

John Abrego was a member of the 1985 Pittsfield Cubs at Wahconah Park. He was a pitcher who in his six game major league career had a record of one win and one loss and a career earned run average of 6.38.

Mike Brumley was a member of the Pittsfield Cubs in 1985. He played in the major leagues with the Chicago Cubs in 1987, the Detroit Tigers in 1989, the Seattle Mariners in 1990, the Boston Red Sox in 1991 and 1992, the Houston Astros in 1993, and the Oakland Athletics in 1994 and back to the Astros for the 1995 season. He appeared in 29 games at second and third base as well as shortstop and had 131 hits, three home runs and 38 runs batted in to go with the career batting average of .206.

Mike Capel was a pitcher who played for the Pittsfield Cubs in 1985 and 1986. He also played for the Chicago Cubs in 1988, the Milwaukee Brewers in 1990 and the Houston Astros in 1991. In 49 games he had a record of three wins and four losses and his earned run average was 4.62.

Steve Engel in 1985 played for the Pittsfield Cubs. He also in 1985 played for the Chicago Cubs which was his only season in the major leagues. In 11 games he had one win and five losses and a 5.57 ERA.

Darrin Jackson played for the Pittsfield Cubs in 1985 and 1986. He was with the Chicago Cubs in 1985 and 1987 to 1989. In 1989, he played for the San Diego Padres whom he stayed with until 1992. He then split the 1993 season between the Toronto Blue Jays and the New York Mets, 1994 was spent with the Chicago White Sox, part of 1997 was with the Minnesota Twins and part was with the Milwaukee Brewers. He also spent 1998 with the Brewers and then went back to the White Sox in 1999. He was an outfielder who appeared in 960 games and had 676 hits, 80 home runs and 317 runs batted in to go with a career batting average of .257.

Jamie Moyer played with the Pittsfield Cubs in 1985. In the major leagues he played with the Chicago Cubs from 1986 to 1988, the Texas Rangers from 1989 to 1990, the St Louis Cardinals and the Baltimore Orioles in 1990. He spent 1991 to 1995 with the Orioles, and then played with the Boston Red Sox in 1996, the Seattle Mariners from 1996 to 2006 and the Philadelphia Phillies from 2006 to 2010. He did earn a spot in the pitching rotation for the Colorado Rockies in 2012. He has pitched in 686 games and has 267 wins and 204 losses. His career earned run average is 4.24. He made the 2003 American League All Star team and also was a member of the 2008 World Champion Philadelphia Phillies. He is a past winner of the Lou Gehrig Award selected by the Phi Delta Theta Fraternity, the Roberto Clemente Award which combines good play and work in the community and the Hutch Award given in memory of Fred Hutchinson, which is awarded to the active player who displays fighting spirit and a competitive desire. He also has won the Branch Rickey Award for exceptional community service and is one of only two pitchers (the other being Hall of Famer Robin Roberts) to give up over 500 career home runs.

Gary Varsho was with the Pittsfield Cubs in 1985 and 1986. He was a pinch hitter and an outfielder who played in the major leagues from

1988 to 1990 with the Chicago Cubs, 1991 and 1992 with the Pitts-burgh Pirates, 1993 the Cincinnati Reds, back to the Pirates in 994 and he finished up his career with the Philadelphia Phillies in 1995. He was 571 games and had 204 hits, including 10 home runs. He also had 84 runs batted in and a batting average of .244.

Rick Amaral was with the Pittsfield Cubs from 1986 to 1988. In the major leagues he played in the outfield as well as playing first and second base. He played with the Seattle Mariners from 1991 to 1998 and the Baltimore Orioles in 1999 and 2000. He was in 727 games and had 493 hits, 11 home runs and 159 runs batted in. He also had a batting average of .277.

Damon Berryhill played at Wahconah Park in 1986 as a member of the Pittsfield Cubs. From 1987 to 1991 he was with the Chicago Cubs, from 1991 to 1993 he was with the Atlanta Braves, 1994 was spent with the Boston Red Sox, 1995 was with the Cincinnati Reds and 1996 was with the San Francisco Giants. He was a catcher and appeared in 683 games. He had 488 hits and 47 home runs and also had 257 runs batted in to go with a .240 batting average.

Les Lancaster was a Pittsfield Cub in 1986. In the major leagues as a pitcher he played with the Chicago Cubs from 1987 to 1991, the Detroit Tigers in 1992 and the St Louis Cardinals in 1993. He pitched in 323 games and had 41 wins, 28 losses and an ERA of 4.05.

Greg Maddux pitched for the Pittsfield Cubs for part of the 1986 season. His major league career saw him play with the Chicago Cubs from 1986 to 1992, the Atlanta Braves from 1993 to 2003, back to the Cubs from 2004 to 2006, the Los Angeles Dodgers for part of 2006, the San Diego Padres from 2007 through part of 2008 and then he finished out his career back with the Dodgers for the rest of 2008. He appeared in 744 major league ball games and had a record of 355 wins and 227 losses. He completed 109 of his starts and had 35 shutouts. His career ERA was 3.16. He led the league in wins in 1992, 1994 and 1995. He was also the league leader in ERA in 1993, 1994, 1995 and 1998. He was a member of the World Champion Atlanta

Braves in 1995 and was an All Star selection in 1988, 92, 94, 95, 96,97,98,99 and 2000. He won the Cy Young award in 1992, 93, 94 and 1995 and also won the Sporting News pitcher of the year for those same Cy Young winning years. He won 19 straight Gold Gloves for fielding excellence as a pitcher. He is a sure bet first ballot Hall of Famer when he becomes eligible.

Paul Noce played for the Pittsfield Cubs in 1986. In the major leagues he played with the Chicago Cubs in 1987 and the Cincinnati Reds in 1990. He was a shortstop/second baseman who appeared in 71 games and had 42 hits including three home runs. He also had a .232 batting average.

Phil Stephenson in 1986 wore the uniform of the Pittsfield Cubs. He played for the Chicago Cubs for part of 1989 and for the rest of 1989 through the 1992 season played with the San Diego Padres. He was a first baseman/outfielder as well as a pinch hitter who appeared in 194 games and had 60 hits, including six home runs and a career batting average of .201.

Rafael Palmeiro played in Pittsfield for the Cubs in 1986. He was a left fielder and a first baseman in the major leagues that played for the Chicago Cubs from 1986 to 1988, the Texas Rangers from 1989 to 1993, the Baltimore Orioles from 1994 through 1998, back to the Rangers for 1999 through 2003 and then back to the Orioles for 2004 and 1005. He appeared in 2,831 games and had 3,020 hits including 568 home runs. He also had 1,835 runs batted in and a career batting average of .288. He was the league leader in runs scored in 1993, in hits and doubles in 1991. He was player of the year in 1999 and also won the Gold Glove in 1997, 1998 and 1999. He was a winner of the Silver Slugger award in 1998 and 1999. He certainly has put up Hall of Fame type numbers. However, he has come under scrutiny because of his steroid use which has certainly hurt his chances for Hall of Fame induction.

Doug Dacenzo was with the Pittsfield Cubs in 1987. He played in the major leagues for the Chicago Cubs from 1988 to 1992, the Texas Rangers in 1993 and the San Diego Padres in 1996. As an outfielder he appeared in 540 games and had 287 hits including five home runs. He had 90 runs batted in and a career batting average of .234.

In 1987 **Mark Grace** was a member of the Pittsfield Cubs. His major league career was spent as a first baseman for the Chicago Cubs from 1988 to 2000, and the Arizona Diamondbacks from 2001 to 2003. In his career which lasted 2,245 games he had 2,445 hits including 73 home runs and 1,146 runs batted in. He had 20,278 fielding chances and made only 110 errors which is a fielding percentage of .995. He was a National League All Star in 1993, 1995 and 1997. He won a Gold Glove for fielding in 1992, 1993, 1995 and 1996. He was also a member of the 2001 World Champion Arizona Diamondbacks,

Dave Pavalas was a Pittsfield Cub in 1987 and played in the major leagues for the Chicago Cubs from 1990 to 1991 and for the New York Yankees in 1995 and 1996. He was a pitcher who appeared in 34 games winning two and losing none and he also had a career ERA of 2.65.

Jeff Pico was a member of the 1987 Pittsfield Cub squad and in the major leagues pitched for the Chicago Cubs from 1988 to 1990. He was in 113 games and had a record of 13 and 12 losses as well as an ERA of 4.24.

Laddie Renfroe played in Pittsfield for the Cubs in 1987 and 1988. In the major leagues he played for the 1991 Chicago Cubs as a pitcher appearing in four games. He had a record of no wins and one loss and his career earned run average was 13.50.

Rick Scheid was a member of the 1987 and 1988 Pittsfield Cubs and then in majors played in Houston for the Astros in 1992 and in Florida for the Marlins in 1994 and 1995. He was a pitcher who appeared in 21 games and had a record of one win and four losses to go with his ERA which was 4.45.

Dwight Smith was a member of the 1987 Pittsfield Cubs squad and then went on to a career in the major leagues where he played with the Chicago Cubs from 1989 to 1993, part of the 1994 season with the California Angels and the rest of 1994 with the Baltimore Orioles. He ended up his career in Atlanta playing for the Braves in 1995 and

1996. He played the outfield as well as pinch hit and he appeared in 813 games where he had 497 hits including 46 home runs and a total of 226 runs batted in. His career batting average was .275 and he was also a member of the 1995 World Champion Atlanta Braves.

Hector Villanueva was a Pittsfield Cub in 1987 and 1988. In the major leagues he played with the Chicago Cubs from 1990 to 1992 and the St Louis Cardinals in 1993. He was a first baseman and a pinch hitter who appeared in 191 games. He had 109 hits including 25 home runs, and he also had 72 runs batted in to go with a batting average of .230.

Jim Bollinger was a member of the 1988 Pittsfield Cubs. As a pitcher in the major leagues he appeared in 186 games with the following teams, the Chicago Cubs from 1992 to 1996, the Montreal Expos in 1997 and the Seattle Mariners in 1998. He had a record of 34 wins and 41 losses and his career ERA was 5.06.

Joe Girardi is now known as the manager of the New York Yankees, but back in 1988 he played baseball with the Pittsfield Cubs. As a catcher he played from 1989 to 1992 with the Chicago Cubs, 1993 to 1995 with the Colorado Rockies, 1996 to 1999 with the New York Yankees, back to the Cubs for the 2000, 2001 and 2002 seasons before finally finishing out his career in 2003 with the St Louis Cardinals. In 1,277 games he had 1,100 hits including 36 home runs. He also had 422 runs batted in and a career batting average of .267. He was a member of the 1996, 1998 and 1999 World Champion New York Yankees and also a member of the 2000 All Star squad. On July 18, 1999 Girardi was the catcher when David Cone of the Yankees threw a perfect game against the Montreal Expos. He was also voted Manager of the Year in 2006 when he was manager of the Florida Marlins. Girardi was also the manager when the Yankees won their 27th World Series title in 2009.

Mike Harkey was a member of the 1988 Pittsfield Cubs. In the major leagues he played with the Chicago Cubs in 1988 and from 1990 to 1993, he was with the Colorado Rockies for part of 1994 and then back to the Cubs of Chicago for the rest of 1994. He split the 1995 season between the Oakland Athletics, California Angels and Los Angeles Dodgers. He was a pitcher and in 131 games he had a record of 36 wins and 36 losses and an earned run average of 4.49.

Joe Kraemer was a Pittsfield Cub for the 1988 season. His two year career in the major leagues was from 1989 to 1990 and it was with the Chicago Cubs. In nine games he had no wins and one loss and a 6.91 ERA.

Ced Landrum played with the Pittsfield Cubs in 1988. In the majors he played with the 1991 Chicago Cubs and the 1993 New York Mets. He was an outfielder, pinch hitter and a pinch runner who appeared in 78 games. He had 25 hits and a .238 batting average.

Kelly Mann played baseball in 1988 as a member of the Pittsfield Cubs. He played for the Atlanta Braves from 1989 to 1990 in a major league career that lasted 18 games. He had nine hits including a home run and a batting average of .173.

Jeff Schwarz was a member of the Pittsfield Cubs for 1988. He then went on to pitch in the major leagues with the Chicago White Sox from 1993 to 1994 and he finished up the 1994 season and his career with the California Angels. In the 54 games he pitched in he had a record of two wins and two losses and a 4.17 ERA.

Jerome Walton spent 1988 at Wahconah Park as a member of the Pittsfield Cubs. He was a centerfielder who went on to a career in the majors that started with the Chicago Cubs in 1989 and went to 1992. Then Walton played with the California Angels in 1993, the Cincinnati Reds from 1994 to 1995, the Atlanta Braves in 1996, the Baltimore Orioles in 1997 and finally the Tampa Bay Devil Rays in 1998. He appeared in 589 games and had 423 hits including 25 home runs. He had 132 runs batted in and a .269 batting average.

Dean Wilkes wore a Pittsfield Cubs jersey in 1988 and then went on to a career in the major leagues with the Chicago Cubs from 1989 to 1990 and the Houston Astros in 1991. He pitched in 25 games and had a record of three wins and 11 losses and a 7.55 ERA.

Alberto Castillo was a member of the 1989 and 1990 Pittsfield Mets. As a catcher he began his major league career with the New York Mets whom he played for from 1995 to1998. He then went on to play with the St Louis Cardinals in 1999, the Toronto Blue Jays in 2000 and 2001 and then the New York Yankees in 2002 the San Francisco Giants in 2003, the Kansas City Royals for 2004 and part of 2005 and the Oakland Athletics for the rest of the 2005 season. He finished out his career in Baltimore with the Orioles in 2007 after playing in 418 games. He was able to get 226 hits including two home runs and had 101 runs batted in and a batting average of .220.

Denny Harriger was a 1989 Pittsfield Met who went on to pitch in four games during the 1990 season with the Detroit Tigers. He had a record of no wins and three losses and a 6.75 ERA.

Pat Howell was with the Pittsfield Mets for the 1989 season and got into 31 games in the majors with the 1992 New York Mets. He had 14 hits and a .187 batting average.

John Johnstone was a member of the 1989 Pittsfield Mets. He pitched in the major leagues with the Florida Marlins from 1993 to 1995, the Houston Astros in 1996, the San Francisco Giants and the Oakland Athletics in 1997. He then went back to the Giants finishing up the 1997 season and stayed in San Francisco until his career ended in 2000. He appeared in 2343 games and had a record of 15 wins and 19 losses and an ERA of 4.01.

Tito Navarro played with the Pittsfield Mets in 1989 and then played in 1993 for the New York Mets in the major leagues. In 12 games he had one hit and a .059 batting average.

Curtis Pride was a Pittsfield Met for the 1989 season. In the majors Pride played left field and pinch hit for the Montreal Expos from 1993 to 1995, the Detroit Tigers from 1996 to 1997, the Boston Red Sox in 1997, the Atlanta Braves in 1998 back with the Red Sox for the 2000 season, back with the Expos for the 2001 season and then the New York Yankees in 2003. He finished his career with the Los Angeles

Dodgers after playing for them from 2004 to 2006. He appeared in 421 games and had 199 hits, 20 home runs and 82 runs batted in. His career batting average was .250.

Dave Telgheder was with the Pittsfield Mets for the 1989 season. As a pitcher in the major leagues he played with the New York Mets from 1993 to 1995, and the Oakland Athletics from 1996 to 1998. In 81 games he had 15 wins and 19 losses and a 5.23 earned run average.

Joe Vitko was a Pittsfield Met in 1989 and had a three game major league career with the New York Mets in 1992. He was a pitcher who went on to have a record of 0 -1 and a career ERA of 13.50.

Jeremy Burnitz was a Pittsfield Met for the 1990 season. As an outfielder in the major leagues he played with the New York Mets from 1993 to 1994, the Cleveland Indians from 1995 to 1996 and the rest of 1996 through the 2001 season with the Milwaukee Brewers. He went back to the Mets for 2002 and 2003 finishing out the 2003 season with the Los Angeles Dodgers. He then played with the Colorado Rockies in 2004, the Chicago Cubs on 2005 and finally he finished out his career with the Pittsburgh Pirates in 2006. He appeared in 1,694 games and had 1,447 hits. There were 315 home runs and 984 runs batted in. He had a .253 career batting average and he was a National League All Star selection in 1999.

Mike Thomas was a member of the Pittsfield Mets in 1990 and in his only major league game he played with the Milwaukee Brewers in 1995.

Pete Walker played at Wahconah Park in 1990 as a member of the Pittsfield Mets. He was a pitcher in the major leagues with the New York Mets in 1995, the San Diego Padres in 1996, and the Colorado Rockies in 2000. He then went back to the Mets in 2001 and 2002 before ending his career in Toronto with the Blue Jays where he played from 2002 to 2006. He appeared in 144 games and had a record of 20 wins and 14 losses and a 4.48 earned run average.

Juan Castillo was with the 1990 Pittsfield Mets and then had a two game major league career in 1994 with the New York Mets. He did not record a won or a loss and had an earned run average of 6.94.

Micah Franklin was a member of the 1991 Pittsfield Mets squad and then went on to play one season in the major leagues with the St Louis Cardinals in 1997. He was an outfielder/hitter who appeared in 17 games and had 11 hits including two home runs and a .324 batting average.

Guillermo Garcia played from 1991 to 1992 with the Pittsfield Mets. In the major leagues he played with the 1998 Cincinnati Reds and the 1999 Florida Marlins. He was a catcher and also a pinch hitter who got into a total of 16 major league baseball games. He had eight hits including two home runs and a .200 batting average.

Ricky Otero was a member of the 1991 Pittsfield Mets who went on to play in the major leagues with the New York Mets for 1995 and the Philadelphia Phillies from 1996 and 1997 as a second baseman. He appeared in 189 games and had 157 hits including 2 home runs and 36 runs batted in to go with his .256 batting average.

Quilvio Veras was a member of the Pittsfield Mets in 1991. His major league career was 767 games long and was spent with the Florida Marlins in 1995 and 1996, the San Padres in 1997 and 1999, and finally the Atlanta Braves in 2000 and 2001. He had 750 hits including 32 homers and 239 runs batted in to go with his .270 batting average.

Hector Carrasco was a Pittsfield Met for the 1991 season. He was a pitcher in the majors who played with the Cincinnati Reds from 1994 to 1997. He also played with the Kansas City Royals in 1997 and then played with the Minnesota Twins from 1998 to 2000. He then went to play in Boston with the Red Sox for 2000 and back to the Twins for the 2001 season, the Baltimore Orioles in 2003, the Washington Nationals in 2005 and the Los Angeles Angels from 2006 to 2007. He was a pitcher in the 647 major league games he appeared in and had a record of 44 wins against 50 losses and a 4.00 ERA.

Edgardo Alfonzo was with the Pittsfield Mets in 1992. He was a member of the New York Mets from 1995 to 2002, the San Francisco Giants from 2003 to 2005, and he split the 2006 season with the Los Angeles Angels and the Toronto Blue Jays. He played second and third base in 1,506 ball games and he was able to get 1532 hits, including 146 home runs. He had 744 runs batted in and a career batting average of .284. He won the Silver Slugger award in 1999 and was a member of the 2000 National League All Star team.

Brian Daubach was on the roster of the 1992 Pittsfield Mets squad. In his major league career he played for the Florida Marlins in 1998, the Boston Red Sox from 1999 to 2002, the Chicago White Sox in 2003, back to Boston and the Red Sox in 2004 and he ended his career with the New York Mets in 2005. He was a first baseman / outfielder who appeared in 661 games. He had 525 hits and hit 93 home runs and had 333 runs batted in and a lifetime batting average of .259. He embarked on a minor league managing career that brought him back to Pittsfield to manage there. He is now the manager of the Hagerstown Suns, a minor league team of the Washington Nationals.

Bill Pulsipher was a pitcher on the 1992 Pittsfield Mets team. In the major leagues he played with the 1995 and 1998 New York Mets, the Milwaukee Brewers in 1998 to 1999, back to the Mets for the 2000 season, the Boston Red Sox and Chicago White Sox in 2001 and the St Louis Cardinals in 2005. He appeared in 106 games and had 13 wins and 19 losses and a career earned run average of 5.15.

Benny Agbayani was a member of the 1993 Pittsfield Mets team. He was a left fielder who played in the major leagues for the New York Mets from 1998 to 2001 and then he split time with the Colorado Rockies and the Boston Red Sox in 2002. He played in 383 games and had 299 hits including 39 home runs and 156 runs batted in to go with a career batting average of .274.

Preston Wilson was a Pittsfield Met for the 1993 season. He was a centerfielder who played for the New York Mets in 1996, the Florida Marlins from 1998 to 2002, and the Colorado Rockies from 2003 to 2005. He also finished out the 2005 season with the Washington Nationals and the Houston Astros. He played with the Astros for part of 2006 as well as the St Louis Cardinals where he finished his career in 2007. He played in 1,108 games and had 1,055 hits including 189 home runs and 668 runs batted in. He had a career batting average of .264 and was also a member of the 2003 National League All Star team. He led the league in runs batted in as well for the 2003 season and was a member of the 2006 World Champion St Louis Cardinals.

Jason Isringhausen pitched in Pittsfield for the Mets in 1993. He played in the majors from 1995 to 1999 (except for 1998 when he was injured) for the New York Mets. He was with the Oakland Athletics from 1999 to 2001, the St Louis Cardinals from 2002 to 2008, the Tampa Bay Devil Rays in 2009 and back to the New York Mets in 2011. He appeared in 674 games and had 48 wins and 53 losses as well as 300 saves and a 3.62 earned run average. He led the league in saves in 2004 and was selected for the All Star team in 2000 and 2005.

Eric Ludwick was a member of the Pittsfield Mets for the 1993 season. In the major leagues he played with the St Louis Cardinals from 1996 to 1997, and he also played part of the 1997 season with the Oakland Athletics. He then went on to play with the Florida Marlins in 1998 and the Toronto Blue Jays in 1999. He appeared in 31 games as a pitcher and had two wins and 10 losses as well as an earned run average of 8.35.

Allen McDill played for the 1993 Pittsfield Mets. As a major league pitcher he played for the, Kansas City Royals in 1997 and 1998, the Detroit Tigers in 2000 and the Boston Red Sox in 2001. In 38 major league ballgames he did not have a win or a loss and had an ERA of 7.79.

Jeff Tam was a member of the Pittsfield Mets in 1993. He played for the New York Mets in 1998, the Cleveland Indians for part of 1999, and then went back to the Mets for the rest of 1999. He then went on to play with the Oakland Athletics from 2000 to 2002, and finished his career with the Toronto Blue Jays in 2003. In the 251 ballgames he pitched in he had seven wins and 14 losses to go with his 3.91 earned run average.

Mike Welch was a Pittsfield Met of the 1993 season and then played in the majors for the 1998 season with the Philadelphia Phillies. He pitched in 10 games and had no wins and two losses as well as an earned run average of 8.27.

Jarrod Peterson was with the Pittsfield Mets for the 1994 season. In the major leagues he played both first and third base for the Detroit Tigers in 2001 and the Kansas City Royals in 2003 in a total of 26 games. He had 15 hits, including two home runs and a batting average of .238.

Jay Payton was with the Pittsfield Mets during the 1994 season. As a major league outfielder he played with the New York Mets from 1998 to 2002, the Colorado Rockies from 2002 to 2003, the San Diego Padres in 2004, the Boston Red Sox in 2005, the Oakland Athletics for the rest of 2005 and all of 2006, the Baltimore Orioles from 2007 to 2008, and then back to the Colorado Rockies for the 2010 season. In the 1,256 games he played in he had 1,159 hits and 119 home runs. He batted in 532 runs and had a career batting average of .279. In 2003 he led the league in putouts as a left fielder and in 2004 he was the league leader in assists as a centerfielder.

Scott Saurbeck played with the Pittsfield Mets in 1994. In the major leagues he was a pitcher with the Pittsburgh Pirates from 1999 to part of 2003, the Boston Red Sox for the rest of 2003, the Cleveland Indians in 2005 and 2006 and the Oakland Athletics in 2007. He recorded 20 wins and 17 losses in 47 major league games. He also finished his career with a 3.28 earned run average.

Vance Wilson was a player of the Pittsfield Mets for the 1994 season. He caught in the major leagues for the New York Mets from 1999 to 2004 and the Detroit Tigers in 2005 and 2006. In the 403 games he appeared in he had 238 hits, 25 home runs and a .250 batting average.

Terrance Long was a member of the Pittsfield Mets during the 1995 season. In the major leagues as an outfielder he played for the New York Mets in 1999, the Oakland Athletics from 2000 to 2003, the San Diego Padres in 2004, the Kansas City Royals in 2005 and the New York Yankees in 2006. He appeared in 840 big league contests and had 824 hits, 69 home runs and 76 runs batted in as well as a .269 batting average.

Ramon Tatis played in 1995 for the Pittsfield Mets. His major league career was with the Chicago Cubs in 1997 and the Tampa Bay Devil Rays in 1998. He pitched in 78 games with a record of one win and one loss and a 6.82 ERA.

Brandon Villafuerte was a member of the 1996 Pittsfield Mets squad. He pitched in the major leagues in 91 games with the Detroit Tigers in 2000, the Texas Rangers in 2001, the San Diego Padres in 2002 and 2003 and the Arizona Diamondbacks in 2004. He had a record one win and seven losses and a 4.12 ERA.

A.J. Burnett played with the 1997 Pittsfield Mets at Wahconah Park. From 1999 to 2005 he was a member of the Florida Marlins and it was during this time that he threw a no hitter versus the San Diego Padres on May 21, 2001. From 2006 to 2008 he was a member of the Toronto Blue Jays and from 2009 to 20011 he was a member of the New York Yankees. He signed a contract to play the 2012 season with the Pittsburgh Pirates. He has pitched in 314 games and has a record of 121 wins and 111 losses His career ERA is 4.10 and he also has 1791 strikeouts. He led the league in shutouts in 2002, games started in 2008 as well as strikeouts and has pitched a total of 21 complete games. He was a member of the 2009 World Champion New York Yankees as well.

Leo Estrella wore the jersey of the 1997 Pittsfield Mets. He pitched in the major leagues for the 2000 Toronto Blue Jays, the 2003 Milwaukee Brewers and the 2004 San Francisco Giants. In the 62 games he pitched in as a major leaguer he had a record of seven wins and three losses and a 4.88 career earned run average.

Jason Phillips was also a member of the 1997 Pittsfield Mets before he began his major league career. From 2001 to 2004 he was a member of the New York Mets, for 2005 he was with the Los Angeles Dodgers, and from 2006 to 2007 he was with the Toronto Blue Jays. He was a catcher/first baseman who appeared in 465 games. He had a total of 344 hits including 30 home runs and 168 runs batted in. His career batting average was .249.

Jason Roach played in Pittsfield as a member of the Pittsfield Mets during the 1997 season. In his two games in the major leagues during the 2003 season as a member of the New York Mets he had a record of no wins and two losses to go with his 12.00 career ERA.

Earl Snyder was a member of the 1998 Pittsfield Mets. He was a first and third baseman who played with the Cleveland Indians in 2002 and the Boston Red Sox in 2004. He appeared in 19 games and had 12 hits including one home run. His career batting average was .203.

Ty Wiggonton was a Pittsfield Met during the 1998 season. In the majors he played first,' second, and third base for the New York Mets from 2002 to 2004, the Pittsburgh Pirates for 2004 and 2005, the Tamp Bay Devil Rays from 2006 to 2007, the Houston Astros from 2007 to 2008, the Baltimore Orioles from 2009 to 2010 and the Colorado Rockies in 2011. He then signed with the Philadelphia Phillies for the 2012 season. In 1,190 games he has 1,087 hits including 158 home runs. He also has 548 runs batted in and a career batting average of .265. He was also selected as a member of the 2010 American League All Star team as a member of the Baltimore Orioles.

Chris Basak was with the Pittsfield Mets during the 2000 season. In his five game major league career during the 2007 season with the New York Yankees he played third base and shortstop and did not record a hit in his only official at bat.

Jamie Cerda was with the 2000 Pittsfield Mets. He was a pitcher in the major leagues who was with the New York Mets from 2002 to 2003 and the Kansas City Royals from 2004 to 2005. He appeared in 132 games and had a record of three wins and nine losses to go with his 4.26 ERA.

Jeff Duncan wore the jersey of the Pittsfield Mets during the 2000 season. He then went on to play for the New York Mets during the 2003 and 2004 seasons. In the 69 games he appeared in as a centerfielder he had 28 hits including a home run and a .182 batting average.

Phillip Barzilla was on the 2001 Pittsfield Astros and then went on to pitch in one major league game with the 2006 Houston Astros. He did not have either a win or a loss and no recorded ERA.

Brooks Conrad was on the Pittsfield Astros for the 2001 season, in the major leagues he pinch hit and played both second and third base. He has appeared in 280 games for the 2008 Oakland Athletics and the 2009 to 2011 Atlanta Braves and split the 2012 season between the Milwaukee Brewers and the Tampa Bay Rays. He has a total of 89 hits, including 18 home runs and his career batting average of .207.

Charlton Jimerson was also a member of the 2001 Pittsfield Astros His major league career was spent with the Houston Astros in 2005 and 2006 and the Seattle Mariners in 2007 and 2008. He was a right fielder and a pinch hitter who appeared in 39 games. He had four hits including two home runs and his batting average was .444.

Todd Self was a member of the 2001 Pittsfield Astros. He had one season in the major leagues and during that 2005 season with the Houston Astros he appeared in 21 games as an outfielder getting nine hits including a home run. His batting average for his career was .200.

In addition to the above named players what follows are brief biographies of players who played in the majors and played in Pittsfield at some point during their careers.

Art Nichols played for the Pittsfield Electrics in 1913. Prior to that as a catcher, first baseman and outfielder he played in the major leagues from 1898 to 1900 with the Chicago Cubs and from 1901 to 1903 with the St Louis Cardinals. In a total of 241 games Nichols had 191 hits, including three home runs, 90 runs batted in and a .245 batting average.

Jock Somerlott in 1913 and 1914 was a Pittsfield Electric baseball player. The first baseman played for two years in the major leagues with the Washington Senators between 1910 and 1911. In 29 games he had 21 hits and a .204 batting average.

Roy "Polly" Wolfe played for the Pittsfield Electrics in 1913 and 1914. As a right fielder in the major leagues he played with the 1912 and 1914 Chicago White Sox. In nine games he had six hits and a .214 batting average.

Robert "Bun" Troy was a pitcher for the Pittsfield team in 1914. In the major leagues he pitched for the Detroit Tigers in a total of one game and ended his career with a record of no wins and one loss with a 5.40 ERA.

Frank Nicholson pitched in the major leagues in 1912 for the Philadelphia Athletics. In the two games he pitched in he had a record of no wins and no losses and a 6.75 ERA. He also pitched in 1914 for the Pittsfield Electrics.

Joe Birmingham played with the Pittsfield Hillies from 1919 to 1920. Prior to that in a 9 year career as a centerfielder for the Cleveland Indians he appeared in a total of 771 games. He had 667 hits including 89 doubles, 27 triples and seven home runs. He also had 265 runs batted in and he scored 284 runs. He ended his major league career with a .253 batting average.

Mickey Devine was a catcher who played for the Philadelphia Phillies in 1918, the Pittsfield Hillies in 1919, the Boston Red Sox in 1920 and the New York Giants in 1925. In his major league career he had 12 hits including four doubles and a .226 batting average.

Gary Fortune pitched for the 1919 Pittsfield Hillies. He also pitched in the major leagues for the 1916 and 1918 Philadelphia Phillies and the 1920 Boston Red Sox. In the 20 games he pitched in he had a record of 0-5 and an ERA of 6.61

Jack Hammond was with the Pittsfield Hillies between 1919 and 1921. He also played with the Cleveland Indians in the major leagues in 1915 and again in 1922. Also during the 1922 season he played with the Pittsburgh Pirates. He was a second baseman who appeared in 45 games and had 22 hits including two doubles and one triple. He also had a lifetime .222 batting average.

Bobby Messenger from 1919 to 1920 was a Pittsfield Hillie. In the major leagues this right fielder played with the Chicago White Sox from 1909 to 1911 and then the St Louis Browns in 1914. He appeared in a total of 54 major league baseball games and had 27 hits including one double and three triples. He had a lifetime batting average of .172.

Ty Pickup was with the Pittsfield Hillies between 1919 and 1920. He played right field in the major leagues with the Philadelphia Phillies in one major league ballgame and had one hit in one at bat for a 1.000 batting average.

Johnny Tillman played four years with the Pittsfield Hillies from 1919 to 1923. Prior to that as a pitcher he pitched in two games for the St Louis Browns in 1915 with a record of 1-0 and a 0.90 ERA.

Frank Kelliher—See Massachusetts Born Players, Somerville, Massachusetts

Colonel Snover was a member of the 1920-1925 Pittsfield Hillies. He was a left handed pitcher who appeared in two games in the major leagues for the 1919 New York Giants. He ended his major league career with a record of 0-1 and a 1.00 ERA.

Bill McCorry was a right handed pitcher who appeared in two games for the 1909 St Louis Browns and he ended up with a record of no wins and two losses and a 9.00 ERA. He also played with the Pittsfield Hillies from 1921-1923

Al Pierotti—See Massachusetts Born Players, Boston, Massachusetts

Ernie Neitzke was an outfielder/pitcher for the 1921 Boston Red Sox. He was credited with batting in 11 games and had six hits in 25 at bats for a .240 batting average. As a pitcher he appeared in two games without a win or a loss and a 6.14 ERA. He played for the Pittsfield Hillies in 1922.

Danny Silva—See Massachusetts Born Players, Everett, Massachusetts

Eddie Zimmerman played third base for two seasons in the major leagues. In 1906 he played with the St Louis Cardinals and in 1911 he was with the Brooklyn Superbas. In 127 games he had 80 hits including 10 doubles, seven triples and three home runs. He also had 37 runs batted in and scored 31 runs himself. He played with the Pittsfield Hillies in 1922.

Neal Ball played second and third base as well as shortstop in a major league career that lasted from 1907 to 1913. He played with the New York Highlanders, Cleveland Indians and the Boston Red Sox. He appeared in 502 games and had 404 hits including 56 doubles, 17 triples and four home runs. He also had a .250 batting average and had 151 runs batted in to go with the 163 runs he scored. He pulled off the first ever unassisted triple play in the major leagues on July 19, 1909 against the Boston Red Sox. He was also a member of the 1923 Pittsfield Hillies.

Chick Gagnon—See Massachusetts Born Players, Millbury, Massachusetts

Hal Leathers had a nine game career in the major leagues as a short-stop/second baseman with the Chicago Cubs in 1920. He had seven hits in 23 at bats including one double and one home run. He also had a .304 batting average. He was a member of the 1923 Pittsfield Hillies.

Bunny Roser was a left fielder for the Boston Braves during the 1922 season. In 32 major league ball games, he had 27 hits including three doubles and four triples and a .239 lifetime batting average. In 1923 he was a member of the Pittsfield Hillies.

Art Wilson was a catcher in the major leagues from 1908 until 1921. From 1908 to 1913 he was with the New York Giants. In 1914 and 1915 he was with the Chi Feds of the Federal League. He played part of 1916 with the Pittsburgh Pirates and then the rest of 1916 and 1917 with the Chicago Cubs. Then from 1918 to 1920 he was with the Boston Braves and ended his career in 1921 with the Cleveland Indians. He appeared in 812 games and had 536 hits including 96 doubles, 22 triples and 24 home runs. He also had 237 runs scored and 226 runs batted in and a lifetime batting average of .261. In 1923 Wilson played with the Pittsfield Hillies.

Mike Wilson was a catcher in the major leagues who appeared in five games for the Pittsburgh Pirates in 1921. He did not have a hit in four at bats and he also played with the 1923 Pittsfield Hillies.

Jimmy Esmond played shortstop for the Cincinnati Reds in 1911 and 1912. In 1914 he played with the Indianapolis Hoosiers of the Federal League and in 1915 played with the Newark Peppers also of the Federal League. For the 461 games he played he had a batting average of .264. He had 406 hits that included 52 doubles, 35 triples and 8 home runs and in 1914 he led the Federal League with 15 triples. In 1924 Esmond played with the Pittsfield Hillies.

Waddy Macphee was a member of the 1922 New York Giants as a third baseman. He appeared in two games and had two hits including a triple for a .286 batting average. He played in Pittsfield in 1924 and 1925 as a member of the Hillies.

Horace Milan was a left fielder who played for the Washington Senators in 1915 and 1917 appearing in 42 games. Milan got 32 hits including four doubles, one triple and he also had 16 runs batted in to go with his .320 batting average. He played for the Pittsfield Hillies in 1924 and 1926.

Moses Solomon was a right fielder who played in two games in the major leagues for the 1923 New York Giants. He had three hits in two games and ended his major league career with a .375 batting average. In 1924 he was a member of the Pittsfield Hillies.

Red Torphy—See Massachusetts Born Players, Fall River, Massachusetts

Shano Collins—See Massachusetts Players, Charlestown, Massachusetts

Lefty Jamerson was a pitcher for one game in the major leagues with the Boston Red Sox in 1924. He did not record either a win or a loss in the game and had a 18.00 ERA. He also then played with the Pittsfield Hillies in 1925 and 1926.

Tom Sullivan—See Massachusetts Players, Boston, Massachusetts

Augie Swentor pinch hit in his only plate appearance for the 1922 Chicago White Sox. He did not get a hit in that at bat. He also played for the 1925 Pittsfield Hillies.

Rowdy Elliott was a catcher for the 1910 Boston Braves, the Chicago Cubs from 1916 to 1918 and the Brooklyn Robins in 1920. In 157 games he had 97 hits including 15 doubles, five triples and one home run. He had 44 runs batted in and a .241 batting average. Elliott was a member of the 1926 Pittsfield Hillies.

Ken Jones pitched in the major leagues for the 1924 Detroit Tigers and the 1930 Boston Braves. In nine games he had a record of 0-1 and a 5.40 ERA. He was a part of the 1926 Pittsfield Hillies.

Sam Mayer played right field and first base and pitched for the 1915 Washington Senators. In the one game he pitched he did not get either the win or the loss or an ERA. While hitting he appeared in 11 games and had seven hits including one home run. His batting average in the major leagues was .241 and he was also a member of the Pittsfield Hillies in 1926 and 1929.

John Perrin was a right fielder who played in four games in the major leagues for the Boston Red Sox in 1921. He had three hits and one run batted in and a .231 batting average. He was a member of the 1926 Pittsfield Hillies.

Red Sheridan had a major league career that was spent with the Brooklyn Dodgers in 1918 and 1920. In the five games he played in he had one hit and a .167 batting average. He played with the Pittsfield Hillies from 1926-1928.

Ed Sperber played right field for the 1924-1925 Boston Braves. In 26 games he had 17 hits, including one home run and 12 runs batted in to go with his .279 batting average. In 1926 Sperber played with the Pittsfield Hillies.

Dan Woodman was a pitcher who played in the major leagues with the Buffalo team of the Federal League in 1914 and 1915 In 18 games he had no wins and no losses and a 2.94 ERA. He was a member of the 1926 Pittsfield Hillies.

Ed Baecht pitched for the Philadelphia Phillies from 1926 to 1928, the Chicago Cubs in 1931 and 1932 and the St Louis Browns in 1937. In 64 big league contests, he had five wins and six losses and a 5.56 earned run average and in 1927 he was a member of the Pittsfield Hillies.

Harry Baldwin was a pitcher with the New York Giants in 1924 and 1925. He had three wins and one loss in 11 games and also had an ERA of 4.41. Baldwin was a member of the 1927 and 1928 Pittsfield Hillies.

Ed Miller played for the 1912 and 1914 St Louis Browns as well as the 1918 Cleveland Indians. He was a right fielder, first baseman and short-stop who appeared in 86 games. He had a total of 39 hits, including five doubles and four triples and his batting average for his major league career was .195. In 1927 Miller was a member of the Pittsfield Hillies.

Frank Parkinson had a four year career in the major leagues form 1921 to 1924, all spent with the Philadelphia Phillies. He appeared in 378 games as a second baseman/third baseman/shortstop. He had 335 hits, 24 home runs and 149 runs batted in as well as a .256 batting average. From 1927 to 1928 he wore the jersey of the Pittsfield Hillies.

Joe Smith (born Salvatore Persico) was a catcher for the 1913 New York Yankees. In 14 games he had five hits, two runs batted in and a .156 batting average. He played in Pittsfield in 1927 with the Hillies.

Red Smith was a shortstop/third baseman for the 1925 Philadelphia Athletics for 20 games. He had four hits and a .286 batting average. He also played for the Pittsfield Hillies during the 1927 season.

Denny Sothern played centerfield for the Philadelphia Phillies in 1926 and then from 1928 to 1930. He finished the 1930 season as a Pittsburgh Pirate and then played for the Brooklyn Dodgers for the 1931 season. In 357 games he had 379 hits, 115 runs batted in and

19 home runs as well as a .280 batting average. His 1927 season was spent with the Pittsfield Hillies.

Lefty Taber pitched for the 1926 and 1927 Philadelphia Phillies recording no wins and one loss in nine games as well as a 10.80 ERA. In 1927 he was a member of the Pittsfield Hillies.

Mule Watson was a member of the Philadelphia Athletics from 1918 to 1919. In 1920 he pitched for the Boston Braves then the Pittsburgh Pirates and back to the Braves for the rest of 1920 as well as 1921, 1922 and part of 1923. He finished 1923 with the New York Giants and finished his career with the Giants in 1924. He pitched in 178 games and had 50 wins and 53 losses and a 4.03 ERA. The 1927 season would see him with the Pittsfield Hillies.

Frank Bennett pitched in five games for the Boston Red Sox in 1927 and 1928. He had no wins and one loss and a 2.70 earned run average for his career. The Pittsfield Hillies were the team he played for in 1928.

Herb Bradley had a three year career as a pitcher for the Boston Red Sox from 1927 to 1929. During the 24 games he pitched in he had one win and three losses and a 5.93 ERA. He played with the Pittsfield Hillies in 1928 and again in 1929.

Ralph Head played for the 1923 Philadelphia Phillies. He was a pitcher and had a 35 game career in the major leagues with two wins and nine losses and a 6.66 ERA. In 1928 he was a member of the Pittsfield Hillies.

Red Shea—See Massachusetts Players, Ware, Massachusetts

Charles Small was a center fielder and pinch hitter for the 1930 Boston Red Sox. In his 25 game career he had three hits, including one double and his career batting average was .167. He spent from 1928 to 1930 with the Pittsfield Hillies.

Harry Wilke was a third baseman who played in three games for the 1927 Chicago Cubs. He was also a member of the Pittsfield Hillies from 1928 to 1930.

Casper Asbjornson—See Massachusetts players, Concord, Massachusetts

Frank Bushey's major league career lasted from 1927 to 1930 and was spent with the Boston Red Sox. He was a pitcher who appeared in 12 games and had a record of no wins and one loss and a 6.32 ERA. From 1928 to 1929 he was a member of the Pittsfield Hillies.

Freddie Moncewicz—See Massachusetts Born Players, Brockton, Massachusetts

Jose Rodriguez was a second baseman/first baseman for the New York Giants from 1916 to 1918. In 58 games he had 24 hits, including three riples and 17 runs batted in. He also had a lifetime batting average of .166. He played for the Hillies of Pittsfield in 1929 and 1930.

Pat Simmons (born Patrick Clement Simoni) was a pitcher in the major leagues with the Boston Red Sox in 1928 and 1929. His 33 game career left him with a lifetime ERA of 3.67 and a record of 0-2. He played at Wahconah Park with the Pittsfield Hillies in 1929 and 1930.

Carl Sumner—See Massachusetts Born Players, Cambridge, Massachusetts

Horace "Hod" Lisenbee was a pitcher in the major leagues with the Washington Senators in 1927 and 1928, the Boston Red Sox in 1929 to 1932, the Philadelphia Athletics in 1936 and the Cincinnati Reds in 1945. In 1927 he led the American League in shutouts with four. He had a record in 207 games of 37 wins and 58 losses with a 4.81 ERA. He called Wahconah Park home for part of 1929 as a member of the Pittsfield Hillies.

Maurice Archdeacon was a centerfielder in the major leagues for the Chicago White Sox from 1923 to 1925. In 127 games he had 128 hits, including 14 doubles and 4 triples as well as a .333 batting average. In 1930 he played with the Pittsfield Hillies.

Jim Bishop played with the Philadelphia Phillies for 1923 and 1924. In 22 games as a pitcher he had a record of 0-4 and a 6.39 ERA and in 1930 he was a member of the Pittsfield Hillies.

Ray Dobens was a pitcher in the major leagues for the 1929 Boston Red Sox. His career was 11 games long and he did not have a win or a loss but had a career ERA of 3.81. 1930 would see him as a member of the Pittsfield Hillies.

Bob Emmerich was a centerfielder and a pinch runner for the 1923 Boston Braves. In 13 games he had two hits and a .083 batting average and he was also a member of the 1930 Pittsfield Hillies.

Bill Holland was a Washington Senator pitcher for one major league season which turned out to be three games for Mr. Holland. He had a record of no wins and one loss and a 11.25 ERA. He was a Pittsfield Electric for the 1941 season.

Glenn Spencer's major league career went from 1928 to 1933. For 1928 and from 1930 to 1932 he was a member of the Pittsburgh Pirates, and in 1933 he played with the New York Giants. In 139 games he had a record of 23 wins and 39 losses and a 4.53 ERA. As for the 1941 season he was a member of the Pittsfield Electrics.

Tony Rensa was a catcher, who in 1930 played with both the Detroit Tigers and the Philadelphia Phillies, and he also played for the Phillies in 1931, 1933 and Rensa was a member of the New York Yankees and from 1937 to 1939 he was a member of the Chicago White Sox. His career was 200 games long and he had 134 hits including 26 doubles, five triples and seven home runs. He also had 65 runs batted in and scored 71 runs. His lifetime batting average was .261. From 1946 to 1947 he was a member of the Pittsfield Electrics.

Gene Hasson was a first baseman for the Philadelphia Athletics in 1937 and 1938. In 47 games he had 49 this including 12 doubles, five triples and four home runs. He also had 26 runs batted in and a .293 batting average. From 1948 to 1949 he was a member of the Pittsfield Electrics/Indians.

Lloyd Brown was a pitcher in the major leagues for the 1925 Brooklyn Dodgers, the Washington Senators from 1928 through 1932, the St Louis Browns and Boston Red Sox in 1933, the Cleveland Indians from 1934 to 1937 and the 1940 Philadelphia Athletics. In 404 games he had a record of 91 wins and 105 losses, a 4.20 ERA and 510 strikeouts. During the 1950 season he played with the Pittsfield Indians.

Dave Gray was a pitcher with the Boston Red Sox in 1964 and in nine games his record was no wins and no losses and a 9.00 ERA. In 1965 he was a member of the Pittsfield Red Sox.

Billy MacLeod—See Massachusetts Born Players, Gloucester, Massachusetts

Pete Smith—See Massachusetts Born Players, Natick, Massachusetts

Ed Connolly was a pitcher for the total of 42 games in the major leagues as he played for the 1964 Boston Red Sox and the 1967 Cleveland Indians. He had a record of six wins and 12 losses and a 5.88 ERA and he also played for the Pittsfield Red Sox in 1967.

Bobby Guindon—See Massachusetts Born Players, Brookline, Massachusetts

Pete Charton appeared as a pitcher in 25 games for the 1964 Boston Red Sox. He had a record of no wins and two losses and a 5.26 ERA. He played also for the 1967 Pittsfield Red Sox.

Galen Cisco played for the Boston Red Sox in 1961 and part of 1962. He also played for the New York Mets from 1962 until 1965, then back to the Red Sox for 1967, and he ended his career with the Kansas City Royals in 1969. In 192 games as a pitcher he had a record of 25 wins and 56 losses and had a 4.56 ERA. He also played with the 1967 Pittsfield Red Sox.

Billy Gardner was with the New York Giants for 1954 and 1955, the Baltimore Orioles from 1956 to 1959, the Washington Senators in 1960, the Minnesota Twins for part of 1961, the New York Yankees for the rest of 1961 and 1962, and the Boston Red Sox for 1962 and 1963. He was a second baseman/third baseman/shortstop who appeared in 1,034 games and had 841 hits including 41 home runs, 159 doubles and 18 triples. He also had 271 runs batted in and he scored 356 runs. He had a lifetime batting average of .237 and in 1957 led the American League in doubles with 36. He was also a member of the 1961 World Champion New York Yankees. He played in Pittsfield in 1967 and 1969.

Bill Schlesinger appeared in one game as a pinch hitter for the 1965 Boston Red Sox and he was also a member of the 1967-1968 Pittsfield Red Sox.

Jose Tartabull was an outfielder and a pinch hitter in the major leagues for the 1962 to1966 Kansas City Athletics, 1966 to 1968 Boston Red Sox and the 1969-1970 Oakland Athletics. In 749 games he had 484 hits, including 56 doubles, 24 triples and two home runs. He scored 247 runs and had 107 runs batted in to go with his career batting average of .261. He played at Wahconah Park with the 1967 Pittsfield Red Sox.

Dave Gray was a pitcher in nine games for the Boston Red Sox in 1964. He did not have a win or a loss and had a 9.00 ERA. He was a member of the 1968-1969 Pittsfield Red Sox.

Russ Nixon was a catcher and a pinch hitter in the major leagues from1957 to 1968. In his career he played in 906 games for the 1957 to 1960 Cleveland Indians, 1960 to 1965 Boston Red Sox, 1966 to 1967 Minnesota Twins and the 1968 Boston Red Sox. He had a total of 670 hits, including 115 doubles, 19 triples and 27 home runs. He scored 215 runs and had 266 runs batted in. His lifetime batting average was .268 and he was a member of the 1968 Pittsfield Red Sox.

Tom Parsons was a pitcher in the major leagues for the 1963 Pittsburgh Pirates and the 1964-1965 New York Mets. He had a record of two wins and 13 losses and a 4.72 ERA. He also played with the 1969 Pittsfield Red Sox and went to the same high school as major leaguers John Lamb and Steve Blass.

Toby Harrah was a second and third baseman as well as a shortstop who played in the major leagues for a total of 2,155 games for the 1969/1971 Washington Senators, 1972-1978 Texas Rangers, 1979-1983

Cleveland Indians, 1984 New York Yankees and the 1985-1986 Texas Rangers. He had a total of 1,954 hits including 307 doubles, 40 triples and 195 home runs. He scored 1,115 runs and had 918 runs batted in. His lifetime batting average was .264 and he was also an American League All Star in 1972, 1975, 1976 and 1982. He played for the Pittsfield Senators in 1970.

Gene Martin was a left fielder and a pinch hitter for the 1968 Washington Senators. In nine games he had four hits, including a home run and a .364 batting average. In 1970 he was a member of the Pittsfield Senators.

Charley Walters was a pitcher for the 1969 Minnesota Twins who appeared in six games and did not record a win or a loss and had an ERA of 5.40. He played in Pittsfield in 1971 and 1972 as a Senator and a Ranger.

Dick Such appeared in 21 games for the 1970 Washington Senators. He had one win and five losses and a 7.56 ERA. He also played for the 1973 Pittsfield Rangers.

Tommy Cruz was a left fielder and a pinch runner in 1973 for the St Louis Cardinals and the 1977 Chicago White Sox for seven games. He did not have a hit in those seven games and he also played for the 1974 Pittsfield Rangers.

Marty Martinez was a second and third baseman and shortstop for a major league career that lasted from 1962 until 1972. He appeared in 436 games for the following teams: 1962 Minnesota Twins, 1967-1968 Atlanta Braves, 1969-1971 Houston Astros, and 1972 St Louis Cardinals/Oakland Athletics/Texas Rangers. He had 230 hits, including 19 doubles and 11 triples and his lifetime batting average was .243. He played at Wahconah Park for the 1975 Pittsfield Rangers.

Lafayette Currence pitched for the 1975 Milwaukee Brewers for eight games. He had a record of no wins and two losses and a 7.71 ERA. He played for the Berkshire Brewers in 1976.

Larry Sorenson pitched for seven teams in a career that lasted from 1977 until 1988. Those teams were the 1977-1980 Milwaukee Brewers,

1981 St Louis Cardinals, 1982-1983 Cleveland Indians, 1984 Oakland Athletics, 1985 Chicago Cubs, 1987 Montreal Expos, and the 1988 San Francisco Giants. He appeared in a total of 346 games for those clubs and had a record of 93 wins and 103 losses and a 4.15 ERA. He was a member of the 1978 American League All Star team and also pitched for the Berkshire Brewers in 1976.

Jeff Cornell pitched in a total of 23 games for the 1984 San Francisco Giants going with a record of one win and three losses and a 6.10 ERA. He also pitched for the 1985 Pittsfield Cubs.

Jeff Jones played in the outfield for the 1983 Cincinnati Reds for a total of 16 games. He had 10 hits including three doubles and had a .227 batting average. In 1985 Jones was a member of the Pittsfield Cubs.

Dickie Noles pitched in the major leagues for the 1979-1981 Philadelphia Phillies, 1982-1984 Chicago Cubs, 1984 Texas Rangers, 1986 Cleveland Indians, 1987 Chicago Cubs/Detroit Tigers, 1988 Baltimore Orioles and the 1990 Philadelphia Phillies. In 277 games he had 36 wins and 53 losses and a 4.56 earned run average for his career. He was a member of the 1980 World Champion Philadelphia Phillies, and he also pitched for the 1987 Pittsfield Cubs.

Al Chambers was a left fielder and a pinch hitter for the Seattle Mariners from 1983 to 1985. In 57 games he had 25 hits, including two home runs and a .208 batting average. He played at Wahconah Park for the 1988 Pittsfield Cubs.

Berkshire County Born In Baseball

Arthur "Art" Madison was born in Clarksburg, Massachusetts on January 14, 1871. He was an infielder for the Philadelphia Phillies in 1895 and the Pittsburgh Pirates team in the National League during the course of his two year major league career. The first game in his career was on September 9, 1895 for the Phillies and the last was on August 22, 1899 for the Pittsburgh Pirates. In 53 games Madison had 44 hits, including five doubles and four triples and a .289 lifetime batting average. He passed away on January 27, 1933 in North Adams, Massachusetts and is buried in the South View Cemetery in North Adams.

Mike Riley "Doc" Powers was a catcher and a first baseman in the major leagues in a career that started on June 12, 1898. For 1898 and part of 1899, he played with the Louisville Colonels. For the rest of 1899 he played with the Washington Senators. From 1901 through part of the 1905 season he played with the Philadelphia Athletics, then he went to the New York Highlanders and back to the Athletics for the rest of his career which lasted until April 12, 1909. In his 647 game career, he had 450 hits that included 72 doubles and 13 triples as well as four home runs. He scored 183 runs and had 199 runs batted in and finished his career with a lifetime batting average of .216. While playing for Connie Mack and the Philadelphia Athletics on April 12, 1909 he crashed into a wall while chasing a foul ball at Shibe Park in Philadelphia. He died two weeks later of internal injuries caused by a post-operative infection. He passed away on April 26, 1909 in Philadelphia, Pennsylvania and is buried in St. Louis Cemetery in Louisville, Kentucky.

Ulysses Franklin "Frank" Grant was born on August 1, 1865 in Pittsfield Massachusetts. He was an African American second baseman who played with the Cuban Giants, Buffalo Bisons, New York Gothams, Page Fence Giants, Cuban X Giants, Philadelphia Giants, back to the New York Gothams, the Colored Capital All Americans and the Genuine Cuban Giants in a career that spanned from 1889 until 1903. He was thought to be the best ballplayer in the 19th century both offensively and defensively. Offensively he had good power as he frequently got both extra base hits and home runs. In fact he was averaging an extra base hit every four times he got up to bat.

On the defensive side of the ball, he had the nickname of "the Colored Dunlap" because many people felt that Grant was the fielding equal of Fred "Sureshot" Dunlap who was one of the slickest fielding second baseman of the era. Grant was always an impressive player when compared to others of the era, but because of segregation in baseball he was never given the chance to showcase his talents in the major leagues. In 1888 sentiments around the league were really against black baseball players, and the only team that was willing to and dared to buck the trend was the Buffalo team of the International League where Grant played. Grant played in the early years of Negro League baseball which paved the way for other Negro League stars like Satchel Paige and Josh Gibson and those two in turn paved the way for the Jackie Robinsons and the Larry Dobys to break down the color barrier in baseball. Grant passed away in Clifton, New Jersey at the age of 67 and was buried in East Ride Lawn Cemetery. He was elected to the Hall of Fame in Cooperstown in 2006.

Jim Garry was born in Great Barrington, Massachusetts on September 21, 1869. He was a pitcher who made his first and only appearance in the major leagues on May 2, 1893 for the Boston Beaneaters. He ended up on the losing end of this game and his ERA was 63.00. He passed away in Pittsfield, Massachusetts on January 12, 1917 and is buried in the Fairview Cemetery in Dalton, Massachusetts.

Peter William "Pete" McBride was a native of Adams, Massachusetts having been born there on June 9, 1875. He was a pitcher who had a two year career in the major leagues which began on September 20,

1898 with the Cleveland Spiders. He later pitched with the St Louis Perfectos where he pitched in eleven games. In the 12 games he appeared in he had a record of two wins and five losses as well as an earned run average of 4.31 to go with 32 strikeouts. He passed away in Adams on July 3, 1944 and is buried in the Maple Cemetery in Adams.

Jack Dwight Chesbro was born in Houghtonville, which is a village in the city of North Adams, Massachusetts, on June 5, 1874. Chesbro began his career in sandlot ball around his hometown in 1892, and then while working for the Middletown State Hospital in Middletown, New York he also played for the hospital team. He made his professional debut with the Albany Senators of the New York State League, then went to the Johnstown Buckskins and the Springfield Maroons. In 1896 Chesbro pitched in the Virginia League with the Roanoke Magicians and finished up the year with the Cooperstown Athletics. His given name was Chesebrough and the Cooperstown paper shortened it so it would fit into the box scores of the games. He began his major league career on July 12, 1899 with the Pittsburgh Pirates pitching for them for a total of four seasons. He pitched in his first game for the New York Highlanders in 1903 and had 21 wins that year. It would be the next year that would mark Chesbro's best year as he won an amazing total of 41 games. During that year he had won 14 games in a row which stood as the Highlander/Yankee team record until it was broken by Roger Clemens in 2001. He also set the team record for strikeouts at 239 and held that record until 1978 when Ron Guidry broke the record. On the downside he is also remembered as the pitcher who threw the wild pitch/passed ball that let the Boston Red Sox defeat the Highlanders for the American League pennant in 1904. His career was highlighted by two National League pennants with the Pirates. He led the National League in wins in 1902 with 28 games and also won 20 or more games five times during his career. He twice led the National League in shutouts as well. He pitched in a total of 392 games completing 260 of them. He also struck out 1,265 batters and had a career earned run average of 2.68. He ended his career with a record of 192 wins and 132 losses.

After a failed attempt at a comeback Chesbro retired to the farm he had purchased in Conway, Massachusetts where he also coached and played some semi- pro baseball. He passed away in Conway on November 6, 1931 and was buried in the Howland Cemetery in Conway. The Veteran's Committee elected Chesbro to the hallowed halls of Cooperstown in 1946.

Stephen "Nails" McGee Arienti was a ball player who made his major league debut for the Brooklyn Superbas on May 15, 1900. In his first major league at bat he hit a home run. He was known as a hardnosed player and being a hot head and his career was shortened by a concussion. He was born in Pittsfield, Massachusetts on July 4, 1880 and is buried in St. Joseph's Cemetery in Pittsfield.

Peter John "Pete" Noonan was born in West Stockbridge, Massachusetts on November 24, 1881. He was a catcher and also played first base for parts of four seasons in the major leagues. He made his debut in the majors for the Philadelphia Athletics on June 20, 1904. He also played with the Chicago Cubs and the St Louis Cardinals, and it was with the Cardinals where he played his last game on October 6, 1907. He appeared in 169 games and had 98 hits including 11 doubles, seven triples and four home runs. He scored 40 runs and had 38 runs batted in and carried a career batting average of .205. He passed away in Great Barrington, Massachusetts on February 11, 1965 and is buried in St. Peter's Cemetery in Great Barrington.

David Francis "Dave" or "Dirty Dave" Murphy was a native of Adams, Massachusetts having been born there on May 4, 1876. He played shortstop and third base in a career that began with the Boston Beaneaters on August 28, 1905 and ended two days later on August 30, 1905. He had two hits in 11 at bats for a .182 batting average. He passed away in Adams, Massachusetts on April 8, 1940 and is buried in the Maple Cemetery in Adams.

Jack Ferry was a pitcher in the major leagues from September 4, 1910 until June 7, 1913. He spent his entire career with the Pittsburgh Pirates appearing in 47 games. He had a record of 10 wins and six

losses and a 3.02 earned run average for his career. He was born
in Pittsfield, Massachusetts on April 7, 1887, and passed away in
Pittsfield on August 29, 1954. He is buried in St. Joseph's Cemetery
in Pittsfield. He is the younger brother of Alfred "Cy" Ferry, who
pitched in the major leagues in 1904 and 1905.

South Williamstown, Massachusetts is the hometown of **Abbott
"Jack" Mills** who was born there on October 23, 1889. He attended
Williams College in Williamstown and then went on to play in the
major leagues from July 1, 1911 until August 19, 1911 with the Cleveland Naps. He was a third baseman who appeared in 13 games in the
majors. He had five hits in 17 at bats for a .294 batting average and
then went on to a successful career as an attorney. He passed away
on June 3, 1973 in Washington, DC and was later cremated.

Howard "Sponge" Storie was born in Pittsfield, Massachusetts on
May 15, 1911. Storie was a catcher who debuted in the major leagues
on September 7, 1931 for the Boston Red Sox. He played in a total
of 12 games for the Sox and ended his major league career on June
5, 1932. He had five hits in 25 at bats for a .200 batting average. He
passed away in Pittsfield, Massachusetts on July 27, 1968 and is
buried in St. Joseph's Cemetery.

Gene Hermanski was born in Pittsfield, Massachusetts on May 11,
1920. After he attended Seton Hall University, he was drafted by the
Philadelphia Athletics in 1939. He debuted in the major leagues on
August 15, 1943 and during the course of his nine year career which
ended on September 22, 1953, he played with the Brooklyn Dodgers,
Chicago Cubs and Pittsburgh Pirates. He was a member of the 1947
Dodger team when Jackie Robinson broke the color barrier in major
league baseball. Showing a sense of humor, he suggested that all of the
Dodgers wear the number 42 so as to confuse any gunman who may
be planning on shooting Robinson. In the 739 games he appeared in,
he had 533 hits in 1960 at bats. Of those hits, 83 were doubles 18 were
triples, and 46 were home runs. He scored 276 runs and had another
259 runs batted in. His career batting average was .272. He played

mostly in the outfield but was also a pinch hitter. He passed away in Homosassa, Florida on August 9, 2010 and was later cremated.

Earl Turner was born in Pittsfield, Massachusetts on May 6, 1923. He made his major league debut as a catcher on September 25, 1948. He played his entire career for the Pirates with his last game being on July 19, 1950. In 75 at bats he had 18 hits including three home runs and his career batting average was .240. He passed away in Lee, Massachusetts on October 20, 1999 and is buried in St. Ann's Cemetery in Lenox, Massachusetts.

Mark Belanger was a native of Pittsfield, Massachusetts having been born there on June 8, 1944. His family lived in Cheshire and Adams before finally settling in Lanesborough. He was a standout athlete at Pittsfield High School in both baseball and basketball. In fact when he graduated from Pittsfield High in 1961 he held the career scoring record in basketball and would hold the record until 2007 when Sedale Jones broke his point total. He had many offers to play college basketball, but chose instead to sign with the Baltimore Orioles for $35,000 as an amateur free agent.

He debuted for the Orioles on August 7, 1965 and played for Baltimore through the 1981 season. During his time in Baltimore, he set team records for games, assists, and double plays and held those records until they were broken by Cal Ripken Jr. He also teamed with Hall of Fame third baseman Brooks Robinson to form an impermeable wall on the left side of the Orioles infield. He was a member of the 1970 World Champion Baltimore Orioles and also was chosen to play in the 1976 All Star game. He won a total of eight Gold Gloves, including six in a row from 1973 through 1978. During the early part of his career before big money really came into baseball, Belanger would spend his winters working at the Besse Clarke Sporting Goods store on North Street in Pittsfield. He ended his career with the Los Angeles Dodgers on October 2, 1982. He was a player representative for the Orioles and the baseball players union and was one of the four players who helped to negotiate a settlement when the players went on strike in

1981. After he retired he worked for the Major League Baseball Players Association as a liaison for the membership. He is ranked 24th in fielding percentage for shortstops ahead of such players as Luis Aparicio, Pee Wee Reese, Rabbit Maranville and Luke Appling, all of whom are in the Hall of Fame. He appeared in 2,016 games and had 1,316 hits including 175 doubles, 33 triples and 20 home runs. He had 389 runs batted in and scored 676 runs himself. He had a career batting average of .228 and his nickname was "The Blade" due to his tall thin build. He passed away in New York City on October 6, 1998 and is buried in St. Joseph's Cemetery in Pittsfield.

Tom Grieve was born on March 4, 1948 in Pittsfield, Massachusetts. After attending Pittsfield High School, he was drafted in the 6th round of the amateur draft by the Washington Senators with whom he debuted on July 5, 1970. He played with the Senators in 1970 and then with the Texas Rangers from 1972-1977, the New York Mets in 1978 and the St Louis Cardinals in 1979. He was a designated hitter and outfielder who appeared in 670 games. In 1907 at bats he had 474 hits including 76 doubles, 10 triples and 65 home runs. He scored 209 runs and had 254 runs batted in, and his lifetime batting average was .249. After his playing career was over, he worked in both the Ranger front office as well as on television as a color commentator. In 1984 Grieve would be named manager of the Rangers and now he is currently a broadcaster for Rangers games. He is also the father of former major leaguer Ben Grieve. Tim Grieve was selected to the Texas Rangers Hall of Fame in 2010.

Jeff Reardon is a native of Dalton, Massachusetts having been born there on October 1, 1955. He attended Wahconah High School and later the University of Massachusetts and his major league career began on June 17, 1979 and ended on May 4, 1994. During the course of his career he played for the New York Mets, Montreal Expos, Minnesota Twins, Boston Red Sox, Atlanta Braves, Cincinnati Reds and finally the New York Yankees. He was drafted right out of high school by the Expos but did not sign, opting to go play college baseball at the University of Massachusetts in Amherst. After college he was not drafted and signed a minor league contract with the New York Mets where he played with the Lynchburg team in the Carolina League. He worked his way through the minor league system and finally made his major league debut with the Mets in 1979. He had a fastball that was clocked at 98 MPH on the radar gun and because of that he was nicknamed "The Terminator."

He was traded to the Expos during the 1981 season and stayed in Montreal through the 1986 season where he made two All Star teams and led the league in saves for the 1985 season. In 1987 Reardon was traded to the Minnesota Twins and was a member of the Twins team that won the 1987 World Series. He was named Rolaids Relief Man of the Year in 1987. He became a free agent after the 1989 season and joined the Boston Red Sox where he became the career save leader, a distinction he held until 1993 when Lee Smith broke his mark. He played in his last major league baseball game on May 4, 1994 and currently ranks 7th on the all-time same list with 367. During his career he appeared in 880 games and had a record of 73 wins and 77 losses and a 3.16 earned run average.

Steven "Turk" Wendell is another Berkshire County resident who made his way to the major leagues. Wendell was born in Pittsfield, Massachusetts on May 19, 1967. He attended Wahconah High School in Dalton, Massachusetts and then went to Quinnipiac College in Hamden, Connecticut. He played with Falmouth in the Cape Cod League and also played with the Dalton Collegians. He began his major league career as a fifth round draft pick for the Atlanta Braves and started his pro career with the Pulaski Braves in the Appalachian League in June of 1988.

He debuted in the major leagues on June 17, 1993 for the Chicago Cubs. He also played for the New York Mets, Philadelphia Phillies and the Colorado Rockies. His final game was on May 14, 2004 and he announced his retirement from baseball in March of 2005 after he failed to earn a roster spot with the Houston Astros. He was a pitcher and certainly not afraid to speak his mind on a variety of subjects.

During the 2000 World Series which pitted the Yankees versus the Mets in a modern day Subway Series, Wendell said this about playing the Yankees: "I don't give a hoot. It won't surprise me; the Yankees have tortured us for years and beating them would be sweet." After the Yankees won they repeatedly toasted Wendell in the clubhouse.

Turk does a lot of charity work especially for children, but shuns the publicity from it. He now owns a hunting and fishing camp in Larkspur, Colorado called the Wykota Ranch. During the course of his career, he appeared in 552 games and had a record of 36 wins and 33 losses to go with 33 career saves and an ERA of 3.93.

Matt White was another of the pitchers from the Berkshires who later went on to pitch in the major leagues after playing at Wahconah High School in Dalton. White was born in Pittsfield, Massachusetts on August 17, 1977. After high school he attended Clemson University in South Carolina. He was drafted in the 15th round of the 1998 amateur draft by the Cleveland Indians. He debuted in the major leagues on May 27, 2003 for the Boston Red Sox and played in his final major league ball game in August 27, 2005 for the Washington Nationals. He also pitched for the Yokohama Bay Stars in Japan and the Uni President 7-Eleven Lions in Taiwan.

In 2003 White bought 50 acres of land from his aunt for $50,000 because she needed money to go into a nursing home. The land is located in Cummington, Massachusetts. He had planned to build a house on the property, but the digging was extremely tough, so he went to get the land surveyed and found that the land was a solid mass of rock called Goshen Stone, which is a very unusual colored variety of mica schist which is found mostly in New England. It is sold as landscaping stone and sells for about $100 a ton. A conservative estimate on the amount of stone on White's property places it at over 24 million tons with a value of $2.5 billion dollars, minus of course what it would cost to get the stone out of the ground. During his career White appeared in seven games and had a record of no wins and two losses to go with an ERA of 16.76.

Jonah Bayliss was born in Adams, Massachusetts on August 13, 1980. He attended the Lawrence Academy in Groton, Massachusetts as well as Trinity College in Hartford, Connecticut. He was drafted in the seventh round of the amateur draft by the Kansas City Royals with whom he debuted on June 21, 2005. He played for the Pittsburgh Pirates in 2006 and 2007 before retiring on August 3, 2007 after compiling a record of five wins and four losses as well as a 6.75 ERA, in the 64 games he pitched in.

Dan Duquette is a native of Dalton, Massachusetts and while he is not a major league baseball player, he has served the sport in many capacities. He did play college baseball and was a catcher on the varsity team at Amherst College.

He got his start in baseball as a scouting assistant with the Milwaukee Brewers. In 1987 the Montreal Expos hired Duquette as their director of player development. In 1991 he became the Expos General Manager taking over for Dave Dombrowski. He built an Expos team that had the best record if baseball in the 1994 season which ended up being strike shortened. Duquette then became General Manager of the Boston Red Sox and was able to build some of the better teams in Red Sox history by acquiring players such as Nomar Garciaparra and Kevin Youklis in the draft and players like Tim Wakefield, Pedro Martinez and Jason Varitek through free agent signings or trades. After his stint with the Red Sox, Duquette started a children's sports academy in Hinsdale, Massachusetts and he also helped start the Israeli Baseball League although the league only lasted one season. He is part owner and president of the Pittsfield Dukes who played in the New England Collegiate Baseball League. On November 8, 2011 he became vice president of baseball operations for the Baltimore Orioles. He is also the cousin of Jim Duquette, who was a former executive for both the Orioles and the Mets, which may cause some interesting discussions. Jim Duquette went to Williams College and Dan Duquette went to Amherst College.

PHOTOGRAPHS/CREDITS

The following is a list of the photographs appearing in this book:

1. Jack Chesbro

2. John Clarkson

3. Mickey Cochrane

4. Candy Cummings

5. Leo Durocher

6. Tom Glavine

7. Frank Grant

8. Tim Keefe

9. Joe Kelly

10. Connie Mack

11. Rabbit Maranville

12. Tom McCarthy

13. Wilbert Robinson

14. Harold "Pie" Traynor

All of these men are or will be (in the case of Tom Glavine) enshrined in the Baseball Hall of Fame and all were born in Massachusetts. The photos are the property of the National Baseball Hall of Fame Library in Cooperstown New York.

Massachusetts-Born Major Leaguers

···

For this part of the book the following is a town by town list of all of the major league players born in Massachusetts along with histories of their major league careers.

ABINGTON

Dan Burke was an outfielder, catcher and a first baseman born in Abington, Massachusetts on October 25, 1868. He debuted in the major leagues on April 18, 1890 for the Rochester Broncos. He also played for the Syracuse Stars and the Boston Beaneaters. He appeared in a total of 42 games for his career which ended on October 1, 1892. He came to bat 126 times and got 22 hits including one double. His career batting average was .175 and he passed away in Taunton, Massachusetts on March 20, 1933. He is buried in Rockland, Massachusetts at the St Patrick's Cemetery.—1890 Rochester Broncos AA Syracuse Stars AA 1892 Boston Beaneaters National NL

Peter John "Pete" Smith was a major league pitcher who was born in Abington on February 26, 1966. He debuted in the major leagues in 1987 for the Atlanta Braves. He also played for the New York Mets, Cincinnati Reds, San Diego Padres and the Baltimore Orioles where he ended his career on September 24, 1998. He had a record as a pitcher of 47 wins and 71 losses to go with a 4.55 career earned run average.—1987-1993 Atlanta Braves NL, 1994 New York Mets NL, 1995 Cincinnati Reds NL, 1997-1998 San Diego Padres NL, and 1987 Baltimore Orioles AL

···

ACUSHNET

John Pardon Taber was a pitcher for the Boston Beaneaters for two games during the 1890 season. He had a record of no wins and one loss in those two games, and he also had a career earned run average of 4.15. He was born in Acushnet, Massachusetts on June 28, 1868 and passed away in Boston, Massachusetts on February 21, 1940. He is buried in Acushnet Cemetery in Acushnet, Massachusetts.

ADAMS

Peter William McBride—see Berkshire County Born Players

David Francis Murphy—see Berkshire County Born Players

AGAWAM

Francis James Rosso was born March 1, 1921 in Agawam, Massachusetts. He was a pitcher and a pinch runner for his career which lasted one season. He debuted for the New York Giants on September 15, 1944 and played in his final game on October 1, 1944. He appeared in two games and did not register either a win or a loss, but had an ERA of 9.00. He passed away in Springfield, Massachusetts on January 26, 1980 and is buried in St Thomas Cemetery in West Springfield, Massachusetts.

AMESBURY

James Henry Bannon was a right fielder who had a three year career in the major leagues which began on June 15, 1893. He played for the St Louis Browns and the Boston Beaneaters appearing in 367 games. He had 450 hits in 1,438 at bats which was good enough for a batting average of .320. He also had 76 doubles, 24 triples and 19 home runs to go with 253 runs batted in. He played his final game on August 12, 1896. He was born in Amesbury, Massachusetts on May 5, 1871 and is the brother of major leaguer Tom Bannon. James Bannon passed away in Glen Rock, New Jersey on March 24, 1948 and is buried in St Mary's Cemetery in Rochester, New Hampshire. 1893 St Louis Browns NL, 1894-1896 Boston Beaneaters NL

Thomas Edward Bannon was born in Amesbury, Massachusetts on May 8, 1869. He was an outfielder and a first baseman for the New York Giants for two seasons after debuting for them on May 10, 1895. He appeared in 39 games and had 44 hits and a career batting average of .265. He passed away on January 26, 1950 in Lynn, Massachusetts and is buried in Lynn at St Joseph 'Cemetery. He is the older brother of James Bannon, who also played in the major leagues.

Patrick Crisham was born in Amesbury on June 4, 1877 and had a career in the major leagues that started on May 5, 1899 for the Baltimore Orioles. His career ended on October 9, 1899. He was a first baseman and a catcher who appeared in 53 games. He had 50 hits in 172 at bats and his career batting average was .291. He died in Syracuse, New York on June 5, 1912 and is buried in Syracuse at the Assumption Cemetery.

AMHERST

John Patrick Henry was born in Amherst, Massachusetts on December 26, 1889. He debuted in the major leagues on July 8, 1910 and played for eight years in the major leagues with the Washington Senators and the Boston Braves. He was a catcher/first baseman who appeared in 687 games and had a career batting average of .207. Of his 397 career base hits, 54 were doubles, 15 were triples and he also hit two home runs to go with 171 runs batted in He died in Fort Huachuca, Arizona on November 24, 1941 and is buried in Evergreen Cemetery in Bisbee, Arizona. 1910-1917 Washington Senators AL, 1918 Boston

ARLINGTON

Dave Shean was born in Arlington, Massachusetts on July 9, 1883. He made his debut in the major leagues on September 10, 1906. During his nine year career in the major leagues he played second base and shortstop appearing in 630 games and getting 495 hits, including 59 doubles, 23 triples and six home runs. He had a career batting average of .228. He played in his final major league baseball game on July 17, 1919. He passed away in Boston, Massachusetts on May 22, 1963 and is buried in Arlington, Massachusetts at St Paul's Cemetery. --1906 Philadelphia Athletics AL, 1908 – 1909 Philadelphia Phillies NL, 1909 -1910 Boston Doves NL,1911 Chicago Cubs NL, 1912 Boston Braves NL, 1917 Cincinnati Reds, 1918-1919 Boston Red Sox AL

Cornelius "Neil" Stynes was a catcher who had a two game major league career. He came to bat eight times and did not record a hit. He was born in Arlington, Massachusetts on December 10, 1868 and played in his first game on September 8, 1890 and his last game was played on September 9, 1890. He died in Somerville, Massachusetts on March 26, 1944 and is buried in St Paul Cemetery in Arlington. 1890 Cleveland Infants PL

Dave Walsh was a left handed pitcher born in Arlington, Massachusetts on September 25, 1960. He debuted in the major leagues on August 13, 1990 and played his final game on October 2, 1990. He appeared in 20 games and had a record of one win no losses with three saves. --1990 Los Angeles Dodgers NL

Fred Winchell pitched for one major league season appearing in four games during the 1909 season. He had no wins and three losses and a 6.28 earned run average. He was born in Arlington, Massachusetts on January 23, 1882 and passed away in Toronto, Canada on August 8, 1958. --1909 Cleveland Naps (Indians) AL

ASHLAND

William McCarthy was a pitcher in the major leagues who was born in Ashland, Massachusetts on April 11, 1882 He played in only one game in the major leagues and did not record either a win or a loss. He died in Boston, Massachusetts on May 29, 1939 and is buried in Concord, Massachusetts at the St. Bernard Parish Cemetery. 1906 Boston Beaneaters

ATHOL

Jimmy Barrett was born in Athol, Massachusetts on March 28, 1875. He played centerfield in the major leagues for nine seasons playing for the Cincinnati Reds, Detroit Tigers, and the Boston Americans/Red Sox after debuting on September 13, 1899. His final big league appearance was on May 13, 1909 and in between he had 962 hits, including 83 doubles, 47 triples and 16 home runs to go with 255 runs batted in and a .291 batting average. He passed away in Detroit, Michigan in October of 1921 and is buried in Detroit's Mount Olivert Cemetery. -- 1899- 1900 Cincinnati Reds NL, 1901-1905 Detroit Tigers AL, 1906 Cincinnati Reds 1907-1908 NL, Boston Americans (Red Sox) AL

ATTLEBORO

Born in Attleboro, Massachusetts pitcher/outfielder **James Burke** played for three major league seasons. In 40 games as a pitcher he had 19 wins and 16 losses and a 3.02 earned run average. In the 49 games he appeared in as an outfielder he had 42 hits and a .309 batting average. --1882-1883 Buffalo Bisons NL, 1884 Boston Reds UA

Eddie Pick was a left fielder and third baseman in a four year major league career that lasted from September 10, 1923 and ended on September 7, 1927. The Attleboro, Massachusetts native was born on May 7, 1899 and appeared in 66 games and had 34 hits, including two home runs. His career batting average was .178. He passed away

in Santa Monica, California on May 13, 1967 and was later cremated.
--1923-1924 Cincinnati Reds NL, 1927 Chicago Cubs NL

AUBURN

Patrick "Pat" Murphy was born in Auburn, Massachusetts on January 2, 1857 and began his major league career as a catcher on September 2, 1887 as a New York Giant. His entire career was spent with the New York Giants and that career ended on October 3, 1890. He appeared in 86 games and had 68 hits, including nine doubles, two triples and one home run to go with 21 runs batted in and a .220 batting average. Murphy passed away in Worcester, Massachusetts on May 16, 1927. He is buried in St. John's Cemetery in Worcester.

BEVERLY

Former big league pitcher **Dave Lundquist** was born in Beverly, Massachusetts on June 14, 1973. He made his major league debut on April 6, 1999. He was a pitcher who appeared in 37 games. He ended up with a record of one win and two losses and a 7.92 earned run average. He played in his last major league game on June 28, 2002. ----1999 Chicago White Sox AL, 2001-2002 San Diego Padres NL

Danny Murphy was born in Beverly, Massachusetts on August 13, 1942. His major league debut was on June 18, 1960 and he played in his last game on October 1, 1970. He was a pitcher as well as an outfielder. His pitching record was four wins and four losses and he ended up with a 4.66ERA. As an outfielder he appeared in 117 games with 23 hits including four home runs and a .177 batting average. --1960-1962 Chicago Cubs NL, 1969-1970 Chicago White Sox AL

Jocko Thompson was born in Beverly, Massachusetts on January 17, 1917. He was a pitcher who made his major league debut on September 21, 1948. His last game was on September 16, 1951 and he ended up with a record of six wins and12 losses and a 4.24 earned run average. He passed away in Olney Maryland on February 3, 1988 and is buried in Gate of Heaven Cemetery in Silver Spring, Maryland, --1948-1951 Philadelphia Phillies NL

Pete Walker was a major league pitcher who was born in Beverly, Massachusetts on April 8, 1969. He made his major league debut on June 7, 1995 and ended his career on July 7, 2006. He had a career record of 20 wins and 14 losses and a 4.48 ERA. -- 1995 New York Mets, 1996 San Diego Padres, 2000 Colorado Rockies, 2001-2002 New York Mets, 2002-2006 Toronto Blue Jays.

BLACKSTONE

Con Dailey was born in Blackstone, Massachusetts on September 11, 1864. He was a catcher, outfielder and first baseman who made his first big league appearance on May 6, 1885. He played in the major leagues for 11 seasons and made his final appearance as a major league baseball player on July 5, 1896. He got into a total of 628 games and had 541 hits, including 74 doubles and 262 runs batted in. He also had a career batting average of .244 and is the brother of Ed Daily who played in the major leagues for six years in the late 1880's. Con Dailey passed away in Brooklyn, New York on June 14, 1928 and is buried in Lutheran All Faith Cemetery in Queens. -- 1885- Providence Grays NL, 1886-1887 Beaneaters NL, 1888-1889 Indianapolis Hoosiers NL, 1890 Brooklyn Ward's Wonders PL, 1891-1895 Grooms NL, 1896 Chicago Cubs NL

Eddie Eayrs was born in Blackstone on November 10, 1890. His major league baseball career debut was on June 30, 1913 and his last game was on October 1, 1921. He was an outfielder, pinch hitter and pitcher. As an outfielder/pinch runner he appeared in 114 games with 83 hits, including five doubles, two triples and one home run. He had a career batting average of .306 and 26 runs batted in. He pitched in a total of 11 games and had a record of one win and two losses to go with his 6.23 career earned run average. He passed away in Warwick, Rhode Island on November 30, 1969 and is buried in Swan Point Cemetery in Providence, Rhode Island. -- 1913 Pittsburgh Pirates NL, 1920-1921 Boston Braves NL, 1921 Brooklyn Robins NL

BOLTON

Wilbert "Uncle Robbie" Robinson was born in Bolton, Massachusetts on June 29, 1864. He debuted in the major leagues on April 19, 1886 and was a member of the famous Baltimore Orioles teams of the late 1890's along with John "Mugsy" McGraw, the Hall of Fame manager for the New York Giants. Robinson was a catcher who spent 17 years in the major leagues, playing in his last game on September 19, 1902. Robinson was in a total of 1,371 games and amassed 1,388 hits including 212 doubles, 51 triples and 18 home runs. He had a total of 722 runs batted in and possessed a career batting average of .273. "Uncle Robby" later went on to manage the Baltimore Orioles for 1 season and the Brooklyn Robins (Dodgers) for 18 seasons. He managed in 2,819 major league games and had a record of 1,399 wins and 1,398 losses. He won two pennants as a manager with the Brooklyn Robins and was inducted in the Baseball Hall of Fame as a manager by the Veterans Committee in 1945. Robinson passed away on August 8, 1934 in Atlanta, Georgia and was buried in the New Cathedral Cemetery in Baltimore, Maryland. He is the younger brother of Fred Robinson who had a three game career in the big leagues in 1884 as a second baseman. -- 1886-1890 Philadelphia Athletics AA, 1890-1891 Baltimore Orioles AA, 1892-1899 Baltimore Orioles NL, 1900 St Louis Cardinals NL, 1902-1903 Baltimore Orioles AL

BOSTON

William "Bill" Anderson was born in Boston, Massachusetts on November 28, 1895 and debuted in the major leagues as a pitcher on September 10, 1925. His last game in the majors was on September 17, 1925 and in his two game career he did not have a recorded win or loss but had a career earned run average of 10.13. He passed away in Medford, Massachusetts on Mach 13, 1983 and is buried in Forest Hill Cemetery in East Derry, New Hampshire. --1925 Boston Braves NL

Jeff Bagwell was a first baseman for his entire big league career which was spent with the Houston Astros. Bagwell was born in Boston, Massachusetts on May 27, 1968 and made his first appearance in a big league uniform on April 8, 1991. During the course of his career Bagwell led the league in runs scored three times (1994, 1999 and 2000), doubles once in 1996 and runs batted in for the 1994 season. He was the National League Rookie of the Year in 1991 and the National League Most Valuable Player in 1994. He was a four time National League All Star (1994, 1996, 1997 and 1999). Bagwell also won a Gold Glove Award for fielding and two Silver Slugger Awards for hitting. He appeared in 2,150 games and had a total of 2,314 hits in 7,797 at bats. He had 488 doubles, 32 triples and 449 home runs. He scored 1,517 runs and drove in 1,529 more runs. He also had a career batting average of .297. He made his final big league appearance on October 2, 2005.

Joe Bean was born in Boston, Massachusetts on March 18, 1874 and debuted with the New York Giants on April 28, 1902. He was a shortstop who appeared in 50 games and had 40 hits including two doubles and one triple. His career batting average was .220. Bean passed away in Atlanta, Georgia on February 15, 1961 and is buried in Atlanta's Westview Cemetery. --1902 NY Giants NL

Utility infielder Mark Bellhorn was born in Boston, Massachusetts on August 23, 1974. He made his major league debut on June 10, 1997. During the course of his career which lasted until September 30, 2007, he appeared in 731 games for the Red Sox, Cubs, Athletics, Rockies, Yankees, Padres and Reds. He had a total of 484 hits, including 113 doubles, 13 triples, and 69 home runs as well as 246 runs batted in. His career batting average was .230, and he was also a member of the 2004 World Champion Boston Red Sox.

John Bergh caught and played centerfield in a major league career that began on August 5, 1876 and ended on June 6, 1880. Bergh was born in Boston on October 5, 1857, and he appeared in 12 games in his career getting a total of 8 hits including 3 doubles. His career batting average was .182. He passed away in Boston on April 17, 1883 and is buried in Holyhood Cemetery in Brookline, Massachusetts. --1876 Philadelphia Athletics NL, 1880 Boston Red Stockings NL

Henry Bostick (born Henry Lipschitz) was born in Boston on January 12, 1895. He had a two game career in the major leagues which began on May 18, 1915 and ended on May 19, 1915. He was a third baseman who didn't record a hit in eight plate appearances. He died in Denver, Colorado on September 16, 1968 and is buried in Fairmont Cemetery in Denver. --1915 Philadelphia Athletics AL

John Butler was born in Boston on July 26, 1879 and was a catcher in the major leagues. His career in the big leagues began on September 28, 1901 and for a time he played under the alias of Fredrick King. He appeared in 44 games and had 16 hits, including two doubles to go with his .134 career batting average. He played his last game in the majors on June 14, 1907. He died in Boston on February 2, 1950 and is buried in Mount Calvary Cemetery in Roslindale, Massachusetts. --1901 Milwaukee Brewers AL, 1904 St Louis Cardinals NL, 1906-1907 Brooklyn Superbas NL

Frank Edward "Kid" Butler was a Boston native having been born in May of 1861. He made his major league debut on May 20, 1884 playing 71 games for the Boston Reds of the Union Association. He was an outfielder/second baseman/shortstop who managed to get 43 hits during his one major league season. His career batting average was .169. Butler passed away in South Boston on April 9, 1921 and was laid to rest in Mount Calvary Cemetery in Roslindale, Massachusetts.

Ed Callahan was an outfielder and a shortstop whose career in the major leagues lasted from July 19, 1884 until October 13, 1884. He was born in Boston on December 11, 1857 and appeared in eight games where he recorded nine total hits and a batting average of .333. He passed away on February 5, 1947 in New York City and is buried in Mount Benedict Cemetery in West Roxbury, Massachusetts. --1884 St Louis Maroons UA, 1884 Kansas City Cowboys UA, Boston Reds UA

Paul Carey was born in Boston on June 8, 1968. He made his major league debut on May 25, 1993 and played his final game in the majors on October 2, 1993. In his only major league season he appeared in 18 games as a first baseman/designated hitter/pinch hitter. He had 10 hits and three runs batted in and a batting average of .213. --1993 Baltimore Orioles AL

Catcher/outfielder Joe Casey was born in Boston, Massachusetts on August 15, 1887. He made his first major league appearance on October 1, 1909 and played his last game on August 24, 1918. During his 50 game career he had 21 hits, including three doubles, he drove in seven runs and had a career batting average of .179. He passed away in Melrose, Massachusetts on June 2, 1966 and is buried in St Patrick Cemetery in Stoneham, Massachusetts. --1909-1911 Detroit Tigers AL, Washington Senators 1918 AL

Right handed pitcher **Carlos Castillo** was born in Boston on April 21, 1975. His first big league appearance was April 2, 1997 and his final appearance was on July 22, 2001. In 111 games he had a record of ten wins and seven losses and a 5.04 earned run average. --1997-1999 Chicago White Sox AL, 2001 Boston Red Sox AL

Alex Cobb is a pitcher in the major leagues who was born in Boston, Massachusetts on October 7, 1987. He made his major league debut on May 1, 2011 and he pitched in nine games that season and had a record of three wins and two losses with a 3.42 ERA. He is still pitching with the Tampa Bay Rays.

Tom Connoley was born in Boston, Massachusetts on December 30, 1892 and made his first appearance in a major league ballgame on May 15, 1915. He spent one season in the majors with the Washington Senators as a third baseman, shortstop and outfielder. He appeared in a total of 50 games and of his 26 hits, three were doubles and two were triples. He also had seven runs batted in and a career batting average of .184. He passed away on May 14, 1966 in Boston and is buried in St. Joseph Cemetery in West Roxbury.

Bill Cooney was a pitcher, right fielder and shortstop who debuted in the major leagues on September 22, 1909. Cooney was born in Boston on April 7, 1883. His final game in the big leagues was on May 6, 1910. Between the two seasons Cooney appeared in 13 games and had six hits in 22 at bats good enough for a .273 batting average. As for his pitching he appeared in three games and did not record a win or a loss, but had a career earned run average of 1.42. He died in Roxbury, Massachusetts on November 6, 1928 and is buried in New Calvary Cemetery in Boston.-- 1909-1910 Boston Doves NL

Dan Cotter was born in Boston on April 14, 1867 and made his major league debut on July 16, 1890. That was his only major league appearance. He was a pitcher who had a record of 0-1 with an ERA of 14.00. He passed away in Dorchester, Massachusetts on September 4, 1935 and is buried in Mount Benedict cemetery in West Roxbury. --1890 Buffalo Bisons PL

Born in Boston, Massachusetts on May 27, 1862 **Ed Crane** was a pitcher as well as a catcher and an outfielder who debuted in the big leagues on April 17, 1884. During the course of his career as a pitcher he had a record of 72 wins and 97 losses as well as a 3.99 earned run average. When Crane appeared at his other positions, he was in 391 games and had a total of 335 hits, including 45 doubles, 15 triples and 18 home runs to go with 84 runs batted in and a batting average of .238. Crane's final appearance was on July 19, 1893. He passed away on September 20, 1896 in Rochester, New York and is buried in Holyhood Cemetery in Brookline, Massachusetts. --1884 Boston Reds UA, 1886 Washington Nationals NL, 1888-1889 New York Giants NL, 1890 New York Giants PL, 1891 Cincinnati Kelly Killers AA, 1891 Cincinnati Reds NL, 1892 New York Giants NL, 1893 New York Giants/Brooklyn Grooms NL

Second baseman/left fielder **Dan Cronin** was born in Boston on April 1, 1857. His first game in the major leagues was on July 9, 1884 and his final game was July 14, 1884. In his short two game career he had one hit and a batting average of .111. He died on November 30, 1885 in

Boston and is buried in Roslindale, Massachusetts at Mount Calvary Cemetery. --1884 Chicago/Pittsburgh UA, 1884 St Louis Maroons UA

Claude Davidson, born in Boston on October 13, 1896 was a second baseman, third baseman and right fielder who made his first major league appearance on April 25, 1918. His last big league game was on September 4, 1919 and during his two year career he appeared in 33 games with 15 hits and 4 runs batted in and a .205 batting average. Davidson passed away on April 18, 1956 in Weymouth, Massachusetts and is buried in Blue Hill Cemetery in Braintree, Massachusetts. --1918 Philadelphia Athletics AL, 1919 Washington Senators AL

Pitcher/outfielder **John "Daisy" Davis** made his major league debut on May 6, 1884. The Boston, Massachusetts native, who was born on November 28, 1858 appeared in 40 games as a pitcher and had an earned run average of 3.78 to go with his record of 16 wins and 21 losses. As a fielder Davis in his 40 games had 22 hits including two doubles and one triple and a .157 batting average. He passed away on November 5, 1902 in Lynn, Massachusetts and is buried in Lynn at the Pine Grove Cemetery. --1884 St Louis Browns AL, 1884-1885 Boston Beaneaters NL

Manny Delcarmen was born in Boston, Massachusetts on February 16, 1982. His major league pitching debut was on July 26, 2005. As of this date he has appeared in 298 games and has a record of 11 wins and eight losses and a career earned run average of 3.97. He was also a member of the 2007 World Champion Boston Red Sox. ----- 2005-2010 Boston Red Sox AL, 2010 Colorado Rockies NL

Boston, Massachusetts is the hometown of **Steve Digman** who was born there on April 16, 1859. His first major league appearance was on June 1, 1880, and his last game was on August 7, 1880. In between he appeared in 11 games and he was an outfielder who had 14 total hits including one double and one triple. His career batting average was .318. He passed away in Boston on July 11, 1881 and is buried in Roslindale at the Mount Calvary Cemetery. --1880 Boston Red Stockings/ Worcester Ruby Legs

Jim Donnelly was a catcher/third baseman who was born in Boston on January 6, 1867. His major league career lasted from July 11, 1884 until July 18, 1884. In the six games he played in he had three hits including a double. His career batting average was .130. He died in Somerville, Massachusetts on December 31, 1933 and is buried in Holy Cross Cemetery in Malden, Massachusetts. -- 1884 Kansas City Cowboys

Dick Donovan was a right handed pitcher in the major leagues who was born in Boston on December 7, 1927. His major league debut was April 24, 1950 and his last big league appearance was on June 12, 1965. He appeared in 345 ballgames and had 122 wins and 99 losses and also had a 3.67 career ERA. He passed away in Weymouth, Massachusetts on January 6, 1997 and is buried in Woodside Cemetery in Cohasset, Massachusetts. --1950-1952 Boston Braves NL, 1954 Detroit Tigers AL, 1955-1960 Chicago White Sox AL, 1961 Washington Senators AL, 1962-1965 Cleveland Indians AL

Cameron Drew was born in Boston on February 12, 1964. He was an outfielder/pinch hitter whose major league career lasted from September 9, 1988 until September 20 1988. He had three hits in the seven games he played in and ended up with a .188 batting average. --1988 Houston Astros

Tom Early was born in Boston on February 17, 1919. He was a pitcher who appeared in his first major-league ball game on September 27, 1938. His last big league pitching appearance was on June 27, 1945. He had a record of 18 wins and 24 losses with a 3.78 earned run average for his career. He passed away on April 5, 1988 in Nantucket, Massachusetts and is buried in that town's St Mary Cemetery. --1938 Boston Braves/Bees NL

Chuck Essegian was a left fielder and pinch hitter during the course of his major league career which began on April 15, 1958. His final game in the major leagues was on September 28, 1963. In between, he played in 404 games and had a total of 260 hits, including 45 doubles, four triples, and 47 home runs. He was also a member of the World Series Champion Los Angeles Dodgers in 1959. He was a Boston native having been born in the Massachusetts capital on August 9, 1931. 1958 Philadelphia Phillies NL, 1959 St Louis Cardinals NL, 1959-1960 Los Angeles Dodgers NL, 1961 Baltimore Orioles AL, 1961 Kansas City Athletics AL, 1961-1962 Cleveland Indians Aland the 1963 Kansas City Athletics AL

George Fair was born in Boston on January 13, 1856. He played in his only major league baseball game in July 29, 1876 and did not record a hit in four at bats. He died on February 12, 1939 in Roslindale, Massachusetts and is buried in St. Joseph Cemetery in West Roxbury. -- 1876 New York Mutuals NL

Turk Farrell was born in Boston on April 8, 1934 and debuted in the major leagues on September 21, 1956 as a pitcher, and his last appearance in a major league uniform was on September 9, 1969. He had a record of 106 wins and 111 losses to go with his 3.45 ERA. He passed away in the United Kingdom on June 10, 1977 and is buried in Forest Park Westheimer Cemetery in Houston Texas.-- 1956-1961 Philadelphia Phillies NL, 1961 Los Angeles Dodgers NL, 1962-1964 Houston Colt 45's NL, 1965-1967 Houston Astros NL, 1967-1969 Philadelphia Phillies NL

John Freeman was born in Boston on January 24, 1901. He was an outfielder who played in his first ballgame in the major leagues on June 27, 1927 and played in his last ballgame in July 4, 1927. He appeared in four games and did not get a hit in any of them. He died in Washington, DC on April 14, 1958 and is buried in St. Joseph Cemetery in West Roxbury, Massachusetts. 1927 Boston Red Sox AL

Sean Gallagher was born in Boston on December 30, 1985. He was a pitcher in the major leagues and has appeared in 91 games with a record of 10 wins and 10 losses and a 5.64 earned run average for his career. 2007-2008 Chicago Cubs NL, 2008-2009 Oakland Athletics, 2009-2010 San Diego Padres, 2010 Pittsburgh Pirates

William Gallagher was born in Boston on February 4, 1874 and made his major league debut as a shortstop on August 19, 1896.

His last game in the majors was on September 1, 1896 and in the 14 games he appeared in he had five hits and a .306 batting average. He died in Worcester, Massachusetts on March 11, 1950 and is buried in Lowell at the St. Patrick Cemetery. 1896 Philadelphia Phillies NL

May 6, 1859 was the birthday of **Franklin W. "Gid" Gardner** of Boston. Gardener played second base and the outfield and also pitched during the course of his major league career that lasted from August 23, 1879 to May 29, 1888. He batted in 199 games and had 178 hits, including 33 doubles, 18 triples, and four home runs to go with his .233 batting average. As a pitcher he appeared in 15 games and had a record of two wins and 12 losses to go with a 3.90 ERA. He passed away in Cambridge, Massachusetts on August 1, 1914 and is buried in the Cambridge City Cemetery in Cambridge, Massachusetts. 1879 Troy Trojans NL, 1880 Cleveland Blues NL,1883-1884 Baltimore Orioles AA, 1884 Chicago /Pittsburgh UA, 1884 Baltimore Monumentals UA, 1885 Baltimore Orioles AA, 1887 Indianapolis Hoosiers NL, 1888 Washington Nationals NL, 1888 Philadelphia Quakers NL, 1888 Washington Nationals NL

Hank Garrity was born in Boston on February 4, 1908. He appeared in his first big league game on July 26, 1931. His last game was on September 26, 1931 and he was in a total of eight games in which he had three hits and a .214 batting average. During his career he was a catcher. He died September 1, 1962 in Boston and is buried in West Roxbury at Saint Joseph Cemetery. 1931 Chicago White Sox AL

Kenny Greer was born on May 12, 1967 in Boston. He was a pitcher who made his first appearance in a major league uniform on September 29, 1993. He played until July 17, 1995 and in nine games he had a record of one win and two losses. His career ERA was 4.85. 1993 New York Mets NL, 1995 San Francisco Giants NL

Pinch hitting, playing first base and being a designated hitter were what **Bob Hansen** did during the course of his major league career which ran from May 10, 1974 until July 10, 1976. In the 82 games that he appeared in, he had 36 hits including five doubles, one triple and two home runs. He was born in Boston on May 26, 1948. 1974/1976 Milwaukee Brewers AL

Pat Hartnet was born in Boston, Massachusetts on October 20, 1863. He was a first baseman who had a career that lasted from April 18ᵗʰ to May 18ᵗʰ 1890. In 14 games he batted .189 with 10 hits including two doubles and a triple. He passed away in Boston on April 10, 1935 and is buried in Holyhood Cemetery in Brookline, Massachusetts. 1890 St Louis Browns AA

Richie Hebner was born in Boston, Massachusetts on November 26, 1947. His first major league appearance was on September 23, 1968. He spent until October 3, 1985 in the big leagues ass a first and third baseman appearing in a total of 1908 games. He had 1,694 hits, including 273 doubles, 57 triples and 203 home runs. He had 890 runs batted in and his lifetime batting average was .276. He was also a member of the 1971 World Champion Pittsburgh Pirates. 1968-1976 Pittsburgh Pirates NL, 1977-1978 Philadelphia Phillies NL, 1979 New York Mets NL, 1980-1982 Detroit Tigers AL, 1982-1983 Pittsburgh Pirates NL, 1984-1985 Chicago Cubs NL

Rich Hill was born in Boston, Massachusetts on March 11, 1980. He is a pitcher who debuted in the majors on June 15, 2005. He has appeared in 110 games with a record of 23 wins and 20 losses and a 4.66 earned run average. 2005-2008 Chicago Cubs NL 2009 Baltimore Orioles AL, 2010-2012 Boston Red Sox AL

Paul Howard was a major league outfielder who was born in Boston, Massachusetts on May 20, 1884. He spent from September 16, 1909 until September 29, 1909 in the majors appearing in a total of six games. He had three hits in 15 at bats and a .200 batting average. He died August 29, 1968 in Miami, Florida and is buried in Winthrop Cemetery in Winthrop, Massachusetts. 1909 Boston Red Sox AL

Christmas Day 1895 was the birthday for **Herb Hunter** of Boston, Massachusetts. Hunter debuted in the major leagues on April 29, 1916 and spent his career in the majors as a leftfielder and a first/third baseman. His last appearance in a big league uniform was on October 1, 1921. In 39 games he had eight hits including one home run. His batting average for his career was .163. He died on July 25, 1970 in Orlando, Florida and is buried at sea. 1916 New York Giants/Chicago Cubs NL, 1917 Chicago Cubs NL, 1920 Boston Red Sox AL, 1921 St Louis Cardinals NL

Jerry Hurley was a catcher and played in the outfield in a career in the major leagues that started on May 1, 1889. His last game was on July 13, 1891. He got into a total of 33 games and had 20 hits including four doubles and two triples. His batting average was .217. Hurley was born in Boston, Massachusetts on June 15, 1863 and passed away in Boston on September 17, 1950. He is buried in Holy Cross Cemetery in Malden, Massachusetts. 1889 Boston Beaneaters NL, 1890 Pittsburgh Burghers PL, Cincinnati Kelly's Killers AA

John Kiely was born in Boston on October 4, 1964. He was a pitcher who first appeared in a major league baseball game on July 26, 1991. His last appearance was on May 2, 1993. His record shows him appearing in 54 games with a record of four wins and five losses and a 4.17 ERA. 1991-1993 Detroit Tigers

Henry Lampe was born in Boston, Massachusetts on September 19, 1872. He was a pitcher who made his big league debut on May 14, 1894. His final game was on August 2, 1895 and in the 89 games that he pitched in he had a record of no wins and three losses with an 8.03 earned run average. He passed away in Dorchester, Massachusetts on September 16, 1936 and is buried in Cedar Grove Cemetery in Dorchester. 1894 Boston Beaneaters NL, 1895 Philadelphia Phillies NL

Walter Lonergan was born in Boston on September 22, 1885 and made his major league debut on August 17, 1911 and his final appearance was on September 22, 1911. In the 10 games he appeared in as a second and third baseman as well as a shortstop he had seven hits and a .269 batting average. He died on January 23, 1958 in Lexington, Massachusetts and is buried in Mount Calvary Cemetery in Roslindale, Massachusetts. 1911 Boston Red Sox AL

Jimmy Macullar was a shortstop and a center fielder in the major leagues that was born in Boston, Massachusetts on January 16, 1855. He made his debut in the majors on May 5, 1879 and played in his final game on October 14, 1886. In between he appeared in 449 games and had 319 hits of which 47 were doubles, 19 were triples and seven were home runs. He scored 246 runs and drove in another 91 runs. His career batting average was .207. He passed away in Baltimore, Maryland on October 14, 1924 and is buried in Baltimore City Cemetery in Baltimore. 1879 Syracuse Stars NL, 1882-1883 Cincinnati Red Stockings AA, 1884-1886 Baltimore Orioles AA

Bunny Madden was born in Boston, Massachusetts on September 14, 1882. Madden went on to play in the major leagues as a catcher debuting on June 3, 1909. He played in 56 games and had 41 hits, including four doubles and two triples to go with his 11 runs batted in and a .287 batting average. He played his final game on September 21, 1911 and later passed away on January 20, 1954 in Cambridge, Massachusetts. He is buried in St. Joseph Cemetery in West Roxbury. 1909-1911 Boston Red Sox AL, 1911 Philadelphia Phillies NL

Mike Mahoney was a pitcher, catcher and first baseman who made his first major-league appearance on May 18, 1897 and played his final game on April 17, 1898. He did not record a win or a loss in his only pitching appearance and he had one hit in nine plate appearances. He was born in Boston on December 5, 1873 and passed away on January 3, 1940 in Boston. He is buried in Mount Calvary Cemetery in Roslindale, Massachusetts. 1897 Boston Beaneaters NL, 1898 St Louis Browns N

December 20, 1944 is the birthday of **Don Mason**. The Boston native was a second and third baseman as well as a pinch hitter in the big leagues. He first appeared in a game on April 14, 1966 and made his final appearance in the lineup on May 30, 1973. He had 143 hits in 336 games. Sixteen of the hits were doubles, three were triples and he had three home runs to go with his .205 batting average. 1966-1970 San Francisco Giants NL, 1971-1973 San Diego Padres NL

Catcher Bill McCarthy was born in Boston on February 14, 1886. His first major league appearance was on June 5, 1905. His career was four games long and his last game was on September 14, 1907. He managed to get one hit in 11 at bats. He died in Washington, DC on February 4, 1929 and is buried in Holyhood Cemetery in Brookline, Massachusetts. 1905 Boston Beaneaters NL, 1907 Cincinnati Reds 1907 NL

Tommy McCarthy was born in Boston, Massachusetts on July 24, 1863. He was an outfielder who made his first big league appearance in a lineup on July 10, 1884. He played in a total of 1,273 games and scored 1,066 runs. He had 1,493 hits including 191 doubles, 53 triples and 44 home runs. He had 732 runs batted in and a lifetime batting average of .292. He led the league in plate appearances in 1889 and 1890 with 656 and 625 appearances and in 1889 he also led the league with 604 at bats. In 1890 he led the league in stolen bases with 83 swipes. McCarthy was thought to be a thinking man when it came to the game of baseball strategy. He was a member of the Boston Beaneaters "Heavenly Twins" outfield along with Hugh Duffy. He passed away on August 5, 1922 in Boston and is buried in Mount Calvary Cemetery in Roslindale. He was inducted into the Baseball Hall of Fame posthumously in 1946 joining his outfield partner Duffy who had been elected the year before in 1945. 1884 Boston Reds UA, 1885 Boston Beaneaters NL, 1886-1887 Philadelphia Quakers NL, 1888-1891 St Louis Browns AA1892-1895 Boston Beaneaters NL, 1896 Brooklyn Bridegrooms NL

Bill McGunnigle was a pitcher and a right fielder in the major leagues that was born in Boston on January 1, 1855. His major league debut was on May 2, 1879 and he played in his final game on August 17, 1882. He pitched in 19 games winning 11 and losing eight with an ERA of 2.81. As a batter he appeared in 56 games with 35 hits and a .173 batting average. He died in Brockton, Massachusetts on March 9, 1899 and is buried in St Patrick Cemetery in Boston. 1879-1880 Buffalo Bisons NL, 1880 Worcester Ruby Legs NL, 1882 Cleveland Blues NL

Alex McKinnon was born in Boston on August 14, 1856. His major league debut was on May 1, 1884 as a first baseman. His final game was on July 4, 1887. He played 1,386 games and scored 209 runs. He had 465 hits, including 82 doubles, 30 triples and 13 home runs. He had 219 runs batted in and a lifetime batting average of .296. He passed away in Charlestown, Massachusetts on July 24, 1887 and is buried in Lowell Cemetery in Lowell, Massachusetts. 1884 New York Gothams NL, 1885-1886 St Louis Maroons NL, 1887 Pittsburgh Alleghenies NL

Lennie Merullo was born in Boston, Massachusetts on May 5, 1917 He made his first big league appearance on September 12, 1941. He was a shortstop who appeared in 639 games. He had 497 hits, including 92 doubles, eight triples and six home runs to go with 152 runs batted in and a .240 batting average. His last game was on August 22, 1947. He is the grandfather of major leaguer Matt Merullo, who was born in Winchester, Massachusetts. 1941-1947 Chicago Cubs NL

Bill Mills was a catcher and a pinch hitter in the majors from May 19, 1944 until June 3, 1944. He appeared in five games and had one hit and a .250 batting average. He was born in Boston, Massachusetts on November 2, 1919. 1944 Philadelphia Athletics AL

Dick Mills was a pitcher who was born in Boston, Massachusetts on January 29, 1945. He debuted on September 7, 1970. He pitched in a total of two games and did not register a win or a loss. He ended his career with a 2.45 ERA. 1970 Boston Red Sox AL

Boston, Massachusetts was home to **Jim Moroney** who was born in the capital of Massachusetts on December 4, 1883. His first time in the major leagues was on April 24, 1906, and his final appearance in a major league uniform as a player was on July 23, 1912. He had two wins and six losses in the 25 games he appeared in and his ERA was 3.69. He died in Philadelphia Pennsylvania on February 26, 1929 and is buried in Holyhood Cemetery in Brookline, Massachusetts. 1906 Boston Beaneaters NL, 1910 Philadelphia Phillies NL, 1912 Chicago Cubs NL

John Morril was born in Boston, Massachusetts on February 19, 1855. He debuted in the major leagues on April 24, 1876 and played until July 8, 1890. He played first and second base while in the majors and he appeared in 1,265 games. He had 1,275 hits of which 239 were doubles, 80 were triples and 43 were home runs. He had a total of 643 runs batted in and scored 821 runs. He had a career batting average of .260. Morril died in Brookline, Massachusetts on April 2, 1932, and he is buried in Brookline at Holyhood Cemetery. 1876-1888 Boston Red Stockings/Beaneaters NL, 1889 Washington Nationals NL, 1890 Boston Reds

Matt Murray was born in Boston, Massachusetts on September 26, 1970. He was a pitcher who got into his first ball game on August 12, 1995 with his final game coming on September 25, 1995. In the six games he appeared in he did not have a win and had three losses. His career ERA was 9.64. 1995 Atlanta Braves NL, 1995 Boston Red Sox AL

Miah Murray was born in Boston, Massachusetts on January 1, 1865 and made his first appearance in a major league lineup on May 17, 1884. He was a catcher/first baseman who appeared in 34 games and had 17 hits and a .142 batting average. His last game in the major leagues was on October 3, 1891. He died in Boston, Massachusetts on January 11, 1922 and is buried in the Holyhood Cemetery in Brookline. 1884 Providence Grays NL, 1885 Louisville Colonels AA, 1888 Washington Nationals NL, 1891 Washington Statesmen AA

Pitcher Fred Newman was born in Boston on February 21, 1942 and debuted in the major leagues on September 16, 1962. In his career he appeared in 108 games and had a record of 33 wins and 29 losses to go with a 3.41 ERA. He was buried in Walnut Hill Cemetery in Brookline after passing away on June 24, 1987 in Framingham, Massachusetts. 1962-1967 California Angels AL

Javier Ortiz was born in Boston on January 22, 1963. He was an outfielder and a pinch hitter who got into his first major league baseball game on June 15, 1990. He played his last game on October 6, 1991 and in between Ortiz had 44 hits in 77 games. He hit two home runs, two triples and nine doubles. He also had 15 runs batted in and a batting average of .275. 1990-1991 Houston Astros

Mike Palm debuted in the majors on July 11, 1948. His last game was on July 21, 1948 and he ended up appearing in three games without a win or a loss. Palm was born in Boston on February 13,

1925 and passed away in Scituate, Massachusetts on July 24, 2011. He is buried in Woodside Cemetery in Cohasset, Massachusetts. 1948 Boston Red Sox AL

March 13, 1918 was the birthday of **Eddie Pellagrini**. Pellagrini was born in Boston, Massachusetts and appeared in his first major league baseball game on April 22, 1946. His last game played was on September 24, 1954. He played second and third base as well as shortstop during his 563 game career. He had a total of 321 hits and of those, 42 were doubles, 13 were triples and 20 were home runs. He had 133 runs batted in and a .226 batting average. He passed away in Weymouth, Massachusetts on October 11, 2006 and is buried in Bourne, Massachusetts at the Massachusetts National Cemetery. 1946-1947 Boston Red Sox, 1948-1949 St Louis Browns AL, 1951 Philadelphia Phillies NL, 1952 Cincinnati Reds NL, 1953-1954 Pittsburgh Pirates NL

Chris Peterson was born in Boston, Massachusetts on November 6, 1970 and made his first appearance in a major league uniform on May 25, 1999. His last game was on June 4, 1999 and he appeared in seven games as a second baseman/shortstop. He had two hits and managed to score one run during his short career. 1999 Colorado Rockies NL

Al Pierotti pitched in the major leagues from August 9, 1920 until April 24, 1921. He was born in Boston, Massachusetts on October 24, 1895 and was in eight major league baseball games. He had a record of 1-2 as well as a 4.05 ERA. He died in Everett, Massachusetts on February 12, 1964 and is buried in Everett at the Glenwood Cemetery. 1920-1921 Boston Braves NL

Tom Raftery was born in Boston, Massachusetts on October 5, 1881. He played right field and his first major league baseball game appearance was on April 18, 1909. His last appearance came on June 27, 1909. In between he managed to get seven hits in 32 plate appearances. Two of the hits were doubles and one was a triple and his batting average was .219. He passed away on New Year's Eve Day 1954 in Boston and is buried in Dorchester North Cemetery in Dorchester, Massachusetts. 1909 Cleveland Naps AL

Bob Reed was a major league pitcher who was born in Boston, Massachusetts on January 12, 1945. He made his big league debut on September 5, 1969. He was in 24 baseball games in the major leagues and had a record of two wins and four losses with a 4.10 ERA. His final game was on September 30, 1970. 1969-1970 Detroit Tigers AL

This next listing is a bit strange as each of the sources I checked all had the same thing listed. They list a ball player by the last name of **Richardson**. All that is known is he made his debut in the major leagues on July 10, 1884 and did not have a hit in four plate appearances. He was also born in Boston although the date is not known. 1884 Chicago/Pittsburgh UA

Sy Rosenthal was an outfielder and a pinch hitter who was born in Boston on November 13 1903. His first game in the major leagues was on September 8, 1925. In his career he had 95 hits in 123 games. He had 17 doubles, five triples and four home runs as well as scoring 40 runs. He had 42 runs batted in to go with his batting average of .266 and his last game in the majors was on September 26, 1926. He died in Boston on April 7, 1969 and is buried in Beth El Cemetery in West Roxbury, Massachusetts. 1925-1926 Boston Red Sox AL

Gus Salve was born in Boston, Massachusetts on December 29, 1885. The first major league game he appeared in was his only game he appeared in and that occurred on September 14, 1908. He was a pitcher and was saddled with the loss that day along with having a 4.11 ERA. He died in Providence, Rhode Island on March 29, 1971 and is buried in St. Thomas Cemetery in Swansea, Massachusetts. 1908 Philadelphia Athletics AL

Marty Shay was born in Boston on April 25, 1896. He was a second baseman and a shortstop that first appeared in a major league game on September 16, 1916. His last game was on September 2, 1924. In 21 games he scored four runs and had 18 hits, including three doubles and one triple to go with a batting average of .240. He died in Worcester, Massachusetts on February 20, 1951 and is buried in Mount Calvary Cemetery in Roslindale. 1916 Chicago Cubs NL, 1924 Boston Braves NL

Centerfielder Mike Slattery was born in Boston, Massachusetts on November 26, 1866. His first big league game was on April 17, 1884 and his final game was on July 23, 1892. He played in 374 games scoring 229 and getting 372 hits, including 44 doubles, 21 triples and eight home runs and when he retired he had a lifetime batting average of .251. He passed away on October 16, 1904 in Boston and is buried in the Holyhood Cemetery in Brookline, Massachusetts 1884 Boston Reds UA, 1888-1889 New York Giants NL, 1890 New York Giants PL, 1891 Cincinnati Reds NL, 1891 Washington Statesmen AA

Art Smith was a pitcher who played in his first major league ball game on June 9, 1932. He played in his last game four days later on June 13, 1932. He appeared in three games and had a record of 0-1 to go with his 11.57 ERA. He was born in Boston, Massachusetts on June 21, 1906 and passed away in Norwalk, Connecticut on November 22, 1995. He was later cremated. 1932 Chicago White Sox AL

Born in Boston, Massachusetts on December 5, 1871, **Tom Smith** was a pitcher and a first baseman who started in the major leagues on June 6, 1894. As a pitcher he played in 25 games and had a record of four wins and seven losses to go with a 6.33 earned run average. When he played first base or hit he had appeared in 29 games and had 17 hits, including two doubles and a triple to go with a .224 batting average. His last major league ball game was on May 12, 1898. He was buried in Mount Calvary Cemetery in Roslindale, Massachusetts after passing away in Dorchester, Massachusetts on March 2, 1929. 1894 Boston Beaneaters NL, 1895 Philadelphia Phillies NL, 1896 Louisville Colonels NL, 1898 St Louis Browns NL

Andy Spognardi played second and third base as well as shortstop in a major league career that lasted from September 2, 1932 until September 25, 1932. In 17 games he scored nine runs and had 10 hits including one double. His career batting average was .294. He died in Dedham, Massachusetts on January 1, 2000 and is buried in Forest Hills Cemetery in Boston. 1932 Boston Red Sox AL

Ed Sprague was a major league pitcher who was born in Boston on September 16, 1945. His first pitching appearance in the major leagues was on April 10, 1968 and his last was on June 5, 1976. In the 198 games that he pitched in he had a record of 17 wins and 23 losses to go with a 3.84 earned run average. He is also the father of Ed Sprague who played in the major leagues as a third baseman from 1991 until 2001. 1968-1969 Oakland Athletics, 1971-1973 Cincinnati Reds NL, 1973 St Louis Cardinals NL, 1973-1976 Milwaukee Brewers Al

Allie Strobel was born in Boston, Massachusetts on June 11, 1884. He played in the major leagues from August 29, 1905 until August 11, 1906. He was a second and third baseman as well as a shortstop that played in 105 games. In those games he had a total of 66 hits, including 10 doubles and one home run and his lifetime batting average was .196. He passed away in Hollywood, Florida on February 10, 1955 and is buried in Hollywood Memorial Gardens in Hollywood, Florida. 1905-1906 Boston Beaneaters NL

Chub Sullivan was born January 12, 1856 in Boston, Massachusetts. He played first base in the major leagues and got his career started on September 24, 1877. In the 112 games he played he scored 55 runs and had 114 hits to go with a .258 batting average. His last game was on July 17, 1880 and he passed away in Boston on September 12, 1881. 1877-1878 Cincinnati Reds NL, 1880 Worcester Ruby Legs NL

Denny Sullivan was a third baseman, played right field and was a catcher in a career that lasted from August 25, 1879 until September 25, 1880. He was born in Boston, Massachusetts on June 26, 1856. During the course of his career he had six hits in six games for a .261 batting average. He passed away in Boston on December 31, 1925 and is buried in New Calvary Cemetery in Boston. 1879 Providence Grays NL, 1880 Boston Red Stockings NL

Mike Sullivan was born in Boston on October 23, 1866 and had his first big league appearance on June 17, 1889. His final game was on October 12, 1899. He pitched in 160 games and had a record of 54 wins and 65 losses and a 5.04 ERA. He died in Boston on June 14, 1906 and

is buried in Mount Calvary Cemetery in Roslindale. Massachusetts.
1889 Washington Nationals NL, 1890 Chicago Colts NL, 1891 Philadelphia Athletics AA, 1891, New York Giants NL, 1892-1893 Cincinnati
Reds NL, 1894 Washington Senators NL, 1894-1895 Cleveland Spiders
NL, 1896-1897 New York Giants NL, 1899 Boston Beaneaters NL

Born on October 18, 1895 in Boston, Massachusetts, **Tom Sullivan**
made his major league pitching debut on May 15, 1922. Two weeks
later he had played in his last game. In the three games he pitched in
he did not record a win or a loss and his ERA was 11.25. He died in
Boston on September 23, 1962 and is buried in Boston's Mount Hope
Cemetery. 1922 Philadelphia Phillies NL

Jerry J. Sweeney was born on August 22, 1857 in Boston, Massachusetts. Sweeney was a first baseman who played in the major
leagues from August 22, 1884 until October 16, 1884. In the 31 games
he played in Sweeney had 34 hits including three doubles. He had a
career batting average of .264. He died on August 25, 1891 in Boston
and is buried in Roslindale, Massachusetts' Mount Calvary Cemetery. 1884 Kansas City Cowboys UA

Bill Tierney was a first baseman and a right fielder in the major
league, who was born in Boston, Massachusetts on May14, 1858.
His career in the major leagues consisted of two games May 2, 1882
and April 24, 1884. He had one hit and a batting average of .125. He
passed away on September 21, 1898 in Boston, Massachusetts and is
buried in the Mount Calvary Cemetery in Roslindale, Massachusetts.
1882 Cincinnati Red Stockings AA, 1884 Baltimore Monumentals UA

George Twombly played in the major leagues from July 19, 1914
until September 1, 1919. He was a first baseman that appeared in 150
games, scoring 35 runs and banging out 88 hits that included one
double and seven triples. He also had a batting average of .211. He
was born in Boston, Massachusetts on June 14, 1892 and passed away
on February 17, 1975 in Lexington, Massachusetts. He was buried
in Puritan Lawn Cemetery in Peabody, Massachusetts. He is also
the older brother of Babe Twombly who played in the major leagues

from April 14, 1920 until October 2, 1921. 1914-1916 Cincinnati Reds NL, 1917 Boston Braves NL, 1919 Washington Senators AL

Jim Wallace was born in Boston, Massachusetts on November 14 1881. He made his major league debut as a right fielder on August 24, 1905 and five days later on August 29, 1905 played in his final game. He appeared in seven games and had six hits including a double for a .207 batting average. He passed away on May 16, 1953 in Revere, Massachusetts and is buried in St Mary's Cemetery in Lynn, Massachusetts. 1905 Pittsburgh Pirates NL

Shortstop Joe Walsh was born in Boston on March 13, 1917 and made his first big league appearance on July 1, 1938. Two days later on July 3, 1938 he played in his final big league game. He did not record a hit in the four games he played. He died in Boston, Massachusetts on October 5, 1996 and is buried in Brookline, Massachusetts at the Walnut Hills Cemetery. 1938 Boston Bees NL

Jim Ward was a catcher in the majors who was in his first ball game at the major league level on August 3, 1876, which was also his only big league game. He had two hits and scored one run in that game and he ended up batting .500 for his career. He died in Boston, Massachusetts on June 4, 1886 and is buried in Mount Benedict Cemetery in West Roxbury. Ward was born in Boston on March 2, 1855. 1876 Philadelphia Athletics NL

Pitcher **Ed Wineapple** played in his only major league ballgame on September 15, 1929. He did not record either a win or a loss in that game. He was born in Boston, Massachusetts on August 10, 1905 and passed away in Delray Beach, Florida on July 23, 1996. 1929 Washington Senators AL

Nick Wise was born in Boston, Massachusetts on June 15, 1866. He was a catcher and a right fielder who appeared in his first ballgame at the major league level on June 20, 1888. That was his only game in the majors and in it he did not have a hit in three plate appearances. Wise died on January 25, 1923 in Boston and is buried in Mount Calvary Cemetery in Roslindale, Massachusetts. 1888 Boston Beaneaters NL

Herman Young was born in Boston, Massachusetts on April 14, 1886. He first appeared in a major league ballgame on June 11, 1911. In his short career which ended on June 23, 1911 Young appeared in six games as a shortstop and a third baseman. He had six hits in nine games and also scored two runs. He batted .240 for his career. He passed away on December 12, 1966 in Ipswich, Massachusetts and is buried in Boston at the Mount Hope Cemetery. 1911 Boston Rustlers NL

Joe Zapustas was a major league outfielder from Boston, Massachusetts who was born on July 25, 1907. He was in his first major league ballgame on September 28, 1933 and played his last game in the majors on September 30, 1933. In the two games he appeared in he had one hit in five at bats for a .200 batting average. He passed away on January 14, 2001 in Brockton, Massachusetts and is buried in St Mary Cemetery in Randolph, Massachusetts. 1933 Philadelphia Athletics AL

BOXFORD

Charlie Fisher was a shortstop and a third baseman who was born in Boxford, Massachusetts on March 10, 1852. He was in his first major league ballgame on June 7, 1884 and one month later on July 7, 1884 he had played in his last game. In the 11 games that he appeared in he had 10 hits, including two doubles and his batting average was .250. He passed away on February 18, 1971 in Eagle, Arkansas and is buried in Eagle Cemetery in Eagle, Arkansas. 1884 Kansas City Cowboys/Chicago Pittsburgh UA

BRADFORD

Dick Blaisdell was born in Bradford, Massachusetts on June 18, 1862. He was a pitcher and a right fielder whose career in the major leagues lasted from June 9, 1884 until June 14, 1884. He pitched in three games and had a record of no wins and three losses to go with his ERA which was 8.65. In four games as a batter he had five hits in 16 plate appearances for a .313 batting average. Blaisdell died on August 20, 1886 in Malden, Massachusetts and is buried in Riverview Cemetery in Groveland, Massachusetts. 1884 Kansas City Cowboys UA

Bradford was also the home for **Bill Moisan** who was born in Bradford on July 30, 1925. He was a pitcher in the major leagues from September 17, 1953 until September 25, 1953. In three big league baseball games he did not record a win or a loss and his career ERA was 5.40. He passed away on Brentwood, New Hampshire on April 9, 2010 and is buried in Willow Grove Cemetery in Newton, New Hampshire. 1953 Chicago Cubs NL

BRIDGEWATER

Bridgewater, Massachusetts is the hometown of Hall of Fame catcher **Gordon Stanley"Mickey" Cochrane**. Cochrane was born in Bridgewater on April 6, 1903. He made his major league debut on April 14, 1925. He was the catcher on the Philadelphia Athletics teams that played in the World Series from 1929 until 1931. That Athletics team won the 1929 and 1930 World Series and many consider that team to be one of the greatest, if not the greatest baseball team of all time. During the course of his career he played in 1,482 games and had a total of 1,652 hits, including 333 doubles, 64 triples and 119 home runs. He scored 1,041 runs and also had 832 runs batted in. He had a career batting average of .320 which is good enough for 55th best all time. He twice led the league in fielding percentage as a catcher and finished his career with a .985 fielding average. He was a two time American League All Star selection as well as a two time winner of the American League Most Valuable Player Award. Cochrane was later traded to the Detroit Tigers and was their player/ manager where he won the American League pennant in his first year as player/manager and in the second year won the World Series giving him a total of three World Series championships. He was elected to the Baseball Hall of Fame in 1947 and later passed away on June 28, 1962 in Lake Forest, Illinois. He was later cremated. 1925-1933 Philadelphia Athletics Al, 19341937 Detroit Tigers AL

BRIGHTON

Dick Kelley was a pitcher in the major leagues from 1964 until 1971. He was born January 8, 1940 in Brighton, Massachusetts and debuted in the major leagues on April 15, 1964. In the 188 games he pitched in he had 18 wins and 30 losses and a 3.39 ERA. His last game in the big leagues was September 28, 1971. He passed away in Northridge, California and was later cremated. 1964-1965 Milwaukee Braves NL, 1966- 1968 Atlanta Braves, 1969/1971 San Diego Padres NL

Jud McLaughlin was a Brighton native having been born there on March 24, 1914. He was in his first major league contest as a pitcher on June 23, 1931 and he played his final game on May 18, 1933. In 16 appearances, he did not have a win or a loss and had a 10.27 earned run average for his career. He passed away in Cambridge, Massachusetts on September 27, 1964 and is buried in the Belmont Cemetery in Belmont, Massachusetts. 1931-1933 Boston Red Sox AL

Hugh Mulcahy was born in Brighton, Massachusetts on September 9, 1913. He was a pitcher who appeared in his first contest on July 24, 1935. From 1941 until 1944 he served in the military and resumed his career in 1945. He played his last game on May 8, 1947. In 220 appearances he had a record of 45 wins and 89 losses and an earned run average of 4.49. He died in Aliquippa, Pennsylvania on October 19, 2001 and is buried in the Beaver Cemetery in Beaver, Pennsylvania. 1935-1940, 1945-1946 Philadelphia Phillies NL, 1947 Pittsburgh Pirates NL

Emil Roy was born in Brighton on May 26, 1907. His career consisted of one major league baseball game and that was on September 30, 1933. Unfortunately he lost in his only mound appearance and ended up with an ERA of 27.00. He passed away on January 5, 1997 in Crystal River, Florida and was later cremated. 1933 Philadelphia Athletics AL

BROCKTON

John Andre was a native of Brockton, Massachusetts having been born there on January 3, 1923. As a pitcher he debuted in the major leagues on April 16, 1955, and three months later on July 16, 1955 he pitched in his last game. In the 22 games that he pitched in he had an ERA of 5.80 and a record of no wins and one loss. He passed away on November 25, 1976 in Barnstable, Massachusetts and is buried in People's Cemetery in Chatham, Massachusetts. 1955 Chicago Cubs NL

Steve "Bye Bye" Balboni is a Brockton, Massachusetts native having been born there on January 16, 1957. He debuted in the major leagues on April 22, 1981 and played in the major leagues for 11 years playing his final game on October 2, 1993. He was a first baseman/designated hitter who appeared in 960 games with 714 hits and 351 runs scored. He had 127 doubles, 11 triples and 181 home runs as well as 495 runs batted in. He also had a lifetime batting average of .229 and he was also a member of the World Champion Kansas City Royals in 1985. 1981-1983 New York Yankees, 1984-1988 AL, Kansas City Royals AL, 1988 Seattle Mariners AL, 1989-1990 New York Yankees AL, 1993 Texas Rangers AL

Harold "Haddie" Gill was born in Brockton, Massachusetts on January 23, 1899. He pitched in only one game in the major leagues and that was on August 16, 1923. He did not get credit for either a win or a loss that day and passed away in Brockton on August 1, 1932 where he is buried in Brockton's Calvary Cemetery. 1923 Cincinnati Reds NL

Major league pitcher **Jim Mann** was born in Brockton, Massachusetts on November 17, 1974. His first pitching appearance was on May 29, 2000 and in 25 pitching appearances he had a record of 0-1 to go with a 4.83 earned run average. His last big league game was on August 1, 2003. 2000 New York Mets, 2001-2002 Houston Astros NL, 2003 Pittsburgh Pirates NL

Freddie Moncewicz was a native of Brockton, Massachusetts having been born there on September 1, 1903. His short career in major league baseball lasted from June 19, 1928 until July 2, 1928. He got into three games and did not record a hit. He passed away on April 23, 1969 in Brockton and is buried in Brockton's Calvary Cemetery. 1928 Boston Red Sox AL

Buck O'Brien was a right handed pitcher who was born in Brockton, Massachusetts on May 9, 1882. His first big league game was on September 9, 1911 and his last game was on August 6, 1913. He had a record of 29 wins and 25 losses during his career including his signature 1912 season where he compiled a record of 20 wins and 13 losses helping the Red Sox to the 1912 World Series title. His career ERA was 2.63 and he passed away on July 25, 1959 in Boston where he is buried in the New Calvary Cemetery. 1911-1913 Boston Red Sox AL, 1913 Chicago White Sox AL

Barney Reilly was born in Brockton, Massachusetts on February 7, 1884. In the major leagues he played second base and right field. His first big league game was on July 2, 1909 and in his 12 game career he had five hits and a batting average of .200. His last game in the major leagues was on September 5, 1909. He passed away on November 15, 1934 in St Joseph, Missouri and is buried in the Mount Olivet Cemetery in St Joseph, Missouri. 1909 Chicago White Sox AL

Brockton, Massachusetts is the home town of **Frank Sexton** who was born there on July 21, 1895. He was a pitcher, left fielder and second baseman in his career which lasted from June 21, 1895 until August 17, 1895. As a pitcher he had a record of one win and five losses and an earned run average of 5.69 in seven games. As a batter he got into 10 games and had seven hits and a batting average of .269. He passed away on January 4, 1938 in Brighton, Massachusetts and is buried in St Patrick Cemetery in Brockton, Massachusetts. 1895 Boston Beaneaters NL

Art Whitney was born in Brockton, Massachusetts on January 16, 1858 and debuted in the major leagues on May 1, 1880. He was a third baseman and a shortstop in a career that ended on August 22, 1891. In the 978 games he played in he scored 475 runs and had 820

hits that included 89 doubles, 32 triples and six home runs. He had 349 runs batted in and a .223 batting average. He died in Lowell, Massachusetts on August 15, 1943 and is buried in Edson Cemetery in Lowell. He is also the younger brother of Frank Whitney. 1880 1880 Worcester Ruby Legs NL, 1881 Detroit Wolverines 1881 NL, 1882 Providence Grays NL, 1882 Detroit Wolverines, 1884-1887 Pittsburgh Alleghenies AA, 1888-1889 NL, 1890 New York Giants PL, 1891 Cincinnati Kelly's Killers AA, 1891 St Louis Browns AA

Frank Whitney was born in Brockton, Massachusetts on February 18, 1856. His debut was on May 17, 1876 and his last game was on August 21, 1876. He was a left fielder who played in 34 games. He scored 27 runs and had 33 hits, including seven doubles, one triples and a batting average of .237. He died in Baltimore, Maryland on October 30, 1943 and is buried in Green Mount Cemetery in Baltimore. 1876 Boston Red Stockings NL

BROOKFIELD

Tom Niland was born in Brookfield, Massachusetts on April 14, 1870 and he debuted in the major leagues on April 19, 1896 as a shortstop and outfielder who appeared in 18 games and scored three runs while knocking out 18 hits including one triple. He also had a lifetime batting average of .176. His final game was on June 6, 1896. He later passed away in Lynn, Massachusetts on April 30, 1950. He is buried in the city of Lynn's St. Mary Cemetery. 1896 St Louis Browns NL

BROOKLINE

Brookline, Massachusetts is the hometown of **Bobby Guindon**, who was born there on September 4, 1943. He was a first[t] baseman/left fielder/pinch runner who got into his first major league ballgame on September 19, 1964. His last game was on September 27, 1964 and he had one double in eight at bats. -- 1964 Boston Red Sox AL

Joe Johnson was born in Brookline on October 30, 1961. He was a right handed pitcher who made his major league debut on July 25, 1985. His last game was on June 21, 1987. In 3 big league seasons he appeared in 62 games winning 20 games and losing 18 with a life time ERA of 4.48. -- 1985-1986 Atlanta Braves NL, 1986-1987 Toronto Blue Jays AL

John Kelleher was born in Brookline, Massachusetts on September 13, 1893. He was a first and third baseman who also played shortstop in a career that started on July 31, 1912. He played in 6 major league seasons and appeared in 235 games. In those games, he had 206 hits, including 29 doubles, eight triples and 10 home runs to go with 89 runs batted in and a .293 batting average. His last game in the major leagues was on April 20, 1924. He passed away in Brighton, Massachusetts on August 21, 1960 and is buried in Brookline, Massachusetts at the Walnut Hills Cemetery.—1912 St Louis Cardinals NL, 1916 Brooklyn Robins NL, 1921-1923 Chicago Cubs NL, 1924 Boston Braves NL

Jim McManus debuted in the major leagues on September 21, 1960 and two weeks later on October 2, 1960 he played in a total of five games and had four hits including a home run for a batting average of .308. He was born in Brookline, Massachusetts on July 20, 1936.—1960 Kansas City Athletics AL

Rick Moloney was born in Brookline, Massachusetts on June 7, 1950. He was a pitcher who was in one big league game and that was on September 20, 1970. He did not have a win or a loss in that contest.—1970 Chicago White Sox AL

Major leaguer **Dave Pickett** was born in Brookline, Massachusetts on May 26, 1874. He played in the major leagues from July 21, 1898 until August 5, 1898. In 14 games he had 12 hits including a double and a lifetime batting average of .279. He died in Easton, Massachusetts on April 22, 1950 and he is buried in Brookline, Massachusetts at the Holyhood Cemetery.—1898 Boston Beaneaters NL

Roy Talcott had a one game major league career that occurred on June 24, 1943. Talcott was born in Brookline, Massachusetts on January

16, 1920. He was a pitcher who did not have either a win or a loss in that game. He passed away on December 6, 1999 in Miami, Florida and is buried in Miami Memorial Park.—1943 Boston Braves NL

BRAINTREE

Jack Manning was born in Braintree, Massachusetts on December 20, 1853. His first start in the major leagues was on April 23, 1873 and he played his last game on October 14, 1886. He was a right fielder as well as a first baseman and a pitcher. His batting statistics show he appeared in 883 games scoring 562 runs with 922 that include 170 doubles, 37 triples and 14 home runs. He also had 360 runs batted in and a batting average of .263. As a pitcher he was involved in '96 where he had a record of 39 wins and 27 losses as well as an ERA of 2.79. He passed away in Boston, Massachusetts on August 15, 1929 and is buried in Boston's New Calvary Cemetery.—1873 Boston Red Stockings NA, 1874 Baltimore Canaries NA, 1874 Hartford Dark Blues NA, 1875 Boston Red Stockings NA, 1876 Boston Red Stockings NL, 1877 Cincinnati Reds NL, 1878 Boston Red Stockings NL, 1880 Cincinnati Reds NL, 1881 Buffalo Bisons NL, 1883-1885 Philadelphia Quakers NL, 1886 Baltimore Orioles AA

CAMBRIDGE

From May 13, 1921 to May 31, 1930 right field, shortstop and second base were the positions that were played by **Bill Barrett**. Barrett, who was born in Cambridge on May 28, 1900 got into 718 games and had 690 hits including 151 doubles, 30 triples and 22 home runs. He scored 318 runs and had 328 runs batted in and a batting average of .288. He passed away on January 26, 1951 in Cambridge where he is buried in the Cambridge City Cemetery.—1921 Philadelphia Athletics AL, 1923-1929 Chicago White Sox AL, 1929-1930 Boston Red Sox AL, 1930 Washington Senators AL

Jason Bere was a pitcher who was born in Cambridge on May 26, 1971. His first game in the major leagues was on May 27, 1993. He

appeared in 211 games and had a record of 71 wins and 65 losses
with a earned run average of 5.14. His final game in the major
leagues was on May 27, 2003.—1993-1998 Chicago White Sox AL,
1998-1999 Cincinnati Reds NL,1999-2000 Milwaukee Brewers NL,
2000 Cleveland Indians AL, 2001-2002 Chicago Cubs NL. 2003
Cleveland Indians AL

Jack Burns was born on August 31, 1907 in Cambridge, Massachusetts. He debuted in the major leagues on September 17, 1930
and played in his final game on September 27, 1936. He was a first
baseman who appeared in 890 games and had 980 hits, including
199 doubles, 31 triples and 44 home runs. He scored 541 runs and
had 417 runs batted in. His lifetime batting average was .280. Burns
passed away on April 18, 1975 in Brighton, Massachusetts and is
buried in Evergreen Cemetery in Brighton.—1930-1936 St Louis
Browns AL, 1936 Detroit Tigers Al

Arthur "Dad" Clarkson was a pitcher in the later part of the 19th
century who was born in Cambridge, Massachusetts on August 31,
1866. His first game in the major leagues was on August 20, 1891 and
his last game in the big leagues was on August 8, 1896. He appeared in
96 games and had a record of 39 wins and 39 losses to go with his 4.90
career ERA. He passed away on February 5, 1911 in Somerville, Massachusetts and is buried in Cambridge City Cemetery. He is also the
brother of John and Walter Clarkson, as well as the cousin of Mert and
Walter Hackett, all of whom played in the major leagues at one time
or another.—1891 New York Giants NL, 1892 Boston Beaneaters NL,
1893-1895 St Louis Browns NL, 1895-1896 Baltimore Orioles NL

John Clarkson, the brother of Arthur and Walter Clarkson, was born
in Cambridge, Massachusetts on July 1, 1861. He made his major
league pitching debut on May 2, 1882 and played in his final game on
July 12, 1894. He was both a pitcher and a first baseman and as a batter in 546 games he had 432 hits, including 73 doubles, 26 triples and
24 home runs. He scored 254 runs and had 232 runs batted in and
a batting average of .219. However it was his pitching record that

made Clarkson one of the game's early stars. In the 531 games that he appeared in he had a record of 328 wins and 178 losses which is a winning percentage of .648 that is good enough for 29th best all time. His 328 wins puts him 12th on the all-time list and his career ERA of 2.81 is good enough for 104th best of all time. Three times he would end up leading the league in wins (1885-53wins, 1887-38 wins and 1889-49 wins). In 1889 he also led the league in earned run average. He led the league three times in strikeouts with (308 in 1885, 237 in 1887 and 284 in 1889). He also led the league in winning percentage in 1889 with a .729 percentage. He led the league in complete games three times (1885-68, 56 in 1887 and 68 in 1889). Twice he would lead the league in shutouts (1885 with 10 and 1889 with 8). Like all pitchers of that era he was a workhorse as is evidenced by him leading the league four times in innings pitched (623.0 innings in 1885, 523.0 innings in 1887, and 483.1 innings in 1888 and 620.0 innings in 1889. In 1889 he won the National League pitching Triple Crown by being on top in wins, strikeouts and ERA. Deservingly he was elected to the Baseball Hall of Fame by the Veterans Committee in 1963. Unfortunately John Clarkson passed away on February 4, 1909 in Belmont, Massachusetts and is buried with his brother Arthur in Cambridge City Cemetery.—1882 Worcester Ruby legs NL, 1884- 1887 Chicago White Stockings NL, 1888-1892 Boston Beaneaters NL, 1893-1892 Cleveland Spiders NL

Like his brothers John and Arthur Clarkson, **Walter Clarkson** was a major-league pitcher who was born in Cambridge, Massachusetts on November 3, 1878. He made his first appearance as a major league pitcher on July 2, 1904. His final game was on April 28, 1908 and in between he appeared in a total of 78 games. He had a record of 18 wins and 16 losses and a 3.17 earned run average. Walter died in Cambridge on October 10, 1946 and is buried with his brothers in Cambridge City Cemetery.—1904-1907 New York Highlanders AL, 1907-1908 Cleveland Naps AL

Pete Cote was both a pinch runner and a pinch hitter who was born in Cambridge, Massachusetts on August 30, 1902. His short career in the major leagues went from June 18, 1926 until June 22, 1926 in the four games he played in he did not have a hit. He passed away in Middleton, Massachusetts on October 17, 1987 and is buried in St Paul Cemetery in Arlington, Massachusetts.—1926 New York Giants NL

Bill Dam was born in Cambridge, Massachusetts on April 4, 1885. His major league career was one game and that was on August 23, 1909. He was a leftfielder in that game and in two at bats he had a double and scored a run. Of course that means his batting average was .500. He passed away on June 22, 1930 in Quincy, Massachusetts and is buried in the Mount Wollaston Cemetery in Quincy.—1909 Boston Doves NL

Patrick Henry "Cozy" Dolan was a native of Cambridge, Massachusetts having been born there on December 3, 1872. His first game in the major leagues was on April 26, 1895 and his final game was on October 5, 1906. Dolan played right field as well as first base and also pitched in the major leagues. As a batter he appeared in 830 games with 855 hits, including 99 doubles, 37 triples and 10 home runs. He also had 315 runs batted in and a batting average of .269. As a pitcher he appeared in 35 games and had a record of 12 wins and 13 losses with a career earned run average of 4.44. Sadly one year after his last game, Dolan passed away on March 29, 1907 in Louisville, Kentucky. He is buried in Arlington, Massachusetts in the St Paul Cemetery.—1895-1896 Boston Beaneaters NL, 1900 -1901Chicago Orphans NL, 1901-1902 Brooklyn Superbas NL, 1903 Chicago White Sox AL, 1903-1905 Cincinnati Reds, 1905-1906 Boston Beaneaters NL

Walter Paul "Doc" Gaurteau was born in Cambridge, Massachusetts on July 26, 1901. His first major league baseball game that he played in was on June 22, 1925. As a second baseman he appeared in 261 games and had 207 hits including 34 doubles and 10 triples. His batting average was .257. His final major league game was on September 29, 1928 and on August 23, 1970, Gaurteau passed away in Salt Lake City, Utah. He is buried in Mount Auburn Cemetery in Cambridge, Massachusetts,--1925 Philadelphia Athletics AL, 1925-1928 Boston Braves NL

Barney Gilligan was a catcher, outfielder and shortstop in a major league career that began on September 25, 1875 and ended on April 27, 1888. In the 521 games that he played in he scored 215 runs. He also had 68 doubles, 23 triples and three home runs and a total of 386 hits. He had a lifetime batting average off .207. He was buried in Pine Grove Cemetery in Lynn, Massachusetts after passing away in Lynn on April 1, 1934. Gilligan was born in Cambridge, Massachusetts on January 3, 1856.—1879-1880 Cleveland Blues NL, 1881-1885 Providence Grays NL, 1886-1887 Washington Nationals NL, and the1888 Detroit Wolverines NL

Catcher/outfielder **Mert Hackett** was born in Cambridge, Massachusetts on November 11, 1859. His first big league game that he played in was on May 2, 1883 and his final game was on October 6, 1887. After appearing in 256 games, Hackett scored 87 runs and had a total of 203 hits that included 42 doubles, 15 triples and eight home runs. His lifetime batting average was .216. He was able to join his brother Walter and his cousins Arthur, John and Walter Clarkson as major leaguers. Hackett died on February 22, 1938 in Cambridge and is buried in St. Paul Cemetery in Arlington.—1883-1885 Boston Beaneaters NL, 1886 Kansas City Cowboys NL, 1887 Indianapolis Hoosiers NL

Walter Hackett was born in Cambridge, Massachusetts on August 15, 1857 and debuted on the major leagues on April 17, 1884. He was a middle infielder who played second base and shortstop. For his career of 138 games, Hackett had 124 hits including 22 doubles and 1 home run and his batting average was .230. He was able to play around the same time as his brother Mert and the three Clarkson cousins. His last game was on October 8, 1885 and he later passed away in Cambridge, Massachusetts on October 2, 1920 and was buried in Arlington, Massachusetts at St Paul Cemetery. --- 1884 Boston Reds UA, 1885 Boston Beaneaters NL

Mack Hillis was born in Cambridge, Massachusetts on July 23, 1901. His major league debut was on September 13, 1924 and as a second and third baseman he appeared in 12 games during his career with the last one being played on September 27, 1928. In those 12 games he had nine hits, including two doubles, three triples and one home run. He had a career batting average of .243. He passed away in Cambridge on June 16, 1961 and was buried in Cambridge City Cemetery.—1924 New York Yankees AL, 1928 Pittsburgh Pirates NL

Tim Keefe was born in Cambridge, Massachusetts on January 1, 1857. Keefe was a right handed pitcher who debuted in the major leagues on August 6, 1880. His last career appearance was on August 15, 1893. He had a record of 342 wins and 225 losses. The 342 wins are good enough for 10th place all time and his career winning percentage of .603 is good enough for 106th best all time. He twice led the league in wins for the year (1886-42 wins and 1888-35 wins). In 1888 he led the league with a .745 winning percentage and he was the league leader in ERA three times (1880- 0.86, 1885 1.58 and 1888 1.74. He led the league twice in complete games (1883- 68 games and 1886- 62 games). In 1888 he led the league in shutouts with eight and in 1883 and 1886 he led the league in innings pitched with 619.0 and 535.0 respectively. In 1883 he had 259 strikeouts and in 1888 335 and both those totals led the league as well. He won the National League pitching Triple Crown in 1888 as well. He passed away in Cambridge, Massachusetts on April 23, 1933 and was posthumously voted in to the Baseball Hall of Fame in Cooperstown by the Veterans Committee in 1964.—1880-1882 Troy Trojans NL, 1883-1884 New York Metropolitans AA, 1884-1889 New York Giants NL, 1890 New York Giants PL, 1891 New York Giants NL, 1892-1893 Philadelphia Phillies NL

Joe Kelly was a leftfielder and a first baseman who was born in Cambridge, Massachusetts on December 9, 1871. He made his first appearance in the major leagues on July 27, 1891. During his 17 year career he appeared in 1,853 games. He scored 1,421 runs which was good enough for 84th all-time and he had 2,220 hits, which included 358 doubles and 194 triples as well as 65 home runs. He also had 1,194 runs batted in and hit .317 for his career, which is good enough for 66th best all time. He stole 443 bases in his career including a league high 87 in 1896. On defense he was stellar as he was fast, was sure- handed and had a powerful throwing arm.

His last major league ball game was on October 8, 1908. He died in Baltimore, Maryland on August 14, 1943 and is buried in Baltimore's New Cathedral Cemetery. He was voted into the hallowed halls of Cooperstown in 1971 by the Veterans Committee.—1891 Boston Beaneaters NL, 1892 Pittsburgh Pirates NL, 1892-1898 Baltimore Orioles NL, 1899-1901 Brooklyn Superbas NL, 1902 Baltimore Orioles AL, 1902-1906 Cincinnati Reds NL, 1908 Boston Doves NL

Karl Kolseth had a six game career in the major leagues that ran from September 30, 1915 until October 3, 1915. Kolseth, who was born in Cambridge, Massachusetts on December 25, 1892, was a first baseman that had six hits including a double and a triple in his career to go with his .261 career batting average. He passed away on May 3, 1956 in Cumberland, Maryland and is buried in St. Peter and Paul Cemetery in Cumberland.—1915 Baltimore Terrapins FL

Toby Lyons was born on March 27, 1869 in Cambridge, Massachusetts. He was a pitcher who got into his first big league ball game on April 18, 1890 and played his last game two weeks later on May 2, 1890. In the three games he pitched in he did not have a win but recorded two losses and an ERA of 10.48.He died in Boston, Massachusetts on August 27, 1920 and is buried in Holy Cross Cemetery in Malden, Massachusetts.—1890 Syracuse Stars AA

May 22, 1886 was the birthday of Cambridge's **Charlie Maloney** who was a major league pitcher for one game on August 10, 1908. He did not have a win or a loss in that game, but did have a career ERA of 4.50. He passed away on January 17, 1967 in Arlington, Massachusetts and is buried in the city of Arlington's St Paul Cemetery.—1908 Boston Doves NL

Major league pitcher **Dewey Metivier** was born in Cambridge, Massachusetts on May 6, 1898. His first appearance in a major league ballgame was on September 15, 1922. Before the end of his career on September 11, 1924 Metivier pitched in 54 games and had a record of 7-7 to go with a 5.74 earned run average for his career. He died on March 2, 1947 in Cambridge and is buried in St. Paul's Cemetery in Arlington, Massachusetts.—1922-1924 Cleveland Indians AL

Fred Mitchell (who was born Fredrick Francis Yapp) was born on June 5, 1878 in Cambridge, Massachusetts. During his career he pitched, was a catcher and also played first base. His first game in the major leagues was on April 27, 1901 and his final game in the majors was on June 15, 1913. As a pitcher he appeared in 97 games and had a record of 31 wins and 50 losses with a 4.10 ERA. His batting stats show him appearing in 202 games with 1,120 hits including 16 doubles and seven triples with a .210 career batting average. He passed away on October 13, 1970 in the town of Newton, Massachusetts and is buried in Stow, Massachusetts at the Brookside Cemetery. 1901-1902 Boston Americans, 1902 Philadelphia Athletics AL, 1903-1904 Philadelphia Phillies NL, 1904-1905 Brooklyn Superbas NL, 1910 New York Highlanders AL, 1913 Boston Braves NL

Carl Sumner had a big league career that lasted from July 25, 1928 until August 21, 1928. As an outfielder he appeared in 16 games and had a total of eight hits that included one double and one triple. His career batting average was .276 and he was buried in Pine Hill Cemetery in Tewksbury, Massachusetts after passing away in Chatham, Massachusetts on February 8, 1999. –1928 Boston Red Sox AL

Vito Tamules was born in Cambridge, Massachusetts on July 11, 1911. He was a pitcher who appeared in his first major league game on September 25, 1934. In the 170 games that he appeared in he had a record of 40 wins and 28 losses as well as a 3.97 earned run average. His last game in the major leagues was on July 25, 1941. He passed away in Nashville, Tennessee on May 5, 1974 and is buried in the Nashville National Cemetery.—1934-1935 New York Yankees AL, 1938 St Louis Browns AL, 1938-1940 Brooklyn Dodgers NL, 1941 Philadelphia Phillies NL, 1941 Brooklyn Dodgers NL

Designated hitter, pinch hitter and first baseman are the positions played by **Joe Vitello** who was born in Cambridge, Massachusetts on April 11, 1970. His major league career began on April 29, 1995 and ended on September 28, 2003. In his 282 game career he had a .248 batting average. He also had 35 doubles, one triple and 26 home runs and a total of 172 hits. He also had 104 runs batted in. – 1995-1999 Kansas City Royals AL, 2000 San Diego Padres NL, 2003 Montreal Expos NL

Eddie Waitkus was a first baseman who was born in Cambridge, Massachusetts on April 4, 1919. He made his major league debut on April 15, 1941 and played in his final game on September 20, 1955. He appeared in 1,140 games and had 1,214 hits in 4,254 at bats. He had 215 doubles, 44 triples and 24 home runs as well as 373 runs batted in. his career batting average was .285. He passed away on September 16, 1972 in Jamaica Plain, Massachusetts and is buried in Cambridge, Massachusetts at the Cambridge City Cemetery. – 1941, 1946-1948 Chicago Cubs NL, 1949-1953 Philadelphia Phillies NL, 1954-1955 Baltimore Orioles AL, 1955 Philadelphia Phillies NL

Austin Walsh was an outfielder in the major leagues who played from April 19, 1914 until October 8, 1914. He was born in Cambridge, Massachusetts on September 1, 1891. In 57 games he had 29 hits including six doubles, one triple and one home run. His career batting average was .240 and he passed away in Glendale, California on January 26, 1955. He is buried in San Fernando Mission Burial Park in Mission Hills, California, --1914 Chicago Chi-Feds FL.

Knuckle ball pitcher **Wilbur Wood** had an 18 year career in the major leagues that began on June 30, 1961 and ended on August 22, 1978. He was born in Cambridge, Massachusetts on October 22, 1941. In his career he appeared in 651 games and had a record of 164 wins and 156 losses and a career earned run average of 3.24. He led the league in wins two times (1972-24wins, 1973-24 wins), he also led the league in innings pitched two times (1972-376.2 innings, and 1973-359.1 innings). He appeared in the 1971, 1972 and 1974 All Star games and in 1972 was voted American League Pitcher of the Year by the Sporting News. He was also Reliever of the Year as voted by the Sporting News for the 1968 season in American League. On July 20, 1973 he started both games of a double header against the Yankees and was the last pitcher in the major leagues to start both games of a double header. 1961-1964 Boston Red Sox AL, 1964-1965 Pittsburgh Pirates NL, 1967-1978 Chicago White Sox AL

George Yankowski was born in Cambridge, Massachusetts on November 22, 1922 and he made his major league debut on August 17, 1942. He was a catcher and a pinch hitter who appeared in 18 games before his career ended on June 28, 1949. He had five hits in 31 plate appearances for a batting average of .161, --1942 Philadelphia Athletics AL, 1949 Chicago White Sox AL

CHARLESTOWN

John Francis "Shano" Collins was born in Charlestown, Massachusetts on December 4, 1885. He was an outfielder and a first baseman in the major leagues in a career that started on April 21, 1910 and ended on May 15, 1925. He played in 1,799 games and had 1,687 hits including 310 doubles, 133 triples and 22 home runs. He scored 747 runs and drove in 709 runs. He also had a batting average of .264. He was a member of the 1917 World Champion Chicago White Sox and also was a member of the infamous 1919 White Sox team that was involved in the fixing of the World Series that year. Shano Collins was never implicated in the scandal and in fact was named as a wronged party in the indictments. The indictments claimed that the conspirators had defrauded him out of $1,784. Collins later went on to manage the Boston Red Sox for the 1931 and part of the 1932 season. He is the grandfather of Bob Gallagher of Newton, Massachusetts who was a major league outfielder and pinch hitter. Collins died September 10, 1955 in Newton, Massachusetts and is buried in St. Mary's Cemetery in Newton, --1910-1920 Chicago White Sox AL, 1921-1925 Boston Red Sox AL

Clarence Dow's lone game in the major leagues came with the Cincinnati Reds on September 22, 1882. He came to bat six times and had two hits and scored one run. He had a lifetime batting average of .333. Dow was born in Charlestown, Massachusetts on October 2, 1854 and he passed away on March 11, 1893 in West Somerville, Massachusetts. He is buried in Woodlawn Cemetery in Everett, Massachusetts.

Sam Gentile was a pinch runner and a pinch hitter in his major league baseball career that went from April 24, 1893 to May 31, 1893. Gentile was born in Charlestown, Massachusetts on October 12, 1916. He had one hit in four plate appearances and had a batting average of .250 for the eight games he played in. Gentile passed away on May 4, 1998 in Everett, Massachusetts and is buried in Woodlawn Cemetery in Everett. --1943-Boston Braves

Harry Pattee was born in Charlestown, Massachusetts on January 17, 1882. He debuted in the major leagues on April 14, 1908 and played in his final game on September 29, 1908. In the 80 games he played for the Brooklyn Superbas as a second baseman, he had 57 hits including five doubles and two triples. He stole 24 bases and had a lifetime batting average of .216. He passed away in Lynchburg, Virginia on July 17, 1971 and was buried in Price Hill Burial Ground in Barrington, Rhode Island.

Fredrick "Dupee" Shaw was a native of the town of Charlestown having been born there on May 31, 1859. He made his debut on the major leagues on June 18, 1883 and played his final game on July 17, 1888. He was a pitcher and a right fielder. As a pitcher he appeared in 211 games and had a record of 83 wins and 121 losses to go with an ERA of 3.10. Batting stats show that he was in 236 games and had 140 hits that included 21 doubles, one triple and one home run. His batting average was .170. He passed away in Wakefield, Massachusetts on January 12, 1938 and was buried at the Glenwood Cemetery in Everett, Massachusetts, --1883-1884 Detroit Wolverines NL, 1884 Boston Reds UA, 1885 Providence Grays NL, 1886-1888 Washington Nationals NL

Jim Sullivan was born in Charlestown, Massachusetts on April 25, 1867. He was a pitcher and made his first major league appearance on April 22, 1891. His career lasted 70 games and he had a record of 26 wins and 28 losses as well as an ERA of 4.50. His last game was on May 6, 1898 and he later passed away on November 29, 1901 in Roxbury, Massachusetts. He is buried in the Holy Cross Cemetery in Malden, Massachusetts, -- 1891 Boston Beaneaters NL, 1891 Columbus Salons AA, 1895-1898 Boston Beaneaters NL

Joe Sullivan played second base and shortstop as well as the outfield in a career that began on April 27, 1893 and ended on September 26, 1896. He appeared in 415 games and had 289 hits, including 45 doubles, 29 triples and 11 home runs. He also had a batting average of .299 and 227 runs batted in. He was born in Charlestown on January 6, 870. He passed away in Charlestown, Massachusetts on November 2, 1897 and is buried in Holy Cross Cemetery in Malden, Massachusetts. -- 1893-1894 Washington Senators NL, 1894-1896 Philadelphia Phillies NL, 1896 St Louis Browns NL

Bobby Wheelock was born in Charlestown on August 6, 1864 and debuted in the major leagues on May 19, 1887. His final game was on September 27, 1891. In 236 games as both a shortstop and an outfielder, he had 25 doubles, four triples and three home runs included in his 209 hits. His batting average for his career was .235 and he died in Boston, Massachusetts on March 13, 1928, and is buried in the Mount Auburn Cemetery in Cambridge, Massachusetts. --1887 Boston Beaneaters NL1890-1891 Columbus Solons AA

CHELMSFORD

First baseman **Tony Lupien** was born in Chelmsford, Massachusetts on April 23, 1917. He debuted in the major leagues on September 12, 1940 and played in his last game on October 3, 1949. He had appeared in 614 games with 632 hits including 92 doubles, 30 triples and 18 home runs. He drove in 230 runs and had a lifetime batting average of .268. He is buried in Norwich, Vermont at the Hillside Cemetery after passing away in Norwich on July 9, 2004 .-- 1940,1942-1943 Boston Red Sox AL, 1944-1945 Philadelphia Phillies NL, 1948 Chicago White Sox AL

CHELSEA

The city of Chelsea was the hometown of **Alex Mustakis** who was born there on March 26, 1909. His first major league baseball game was on July 7, 1940. As a pitcher he appeared in his last game on August 3, 1940. In the six games he pitched he had a record of no wins and one loss and a 9.00 ERA. He passed away on January 17, 1970 in Scranton, Pennsylvania and is buried in Cathedral Cemetery in Scranton. --1940 Boston Red Sox AL

January 26 1844 was the birthday of Chelsea, Massachusetts's **Tom Pratt.** He played first base in his only big league appearance on October 18, 1871. He had two hits and scored two runs and ended up with a .333 batting average. He passed away on September 28, 1908 in Philadelphia, Pennsylvania and is buried in Philadelphia's Laurel Hill Cemetery. --1871 Philadelphia Athletics UA

Walt Whittaker was born in Chelsea, Massachusetts on June 11, 1894. He was only in the big leagues for one game and that game was on July 6, 1916. He did not have a won or a loss and gave up one run in the two innings he pitched so his career ERA was 4.50. He passed away on August 7, 1965 in Pembroke, Massachusetts and is buried in Bryantville, Massachusetts at the Mount Pleasant Cemetery—1916 Philadelphia Athletics AL

Ames "Red" Woodhead was a third baseman in the major leagues from April 15, 1873 until September 10, 1879. He appeared in 35 games and had 21 hits and a batting average of .154. He was born in Chelsea, Massachusetts on July 9, 1851 and passed away in Boston on September 7, 1979. He is buried in the Bennington Street Cemetery in East Boston—1873 Baltimore Marylands NA, 1879 Syracuse Stars NL

CHICOPEE

Ray Fitzgerald was born in Chicopee, Massachusetts on December 5, 1904. His major league baseball career was one game and that was on April 18, 1931. He pinch hit in his only plate appearance and did not reach base. He passed away on September 6, 1977 in Westfield, Massachusetts and is buried in St. Mary's Cemetery in Westfield—1931 Cincinnati Reds NL

Chicopee, Massachusetts native **Mike Hickey** was born on December 25, 1871 and played the only game of his baseball career in the majors on September 14, 1899 for the Boston Beaneaters. He played second base and had one hit in three plate appearances. He passed away on June 11, 1918 in Springfield, Massachusetts and is buried in the Calvary Cemetery in Chicopee, Massachusetts.

Ed Trumbell was a catcher/pitcher in his major league career with the Washington Nationals in 1884. His career lasted from May 10, 1884 until July 28, 1884. He appeared in 10 games as a pitcher and had a record of one win and nine losses and a 4.71 ERA. His batting statistics show him appearing in 25 games and getting 10 hits, including two doubles for a .116 batting average. Trumbell was born in Chicopee, Massachusetts on November 3, 1860 and died on January 14, 1937 in Kingston, Pennsylvania. He was buried in St. Patrick's Cemetery in Chicopee, Massachusetts.

CHICOPEE FALLS

Stan Partenheimer was a pitcher in the major leagues from May 27, 1944 until September 11, 1945. He appeared in nine games without recording a win or a loss and he ended up with a career ERA of 6.91. He was born in Chicopee Falls, Massachusetts on October 21, 1922 and is the son of former major league third baseman Steve Partenheimer. Stan passed away on January 28, 1989 in Wilson, North Carolina and is buried in the Evergreen Memorial Gardens in Wilson. –1944 Boston Red Sox AL, 1945 St Louis Cardinals NL

CLARKSBURG

Art Madison—SEE BERKSHIRE COUNTY BORN PLAYERS

CLINTON

Clinton, Massachusetts is the hometown of **Billy Burke** who was a major league pitcher from April 30, 1910 until September 26, 1911.

Burke appeared in 21 games and had one win and one loss to go with his career ERA of 4.81. He was born in Clinton on July 11, 1889, and passed away on February 9, 1967 in Worcester, Massachusetts. He is buried in St. John's Cemetery in Lancaster, Massachusetts—1910-1911 Boston Doves/Rustlers NL

Frank Connaughton was born in Clinton, Massachusetts on January 1, 1869 and made his major league debut on May 28, 1894. He played shortstop, left field and was a catcher in a 146 game career that ended on October 5, 1906. He had a total of 150 hits that included 12 doubles, four triples and four home runs along with 77 runs batted in and a career batting average of .283. – 1894 Boston Beaneaters NL, 1896 New York Giants NL, 1906 Boston Beaneaters NL

Left handed pitcher **Tim Fortugno** was born on April 11, 1962 in Clinton, Massachusetts. In the 76 games he appeared in from July 20, 1992 until July 26, 1995 he had a record of three wins and four losses and a 5.06 ERA –1992 California Angels AL, 1994 Cincinnati Reds NL, 1995 Chicago White Sox AL

Malachi Kitteridge was a catcher in the major leagues from April 19, 1890 until August 6, 1906. He appeared in 1216 games and had a batting average of .219. He had 882 hits that included 108 doubles, 31 triples and 17 home runs. He also had 391 runs batted in and scored 375 runs. He was born in Clinton, Massachusetts on October 12, 1869 and passed away in Gary, Indiana on June 23, 1928. He is buried in Bucksport Maine.—1890-1897 Chicago Colts, 1898-1899 Louisville Colonels, 1899 Washington Senators NL, 1901-1903 Boston Beaneaters NL, 1903-1906 Washington Senators, 1906 Cleveland Naps AL

Jack McGreachey was born in Clinton, Massachusetts on May 13, 1864. He made his major league debut as an outfielder on June 17, 1886. He got into 608 games before his career ended on August 24, 1891. In those 608 games he had 604 hits including 106 doubles, 18 triples and nine home runs and 276 runs batted in and he also had a career batting average of .245. He died on April 5, 1930 in Cambridge, Massachusetts and is buried in the Woodlawn Cemetery in Clinton.—1886 Detroit Wolverines NL, 1886 St Louis Maroons NL, 1887-1889 Indianapolis Hoosiers NL, 1890 Brooklyn Ward's Wonders PL, 1891 Philadelphia Athletics AA, 1891 Boston Reds AA, 1891 Philadelphia Athletics AA

From October 8, 1885 until September 24, 1903 **Jimmy Ryan** played the outfield in the major leagues. He appeared in 2,014 games and had a total of 1,643 hits that included 451 doubles, 157 triples and 118 home runs. He had a career batting average of .308. He also led the league with 182 hits, 33 doubles and 16 home runs during the 1888 season. He was born in Clinton, Massachusetts on February 11, 1863 and died in Chicago, Illinois on October 29, 1923. He is buried in the Calvary Catholic Cemetery in Evanston, Illinois.—1885-1889 Chicago White Stockings NL, 1890 Chicago Pirates PL,1891-1900 Chicago Colts/Orphans NL, 1902-1903 Washington Senators AL

CONCORD

Casper Asbjornson was born in Concord, Massachusetts on June 19, 1909. He debuted in the major leagues on September 17, 1928 and played his final game on August 31, 1932. He got into 97 games as a pinch hitter and a catcher and had 52 hits, of which there were 10 doubles, one triple and one home run. He had 27 runs batted in and a batting average of .235. He died in Williamsport, Pennsylvania on January 21, 1970 and is buried in Wildwood Cemetery in Williamsport.—1928-1929 Boston Red Sox, 1931-1932 Cincinnati Reds

Tom Glavine was born in Concord, Massachusetts on March 25, 1966. The southpaw made his pitching debut on August 17, 1987 and pitched in the major leagues until August 14, 2008, a total of 22 major league seasons. He finished his career with a record of 305 wins and 203 losses for a winning percentage of .600, and he had a career ERA of 3.54. He was the National League leader in wins five times (1991-20, 1992-20, 1993-22, 1998-20 and 2000-21). In 1991 he led the league with nine complete games and in 1992 he was the league leader in shutouts with five. He was the league leader in games started six times proving his durability

(1993-36, 19996-36, 1999-35, 2000-35, 2001-35 and 2002-36). He was a 10 time selection as a National League All Star (1991-1993, 1996-1998, 2000, 2002, 2004, and 2006). He won the National League CY Young Award in 1991 and 1998, and was the 1991 and 2000 National League Pitcher of the Year as chosen by the Sporting News. He also won the 1995 National League Babe Ruth Award for pitching in the World Series and was also voted World Series MVP in 1995. Four times he won the Silver Slugger Award for best hitting pitcher (1991, 1995, 1996 and 1998). He was a member of the 1995 World Series Champion Atlanta Braves and is a sure bet as a first ballot Hall of Fame entrant, and he is also the older brother of Mike Glavine who also pitched in the major leagues.—1987-2002 Atlanta Braves, 2003-2007 New York Mets, 2008 Atlanta Braves

Mike Glavine, the younger brother of Tom Glavine, was also born in Concord Massachusetts, with his birthday being January 24, 1973. He was a first baseman and a pinch hitter who debuted on September 14, 2003 and played his last game two weeks later on September 28, 2003. In the six games he played in, he had one hit in seven at bats for a .143 batting average.—2003 New York Mets

Outfielder **Dick Loftus** was born in Concord, Massachusetts on March 7, 1901 and made his first big league appearance on April 20, 1924. His final appearance in a major league uniform was on September 14, 1925. He appeared in 97 games and 53 hits. He had 21 runs batted in and a lifetime batting average of .250. He passed away in his hometown of Concord on January 21, 1972 and is buried in the St. Bernard Parish Cemetery in Concord. –1924-1925 Brooklyn Robins

DALTON

Jeff Reardon—SEE BERKSHIRE COUNTY BORN PLAYERS

Turk Wendell—SEE BERKSHIRE COUNTY BORN PLAYERS

DANVERS

Ed Caskin was born in Danvers, Massachusetts on December 30, 1851 and made his first appearance in the major leagues on May 1, 1879. He played shortstop, third base and catcher during his career which went from May 1, 1879 until September 24, 1886. In 482 games he had 427 hits that included 50 doubles, 10 triples and two home runs. He also had driven in 163 runs and his lifetime batting average was .228. He was buried in Danvers at St. Mary's Cemetery after passing away in his hometown on October 24, 1924.—1879-1881 Troy Trojans NL, 1883-1884 New York Gothams NL, 1885 St Louis Maroons NL, and 1886 New York Giants NL

Connie Creeden's major league career was from April 28, 1943 until May 5, 1943. Creeden, who was born in Danvers, Massachusetts on July 21, 1915, was a pinch hitter during his five game major league career. He had one hit and one run batted in and his batting average was .250. He died in Santa Ana, California on November 30, 1969 and is buried in the Good Shepherd Cemetery in Huntington Beach, California. –1943 Boston Braves

Second baseman **Thorndike Proctor "Thorny" Hawkes** was born in Danvers, Massachusetts on October 15, 1852. His first appearance in a major league uniform was on May 1, 1879 and he played until August 2, 1884. In the 102 games that Hawkes played in, he had 94 hits that included 10 doubles and three triples. He also batted in 20 runs and carried a .234 batting average. Hawkes passed away in Danvers on February 2, 1929 and is buried in the Holton Street Cemetery in Danvers. –1879 Troy Trojans NL, 1884 Washington Nationals AA

Dan Woodman was a right handed pitcher in the major leagues from July 10, 1914 until May 12, 1915. He was born in Danvers, Massachusetts on July 8, 1893 and passed away in Danvers on December 14, 1969. He is buried in the Holton Street Cemetery in Danvers. During the course of his career he was in 18 games and did not record a win or a loss, but did have a respectable 2.94 ERA. –1914 Buffalo Feds FL, 1915 Buffalo Blues FL

DEDHAM

Dedham, Massachusetts is the home of major leaguer **Henry "Buck" Danner** who played for one week in the major leagues from September 17, 1924 until September 24, 1924. Danner had three hits in 12 at bats for a .250 batting average. He was born in Dedham, Massachusetts on June 8, 1891 and passed away in Boston on September 21, 1949. He is buried in Dedham at the Brookdale Cemetery. –1915 Philadelphia Athletics AL

Utility infielder **Bill Hunnefield** was born in Dedham on January 5, 1899 and made his first appearance in the major leagues on April 17, 1926. He played second and third bases, as well as shortstop in a career that saw him play a total of 511 games with the last one being on September 27, 1931. In those 511 games he had a total of 452 hits including 75 doubles, nine triples and nine home runs. He scored 230 runs and batted in another 144. His career batting average was .272. He died in Nantucket, Massachusetts on August 28, 1976 and he was later cremated. – 1926-1930 Chicago White Sox AL, 1931 Cleveland Indians AL, Boston Braves NL, New York Giants NL

Howard "Lefty" Mills was born in Dedham, Massachusetts on May 12, 1910. As a pitcher in the major leagues, he appeared in 96 games for the St Louis Browns from June 10, 1934 until August 29, 1940. He had a record of 15 wins and 30 losses and a career ERA of 6.06. Mills passed away in Riverside, California on September 23, 1982 and is buried in Green Hill Memorial Park in Rancho Palos Verdes, California.

DORCHESTER

Bob Brown was born in Dorchester, Massachusetts on April 1, 1911. He played in his first major league baseball game on April 21, 1930 and his last on May 3, 1936. In 79 games as a pitcher he had a record of 16 wins and 21 losses and a 4.48 career ERA. He passed away on August 3, 1990 in Pembroke, Massachusetts and is buried in St Joseph Cemetery in West Roxbury—1930-1936 Boston Braves/Bees

October 30, 1874 was the birthdate of **Simon "Sammy" Curran** who pitched in only one game in the major leagues. The Dorchester Massachusetts native threw in his only game on August 1, 1902 for the Boston Beaneaters. He did not get credit for the win or the loss, but had an ERA of 1.35 after pitching for 6 and 2/3 innings. Curran died on May 19, 1936 in Dorchester and is buried in Holy Cross Cemetery in Malden, Massachusetts.

Ed Gallagher was a left-handed pitcher who debuted in the major leagues on July 8, 1932, his last game in the majors was September 24, 1932. He pitched in parts of nine games and did not have a win but as saddled with three losses and an ERA of 12.55. He was born in Dorchester, Massachusetts on November 28, 1910 and passed away in Hyannis, Massachusetts on December 22, 1981. He is buried in the Mosswood Cemetery in Cotuit, Massachusetts – 1932 Boston Red Sox

Bob Giggie was born on August 13, 1933 in Dorchester; his major league career lasted from April 18, 1959 until July 24, 1962. In 30 games as a pitcher, he recorded three wins and one loss and a 5.18 ERA. –1959-1960 Milwaukee Braves NL, 196-/1962 Kansas City Athletics AL

Pinch hitting/pinch running and playing second base were what **Bill Marshall** did in a major league career that lasted from June 20, 1931 until September 21, 1934. Marshall, who was born in Dorchester, Massachusetts on February 14, 1911 played in seven games and had one hit in eight at bats. He passed away on May 5, 1977 in Sacramento, California and is buried in St. Mary's Catholic Cemetery in Sacramento. –1931 Boston Red Sox AL, 1934 Cincinnati Reds NL

Born on December 21, 1884 **Steve White** made his first appearance in a major league baseball game on May 29, 1912. The Dorchester, Massachusetts native's final game in the big leagues was on July 5, 1912. He was a pitcher who in four major league ballgames did not have a win or a loss, but had a career ERA of 5.40. He died in Braintree, Massachusetts on January 25, 1975 and is buried in St. Mary's Cemetery in Randolph, Massachusetts. – 1912 Washington Senators AL, 1912 Boston Braves NL

DOUGLAS

Mike Brannock was a third baseman who played in the major leagues from October 21, 1871 until August 28, 1875. He was born in Douglas, Massachusetts on October 25, 1851 and appeared in five games during his career for the Chicago White Stockings of the National Association. He had two hits in 23 at bats for a .087 batting average. He passed away on October 7, 1881 in Chicago, Illinois and is buried in Calvary Catholic Cemetery in Evanston, Illinois

DRACUT

Right fielder **Art Sladen** was born in Dracut, Massachusetts on October 28, 1859. His career in the major leagues was from August 22-August 25, 1884. He did not record a hit in seven at bats. He passed away on February 14, 1914 in Dracut and is buried in the Edson Cemetery in Lowell, Massachusetts. –1884 Boston Reds UA

DUDLEY

John "Doc" Stafford was a pitcher and a right fielder during the course of his major league career which ran from June 15, 1893 until July 7, 1893. He appeared in two games as a pitcher and recorded no wins and one loss with a 14.14 ERA. Batting he appeared in two games with no hits. He was born in Dudley, Massachusetts on April 7, 1870 and passed away on July 3, 1940 in Worcester, Massachusetts. He is buried in Calvary Cemetery in Dudley, Massachusetts. He is the brother of James "General Stafford who had a nine year major league career from August 27, 1898 until October 12, 1899. – Cleveland Spiders NL

Jerry Turbidy was born in Dudley, Massachusetts on July 4, 1852. His first big league appearance was on July 27, 1884 and his final appearance was on August 13, 1884. As a shortstop he appeared in 13 games and had four doubles included in his 11 total hits. He scored five runs and had a batting average of .224. He passed away in Webster, Massachusetts on September 5, 1920 and is buried in Dudley at the Calvary Cemetery. –1884 Kansas City Cowboys UA

EAST BOSTON

Joe Callahan was a pitcher in the major leagues who was born in East Boston, Massachusetts on October 8, 1916. He pitched in the major leagues from September 13, 1939 until June 15, 1940. In 10 games that he pitched in he had a record of one win and two losses and an ERA of 6.40. He passed away on South Boston on May 24, 1949 and is buried in New Calvary Cemetery in Boston. –1939-1940 Boston Bees NL

EAST BRIDGEWATER

Tom Hernon was born in East Bridgewater, Massachusetts on November 4, 1866. He made his debut in the major leagues on September 13, 1897 and three days later played in his last game on September 15, 1897. In the four games he appeared in as a left fielder he had one hit in 16 at bat while batting in two runs and scoring two more runs. He passed away on February 4, 1902 in New Bedford, Massachusetts and is buried in St. Mary's Cemetery in New Bedford. –1897 Chicago Colts NL

EAST BROOKFIELD

Corneilius Alexander McGillicudy had a 10 year major league career as a catcher, first baseman and right fielder. He was born in East Brookfield, Massachusetts on December 22, 1862. He appeared in 724 major league baseball games and had 698 hits in 2,698 at bats. He had 79 doubles, 28 triples and five home runs and 265 runs batted in and a career batting average of .244.

But he may be better known as Connie Mack, the longtime owner and manager of the Philadelphia Athletics. Mack had previously been the player/manager of the Pittsburgh Pirates from 1894 until 1896. Mack managed in the minor leagues from 1897 to 1900 in the Western League, which was headed by Ban Johnson who would found the American League in 1901. Mack was one of Johnson's early supporters until Johnson's dictatorial ways led baseball to create the position of commissioner, and then in 1901 Mack took over the reins of the Philadelphia Athletics whom he managed from 1901 until 1950, an unprecedented 50 year run as manager of one ball club. His Athletic teams would win nine American League pennants and five World Series titles. In fact the 1929 to 1931 Philadelphia Athletics team is considered by many to be one of the greatest teams ever assembled.

Of course Mack also had one of the greatest infields ever assembled in the early years of his managerial reign as he would have Stuffy McGinnis at first, Eddie Collins at second, Jack Barry at shortstop and Frank Baker at third base. This quartet of players would be known as the $100,000 infield because Mack had said he would not even sell them for that price which would be considered sizeable in the early part of the 20th century. Mack never managed in a uniform as he always wore a suit while on the bench. He is the all-time leader in managerial wins with 3,731 which is almost 1,000 wins more than the man in second place, the legendary John McGraw. Mack was so revered by Philadelphia that Shibe Park where the Athletics played was renamed Connie Mack Park to honor the long time skipper.

Mack was selected to the Baseball Hall of Fame in 1937 by the Centennial Committee as a manager and was part of the first induction class in 1939. He passed away on February 8, 1956 in Philadelphia and is buried in Holy Sepulchre Cemetery in Cheltham, Pennsylvania. –1886-1889 Washington Nationals NL, 1890 Buffalo Bisons P, 1891-1896 Pittsburgh Pirates NL

EAST DOUGLAS

Henry Coppola was a right handed pitcher in the major leagues who was born in East Douglas, Massachusetts on August 4, 1912. He made his major league debut on April 19, 1935 and pitched in his last game on May 7, 1936. In the 25 games he pitched in, he had three wins and four losses and a 5.65 ERA. He passed away in Norfolk, Massachusetts on July 10, 1990 and is buried in St. Douglas Cemetery in Douglas, Massachusetts. –1935-1936 Washington Senators AL

EASTHAMPTON

Catcher Pete Lapan was born in Easthampton, Massachusetts on June 25, 1891. He made his first major league appearance on September 16, 1922. In his career which ended on May 5, 1923, he appeared in 13 games and had 11 hits including one double and one home run. He also had a batting average of .306. He died in Norwalk, California on January 5, 1953 and is buried in Los Angeles National Cemetery in California. -- 1922-1923 Washington Senators AL

ESSEX

Third baseman **Fletcher Low** was born in the town of Essex, Massachusetts on April 7, 1893. He career in the major leagues was one day and that was October 7, 1915. In four plate appearances he hit a triple and drove in a run and his lifetime batting average was .250. He passed away in Hanover, New Hampshire on June 6, 1973 and is buried in Hanover's Dartmouth Cemetery. –1915 Boston Braves NL

EVERETT

George Brickley was born in Everett, Massachusetts on July 19, 1894 and debuted in the major leagues on September 26, 1913. He appeared in five games and had two hits, one of which was a triple. This major league right fielder had a career batting average of .167 and his final major league appearance was on October 1, 1913. He passed away on February 23, 1947 in Everett, Massachusetts and he is buried in the Holy Cross Cemetery in Malden, Massachusetts. –1913 Philadelphia Athletics

James "Hub" Hart was born in Everett, Massachusetts on February 2, 1878. He was a catcher in the major leagues and his first appearance in a big league ballgame was on July 16, 1905. He was in a total of 57 games and his last game was on October 5, 1907. He had 27 hits including one double and 11 runs batted in to go with a .213 batting average. He passed away on October 10, 1960 in Fort Wayne Indiana and is buried in that city's Green Lawn Memorial Park. –1905-1907 Chicago White Sox

Centerfielder Barney Olsen was born in Everett, Massachusetts on September 11, 1919. He made his major league debut on August 23, 1941 and played in his final game on September 28, 1941. In the 24 ballgames he appeared in he had 23 hits in 71 at bats. Of those 21 hits, six were doubles, one was a triple and one was a home run. He had a batting average of .288 and also had four runs batted in. Olsen died in Everett on March 30, 1977 and is buried in Malden, Massachusetts at the Holy Cross Cemetery. – 1941 Chicago Cubs NL

John "Lefty" Shea was born in Everett, Massachusetts on December 27, 1904. He was a pitcher who appeared in his only major league game on June 30, 1928. He did not get a win or a loss and his career ERA was 18.00. He passed away on November 30, 1956 in Malden and is buried in the Holy Cross Cemetery in Malden. – 1928 Boston Red Sox Al

Everett, Massachusetts was the home of major league third baseman **Danny Silva** who was born there on October 5, 1896. In his only major league ballgame on August 11, 1919 he had one hit in four at bats. He passed away in Hyannis, Massachusetts on April 4, 1974 and is buried in the Mosswood Cemetery which is in Cotuit, Massachusetts. –1919 Washington Senators

FAIRHAVEN

Jim Cudworth was born in Fairhaven, Massachusetts on August 22, 1858. His first appearance in a major league baseball game was on July 27, 1884 and his last was on September 10, 1884. He played first base and centerfield as well as pitched in his career. As a pitcher in the two games that he pitched he had a record of no wins and no losses and a 4.24 ERA. His batting statistics show him appearing in 32 games where he had a batting average of .147. In 116 at bats he had 17 hits that included three doubles and one triple. He died on December 21, 1943 in Middleboro, Massachusetts and is buried in the Clark cemetery in Lakeville, Massachusetts. –1884 Kansas City Cowboys UA

FALL RIVER

Second baseman **Benny Bowcock** was born in Fall River, Massachusetts on October 28, 1879. His first major league ballgame was on September 18, 1903 and 10 days later on September 28, 1903 he played in his last game. In the 14 games he played in he had 16 hits in 50 at bats. Of those hits, three were doubles, one was a triple and one was a home run. Bowcock passed away on June 16, 1961 in Taunton, Massachusetts and was later buried in St. Mary's Cemetery in the town of Taunton, Massachusetts. – 1903 St Louis Browns AL

Charlie Buffinton (was born Charles G Buffington) was born in Fall River, Massachusetts on June 14, 1861. His first appearance in a major league baseball game was on May 17, 1882 and his last appearance was on June 28, 1892. Buffinton played first base, the outfield and pitched during the course of his career. As a pitcher he appeared in 414 games and had a record of 233 wins and 152 losses. His career earned run average was 2.96 and seven times during the course of his career he won 20 or more games including 1884 when he won 48 games in a season. In 1891 Buffinton led the league in winning percentage when he went with a record for 29 wins and nine losses good enough for a .763 winning percentage. When he batted he was in a total of 586 games and he scored 245 runs and had 255 runs batted in. He had 543 hits including 67 doubles, 17 triples and seven home runs. His lifetime batting average was .245. Buffinton died on September 23, 1907 in Fall River and was buried in Oak Grove Cemetery in Fall River.— 1882-1884Boston Red Stockings NL, 1885-1886 Boston Beaneaters NL 1887-1889 Philadelphia Athletics NL, 1890 Philadelphia Quakers PL, 1891 Boston Reds AA, 1892 Baltimore Orioles NL

Art Butler was born Arthur Edward Bouthiller on December 19, 1887 in Fall River, Massachusetts. He was a shortstop/second baseman and outfielder who debuted in the major leagues on April 14, 1911. His last game in the big leagues was on October 1, 1916. During that time Butler had 311 hits and a batting average of .241. Of those hits 44 were doubles, 13 were triples and three were home runs. He died in Fall River on October 7, 1984 and is buried in Fall River at the Notre Dame Cemetery. – 1911 Boston Rustlers NL, 1912-1913 Pittsburgh Pirates NL, 1914-1916 St Louis Cardinals NL

Fall River, Massachusetts was the home of **Tom Cahill** who was born there in October of 1868. He was a catcher, shortstop and left fielder whose career began in the major leagues on April 9, 1891 and ended on October 4, 1891. Cahill's career hit total was 109 and out of that 17 were doubles, seven were triples and three were home runs. His career batting average was .253 and he also scored 68 runs. He was buried in St. John's Cemetery in Fall River after passing away on December 25, 1894 in Scranton, Pennsylvania

Tom Drohan was born in Fall River, Massachusetts on August 26, 1887. He made his pitching debut in the major leagues on May 1, 1913 and two weeks later on May 16, 1913 pitched in his final game. In the two games he pitched in he did not have a win or a loss and his career ERA was 9.00. He passed away on September 17, 1926 in Kewanee, Illinois and is buried in that town's Pleasant View Cemetery. –1913 Washington Senators AL

Frank Fennelly of Fall River, Massachusetts was born on February 18, 1860 and he made his major league debut on May 1, 1884. He was a shortstop who appeared in a total of 786 games in his career. In those games he scored 609 runs and drove in 408 more runs. He also had a total of 781 hits, of which 102 were doubles, 82 were triples and 34 were home runs. His lifetime batting average was .257. In 1889 Fennelly led the league in runs batted in with 89 and in 1886 he led the league in getting hit by a pitch when that happened to him 18 times. His final game in the majors was on June 18, 1890 and on August 4, 1920 he passed away in Fall River where he was later buried in St. Patrick's Cemetery. – 1884 Washington Nationals AA, 1884-1888 Cincinnati Red Stockings AA, 1888-1889 Philadelphia Athletics AA, 1890 Brooklyn Gladiators AA

From June 5, 1983 until September 27, 1997 **Greg Gagne** was a shortstop in the major leagues. During that time frame he appeared in 1,798 games and had 1,440 hits. Those hits included 298 doubles, 50 triples and 111 home runs. He scored 712 home runs and had 604 runs batted in. Gagne also had a career batting average of .254 and was a member of the World Champion Minnesota Twins in 1987 and 1991. He was born in Fall River, Massachusetts on November 12, 1961. – 1983-1992 Minnesota Twins AL, 1993-1995 Kansas City Royals AL, 1996-1997 Los Angeles Dodgers NL

Tom Gastall was a catcher and a pinch hitter who was born in Fall River, Massachusetts on June 1, 1932. He debuted in the major leagues on June 21, 1955 and played until September 19, 1956. In 52 games he had three doubles and a total of 15 hits and a .181 batting average. One day after his final game in the major leagues he passed away in the town of River Beach, Maryland and he was later buried in Fall River at St. Patrick's Cemetery1955-1956 Baltimore Orioles AL

Russ Gibson, who was born in Fall River, Massachusetts on May 6, 1939, was a catcher in the major leagues from April 14, 1967 until September 6, 1972. His 264 game career showed he had 181 hits that included 34 doubles, four triples and eight home runs. He also had 78 runs batted in and a batting average of .228. He passed away in Swansea, Massachusetts on July 7, 2008 where he is buried in that town's Mt Hope Cemetery. –1967-1969 Boston Red Sox AL, 1970-1972 San Francisco Giants NL

Brandon Gomes has played in the major leagues since May 3, 2011. He was born in Fall River, Massachusetts on July 15, 1984 and in his two year pitching career with the Tampa Bay Rays he has compiled a record of 4-3 with a 3.62 ERA.

Joe Harrington was a shortstop as well as second and third baseman who played in the major leagues September 10, 1895 to July 20, 1896. In the 72 games he played, he scored 47 runs and had 38 runs batted in. Of his 58 hits in the major leagues, he had five doubles and five triples and three home runs. He also had a batting average of .220. He was born in Fall River, Massachusetts on December 21, 1869 and passed away on September 12, 1933 in Fall River where he is buried in St. Patrick's Cemetery in Fall River. – 1895-1896 Boston Beaneaters NL

Second and third base were the positions played by **Matt Howard** in his major league career that lasted from May 17, 1996 until September 18, 1996. In the 35 games he played he had 11 hits including one double, and one home run. His batting average was .204. Howard was born in Fall River, Massachusetts on September 27, 1967. –1996 New York Yankees AL

Allen Levrault was born in Fall River, Massachusetts on August 15, 1977 and made his major league debut on June 13, 2000. As a pitcher he appeared in 56 games and had an ERA of 5.59 and a record of seven wins and 11 losses. His last game in the majors was on June 27, 2003. –2000-2001 Milwaukee Brewers NL, 2003 Florida Marlins NL

January 31, 1862 was the birthday of **Jim Manning** of Fall River, Massachusetts. Manning played the outfield, second base and shortstop in a career that lasted from May 16, 1884 until October 13, 1889. He got into a total of 364 games and scored 188 runs while having 149 runs batted in. He had 39 doubles, 25 triples and eight home runs in his total of 298 hits. His career batting average was .215. He passed away in Edinburg, Texas on October 22, 1929 and is buried in the

North End Burial Ground in Fall River. –1884-1885 Boston Beaneaters NL, 1885-1887 Detroit Wolverines NL, 1889 Kansas City Cowboys AA

Major league pitcher **Mike McDermott** was born in Fall River, Massachusetts on May 6, 1864. His career in the major leagues went from September 2, 1889 until October 13, 1889. In the nine games he appeared in he had a record of one win and eight losses as well as a career ERA of 4.16. He passed away on May 7, 1947 in Fall River and was buried in St. Patrick's Cemetery in that city. –1889 Louisville Colonels AA

Fall River, Massachusetts was home to centerfielder and pitcher **Christopher McFarland**, who was born in Fall River on August 17, 1861. McFarland's career was from April 19, 1884 to April 29, 1884. His batting statistics show that he had three hits in 14 at bats and that one of the hits was a double. His career batting average was .214. As a pitcher in the one game he pitched he was saddled with the loss and ended up with a career ERA of 15.00, McFarland passed away on May 24, 1918 in New Bedford, Massachusetts and is buried in Fall River's Oak Grove Cemetery. – 1884 Baltimore Monumentals UA

Ambrose "Amby" Murray was a pitcher in the major leagues from July 5, 1936 until July 19, 1936. In the four games he pitched in he had a record of no wins and no losses and a 4.09 ERA. He was born June 4, 1913 in Fall River and he passed away in Port Salernom, Florida on February 6, 1997. He was later cremated.—1936 Boston Bees NL

Jerry "Rem Dawg" Remy was born in Fall River, Massachusetts on November 8, 1952. He was a second baseman who got his first start in the major leagues on April 7, 1975. In a career that ended on May 18, 1984 Remy had 1,226 hits in 4,455 at bats for a career batting average of .275. Of those hits, 140 were doubles, 38 were triples and seven were home runs. He had 329 runs batted in and scored 605 runs. He was a member of the 1978 American League All Star team and is now a well-known sportscaster who calls the Boston Red Sox game on NESN. –1975-1977 California Angels

Dick Siebert was a first baseman and a left fielder who was born in Fall River, Massachusetts on February 19, 1912. He played in the major leagues from September 7, 1932 until September 23, 1945. In 1,035 games Siebert had 1,104 hits that included 204 doubles, 40 triples and 32 home runs. He scored 439 runs himself and had 482 runs batted in. His career batting average was .282. He was a member of the 1943 American League All Star team as well. He passed away in Minneapolis, Minnesota on December 9, 1978 and is buried in that city's Lakewood Cemetery. He is the father of Paul Siebert who pitched in the major leagues from1974 until 1978. –1932/1936 Brooklyn Dodgers NL, 1937-1938 St Louis Cardinals NL< 1938-1945 Philadelphia Athletics AL

Catcher Charles "Butch" Sutcliffe was born in Fall River, Massachusetts on July 22, 1915. He was in the major leagues from August 28, 1938 when he played his first game until September 11, 1938 when he played his last game. In his four game career he had one hit in four at bats and a .250 batting average. He passed away in Fall River on March 2, 1994 and is buried in Oak Grove Cemetery in Fall River.—1938 Boston Bees NL

Walter "Red" Torphy was a first baseman in the major leagues from September 25, 1920 until October 3, 1920. He had three hits in 15 at bats and two of those hits were doubles. His career batting average was .200. He was born in Fall River, Massachusetts on November 6, 1891 and passed away on his hometown in February 11, 1980, where he was later buried in the St. Patrick Cemetery. – 1920 Boston Braves NL

Louis "Luke" Urban was a Fall River, Massachusetts native having been born there on March 22, 1898. He debuted in the major leagues on July 19, 1927 as a catcher and he played in his final game on June 21, 1928. In his 50 game career he had 35 hits including five doubles and his career batting average was .273. He died in Somerset, Massachusetts on December 7, 1980 and was later buried in Notre Dame Cemetery in Fall River. – 1927-1928 Boston Braves NL

FALMOUTH

Steve Cishek was born in Falmouth, Massachusetts on June 18, 1986. He pitched in his first ballgame on September 26, 2010 and through the 2012 season he had a record of 7-3 to go with an ERA of 2.57. He has spent his baseball career with the Florida/Miami Marlins of the National League.

FITCHBURG

George Barnacle was born in Fitchburg, Massachusetts on August 26, 1917. In the major leagues he pitched from September 6, 1939 until April 19, 1941. In the 20 games that Barnacle pitched in, he had a record of three wins and three losses and a 6.55 ERA. He passed away on October 10, 1990 in Largo, Florida and is buried in the All Faith's Cemetery in St Petersburg Florida. –1939-1941 Boston Bees/Braves

Jimmy "Nixey" Callahan was a left fielder, third baseman and a pitcher who played in the major leagues from May 12, 1894 until July 29, 1913. In the 923 games he was credited for batting in, Callahan had 901 hits including 135 doubles, 46 triples and 11 home runs as well as 394 runs batted in and 442 runs scored. His career batting average was .272. As a pitcher Callahan appeared in a total of 195 games and had a record of 99 wins and 73 losses to go with a 3.39 career earned run average. During the 1898 and 1899 season Callahan recorded 20 and 21 wins respectively. He was born in Fitchburg, Massachusetts on March 18, 1874 and passed away on October 4, 1934 in Boston. He is buried in St. Bernard's Cemetery in Fitchburg, Massachusetts. – 1894 Philadelphia Phillies NL, 1897-1900 Chicago Colts/Orphans NL, 1901-1913 Chicago White Sox AL

Catcher and left fielder **Gene Derby** was born in Fitchburg, Massachusetts on February 3, 1860. His major league career was from September 3, 1885 until September 30, 1885. In the 10 games he played in he had four hits and also scored four runs. His career batting average was .129, and he also had two runs batted in. He passed away on Waterbury,

Connecticut on September 13, 1917 and is buried in the Glens Falls Cemetery in Glens Falls, New York.- 1885 Baltimore Orioles AA

Fitchburg is also the hometown of **John Keefe** who pitched in the major leagues from April 28, 1890 until October 11, 1890. In his 43 game career Keefe had a record of 17 wins and 24 losses and a 4.32 ERA. He was born on July 16, 1867 in Fitchburg and passed away there on August 10, 1937. He is buried in Fitchburg's St. Bernard Cemetery. – 1890 Syracuse Stars AA

Catching and third base were the positions of **Pat Moran** in his career. Moran, who was born in Fitchburg, Massachusetts on February 7, 1876, got his start in the major leagues on May 15, 1901 and he played in his final game on June 5, 1914. For the 818 games he played, he had 262 runs batted in and also scored 198 runs himself. He had 618 hits that included 102 doubles, 24 triples and 18 home runs. His lifetime batting average was .235. He was a member of the 1907 World Champion Chicago Cubs as well. He died in Orlando, Florida on March 7, 1924 and is buried in St. Bernard's Cemetery in Fitchburg. –1901-1905 Boston Beaneaters NL, 1906-1909 Chicago Cubs NL, 1910-1914 Philadelphia Phillies NL

March 25, 1856 was the birthday of **Martin Powell**. The Fitchburg, Massachusetts native was a first baseman who started his big league career on June 18, 1881 and ended it on August 10, 1884. In 279 games he had 213 hits that included 43 doubles, 11 triples and three home runs as well as 115 runs batted in. He died on February 5, 1888 in Fitchburg and is buried in the St. Bernard's Cemetery in Fitchburg. –1881-1883 Detroit Wolverines NL, 1884 Cincinnati Outlaw Reds UA

Ray Tift pitched in the major leagues from August 7, 1907 until September 2, 1907. In four games he had a record of 0-0 with a 4.74 ERA. He was born in Fitchburg on June 12, 1884, and he later passed away on March 29, 1945 in Verona, New Jersey. He is buried in the Rosedale Cemetery in the town on Linden, New Jersey. – 1907 New York Highlanders AL

June 20, 1889 is the birthday of **Ed Warner** of Fitchburg, Massachu-
setts. Warner played in the major leagues from July 2, 1912 until
August 26, 1912. He pitched in 11 games and had a record of one win
and one loss and an ERA of 3.60. He passed away in New York, New
York on February 5, 1954 and is buried in the Forest Hill Cemetery in
Fitchburg.—1912 Pittsburgh Pirates NL

FRAMINGHAM

Stan Benjamin was an outfielder and a first baseman who made his
major league debut on September 16, 1939. He played in his final game
on September 16, 1945. In his 241 game career he had 176 hits that
included 32 doubles, 11 triples and five home runs. His lifetime batting
average was .229. He was born in in Framingham, Massachusetts on
May 20, 1914 and passed away in Harwich, Massachusetts on December
24, 2009. He is buried in Green River Cemetery in Greenfield, Massachusetts. –1939-1942 Philadelphia Phillies NL, 1945 Cleveland Indians AL

Utility infielder **Lou Merloni** was born in Framingham, Massachusetts on April 6, 1971 He made his major league debut on May
10, 1998 and played in his final game on June 4, 2006. He played
second and third base as well as shortstop in a career that lasted for
423 games. In those games Merloni had 294 hits that included 67
doubles, seven triples and 14 home runs. His career batting average
was .271. –1998-2002 Boston Red Sox AL, 2003 San Diego Padres 2003
NL, 2003 Boston Red Sox AL, 2004 Cleveland Indians AL, 2005 Los
Angeles Angels AL, 2006 Cleveland Indians AL

Jeff Plympton was born in Framingham, Massachusetts on November
24, 1965. His first appearance in a major league ballgame was as a
pitcher on June 15, 1991 and his final appearance was on September
16, 1991. In four games he did not record a win or a loss and his ERA
was 0.00 – 1991 Boston Red Sox AL

John Quinn had a career in the major leagues that lasted only one game
and that game was on October 9, 1911. He was a catcher in that game

and in two at bats he did not have a hit. He was born in Framingham, Massachusetts on September 12, 1885 and he passed away on April 9, 1956 in Marlborough, Massachusetts. He is buried in St. Mary's Cemetery in Mansfield, Massachusetts. – 1911 Philadelphia Phillies NL

Dave Schuler was born in Framingham on October 4, 1953. He was a pitcher who debuted in the major leagues on September 17, 1979 and ended his career on October 2, 1985. In 18 games he had no wins and one loss and his career earned run average was 5.40. 1979-1980 California Angels AL, 1985 Atlanta Braves NL

Harold Joseph "Pie" Traynor was born in Framingham, Massachusetts on November 11, 1898. He debuted in the major leagues on September 15, 1920 and spent his entire playing career with the Pittsburgh Pirates. In 1941 games Traynor had 2,416 hits that included 371 doubles, 164 triples and 58 home runs. He also had scored 1,183 runs and had 1,273 runs batted in. Inn 1923, 25, 27,28,29,30 and 31, he had 100 or more runs batted in and in 1923 he led the league in triples with 19. He was also a member of the 1925 World Champion Pittsburgh Pirates and was a two time National League All Star selection. His lifetime batting average of .320 is good enough for 54th best of all time. He played his final game in Pittsburgh on August 14, 1937 and was later elected to the Baseball Hall of Fame in 1948. From 1944 until 1966 he was the Pirates radio broadcaster and he was ranked 70th on the Sporting News 100 best baseball players of all time. He passed away in Pittsburgh on March 16, 1972 and is buried in Homewood Cemetery in Pittsburgh.

Major league pitcher **Ken Turner** was born in Framingham, Massachusetts on August 17, 1943. He made his major league debut June 11, 1967 and pitched in his final game on July 16, 1967. In 13 big league appearances he had a record of 1 win and 2 losses and a 4.45 ERA. – 1967 California Angels

Lance Zawadzki was a shortstop and a second baseman as well as a pinch hitter in a major league career that started on May 2, 2010. He has appeared in 20 games and has a total of seven hits. He has also scored four runs. He was born in Framingham, Massachusetts on May 25, 1985 –2010 San Diego Padres NL

FRANKLIN

Al Boucher was born in Franklin, Massachusetts on November 13, 1881. He was a third baseman who got into this first major league baseball game on April 16, 1914. His final game was on October 8, 1914. In the 147 games he appeared in he had 119 hits including 26 doubles, four triples and two home runs. He also had 49 runs batted in and a career batting average of .231. He passed away in Torrance, California on June 23, 1974 and is buried in Holy Cross Cemetery and Mausoleum in Culver City, California. – 1914 St Louis Terriers FL

Eddie Grant was born in Franklin, Massachusetts on May 21, 1883. He played third base and shortstop in his career which began on August 4, 1905 and ended on October 6, 1915. He was one of the better third basemen in the league at the time. He did not hit for a lot of power, but he was a crackerjack around the hot corner. His career batting average was .249, and he had a total of 844 hits including 79 doubles, 30 triples and five home runs. He also drove in 277 runs. Grant retired in 1915 and had made plans to work at the law practice he had in the Boston area. However, all that was interrupted by World War I and Grant became the first major league player active or inactive to enlist in the military. While he was on patrol in the Argonne Forest in France, a shell came through the trees and wounded two of Grant's lieutenants. As Grant was calling for stretchers and medics, he was struck and killed instantly by a shell. He was buried in the Argonne Forest only a short distance from where he was killed. He is now buried in the Meuse Argonne American Cemetery in Romagne, France. The date of his death was October 2, 1918. On Memorial Day in 1921 there was a monument of Grant that was unveiled at the Polo Grounds in New York City. He was also honored by having a highway in the Bronx named after him as well as the baseball field at Dean Junior College. He also has two

American Legion Posts named after him as well. – 1905 Cleveland Naps AL, 1907-1910 Philadelphia Phillies NL, 1911-1913 Cincinnati Reds NL,1913-1915 New York Giants NL

GEORGETOWN

Fred Tenney was a first baseman, outfielder and catcher in the major leagues from June 16, 1894 until October 7, 1911. Tenney appeared in a total of 1,994 games and had a total of 2,231 hits. Of those hits 270 were doubles, 77 were triples and 22 were home runs. He also had 688 runs batted in and a lifetime batting average of .294. It was thought by many people that Tenney ranked only behind Hal Chase when it came to fielding prowess by a first baseman in the "Deadball Era." He was born in Georgetown, Massachusetts on November 26, 1871, and he was buried in Harmony Cemetery in Georgetown after passing away in Boston on July 3, 1952. –1894-1906 Boston Beaneaters NL, 1907 Boston Doves NL, 1908-1909 NY Giants NL, 1911 Boston Rustlers NL

GLOUCESTER

Hank Camelli was born in Gloucester, Massachusetts on December 9, 1914. In his major league career which ran from October 3, 1943 until September 28, 1947, he was a catcher who appeared in 159 games and had a total of 86 hits that included 15 doubles, four triples and two home runs. He also had a .229 batting average and 26 runs batted in. He passed away in Wellesley, Massachusetts on July 14, 1996 and he is buried in Woodlawn Cemetery. –1943-1946 Pittsburgh Pirates NL, 1947 Boston Braves NL

Alfred "Fred" Doe pitched for one week in the major leagues from August 23, 1890 until August 30, 1890. Doe, who was born in Gloucester, Massachusetts on April 18, 1864, had a record of no wins and one loss as well as a career ERA of 9.00. He passed away on October 4, 1938 and was buried in the Oak Grove Cemetery in Gloucester, Massachusetts. Doe also spent many years as a player and a manger in the old New England League and it was through his efforts and many others that it would end up being possible to play baseball on Sundays in Massachusetts. – 1890 Buffalo Bisons/ Pittsburgh Burghers PL

Gloucester, Massachusetts was the birthplace of **Billy MacLeod** on May 13, 1942. He was a pitcher in the major leagues from September 13, 1962 until September 22, 1962. He only appeared in two games in the major leagues and had a record of no wins and one loss to go with the 5.40 ERA he had for his career.—1962 Boston Red Sox AL

John Phalen "Stuffy" McInnis was born in Gloucester, Massachusetts on September 19, 1890. He was a first baseman who began his major league career on April 12, 1909. Between that date in April and August 1, 1927 McInnis appeared in a total of 2,128 games and had a total of 2,405 hits including 312 doubles, 101 triples and 20 home runs. He scored 872 runs and had 1,062 runs batted in. He only struck out 251 times in 8,634 plate appearances and he had a .307 batting average, which is good enough to place him 126th on the all-time list for that statistic. It was as a fielder that McInnis really shined, as he handled 21,360 chances at first base and made only 160 errors, which is good enough for 89th place as that figured out to a .993 average. He was a member of the 1911 and 1913 World Champion Philadelphia Athletics, the 1918 World Champion Boston Red Sox and the World Champion Pittsburgh Pirates of 1925. When McInnis was a member of the Philadelphia Athletics he was a member of the famous $100,000 infield along with Eddie Collins, Jack Barry and Frank "Home Run" Baker. McInnis was the youngest member of that infield. He later coached at the collegiate level at Harvard University. He passed away in Ipswich, Massachusetts on February 16, 1960 and is buried in the Rosedale Cemetery in Manchester, Massachusetts. –1909-1917 Philadelphia Athletics AL, 1918- 1921 Boston Red Sox AL, 1922 Cleveland Indians AL, 1923-1924 Boston Braves NL, 1925-1926 Pittsburgh Pirates NL, 1927 Philadelphia Phillies NL

Ralph Foster "Cy" Perkins caught in the major leagues from September

15, 1915 until September 30, 1934. In the 1,171 games he appeared in, he had 933 hits that included 175 doubles, 35 triples and 30 home runs. He also had 409 runs batted in and he scored 329 runs himself. His lifetime batting average was .259. He was born in Gloucester, Massachusetts on February 27, 1896 and passed away in Philadelphia, Pennsylvania on October 2, 1963. He is buried in the Oak Grove Cemetery in Gloucester, Massachusetts. –1915-1930 Philadelphia Athletics AL, 1931 New York Yankees AL, 1934 Detroit Tigers AL

GRAFTON

May 23, 1885 was the birthday of **Hugh Bradley**, a right fielder and first baseman who hailed from Grafton, Massachusetts. He played in the major leagues from April 25, 1910 until September 7, 1915. In the 277 games he appeared in he had 238 hits. 46 of the hits were doubles, 12 were triples and two were home runs. He had 117 runs batted in and he scored 84 runs himself. His lifetime batting average was .261. He passed away on January 26, 1949 in Worcester, Massachusetts and he is buried in Worcester's St John's Cemetery. He is also the nephew of George "Foghorn" Bradley who played in the major leagues from August 23, 1876 until October 21, 1876. – 1910-1912 Boston Red Sox AL, 1914-1915 Pittsburgh Rebels FL, 1915 Brooklyn Tip-Tops FL, 1915 Newark Pepper FL

Warren "Hick" Carpenter was born in Grafton, Massachusetts on August 16, 1855. He played in his first major league game on May 1, 1879 and played in his last game on July 31, 1892. He was a first and third baseman that had a total of 1,202 hits that included 142 doubles, 47 triples and 18 home runs. He had 543 runs batted in and had a .259 batting average. In 1882 he led the league in hits with 120 and runs batted in with 67. He passed away on April 18, 1937 in San Diego, California and is buried in that city's Mount Hope Cemetery. – 1879 Syracuse Stars NL, 1880 Cincinnati Reds NL, 1881 Worcester Ruby Legs NL, 1882-1889 Cincinnati Red Stockings AA, 1892 St Louis Browns

Asa Straton was born in Grafton, Massachusetts on February 10, 1853. His career in major league baseball lasted one game and the date on that game was June 17, 1881. He was a shortstop that played for the Worcester Ruby Legs that day going one for four which was good enough for a .250 batting average. He passed away in Fitchburg, Massachusetts on August 13, 1925 and is buried in Grafton's Riverside Cemetery.

GREAT BARRINGTON

Jim Garry—SEE BERKSHIRE COUNTY BORN PLAYERS

GREENFIELD

Peter Bergeron was born in Greenfield, Massachusetts on November 9, 1977. He played centerfield in the major leagues from September 7, 1999 until April 18, 2004. He was in a total of 308 games and had 249 hits in 1,103 at bats. He had 41 doubles, 13 triples and eight home runs. He was also able to score 171 runs and had a career batting average of .226. –1999-2004 Montreal Expos NL

Steve Partenheimer was a third baseman in the major leagues who was born in Greenfield, Massachusetts on August 30, 1891. June 28, 1913 was his only appearance in a major league baseball game and it came as a third baseman for the Detroit Tigers. He did not have a hit in three at bats. He passed away in Mansfield, Ohio on June 16, 1971 and is buried in his home town of Greenfield at the Green River Cemetery. He is also the father of Stan Partenheimer, who played in the major leagues in 1944 and 1945.

Greenfield, Massachusetts native **Dave Wissman** was a left fielder and a pinch hitter who played in the major leagues from September 15, 1964 until October 4, 1964. He had four hits in 16 games for a .148 batting average and he was born in Greenfield on February 17, 1941. –1964 Pittsburgh Pirates NL

GROVELAND

Jim McGinley was a pitcher in the major leagues from September 22, 1904 until May 5, 1905. McGinley was born in Groveland, Massachusetts on October 2, 1878 and in the four games he appeared in he had a record of two wins and two losses and a 3.30 ERA. He passed away in Haverhill, Massachusetts and is buried in Riverview Cemetery in Groveland. 1904-1905 St Louis Cardinals NL

June 15, 1897 in Groveland, Massachusetts was the birthday of **Edwin "Cy" Twombly**. He debuted in the major leagues on June 25, 1921 and pitched in his final game on August 17, 1921. He was a pitcher and in the seven games he appeared in he had a record of one win and two losses and a 5.86 ERA. He died on December 3, 1974 in Savannah, Georgia and is buried in Lexington, Virginia at the Stonewall Jackson Cemetery. –1921 Chicago White Sox AL

HARDWICK

Left fielder **Jack McCarthy** was born in Hardwick, Massachusetts on March 26, 1869. He played in the major leagues from August 3, 1893 until May 25, 1907. In the 1,092 games that he played in, he had 1,205 hits that included 171 doubles, 66 triples and eight home runs. He also had 476 runs batted in and scored 551 runs. His career batting average was .287. –1893-1894 Cincinnati Reds NL, 1898-1899 Pittsburgh Pirates NL, 1900 Chicago Orphans NL, 1901-1903 Cleveland Naps AL, 1903-1905 Chicago Cubs NL, 1906-1907 Brooklyn Superbas NL

HAVERHILL

Sam Fishburn was born in Haverhill, Massachusetts on May 15, 1893. He made his major league debut on May 30, 1919 and played first and second base as well as pinch running for his career which ended on July 19, 1919. In nine games he had one single and one double and two runs batted in. His batting average was .333. He passed away on April 11, 1965 in Bethlehem, Pennsylvania and was buried in the Cedar Hill Memorial Park in Allentown, Pennsylvania. – 1919 St Louis Cardinals NL

Hal Janvrin (also known as Harold Childe) was born in Haverhill on August 27, 1892. He played first and second base as well as shortstop in a career that started on July 9, 1911 and ended on October 1, 1922. He was in a total of 792 games and had 515 hits that included 68 doubles, 18 triples and eight home runs. He also drove in 210 runs and had scored 250 runs himself. His life time batting average was .232. He was also a member of the 1915 and 1916 World Champion Boston Red Sox. He passed away in Boston on March 1, 1962 and is buried in the Exeter Cemetery in Exeter, New Hampshire. – 1911-1917 Boston Red Sox AL, 1919 Washington Senators AL, 1919-1921 St Louis Cardinals NL, 1921-1922 Brooklyn Robins NL

Danny Mahoney was born on September 6, 1888 in Haverhill, Massachusetts. He appeared in only one game for the Cincinnati Reds in 1911 and did not record and official at bat in the game. He passed away on September 28, 1960 in Utica, New York and is buried in the St Bernard Cemetery in Waterville, New York

Major league catcher and first baseman **Jack Ryan** was born in Haverhill, Massachusetts on November 12, 1868. He debuted in the big leagues in September 2, 1889 and played in his final game on October 4, 1913. In 616 games he was credited with 476 hits including 69 doubles, 29 triples and four home runs. He scored 245 runs and had 189 runs batted in. His lifetime batting average was .217. He passed away on August 21, 1952 in Boston and is buried in the St. James Cemetery in Haverhill. – 1889-1891 Louisville Colonels AA, 18894-1896 Boston Beaneaters NL, 1898 Brooklyn Bridegrooms NL, 1899 Baltimore Orioles NL,1901-1903 St Louis Cardinals NL, 1912-1913 Washington Senators AL

Mike Ryan was born in Haverhill, Massachusetts on November 25, 1941 and played in the big leagues from October 3, 1964 until September 10, 1974. In 636 games he had 370 hits. He had 60 doubles, 12 triples and 28 home runs. He scored 146 runs and had 161 runs batted in. His lifetime batting average was .193. –1964-1967 Boston Red Sox AL, 1968-1973 Philadelphia Phillies NL, 1974 Pittsburgh Pirates NL

Mike Welch was a pitcher in the major leagues who debuted on July 17, 1998. He played in his final game on September 27, 1998. He appeared in 10 games and had an ERA of 8.27 and a record of zero wins and two losses. He was born in Haverhill, Massachusetts on August 25, 1972. – 1998 Philadelphia Phillies

Frank Wyman made his major league debut on June 10, 1884. During his career he was a pitcher, outfielder and first baseman. Batting he is credited with appearing in 32 games with 30 hits, four of which were doubles. He scored 17 runs and had a .227 batting average. Pitching he played in three games and had a record of no wins and one loss as well as a 6.86 ERA. He played his last game in the major leagues on August 9, 1884. He was born in Haverhill on May 10, 1862 and is buried in the Linwood Cemetery in Haverhill after passing away on February 4, 1916 in Everett, Massachusetts. –1884 Kansas City Cowboys/Chicago Pittsburgh UA

HOLBROOK

Holbrook, Massachusetts is the birthplace of **Ollie Hanson** who was a pitcher in the major leagues. Hanson was born on January 19, 1896 and played in the major leagues from April 27, 1921 until May 5, 1921. He had a record of no wins and two losses and an ERA of 7.00. He passed away in Clifton, New Jersey on August 19, 1951 and is buried in Patterson, New Jersey at Cedar Lawn Cemetery. – 1921 Chicago Cubs NL

HOLDEN

Bruce Taylor was born in Holden, Massachusetts on April 16, 1953. He was a pitcher who debuted in August 5, 1977 and appeared in 30 games with the final game being on May 22, 1979. He had a record of two wins and two losses and an ERA of 3.86. –1977-1979 Detroit Tigers

HOLYOKE

Bob Adams was born in Holyoke, Massachusetts on July 24, 1901. His pitching career was two games long, September 22 and September 23 1925. He did not record a win or a loss and his career ERA was 7.94. He passed away in Lemoyne, Pennsylvania on October 17, 1996. –1925 Boston Red Sox AL

Richard "Dick" Burns was born in Holyoke, Massachusetts on December 26, 1863. He pitched and played the outfield in his career which ran from May 3, 1883 until July 23, 1885. In 58 games as a pitcher he had a record of 25 wins and 27 losses, including one season when he won 23 games and lost 15. His career ERA was 3.07. As a batter he is credited with being in 130 games with 97 hits. Of those hits, 26 were doubles, 14 were triples and four home runs. In the 1884 season he was the Union Association leader in triples with 13. He had a lifetime batting average of .267. He died November 16, 1937 in Holyoke and is buried in Calvary Cemetery in Holyoke, Massachusetts. – 1883 Detroit Wolverines NL, 1884 Cincinnati Outlaw Reds UA, 1885 St Louis Maroons NL

Patrick "Pat or Doc" Carney was a right fielder and a pitcher who was born in Holyoke, Massachusetts on August 7, 1876. He made his major league debut on September 20, 1901 and played in his final game on August 31, 1904. In the 338 games he was credited for batting in, he had 308 hits including 36 doubles, 11 triples and three home runs. He had 143 runs scored and 131 runs batted in and a .247 batting average. As a pitcher he appeared in 16 games with a record of four wins and 10 losses and a 4.69 ERA. He passed away in Worcester, Massachusetts on January 9, 1953 and is buried in St. John's Cemetery in Worcester. –1901-1904 Boston Beaneaters NL

Jerome "Jerry" Conway was born in Holyoke, Massachusetts on June 7, 1901. His first and only appearance in a major league baseball game was on August 31, 1920 and he did not record a win or a loss or allow a run in the two innings he pitched. He died April 16, 1980 in Holyoke, Massachusetts and is buried in the city of Holyoke's St. Jerome's Cemetery. – 1920 Washington Senators AL

Holyoke is also the home town of James **Joseph "Skip" Dowd** who was a major league pitcher for one game on July 5, 1910. He did not figure in the win or the loss that day. He was born February 16, 1889 and passed away in Holyoke on December 20, 1960. He is buried in St. Jerome's Cemetery. – 1910 Pittsburgh Pirates NL

Tommy "Buttermilk Tommy" Dowd was an outfielder and a second baseman who was born in Holyoke, Massachusetts on April 20, 1869. He made his major league debut on April 8, 1891 and played in his final game on September 28, 1901. He appeared in 1,321 games and had 1,493 hits and 903 runs scored. He had 168 doubles, 88 triples and 24 home runs. He also had 501 runs batted in and a lifetime batting average of .271. He was the first ever batter for the Boston Americans (later to become the Red Sox) as he led off in a game on April 26, 1901 against the Baltimore Orioles. Dowd passed away on July 3, 1933 in Holyoke and is buried in Calvary Cemetery in Holyoke. –1891 Boston Reds AA, 1891 Washington Statesmen AA, 1892 Washington Senators NL,1893-1897 St Louis Browns NL, 1897 Philadelphia Phillies NL, 1898 St Louis Browns NL, 1899 Cleveland Spiders NL, 1901 Boston Americans AL

Jack Hannifin was born in Holyoke, Massachusetts on February 25, 1883. He made his first start in a major league baseball game on April 19, 1906 and he remained a major leaguer until October 7, 1908. He was a shortstop as well as a first and third baseman. In 158 games he scored 50 runs and had 94 hits, of which there were 13 doubles, six triples and three home runs. He also had a .214 batting average and drove in 40 runs. He was buried in St. Jerome's Cemetery in Holyoke after he passed away on October 27, 1945 in Northampton, Massachusetts. –1906 Philadelphia Athletics AL, 1906-1908 New York Giants NL, 1908 Boston Doves NL

Fran Healy was born in Holyoke, Massachusetts on September 6,

1946 and caught in the major leagues from September 3, 1969 until April 21, 1978. Healy appeared in 470 games and had 332 hits including 60 doubles, six triples and 20 home runs. He also had 141 runs batted in and a .250 batting average. He is the nephew of Francis Healy who was a major league baseball player from 1930 until 1934. –1969 Kansas City Royals AL, 1970-1972 San Francisco Giants NL, 1973-1976 Kansas City Royals AL, 1976-1978 New York Yankees AL

Francis Healy was born in Holyoke, Massachusetts on July 29, 1910. He began his career in the major leagues on April 29, 1930 and played in the majors until September 26, 1934. He was a catcher and a pinch hitter who was in 42 games and had 13 hits including three doubles. He batted .241 for his career. He died in Springfield, Massachusetts on February 12, 1997 and is buried in St. Jerome's Cemetery in Holyoke. He is the uncle of Fran Healy, who played in the major leagues from 1969 to 1978. – 1930-1932 New York Giants NL, 1934 St Louis Cardinals NL

Frank Leja was a first baseman and pinch hitter and pinch runner who played in the major leagues from May 1, 1954 until April 29, 1962. In 26 games he had one hit and scored three runs. His career batting average was .043. He was born in Holyoke, Massachusetts on February 7, 1936 and passed away in Boston, Massachusetts on May 3, 1991. He is buried in Greenlawn Cemetery in Nahant, Massachusetts. – 1954-1955 New York Yankees, 1962 Los Angeles Angels AL

Joe "Scooch" Lucey was born in Holyoke on March 27, 1897 and debuted in the major leagues on July 6, 1920. He played in the majors as a shortstop and second baseman as well as pitching with his final appearance being June 25, 1925. In the seven games he pitched in he had a record of no wins and one loss and a 9.00 ERA. As a batter he was credited with appearing in 13 games and had two hits for a batting average of .111. He passed away in Holyoke, Massachusetts on June 30, 1980 and is buried in Calvary Cemetery in Holyoke. –1920 Boston Red Sox AL, 1925 New York Yankees AL

Mike Lynch was born in Holyoke, Massachusetts on June 28, 1880 and debuted on June 21, 1904 in the major leagues. His final appearance was on September 25, 1907 and he was a pitcher who appeared in 97 games. His lifetime record was 43 wins and 32 losses and he had an ERA of 3.05. He passed away in Garrison, New York on April 2, 1927 and is buried in St Francis Cemetery in Pawtucket, Rhode Island. –1904-1907 Pittsburgh Pirates NL, 1907 New York Giants NL

Right fielder **Roger "Noonie" Marquis** was born in Holyoke, Massachusetts on April 5, 1937. He appeared in his only big league game on September 25, 1955 for the Baltimore Orioles. He did not get a hit in his only at bat. He passed away on July 19, 2004 in Holyoke, Massachusetts and is buried in Notre Dame Cemetery in South Hadley, Massachusetts.

Eddie Mayo was also known by the nickname of "Hotshot" and he was born in Holyoke on April 15, 1910. He played in the major leagues from May 22, 1936 until October 3, 1948. He played second and third base and appeared in 834 games. He had a total of 759 hits that included 119 doubles, 16 triples and 26 home runs. He also scored 350 runs and had 287 runs batted in. His lifetime batting average was .252 and he was also a member of the 1945 World Champion Detroit Tigers. He passed away on November 27, 2006 in Banning, California and he was later cremated. –1936 New York Giants NL, 1937-1938 Boston Bees NL, 1943 Philadelphia Athletics AL, 1944-1948 Detroit Tigers AL

October 12, 1912 was the birthday of **Ed Moriarty** of Holyoke, Massachusetts. Ed was a second baseman and a pinch hitter in the major leagues. He had a career that lasted from June 21, 1935 until May 12, 1936. In his 14 game career Moriarty had 12 hits including two doubles, one triple and one home run. He had a batting average of .300. He died on September 29, 1991 in Holyoke and is buried in Calvary Cemetery in Holyoke. –1935-1936 Boston Braves/Bees NL

Gene Moriarty was born in Holyoke, Massachusetts on January 6, 1863. His major league debut came on June 18, 1884 and his career lasted until October 15, 1892. He played leftfield and third base and also appeared in three games as a pitcher with a record of zero wins and two losses and a 5.74 ERA. Batting statistics show him in 72 games scoring 26 runs and having 23 runs batted in. He had 41 hits, including five doubles, three triples and three home runs with a .152 batting average. –1884 Boston Beaneaters NL,1884 Indianapolis Hosiers AA, 1885 Detroit Wolverines NL, 1892 St Louis Browns NL

Ray Nelson, who was a major league baseball player as a second baseman, was born in Holyoke, Massachusetts on August 4, 1875. May 6, 1901 to August 16, 1901 was the extent of his career in the major leagues. He was in 39 games and had 26 total hits that included two doubles. His lifetime batting average was .200 and he died in Mount Vernon, New York on January 8, 1961.—1901 New York Giants NL

Dennis O'Neil was born in Holyoke, Massachusetts on November 22, 1886. His major league career as a first baseman was from June 18, 1893 until July 26, 1893. In seven games he had three hits and scored three runs with a .120 batting average. He passed away on November 15, 1912 in Rushville, Indiana and is buried in St. Jerome's Cemetery in Holyoke. –1893 St Louis Browns NL

Tommy "Foghorn" Tucker was a major league first baseman who played from April 16, 1887 until September 13, 1899. He appeared in 1,688 games and had 1,882 hits including 240 doubles, 85 triples and 42 homeruns. He scored 1,084 runs and had 932 runs batted in and a lifetime batting average of .290. In 1889 he led the American Association in hits with 196, and was also the league leader in batting with a .372 average. Tucker passed away on October 22, 1935 in Montague, Massachusetts and is buried in the Calvary Cemetery in Holyoke. –1887-1889 Baltimore Orioles AA, 1890-1897 Boston Beaneaters NL, 1897 Washington Senators NL, 1898 Brooklyn Bridegrooms NL, 1898 St Louis Browns NL, 1899 Cleveland Spiders NL

Mark Wohlers was a pitcher in the major leagues from August 17, 1991 until September 28, 2002. He appeared in 533 major league ballgames and had a record of 39 wins and 29 losses, 119 saves and a 3.97 ERA. He was a member of the Atlanta Braves during the 1990's when they were the dominant National League ball club. He was a member of the Braves in 1995 when they won the World Series Championship and was also a member of the 1996 National League All Star team.

He was born in Holyoke on January 23, 1970.—1991-1999 Atlanta Braves NL, 2000-2001 Cincinnati Reds NL, 2001 New York Yankees AL, 2002 Cleveland Indians AL.

HYDE PARK

Willard "Bill" Morrell was born in Hyde Park, Massachusetts on April 9, 1893 and made his debut in the major leagues as a pitcher on April 20, 1926. He pitched in the majors until August 5, 1931 and appeared in a total of 48 games. He had a record of eight wins and six losses to go with a 4.64 ERA. He passed away in Birmingham, Alabama on August 5, 1975 and is buried in Birmingham at the Elmwood Cemetery. –1926 Washington Senators AL, 1930-1931 New York Giants NL

IPSWICH

Joseph Burns was born in Ipswich, Massachusetts on March 26, 1889. His first appearance in the major leagues was on June 19, 1910 and he was a left fielder who appeared in five games with the last game being on September 23, 1913. He had six hits on 14 at bats and a .429 batting average. He passed away in Beverly, Massachusetts on July 12, 1987 and is buried in the Highland Cemetery in Ipswich.

Chet Nourse was an Ipswich native having been born there on August 7, 1887. He debuted in the major leagues on July 27, 1909 and pitched in the major leagues until August 4, 1909. In three games he did not record a win or a loss and had a 7.20 ERA. He passed away on Clearwater, Florida on April 20, 1958 and is buried in the Oak Hill Cemetery in Newburyport. – 1909 Boston Red Sox AL

JAMAICA PLAIN

Leo Callahan was an outfielder in the major league from April 9, 1913 until September 28, 1919. He only played in the 1913 and 1919

season appearing in a total of 114 games. He had 17 doubles, five triples and one home run and scored 32 runs himself. He also had a batting average of .221. He was born in Jamaica Plain, Massachusetts on August 9, 1890 and passed away in Erie, Pennsylvania on May 2, 1982. He was buried in the Calvary Cemetery in Oil City, Pennsylvania. – 1913 Brooklyn Superbas NL, 1919 Philadelphia Phillies NL

John "Tip" Tobin was born in Jamaica Plain on September 15, 1906. He was a pinch hitter who made his only appearance in a major league ballgame on September 22, 1932. He passed away in Rhinebeck, New York on August 6, 1983. – 1932 New York Giants NL

Clarence "Babe" Twombly was born in Jamaica Plain on January 18, 1896. His major league debut was on April 14, 1920. He was an outfielder and a pinch hitter for his career which ended on October 2, 1921. He played in 165 baseball games and scored 47 runs and had 32 runs batted in. He also had a total of 109 hits that included nine doubles, two triples and three home runs to go with his lifetime batting average of .304. He was also the brother of George Twombly who played in the major leagues from 1914 until 1919. Babe Twombly passed away on November 23, 1974 in San Clemente, California and is buried in Glendora, California at the Oakdale Memorial Park. –1920-1921 Chicago Cubs

LAKEVILLE

Cyril "Cy" Morgan was born in Lakeville, Massachusetts on November 11, 1895. He was a pitcher who appeared in his first baseball game on the major league level on June 8, 1921 and then played until May 1, 1922. In 19 appearances Morgan had a record of one win one loss and a 7.39 earned run average. He died in Lakeville on September 11, 1946 and is buried in East Harwich Cemetery in East Harwich, Massachusetts. –1920-1921 Boston Braves

LAWRENCE

Johnny Broaca was born in Lawrence, Massachusetts on October 3, 1909. He pitched in the major leagues from June 2, 1934 until September 23, 1939. In 121 games Broaca had a record of 44 wins and 29 losses and a 4.08 ERA. He died in Lawrence on May 16, 1985 and is buried in the Immaculate Conception Cemetery in Lawrence. 1934-1937 New York Yankees AL, 1939 Cleveland Indians AL

James Patrick "Doc" Casey was born in Lawrence, Massachusetts on March 15, 1870. His first appearance in a major league baseball game was on September 14, 1898. He played third base until his final game which was on October 5, 1907. He played in 1,114 games and had 1,122 hits that included 137 doubles, 52 triples and nine home runs. He scored 584 runs and had 354 runs batted in, and his lifetime batting average was .258. He passed away on December 31, 1936 in Detroit, Michigan and is buried in the Mount Olivet Cemetery in Detroit. – 1898-1899 Washington Senators NL, 1899-1900 Brooklyn Superbas NL, 1901-1902 Detroit Tigers AL, 1903-1905 Chicago Cubs NL, 1906-1907 Brooklyn Superbas NL

John Crowley was born in Lawrence, Massachusetts on January 12, 1862. He was a catcher and played in his first game on May 1, 1884. He played in 48 major league baseball games with the last one being on September 10, 1884. He had a lifetime batting average of .244 and had a total of 41 hits that included seven doubles and three triples. He passed away on September 23, 1896 in Lawrence and is buried in St. Mary's Cemetery in Lawrence. 1884 Philadelphia Quakers NL

William "Wild Bill" Donovan was born in Lawrence, Massachusetts on October 13, 1876. During the course of his major league career which began on April 22, 1898 and ended on September 2, 1918, Donovan played the outfield and first base as well as pitched. When he was credited with batting in a game he appeared in 459 games and had 251 hits that included 30 doubles, 11 triples and seven home runs. His batting average was .193. He was a much better pitcher as he had a record of 185 wins and 139 losses in 378 games. His career

ERA was a respectable 2.69 and he twice won 20 or more games in a season (1901- 25 wins, 1907 25 wins). In 1901 he was the league leader in wins with 25, and games appeared in with 45. In 1903 he was the American League leader in complete games with 34 and in 1907 when he went with a record of 25 wins and only four losses, he was the league leader in winning percentage with a .862 wins percentage. Donovan had come up with a sore arm during the 1912 season, and in 1913 and 1914 he appeared in 17 games as a pitcher in the minor leagues with the Providence team of the International League and one of the men he managed was a young man by the name of Babe Ruth. Donovan also managed in the major leagues with the New York Yankees from 1915 through 1917 in the American League and the Philadelphia Phillies in the National League in 1921. Donovan died on December 9, 1923 in Forsyth, New York when he was involved in a terrible train accident. There were three trains in a line and the first[t] train struck a car left abandoned on the tracks. The second train stopped to assist the first train and the third train struck the second train partly due to the heavy fog on the train tracks. Donovan was killed instantly. He was buried in Holy Cross Cemetery in Yeadon, Pennsylvania. – 1898 Washington Senators NL, 1899-1902 Brooklyn Superbas NL, 1903-1912 Detroit Tigers AL, 1915-1916 New York Yankees AL, 1918 Detroit Tigers AL

"Jocko" Flynn was born in Lawrence, Massachusetts on June 30, 1864. His first appearance in a major league baseball game was May 1, 1886 and his last was on May 23, 1887. He was a pitcher and a right fielder during the course of his major league career. As a pitcher Flynn had a record of 23 wins and six losses and an ERA of 2.24. His record that year was good enough to lead the league in winning percentage as 23 wins and six losses figures out to a winning percentage of .793. As for batting, he was credited with appearing in 58 games and having 41 hits that included six doubles two triples and four home runs. His lifetime batting average was .200. He passed away on December 31, 1907 in Lawrence and is buried in the Immaculate Conception Cemetery in the city of Lawrence. –1886-1887 Chicago Cubs NL

Left fielder **Mike Jordan** was born in Lawrence on February 7, 1863. He played in the major leagues from August 21, 1890 to October 3, 1890. In 37 games he had 12 hits including one double and a lifetime batting average of .096. He passed away on September 25, 1940 in Lawrence and is buried in Lawrence's Immaculate Conception Cemetery. – 1890 Pittsburgh Alleghenies NL

Frank McManus was born in Lawrence on September 21, 1875 and played in the major leagues from September 15, 1899 until October 8, 1904 as a catcher. He appeared in only 14 games and had eight hits including a double for a lifetime batting average of .229. He passed away in Syracuse, New York on September 1, 1923 and is buried in St. Mary's Cemetery in Lawrence. – 1899 Washington Senators NL, 1903 Brooklyn Superbas NL, 1904 Detroit Tigers AL, 1904 New York Highlanders AL

George "Prunes" Moolic was born in Lawrence, Massachusetts on March 12, 1867. He played in his first game in the majors on May 1, 1886 and his last game was on September 7, 1886. His short career was spent as a catcher and a right fielder. Of the eight total hits he had, three were doubles and he had a batting average of .143. He passed away on February 19, 1915 in Lawrence and is buried in St. Mary's Cemetery in Lawrence. – 1886 Chicago White Stockings NL

LEE

Frank Dwyer—SEE BERKSHIRE COUNTY BORN PLAYERS

LEOMINSTER

Lew "Blower" Brown was born in Leominster, Massachusetts on February 1, 1858. His first major league baseball game was on June 17, 1876 and he played in the big leagues as a catcher, right fielder and first baseman until October 18, 1884. In 376 games he had 379 hits including 83 doubles, 31 triples and 10 home runs. He had 169 runs batted in and scored 205 runs. His batting average for his career was

.269. He passed away on January 15, 1889 in Boston and is buried in that city's Forest Hills Cemetery. –1876-1877 Boston Red Stockings NL, 1878-1879 Providence Grays NL, 1879 Chicago White Stockings NL, 1881 Detroit Wolverines NL, 1881 Providence Grays NL, 1883 Boston Beaneaters NL, 1883 Louisville Eclipse AA, 1884 Boston Reds UA

Mike Gordon was born on September 11, 1953 in Leominster. He was a catcher who began his career in the major leagues on April 7, 1977 and played until July 9, 1978. He appeared in 12 games and had two hits for a .071 batting average. – 1977-1978 Chicago Cubs NL

LEXINGTON

John "Dinny" McNamara was born in Lexington, Massachusetts on September 16, 1905. His big league debut was on July 2, 1927 and he played in his final game on May 30, 1928. He was an outfielder as well as a pinch runner and he had one hit in 13 at bats. He died on December 20, 1963 and is buried in St. Bernard's Cemetery in Concord, Massachusetts. – 1927-1928 Boston Braves NL

LOWELL

Mike Balas (who was born Mitchell Francis Balaski) was born in Lowell, Massachusetts on May 9, 1910. He was a pitcher who played in his only big league game on April 27, 1938. He did not record a win or a loss and his ERA was 6.75. Even though Balas only had a one game career, he was better known as a conscientious objector during World War II. Most of the other ball players during this time served in some capacity, but not Balas. In 1942 because of his beliefs against war, he was prosecuted for disobeying the Selective Service Act. Even though both his father and his brother both registered for the draft, Balas sought refuge citing his religious beliefs (Jehovah Witness). He passed away in Westfield, Massachusetts on October 15, 1996 and he was later cremated. – 1938 Boston Bees NL

John Barrett was an outfielder in the major leagues from April 14, 1942 until September 26, 1946. He was in a total of 588 games, and he had 454 hits including 82 doubles, 32 triples and 23 home runs. He also had 220 runs batted in and scored 303 runs himself. His lifetime batting average was .251. He was the National League leader in triples and steals in 1944 with 19 triples and 28 steals. He was born December 18, 1915 in Lowell, Massachusetts and he passed away in Seabrook Beach, New Hampshire on August 17, 1974. He is buried in Ridgewood Cemetery in North Andover, Massachusetts. –1942-1946 Pittsburgh Pirates NL, 1946 Boston Braves NL

Second base, third base and shortstop were the positions played by **Frank Bonner** in a major league career that ran from April 26, 1894 until June 25, 1903. In his career he appeared in 246 games, while scoring 115 runs and driving in 115 runs. Of his 244 hits 44 were doubles, eight were triples and four were home runs. His lifetime batting average was .257 and he was born in Lowell, Massachusetts on August 20, 1869. He passed away in Kansas City, Missouri on December 31, 1905 and is buried in Mount St. Mary's Cemetery in Kansas City. –1894-1895 Baltimore Orioles NL, 1895 St Louis Browns NL, 1896 Brooklyn Bridegrooms NL, 1899 Washington Senators NL, 1902 Cleveland Broncos AL, 1902 Philadelphia Athletics AL, 1903 Boston Beaneaters NL

Lowell, Massachusetts was the birthplace of **William "Bill" Conway** whose birthday was on November 28, 1861. Conway was a catcher who made his first appearance in the major leagues on July 28, 1884 and played until August 29, 1886. In eight games he had two hits in 18 at bats for a .111 batting average. He died in Somerville, Massachusetts on December 18, 1943 and is buried in St. Paul's Cemetery in Arlington, Massachusetts. He is the brother of Dick Conway who pitched and played outfield in the major leagues from 1886 until 1888. – 1884 Philadelphia Quakers NL, 1886 Baltimore Orioles AA

Dick Conway was born in Lowell, Massachusetts on April 25, 1866. His first major league appearance was on July 22, 1886 and his last was October 8, 1888. He pitched and played the outfield and his pitching stats showed him winning 15 games and losing 24, while carrying a 4.78 ERA for the 41 games he pitched in. As for batting in the 58 games, he had 47 hits that included six doubles and one triple and a lifetime .230 batting average. He was the brother of Bill Conway who played in the major leagues from 1884 until 1886. Dick Conway passed away in Lowell on September 9, 1926 and is buried in St. Mary's Cemetery on Lawrence Massachusetts. --- 1886 Baltimore Orioles AA, 1887-1888 Boston Beaneaters NL

Jack Corcoran was born in Lowell, Massachusetts on May 15, 1858. He debuted in the major leagues on May 1, 1884 and during his career which ended on October 13, 1884, he played as a catcher, second baseman and outfielder in a total of 52 games. He had four doubles and three triples and a total of 39 hits in 185 at bats. He also had a lifetime batting average of .211. He passed away on December 28, 1935 in Jersey City, New Jersey and is buried in the Jersey City Cemetery.—1884 Brooklyn Atlantics AA

John "Denny" Driscoll was born in Lowell, Massachusetts on November 19, 1855. He was a center fielder and a pitcher in a career that lasted from July 1, 1880 until June 28, 1884. As a pitcher he was in a total of 83 games and had a record of 38 wins and 29 losses as well as a 3.08 career ERA. In 1882 he posted a record of 13 wins and 9 losses and had a league leading 1.21 ERA for the Pittsburgh Alleghenys. As a batter he was credited with appearing in 95 games and had 57 hits in 341 at bats for a .167 batting average. Included in his hit total were six doubles, one triple and one home run. He passed away in Lowell on July 11, 1886 and is buried in St Patrick Cemetery in Lowell.—1880 Buffalo Bisons NL, 1882-1883 Pittsburgh Alleghenys AA, 1884 Louisville Eclipse AA

Jack Firth was born in Lowell, Massachusetts on May 6, 1855 and had a one game major league career as a pitcher. The only game he pitched and played in was on August 15, 1884, and he did not get a win or a loss in the game and he ended up with a 8.00 ERA. –1884 Richmond Virginians AA

Ed "Sleepy" Flanagan was born in Lowell, Massachusetts on September 15, 1861. He played first base during his major league career which went from April 16, 1887 until October 8, 1889. In the 42 games he played he had 42 hits including 12 doubles, three triples and one home run. He batted .250 for this career and also scored 23 runs. He passed away on November 10, 1926 in Lowell and is buried in that city's St. Patrick's Cemetery. –1887 Philadelphia Athletics AA, 1889 Louisville Colonels AA

Bob Ganley was an outfielder who played in the major leagues from September 1, 1905 until September 27, 1909. He played in 572 games and had 540 hits in 2,129 at bats. 44 of those hits were doubles, 24 were triples and two were home runs. He scored 246 runs and had 123 runs batted in and a .254 batting average. He was born in Lowell on April 23, 1875 and passed away on October 9, 1945 in Lowell where he is buried in the St Patrick Cemetery. –1905-1906 Pittsburgh Pirates NL, 1907-1909 Washington Senators AL, 1909 Philadelphia Athletics AL

John Grady played from May 10, 1884 until May 24, 1884. Grady who was born in Lowell, Massachusetts on June 18, 1860, was a first baseman and a centerfielder who appeared in nine games. His 11 major league hits included three doubles and he had a lifetime batting average of .306. He died in Lowell on July 15, 1893 and is buried in the St Patrick Cemetery in Lowell. –1884 Altoona Mountain City AA

Bill Merritt was born in Lowell, Massachusetts in July 30, 1870. He was a first baseman and a catcher who began his career in the major leagues in August 8, 1891 and ended it on October 15, 1899. In 401 games he had 384 hits that included 40 doubles, 12 triples and eight home runs. He scored 182 runs and had 196 runs batted in and a .272 batting average. He passed away in Lowell on November 17, 1937 and is buried in St. Patrick's Cemetery in Lowell. – 1891 Chicago Colts NL, 1892 Louisville Colonels NL, 1893-1894 Boston Beaneaters NL, 1894 Pittsburgh Pirates NL, 1894-1895 Cincinnati Reds NL, 1895-1897 Pittsburgh Pirates NL, 1899 Boston Beaneaters NL

Robert Person was born in Lowell, Massachusetts on October 6, 1969. His first start in the major leagues was September 18, 1995 and his career ended on June 7, 2003. His career record in 206 pitching appearances was 51 wins and 42 losses and a 4.64 ERA. –1995-1996 New York Mets NL, 1997-1999 Toronto Blue Jays AL, 1999-2002 Philadelphia Phillies NL, 2003 Boston Red Sox AL

Joseph "Skippy" Roberge played shortstop, as well as second and third base in a major league career that lasted from July 18, 1941 until June 15, 1946. In 177 games he had a total of 112 hits that included 19 doubles, three triples and three home runs. He scored 35 runs and had 47 runs batted in. His lifetime batting average was .220. He was born in Lowell, Massachusetts on May 19, 1917 and passed away on June 7, 1993 in Lowell where he is buried in St. Joseph's Cemetery. – 1941-1942/1946 Boston Braves NL

Catcher Charlie Snow was born in Lowell, Massachusetts on August 3, 1849. He played in only one major league baseball game with that game being on October 1, 1874. He had one hit in his only at bat and ended up with a 1.000 batting average. He later passed away on August 27, 1929 in Brooklyn, New York and is buried in the Green-Wood Cemetery in Brooklyn. –1874 Brooklyn Atlantics NA

Marty Sullivan was born in Lowell, Massachusetts on October 20, 1862. He was a left fielder in the major leagues whose playing career was from April 30, 1887 until August 17, 1891. In the 398 games that he played in, he had 441 hits in 1,618 at bats. He had 56 doubles, 32 triples and 26 home runs included in that hit total and he also had 220 runs batted in and scored another 280 runs himself. His career batting average was .273. He died on January 6, 1894 in Lowell and is buried in St. Patrick's Cemetery in Lowell. – 1887-1888 Chicago White Stockings NL, 1889 Indianapolis Hoosiers NL, 1890-1891 Boston Beaneaters NL, 1891 Cleveland Spiders NL

LYNN

Harry "The Golden Greek" Agganis was born in Lynn, Massachusetts on April 20, 1929. He debuted in the major leagues on April 13, 1954 as a first baseman and played in his last game on June 2, 1955. He was a two sport star at Boston University where he played baseball and football. He enlisted in the United States Marine Corps after the 1949 college football season. He received a dependency discharge and then went back to college at Boston University. He played in only 157 major league baseball games and had 135 hits including 35 doubles, nine triples and 11 homers. He scored 65 runs and had 69 runs batted in. After he ended his rookie season, he had led the American League in assists and fielding percentage. He ended up in the hospital after complaining that he had chest pains and a bad fever and was diagnosed with pneumonia and on June 27, 1955 he passed away in Cambridge, Massachusetts from a pulmonary embolism and was buried in the Pine Grove Cemetery in Lynn. – 1954-1955 Boston Red Sox AL

Stan "Polo" Andrews was born in Lynn, Massachusetts on April 17, 1917 and was a catcher when he made his major league debut on June 11, 1939. His final appearance in a major league baseball game was on September 30, 1945 and in the 70 games that he appeared in he had 32 hits including two doubles, one triple and one home run. His life time batting average was .215. He passed away in Bradenton, Florida on June 10, 1995. – 1939-1940 Boston Bees NL, 1944-1945 Brooklyn Dodgers NL, 1945 Philadelphia Phillies NL

George "Curly" Bullard was born in Lynn, Massachusetts on October 24, 1928. He was a shortstop and a pinch runner in a short major league career that only went from September 17, 1954 until September 25, 1954. He did not have a hit in his only official time at bat. He passed away in Lynn, Massachusetts on December 23, 2002 and is buried in the Puritan Lawn Memorial Park which is in Peabody, Massachusetts. – 1954 Detroit Tigers AL

Les Burke was a second and third baseman as well as a pinch hitter during the course of his major league baseball career which ran from May 2, 1923 until September 15, 1926. In the 194 games he played in, he had 131 hits including 17 doubles and seven triples and a .259 batting average. He was born in Lynn, Massachusetts on December 18, 1902 and passed away on December 23, 2002 in Lynn. He is buried in the Puritan Lawn Memorial Park in Peabody, Massachusetts.—1923-1926 Detroit Tigers AL

John Deering pitched in the major leagues from May 12, 1903 until September 25, 1903 He had a record of seven wins and seven losses and a 3.80 ERA. He was born in Lynn, Massachusetts on June 25, 1878 and passed away in Beverly, Massachusetts on February 15, 1943. He is buried in the town of Beverly at St. Mary's Cemetery. – 1903 Detroit Tigers AL, 1903 New York Highlanders AL

Josh Fogg was born in Lynn, Massachusetts on December 13, 1976 He was a pitcher who debuted in the majors on September 2, 2002 and pitched until October 4, 2009. In 243 games he had a record of 62 wins and 69 losses and a 5.03 ERA—2001Chicago White Sox AL, 2002-2005 Pittsburgh Pirates NL, 2006-2007 Colorado Rockies NL, 2008 Cincinnati Reds NL, 2009 Colorado Rockies NL

Irving "Bump" Hadley was born in Lynn, Massachusetts on July 5, 1904. He was a pitcher in the major leagues from April 20, 1926 until September 16, 1941. In the 528 games that he appeared in as a pitcher, he had a record of 161 wins and 165 losses with an ERA of 4.24. For the 1931 Washington Senators, he led the league in games appeared in as a pitcher with 55, with the St Louis Browns in 1933 he led the league in innings pitched with 316.2, and with the New York Yankees in 1936 when he had 14 wins and only four losses, he led the league in winning percentage with .778. He was a member of the 1936, 1937 and 1939 World Champion New York Yankees as well. He also may be better known as the pitcher who fractured Mickey Cochrane's skull with a pitch, which effectively ended Cochrane's career. Hadley passed away on February 15, 1963 in Lynn, Massachusetts and is buried in the Swampscott Cemetery in Swampscott, Massachusetts.—1926-1931 Washington Senators AL, 1932 Chicago

White Sox AL, 1932-1934 St Louis Browns AL, 1935 Washington Senators AL, 19361940 New York Yankees AL, 1941 New York Giants NL, 1941 Philadelphia Athletics AL

Lynn, Massachusetts is the hometown of **Jim Hegan** who was a catcher in the big leagues from September 9, 1941 until July 4, 1960 He did spend three years early in his career in the service during World War II. In the 1,666 games he appeared in he had 1,087 hits including 187 doubles, 46 triples and 92 home runs. He also scored 550 runs and had 525 runs batted in. He had a lifetime batting average of .228 and was a member of the 1947, 1949, 1950, 1951 and 1952 American League All Star teams and he was also a member of the 1948 World Champion Cleveland Indians. He is the father of Mike Hegan who played first base and the outfield in the majors from1964 until 1977. Jim Hegan was born in Lynn, Massachusetts on August 3, 1920 and passed away on July 17, 1984 in Lynn. He is buried in the Swampscott Cemetery in Swampscott, Massachusetts. –1941-1942 Cleveland Indians AL, 1946-1957 Cleveland Indians AL, 1958 Detroit Tigers AL, 1958-1959 Philadelphia Phillies NL, 1959 San Francisco Giants NL, 1960 Chicago Cubs NL

Second baseman **Les Hennessy** was born in Lynn, Massachusetts on December 12, 1893. His career in the major leagues lasted from July 4, 1913 until July 20, 1913. He had three hits in 22 at bats for a .136 batting average. He passed away in New York, New York on November 20, 1976 and was buried in St. Joseph's Cemetery in Lynn. –1913 Detroit Tigers AL

Ken Hill was born in Lynn, Massachusetts on December 14, 1965. He made his first appearance in the major leagues on September 3, 1988 and pitched in the majors until April 18, 2001. In 332 games pitched he had a record of 117 wins and 109 losses and an ERA of 4.06. In the strike shortened 1994 season he led the National League in wins with 16 and in 1996 he led the American League in shutouts with three. He was a member of the 1994 National League All Star team and finished second in the Cy Young Award voting in 1994. –1988-1991

St Louis Cardinals NL, 1992-1994 Montreal Expos NL, 1995 St Louis Cardinals NL, 1995 Cleveland Indians AL, 1996-1997 Texas Rangers AL, 1997-2000 Anaheim Angels AL, 2000 Chicago White Sox AL, 2001 Tampa Bay Devil Rays AL

November 18, 1965 was the birthday of Lynn, Massachusetts native **Chris Howard**. He made his pitching debut in the major leagues on September 21, 1993 and ended up pitching in his final game on September 20, 1995. In 44 games he had a record of two wins and no losses and a 3.13 earned run average. 1993 Chicago White Sox AL, 1994 Boston Red Sox AL, 1995 Texas Rangers AL

Mike Pazik was born in Lynn, Massachusetts on January 26, 1950 and debuted in the majors on May 11, 1975. He then pitched in his final game on April 27, 1977 and in between he had a record of one win and four losses with a 5.79 ERA after appearing in 13 games. –1975-1977 Minnesota Twins AL

Irving Porter was an outfielder in the major leagues for one game and one game only with the date of the game being August 20, 1914. He was credited with one hit in four at bats for a .250 batting average. He was born in Lynn, Massachusetts on May 17, 1888 and passed away on February 20, 1971 in Lynn where he was later buried in St. Joseph's Cemetery in Lynn. –1914 Chicago White Sox AL

John "Blondy" Ryan was born in Lynn, Massachusetts on January 6, 1906. He was a shortstop and also played both second and third base in a career in the major leagues that lasted from July 13, 1930 until July 31, 1938. He played in 386 games and had a lifetime batting average of .239. He had a total of 318 hits including 36 doubles, 13 triples and eight home runs. He scored 127 runs and had 133 runs batted in, and he was a member of the 1933 World Series Champion New York Giants. He passed away in Swampscott, Massachusetts on November 28, 1959 and is buried in Lynn, Massachusetts at St. Joseph's Cemetery. –1930 Chicago White Sox AL, 1933-1934 New York Giants NL, 1935 Philadelphia Phillies NL, 1935 New York Yankees AL, 1937-1938 New York Giants NL

Al Weston was a pinch hitter when he played in the major leagues from June 29, 1929 until July 8, 1929. He did not have a hit in three plate appearances. He was born in Lynn, Massachusetts on December 11, 1905 and passed away in San Diego, California on November 13, 1997 and was later cremated. 1929 Boston Braves NL

August 20, 1920 was the date that **Tom Whelan** made his only appearance in a major league baseball game. He was a first baseman who did not have a hit in two plate appearances. He was born in Lynn, Massachusetts on January 3, 1894 and passed away in Boston on June 26, 1957. He was buried in Lynn at St. Joseph's Cemetery. – 1920 Boston Braves NL

MALDEN

Gary Disarcina was born in Malden, Massachusetts on November 19, 1967. He made his first appearance in a major league baseball game on September 23, 1989 and played in his final game on May 8, 2000. He was a shortstop for his entire 1,086 game career, which was a career where he had 966 hits that included 186 doubles, 20 triples and 28 home runs. He scored 444 runs and had 355 runs batted in. His lifetime batting average was .258. He was also a member of the 1995 American League All Star team. –1989-2000 California/ Anaheim Angels AL

Foster "Babe" Ganzel was an outfielder in the major leagues from September 19, 1927 until May 10. 1928. Ganzel had a total of 23 hits in his career including five doubles, two triples and one home run. He also had a batting average of .311 for his career. He was born in Malden, Massachusetts on May 22, 1901 and passed away on February 6, 1978 in Jacksonville, Florida. He is the son of Charlie Ganzel who played in the major leagues from September 27, 1884 until September 21, 1897 and the nephew of John Ganzel who played in the major leagues from April 21, 1898 until September 30, 1908. – 1927-1928 Washington Senators AL

Steve Lombardozzi was born in Malden, Massachusetts on April 26, 1960. He was a second baseman in the major leagues from July 12, 1985 until April 11, 1990. In 446 games he had a total of 294 hits including 61 doubles, 12 triples and 20 home runs. He scored 153 runs and had 107 runs batted in to go with a .233 batting average for his career. He was a member of the 1987 World Champion Minnesota Twins and is the father of Steve Lombardozzi Jr who has been pitching in the major leagues since September of 2011. –1985-1988 Minnesota Twins AL, 1989-1990 Houston Astros NL

Kevin McGlinchy was born in Malden, Massachusetts on June 28, 1977. He made his major league pitching debut on April 5, 1999 and played until September 28, 2000. In his career he had a record of seven wins and three losses in the 744 games he appeared in. He also had a career ERA of 2.75. – 1999-2000 Atlanta Braves NL

Dave Morey was born in Malden, Massachusetts on February 25, 1889. His career as a pitcher in the major leagues was from July 4, 1913 until July 17, 1914. In the two games he appeared in he did not get credit for either the win or the loss, but ended up with a career earned run average of 4.50. He passed away on January 4, 1986 in Oak Bluffs, Massachusetts and is buried in the Oak Grove Cemetery in Vineyard Haven, Massachusetts. – 1913 Philadelphia Athletics AL

Frank "Squash" Wilson was born in Malden, Massachusetts on April 20, 1901. He debuted in the major leagues on June 20, 1924 and played until July 2, 1928. Wilson got into 168 games as a leftfielder and a pinch hitter. He had 120 hits in 488 at bats for a .246 batting average. 19 of the hits were doubles, four were triples and one was a home run. He also had 38 runs batted in and scored 46 runs himself. He passed away on November 25, 1974 in Leicester, Massachusetts and is buried in that town's Pine Grove Cemetery. –1924-1926 Boston Braves NL, 1928 Cleveland Indians AL, 1928 St Louis Browns AL

MANSFIELD

Joe Vernon was born in Mansfield, Massachusetts on November 25, 1889. He was a pitcher in the major leagues from July 20, 1912 until May 15, 1914. He was only in two major league baseball games and did not record a win or a loss, and he ended up with a career earned run average of 11.05. He passed away on March 13, 1955 in Philadelphia, Pennsylvania and is buried in the Milltown Rural Cemetery in Brewster, New York. –1912 Chicago Cubs NL, 1914 Brooklyn Tip Tops FL

MARBLEHEAD

Joe Graves played only one game in the major leagues, that being on September 26, 1926. He was a third baseman who did not have a hit in five plate appearances. He was born in Marblehead, Massachusetts on February 26, 1906 and passed away on December 22, 1980 in Salem, Massachusetts. He is buried in the Waterside Cemetery in Marblehead and is also the brother of Sid Graves who played in the major leagues in July and August of 1927.—1926 Chicago Cubs NL

Samuel "Sid" Graves was a center fielder and a pinch hitter in the major leagues who played from July 23, 1927 until August 5, 1927. He had five hits in seven games including one double and one triple and he had a batting average of .250 for his career. He was born in Marblehead, Massachusetts on November 30, 1901 and passed away on December 26, 1983 in Biddeford, Maine. He was buried in the Hope Cemetery in Kennebunk, Maine. He was also the older brother of Joe Graves who played in the majors in one game in 1926. –1927 Boston Braves NL

MARLBOROUGH

John Buckley was a pitcher in the major leagues for 10 days from July 15, 1890 until July 25, 1890. He was a native of Marlborough, Massachusetts having been born there on March 20, 1874. In the four games he pitched in he had a record of one win and three losses and a 7.68 ERA. He died in Westborough, Massachusetts and is buried in the Immaculate Conception Cemetery in Marlborough, Massachusetts. –1890 Buffalo Bisons PL

Frank Quinlan was born in Marlborough, Massachusetts on March 9, 1869 and he made his major league debut which coincidentally was his only major league appearance on October 5, 1891. He was a catcher and a left fielder that did not have a hit in five plate appearances. He died in Brockton, Massachusetts on May 4, 1904 and is buried in the Immaculate Conception Cemetery in Marlborough, Massachusetts. – 1891 Boston Reds AA

MEDFORD

George "Foghorn" Bradley was born in Medford, Massachusetts on July 1, 1855. He was a pitcher and a right fielder in a career that had its start on August 23, 1876 and ended on October 21, 1876. When he was credited with pitching, Bradley had a record of 9 wins and 10 losses and a 2.49 ERA in the 22 games he pitched in. In games where he was credited with batting, he had 19 hits including two doubles and one triple in 82 at bats, which gave him a career batting average of .232. He passed away in Philadelphia, Pennsylvania on March 31, 1900 and is buried in the Forest Hills Cemetery in Huntingdon Valley, Pennsylvania. He is also the uncle of Hugh Bradley who played in the major leagues from 1910 until 1915. –1876 Boston Red Stockings NL

Joseph P. Coleman was born in Medford, Massachusetts on July 30, 1922. He made his debut as a pitcher in the major leagues on September 19, 1942 and played in the major leagues until September 7, 1955. In 223 major league baseball games he had a record of 52 wins and 76 losses and a career ERA of 4.38. He also was a member of the 1948 American League All Star team. He passed away in Fort Myers, Florida on April 9, 1997 and is buried in the Fort Myers Memorial Gardens. He is the father of Joe Coleman who played in the major leagues from 1965 to 1979, and the grandfather of Casey Coleman who debuted in the major leagues on

August 2, 2010. – 1942/1946-1953 Philadelphia Athletics AL, 1954-1955 Baltimore Orioles AL, 1955 Detroit Tigers AL

Joe H. Coleman was born in Medford, Massachusetts on February 3, 1947 and pitched in the major leagues from September 28, 1965 until September 24, 1979. In his major league career of 484 games, Coleman had a record of 142 wins and 135 losses to go with his career ERA of 3.70. He also had 18 shutouts in his career and was a member of the 1972 American League All Star team. He is the son of Joseph P. Coleman, who pitched in the majors from1942 until 1955, and the father of Casey Coleman who began his career in the major leagues on August 2, 2010.

Jim Driscoll was a shortstop, a second baseman and a pinch hitter in his major league career which began on June 7, 1970 and ended on May 26, 1972. He appeared in 36 games and had 10 hits with one of the hits being a home run. His lifetime batting average was .143 and he was born in Medford, Massachusetts on May 14, 1944. – 1970 Oakland Athletics AL, 1972 Texas Rangers AL

Howard "Cap" or "Kid" Fahey was born in Medford, Massachusetts on June 24, 1892 and played in the major leagues from July 23, 1912 until September 14, 1912. He was a utility infielder who played second and third base as well as shortstop. He did not have a hit in eight at bats. He passed away in Clearwater, Florida on October 24, 1971 and is buried in Oak Grove Cemetery in Medford. –1912 Philadelphia Athletics AL

William "Bill" Mombouquette was born in Medford, Massachusetts on August 11, 1936. He made his major league pitching debut on July 18, 1958 and made his final appearance in a major league ball game on September 3, 1968. In between his first and last games he appeared in 343 games and had a record of 114 wins and 112 losses with a 3.68 earned run average for his career. He won 20 games in the 1963 season and also threw a no hitter on August 1, 1962 against the Chicago White Sox, while he was pitching for the Boston Red Sox. He was a member of the American League All Star team in 1960, 1962 and 1963. –1958- 1965 Boston Red Sox AL, 1966-1967 Detroit Tigers AL, 1967-1968 New York Yankees AL, 1968 San Francisco Giants NL

Mike Pagliarulo was a third baseman in the major leagues from July 7, 1984 until October 1, 1995. He appeared in 1,246 games and had 942 hits in 390 at bats for a .241 batting average. Of those 942 hits 206 were doubles, 18 were triples and 134 were home runs. He had scored 462 runs and also had 505 runs batted in. He was a member of the 1991 World Champion Minnesota Twins as well. – 1984-1989 New York Yankees AL, 1989-1990 San Diego Padres NL, 1991 -1993 Minnesota Twins AL, 1993 Baltimore Orioles AL, 1995 Texas Rangers AL

Bob Tufts was born in Medford, Massachusetts on November 2, 1955. He was a pitcher who began his major league career on August 10, 1981 and ended it on May 6, 1983. In the 27 games he pitched in he had two wins and no losses and a 4.71 ERA. – 1981 San Francisco Giants NL, 1982-1983 Kansas City Royals AL

MEDWAY

Albert "Allie" Moulton was born in Medway, Massachusetts on January 16, 1886. His major league career began on September 25, 1911 and ended on September 30, 1911. He was a second baseman who played in a total of four games and had one hit as well as one run batted in. He also scored four runs himself and had a lifetime batting average of .067. It is important and even amazing that Moulton was even able to play major league baseball because his father was of European and African ancestry, and due to the customs and practices of the day Moulton was considered to be a Negro which in the days of Jim Crow in baseball was considered taboo. Moulton ended up bouncing around the minor leagues for a number of years before finally settling in as a machine tool engineer. He passed away on July 10, 1968 in Peabody, Massachusetts and is buried in the Pine Grove Cemetery in Warner, New Hampshire.—1911 St Louis Browns AL

MELROSE

Geoff Combe was born in Melrose, Massachusetts on February 1, 1956. He debuted in the major leagues as a pitcher on September 2, 1980 and pitched in his final game on October 2, 1991. In 18 games he had a record of one win and no losses and a 8.51 ERA. 1980-1981 Cincinnati Reds NL

Melrose was the hometown on **Joe Harris** who was born there on October 5, 1907. He was a pitcher who played from September 22, 1905 until October 5, 1907. In the 45 games he pitched in he had a record of three wins and 30 losses and a 3.35 earned run average for his career. He passed away in Melrose on April 12, 1966 and was buried in the Wyoming Cemetery in Melrose. –1905-1907 Boston Americans AL

Steve Lomasney was a catcher in the major leagues for only one game and that was on October 3, 1999. He did not have a hit in two at bats. He was born in Melrose, Massachusetts on August 29, 1977. – 1999 Boston Red Sox AL

MERRIMAC

Dennis Berran played left field in the major leagues on August 11, 1912 which was his only major league appearance. He had one hit and scored one run in four times at bat and his batting average was .250. He was born in Merrimac, Massachusetts on October 8, 1887 and passed away on April 28, 1943 in Boston. He is buried in the New Calvary Cemetery in Boston. –1912 Chicago White Sox AL

METHUEN

Steve "Bedrock" Bedrosian was born in Methuen, Massachusetts on December 6, 1957. He was a pitcher whose first appearance in a major league baseball game was on August 14, 1981. In 732 games he had a record of 76 wins and 79 losses, an ERA of 3.38 and 184 saves. As a member of the Philadelphia Phillies in 1987, he was the National League leader in saves with 40. He was a National League All Star in 1987 as well and he was also the winner of the 1987 Cy Young Award as well as the Rolaids Relief Winner in 1987 too. Bedrosian was a member of the 1991 World Champion Minnesota Twins. His final appearance in the majors was on August 9, 1995. – 1981-1985 Atlanta Braves NL, 1986-1989 Philadelphia Phillies NL, 1989-1990 San Francisco Giants NL, 1991 Minnesota Twins AL, 1993-1995 Atlanta Braves NL

Major league pitcher **Mike Rochford** was born in Methuen on March 14, 1963. He made his first pitching appearance on September 3, 1988 and played in his final game on April 16, 1990. In eight games he had a record of no wins and one loss to go with his ERA which was 9.58. –1988-1990 Boston Red Sox AL

George Wheeler (born George L Heroux) was born in Methuen, Massachusetts on July 30, 1869. His pitching career spanned from September 18, 1896 until May 30, 1899. In 50 big league contests Wheeler had a record of 21 wins and 20 losses and an ERA of 4.24. He passed away on March 21, 1946 in Santa Ana, California and was later cremated. – 1896-1899 Philadelphia Phillies NL

MILFORD

Frank Fahey was a left fielder and a pitcher who was born in Milford, Massachusetts on January 22, 1896. His career in the major leagues was from April 25, 1918 until June 10, 1918. His pitching line shows him without a win or a loss in the three games he pitched in and he ended up with a career earned run average of 6.00. As for batting, he was credited with appearing in 10 games and he had three hits including a double in 17 at bats for a .176 batting average. He passed away in Boston on March 19, 1954 and is buried in St. Mary's Cemetery in Uxbridge. – 1918 Philadelphia Athletics.

Art Kenney was born in Milford on April 29, 1916 and debuted as a pitcher on July 1, 1938 with his career lasting only until July 4, 1938.

He did not have a decision on the two games he pitched and his career ERA was 15.53. – 1938 Boston Bees NL

Ralph Lumenti was born in Milford, Massachusetts on December 21, 1936. He pitched in the major leagues from September 7, 1957 until September 27, 1959. He had a record of one win and three losses as well as a 7.29 ERA. –1957-1959 Washington Senators AL

From April 21, 1890 until July 29, 1893, **Tom Vickery** was a pitcher in the major leagues. He had a record of 42 wins and 41 losses as well as a 3.75 ERA for his career which consisted of 97 games. He was a winner of 24 games during the 1890 season although he also led the league in hitting a batter when he hit 29 batters during the 46 games he pitched in that year. He passed away on March 21, 1921 in Burlington, New Jersey and he is buried in the Odd Fellows Cemetery in Burlington, New Jersey. –1890/1893 Philadelphia Phillies NL, 1891 Chicago Colts NL, 1892 Baltimore Orioles NL

MILLBURY

Henry "Chick" Gagnon was born in Millbury, Massachusetts on September 27, 1897. He was a shortstop and a pinch runner/hitter in his major league career which ran between June 27, 1922 and July 10, 1924. He was in 14 games and had two hits in nine at bats. His batting average was .222. He passed away in Wilmington, Delaware on April 30, 1970 and is buried in St. John's Cemetery in Worcester, Massachusetts – 1922 Detroit Tigers AL, 1924 Washington Senators AL

MILLERS FALLS

Doug Smith was born in Millers Falls, Massachusetts on May 25, 1892. He played in only one major league baseball game and that was on July 10, 1912 and he was a pitcher. He did not get the win or the loss in the game and his career ERA was 3.00 He passed away in Greenfield, Massachusetts on September 19, 1973 and is buried in the Highland Cemetery in Millers Falls. –1912 Boston Red Sox AL

MILLVILLE

Tim McNamara was born in Millville, Massachusetts on November 20, 1898. He pitched in the major leagues from June 27, 1922 until May 15, 1926. He had a record of 14 wins and 29 losses and an ERA of 4.78 in his career which was 98 games long. He died November 5, 1994 in North Smithfield, Rhode Island and is buried in St Charles's Cemetery in Blackstone, Massachusetts. – 1922-1925 Boston Braves NL, 1926 New York Giants NL

MILTON

Charlie Devens was born in Milton, Massachusetts on January 1, 1910. He was a pitcher who appeared in his first major league baseball game on September 24, 1932. His final appearance in a major league ballgame was on September 26, 1934. In the 16 games he pitched in he had a record of 5-3 as well as a 3.73 ERA. He passed away on August 13, 2003 in Scarborough, Maine and is buried in the Mount Auburn Cemetery in Cambridge, Massachusetts. –1932-1934 New York Yankees AL

Elburt "Elbie" Fletcher was a major league third baseman from September 16, 1934 until October 2, 1949. He appeared in 1,415 games and had a total of 1,323 this that included 228 doubles, 58 triples and 79 home runs. He had 616 runs batted in and scored 723 runs. He was a member of the National League All Star team in 1943, and led the league in bases on balls in 1940 with 119 walks and again in 1941 with 118 walks. He was born in Milton, Massachusetts on March 18, 1916 and passed away on March 9, 1994 in Milton where he is buried in the Milton Cemetery. –1934-1939 Boston Braves/Bees NL, 1939-1943, 1946-1947 Pittsburgh Pirates NL, 1949 Boston Braves NL

Chris Mahoney was born in Milton, Massachusetts on June 11, 1885. He played centerfield and pitched in a career that began on July 12, 1910 and ended on October 8, 1910. His pitching record showed him with a record of no wins and one loss in the two games he pitched in. He also had a career earned run average of 3.27. As a batter he was credited with appearing in three games with one hit in seven at bats and a .143 batting average. He died on July 15, 1954 in Visalia, California where he is buried in the Visalia Cemetery. 1910 Boston Red Sox AL

NATICK

John Fitzgerald was born in Natick, Massachusetts on May 30, 1870. He pitched in the major leagues from July 18, 1891 until October 5, 1891. In the six games that he pitched in he had a record of one win and one loss and a 5.63 ERA. He passed away on March 31, 1921 in Boston and was buried in the New Calvary Cemetery in Boston. – 1891 Boston Reds AA

Walt Hriniak was a catcher and a pinch hitter in the major leagues from September 10, 1968 until September 30, 1969. In 47 games he had 25 hits in 99 at bats which is a lifetime batting average of .253. He later was the hitting coach of the Boston Red Sox and then the Chicago White Sox. Then in 1995 he opened up his own hitting school and became a private instructor. – 1968-1969 Atlanta Braves NL, 1969 San Diego Padres NL

Frank Mahar was born in Natick, Massachusetts on December 4, 1878. His only game in major league baseball was on August 29, 1902. He was a left fielder who only had one at bat and he did not get a hit. He passed away in Somerville, Massachusetts and is buried in the Forest Dale Cemetery in Malden, Massachusetts. --- 1902 Philadelphia Phillies NL

Pat Pettee was born in Natick, Massachusetts on January 10, 1863. He played in the major leagues from April 8, 1891 until April 14, 1891. In two games he did not record a hit in five at bats. He passed away on October 9, 1934 in Natick and is buried in St. Patrick's Cemetery in that town. – 1891 Louisville Colonels AA

Pete Smith pitched in the major leagues from September 13, 1962 until September 28, 1963. He had a record of no wins and one loss in the seven games he pitched in. He also had a 6.75 earned run average for his career. He was born in Natick, Massachusetts on March 19, 1940. – 1962-1963 Boston Red Sox AL

NEW BEDFORD

Bob Allietta was a catcher in the major leagues from May 6, 1975 until September 28, 1975. He appeared in 21 games, and of his eight major league hits one was a double and one was a home run. His lifetime batting average was .178. Allietta was born in New Bedford, Massachusetts on May 1, 1952. – 1975 California Angels AL

Outfield, shortstop and second base were where **Jim Canavan** played during the course of a career in the major leagues that ran from April 8, 1891 until July 13, 1897. In 541 games Canavan had 464 hits that included 63 doubles, 49 triples and 30 home runs. He also scored 326 runs and had 291 runs batted in. His lifetime batting average was .224. He was born in New Bedford, Massachusetts on November 26, 1866 and passed away in New Bedford on May 27, 1949. He is buried in New Bedford's St. Mary's Cemetery. –1891 Cincinnati Kelly's Killers AA, 1891 Milwaukee Brewers AA, 1892 Chicago Colts NL, 1893-1894 Cincinnati Reds NK, and 1897 Brooklyn Bridegrooms NL

John "Daff" Gammons was born in New Bedford, Massachusetts on March 17, 1876. His major league career spanned form April 23, 1901 until June 26, 1901. In that career he was a left fielder and second and third baseman as well. In 28 games he had 18 hits including one triple and his lifetime batting average was .194. He passed away on March 24, 1963 in East Greenwich, Rhode Island and is buried in the Oak Grove Cemetery in New Bedford, Massachusetts. –1901 Boston Beaneaters NL

Brian Rose was born in New Bedford, Massachusetts on February 13, 1976. His career in the majors was spent as a pitcher and went from July 25, 1997 until May 30, 2001. In 68 games he had a record of 15 wins and 23 losses in 68 games. His career ERA was 5.86. –1997-2000 Boston Red Sox AL, 2000 Colorado Rockies NL 2001 New York Mets NL, 2001 Tampa Bay Devil Rays AL

NEWBURYPORT

Kyle Abbott was born in Newburyport, Massachusetts on February 18, 1968. He made his major league debut on September 10, 1991 and then ended up pitching in his final game on August 24, 1996. In 57 games he had a record of four wins and 17 losses and an earned run average for his career of 5.20. –1991 California Angeles AL, 1992 Philadelphia Phillies NL, 1995 Philadelphia Phillies NL, 1996 California Angels AL

Pat "Whoops" Creeden was a pinch hitter and a shortstop in the major leagues for a one week period from April 14, 1931 until April 21, 1931. He did not have a hit in the five games he played in. He was born in Newburyport, Massachusetts on May 23, 1906 and passed away on April 20, 1992 in Brockton, Massachusetts. He is buried in the Calvary Cemetery in Brockton, Massachusetts. – 1931 Boston Red Sox AL

Angelo "Junior" Dagres was a right fielder and a pinch hitter for two weeks in the major leagues. He played from September 11, 1955 until September 25, 1955. In 8 games he had four hits in 15 at bats. He also had three runs batted in and scored five runs himself. His lifetime batting average was .267. He was born in Newburyport, Massachusetts on August 22, 1934. –1955 Baltimore Orioles AL

NEWTON

Bob Barr was born in Newton, Massachusetts on March 12, 1908. He was a pitcher in the major leagues from September 11, 1935 until September 14, 1935. He did not have either a win or a loss in the two games he pitched in and his career earned run average was 3.86. He passed away on July 25, 2002 in Dover, New Hampshire and is buried in the Pine Grove Cemetery in Barrington, New Hampshire. –1935 Brooklyn Dodgers NL

September 9, 1961 in Newton Massachusetts was the birthday of major league pitcher **Jim Corsi**. He began his career in the major leagues on June 28, 1988 and ended his career on October 3, 1999. He had a record

of 22 wins and 24 losses and a career ERA of 3.25. –1988-1989 Oakland
Athletics AL, 1991 Houston Astros NL, 1992 Oakland Athletics AL,
1993 Florida Marlins NL, 1995-1996 Oakland Athletics AL, 1997-1999
Boston Red Sox AL, 1999 Baltimore Orioles AL

John Curtis was born in Newton, Massachusetts on March 19, 1948.
He pitched in the major leagues in a career that began on August 13,
1970 and ended on September 28, 1984. In the 438 games he pitched
in he had a record of 89 wins and 97 losses as well as an ERA of 3.96.
–1970-1973 Boston Red Sox AL, 1974-1976 St Louis Cardinals NL,
1977-1979 San Francisco Giants NL, 1980-1982 San Diego Padres NL,
1982-1984 California Angels AL

Lawrence "Law" Daniels was born in Newton, Massachusetts on
July 14, 1862. He was a catcher and also played the outfield and first
base in a career that began on April 25, 1887 and ended on October
7, 1888. In 109 major league baseball games Daniels had 86 total hits
that included one double, one triple and two home runs. He scored
55 runs and had 60 runs batted in and he also had a career batting
average of .225. He was buried in the Calvary Cemetery in Waltham
after he passed away on January 7, 1929 in Waltham, Massachusetts.
–1887 Baltimore Orioles AA, 1888 Kansas City Cowboys AA

Pitcher Sean Depaula was born in Newton, Massachusetts on November
7, 1973. He pitched in a total of 29 major league ballgames from August 231,
1999 until August 1, 2002. He had a record of one win and one loss and an
ERA of 6.75. 1999-2000 Cleveland Indians, 2002 Cleveland Indians AL

Hal Deviney was a pitcher in the major leagues who pitched in only
one game with the date of the game being July 30, 1920. He did not
record a win or a loss and possessed a career ERA of 15.00. He was born
in Newton, Massachusetts on April 11, 1893 and died in Westwood,
Massachusetts on January 4, 1933. He is buried in the Brookdale Cemetery in Dedham, Massachusetts. –1920 Boston Red Sox AL

Bob Dresser, who was born in Newton, Massachusetts on October 4,
1878, pitched in his only major league baseball game on August 13, 1902

for the Boston Beaneaters of the National League. His record showed him with no wins and one loss and a career earned run average of 3.00. He passed away in Duxbury, Massachusetts on July 27, 1924 and is buried in the Mount Wollaston Cemetery in Quincy, Massachusetts.

The outfield and pinch hitting was where **Bob Gallagher** spent a major league career that lasted from May 17, 1972 until September 26, 1975. In 213 ballgames he had 56 hits that included six doubles, one triple and two home runs. He also scored 34 runs and had a batting average of .220. He was born in Newton, Massachusetts on July 7, 1948 and is also the grandson of Shano Collins who played in the major leagues between 1910 and 1925. – 1972 Boston Red Sox AL, 1973-1974 Houston Astros NL, 1975 New York Mets NL

Norman "Jumbo" Roy was a pitcher in the major leagues from April 23, 1950 until September 27, 1950. In 19 games he had a record of 4-3 as well as a career ERA of 5.13. He was born in Newton, Massachusetts on November 15, 1928 and passed away on March 22, 2011 in Nashua, New Hampshire. He is buried in St. Patrick's Cemetery in Hudson, New Hampshire. –1950 Boston Braves NL

NEWTONVILLE

Warren Huston was born in Newtonville, Massachusetts on October 31, 1913. He was a second baseman as well as a third baseman and shortstop in a major league career that ran from June 24, 1937 until September 4, 1944.In the 71 games he played in he had 18 hits including four doubles and a lifetime batting average of .165. He passed away on August 20, 1999 in Wareham, Massachusetts and was later cremated.—1937 Philadelphia Athletics AL, 1944 Boston Braves NL

NORTH ABINGTON

Michael Driscoll was born in North Abington, Massachusetts on October 19, 1892. He pitched in his only major league baseball game on July 6, 1916 and was saddled with the loss in the game as well as a 5.40 earned run average. He died in Foxboro, Massachusetts on March 22, 1953 and is buried in the Immaculate Conception Cemetery in Easton, Massachusetts. – 1916 Philadelphia Athletics AL

Jim "Sid" Hickey pitched in the major leagues from April 25, 1942 until July 31, 1944. He had a record of no wins and one loss in nine games and his earned run average was 6.75. He was born in North Abington, Massachusetts on October 22, 1920 and passed away on September 20, 1997 in Manchester, Connecticut. He was later buried in St. Patrick's Cemetery in Rockland, Massachusetts. –1942-1944 Boston Braves NL

NORTH ADAMS

Jonah Bayless—SEE BERKSHIRE COUNTY BORN PLAYERS

Jack Chesbro—SEE BERKSHIRE COUNTY BORN PLAYERS

NORTH ANDOVER

Harry MacPherson was a pitcher in the major leagues who pitched in his only ballgame on August 14, 1944. He did not have either a win or a loss and did not give up an earned run in the only inning he pitched. He was born in North Andover, Massachusetts on July 10, 1926. – 1944 Boston Braves NL

NORTH BROOKFIELD

William "Bill" Bergen was born in North Brookfield, Massachusetts on June 13, 1878. He was in the major leagues from May 6, 1901 until September 20, 1911. He was primarily a catcher and he appeared in a total of 947 games. In those games he had a total of 516 hits including 45 doubles, 21 triples and two home runs. He scored 138 runs and also had 193 runs batted in. His lifetime batting average was .170.

He passed away in Worcester, Massachusetts on December 19, 1943 and is buried in St. John's Cemetery in Worcester. He is the younger brother of Marty Bergen who played in the major leagues from 1896 until 1899. –1901-1903 Cincinnati Reds NL, 1904-1911 Brooklyn Superbas/Dodgers NL

Marty Bergen, the older brother of Bill Bergen, was also born in North Brookfield on October 25, 1871. He was a catcher just like his younger brother and Marty's career started on April 17, 1896 and ended on October 15, 1899. He played in 344 games and had a total of 339 hits including 44 doubles, 15 triples and 10 home runs. He also had 176 runs batted in and scored 180 runs himself. His batting average for his career was .265. He passed away in North Brookfield, Massachusetts on January 19, 1900 and is buried in St. Joseph's Cemetery in North Brookfield.—1896-1899 Boston Beaneaters NL

NORTH SCITUATE

Bill Vargus was a pitcher who appeared in a major league baseball game for the first time on June 23, 1925. His career ended 15 games later on June 26, 1926. He had a record of one win and one loss and a 3.89 ERA for his career. He was born in North Scituate on November 11, 1899 and passed away on February 12, 1979 in Hyannis, Massachusetts. He was later buried in the Mount Wollaston Cemetery in Quincy, Massachusetts. – 1925-1926 Boston Braves NL

NORTH TRURO

Daniel "Deacon Danny" MacFayden was born in North Truro, Massachusetts on June 10, 1905 and he then made his major league debut on August 25, 1926 and went on to play in 465 baseball games with the last game being on September 13, 1943. He had a record of 132 wins and 159 losses and a career ERA of 3.96. In 1929 he led the American League with four shutouts. He passed away on August 26, 1972 in Brunswick, Maine and is buried in the Old North Cemetery in North Truro. – 1926-

1932 Boston Red Sox AL, 1932-1934 New York Yankees AL, 1935 Cincinnati Reds NL, 1935-1939 Boston Braves NL, 1940 Pittsburgh Pirates NL, 1941 Washington Senators AL, 1943 Boston Braves NL

NORTHAMPTON

Joe Bokina was born in Northampton, Massachusetts on April 4, 1910. He made his first major league appearance on April 16, 1936 and his last game came three weeks later on May 9, 1936. He was a pitcher who had a record of no wins and two losses in five games. His career ERA was 8.64. Bokina passed away on October 25, 1991 in Chattanooga, Tennessee. He is buried in Lake Hill Gardens in Trenton, Georgia. – 1936 Washington Senators AL

Stu Miller was a pitcher in the major leagues from August 12, 1952 until April 23, 1968. He appeared in a total of 704 ballgames and had a record of 105 wins and 103 losses. His earned run average for his career was 3.24. In 1958 he led the National League in ERA with an average of 2.47. He also led the National League in saves with 17 during the 1961 season and led the American League with 27 saves during the 1963 season. He finished his career with 154 saves. He was also a member of the 1961 and 1962 National League All Star teams. Miller was born in Northampton, Massachusetts on December 26, 1927 – 1952-1956 St Louis Cardinals NL, 1956 Philadelphia Phillies NL, 1957 New York Giants NL, 1958-1962 San Francisco Giants NL, 1963-1967 Baltimore Orioles AL, 1968 Atlanta Braves NL

NORTHBRIDGE

Glen Adams was born in Northbridge, Massachusetts on October 4, 1947. His major league career was spent as a designated hitter, pinch hitter and an outfielder. His career in major league baseball began on May 4, 1975 and ended on October 3, 1982. He got a total of 452 hits in 661 games. Of those hits 79 were doubles, five were triples and 34 were home runs. He had 225 runs batted in and scored 152 runs himself. He also had a lifetime batting average of .280. –1975-1976 San Francisco Giants NL, 1977-1981 Minnesota Twins AL, 1982 Toronto Blue Jays NL

Lou Lucier was born in Northbridge, Massachusetts on March 23, 1918. He appeared in his first major league contest on April 23, 1943 and his last game on June 13, 1945. He was a pitcher who ended his career with a record of three wins, five losses and a career ERA of 3.81.—1943-1944 Boston Red Sox AL, 1944-1945 Philadelphia Phillies NL

NORTHFIELD

Connie "Stone Face" Murphy was a catcher in the major leagues from September 17, 1893 until September 30, 1894. In his seven game career, he had three hits including a double and also had a .143 batting average. He was born in Northfield, Massachusetts on November 1, 1870 and passed away on December 14, 1945 in New Bedford, Massachusetts where he is buried in St. Mary's Cemetery in New Bedford. –1893-1894 Cincinnati Reds NL

NORWOOD

Pinch hitting and pitching were what **Charlie Bowles** did in a major league career that lasted from September 25, 1943 until September 19, 1945. His pitching record showed he had 1 win and 4 losses with an ERA of 4.38 in 10 games. When he batted he was credited with appearing in 16 games and had six hits, one of which was a double. His lifetime batting average was .207. He was born in Norwood, Massachusetts on March 15, 1917. He passed away in Newton, North Carolina on December 23, 2003 and was later cremated. – 1943-1945 Philadelphia Athletics AL

Marty Callagan was born on June 9, 1900 in Norwood, Massachusetts. He made his major league debut as an outfielder on April 13, 1922 and played his final game on September 28, 1930. He was in a total of

295 games and had 205 hits including 28 doubles and 13 triples. He also scored 106 runs and had 74 runs batted in to go with his career batting average of .267. He passed away on June 23, 1975 in Norfolk, Massachusetts and was buried in the Highland Cemetery in Norwood. – 1922-1923 Chicago Cubs NL, 1928/1930 Cincinnati Reds NL

March 11, 1925 was the birthday of Norwood, Massachusetts native **Ray Martin**. Martin began his major league career on August 15, 1943 and played in his final game on April 25, 1948. He was a pitcher who played in five games and had a record of one win and no losses and a respectable 2.45 career earned run average. – 1943/1947-1948 Boston Braves NL

Allen Ripley was born in Norwood, Massachusetts on October 18, 1952. His first major league appearance was on April 10. 1978 and his last game in the major leagues was on September 24, 1982. In 101 games he had a record of 23 wins and 27 losses as well as an ERA of 4.52. He was also the son of Walt Ripley who pitched in the major leagues during the 1935 season. –1978-1979 Boston Red Sox AL, 1980-1981 San Francisco Giants NL, 1982 Chicago Cubs NL

Mike Smith made his major league pitching debut on April 26, 2002 and pitched in his final game on August 6, 2006. In 15 games he had a record of no wins and three losses and a 7.04 ERA.—2002 Toronto Blue Jays AL, 2006 Minnesota Twins AL

Bill Travers was born in Norwood, Massachusetts on October 17, 1952. His first appearance in a major league ball game was on May 19, 1974 and he pitched in the big leagues until his final game on July 17, 1983. He had a record of 65 wins and 71 losses and a 4.10 career ERA after appearing in 205 games. He was a member of the 1976 American League All Star team. –1974-1980 Milwaukee Brewers NL, 1981/1983 California Angels AL

OAKDALE

Charles Andrew "Duke" Farrell was born in Oakdale, Massachusetts on August 31, 1866. He played in his first big league ball game on April 21, 1888 and his last on June 13, 1905. He was a catcher, third baseman and an outfielder who appeared in 1,565 games and he had 1,572 hits that included 211 doubles, 123 triples and 52 home runs. He also had 916 runs batted in and he scored another 829 runs. In 1891 Farrell led the league in home runs with 12 and in runs batted in with 110. He was a member of the 1903 World Champion Boston Americans (who later became the Red Sox). He passed away in Boston, Massachusetts on February 15, 1925. He is buried in the Immaculate Conception Cemetery in the city of Marlborough, Massachusetts. – 1888-1889 Chicago White Stockings NL, 1890 Chicago Pirates PL, 1891 Boston Reds AA, 1892 Pittsburgh Pirates NL, 1893 Washington Senators NL, 189401896 New York Giants NL, 1896-1899 Washington Senators NL, 1899-11902 Brooklyn Superbas NL, 1903-1905 Boston Americans AL

ORANGE

Whitey Witt was born Ladislaw Waldemar Wittkowski in Orange, Massachusetts on September 28, 1895. He played the outfield as well as shortstop and second base in a career that went from April 12, 1916 until August 19, 1926. He appeared in 1,139 games and had a total of 1,195 hits. Included in his hit total were 144 doubles, 62 triples and 18 home runs. He had 302 runs batted in and scored 602 runs himself. His lifetime batting average was .287 and he was a member of the 1923 World Champion New York Yankees. He passed away in Salem County, New Jersey on July 14, 1988 and was later buried in Woodstown, New Jersey at St. Joseph's Church Cemetery. – 1916-1921 Philadelphia Athletics AL, 1922-1925 New York Yankees AL, 1926 Brooklyn Robins NL

PALMER

Bill Dunlap was born in Palmer, Massachusetts on May 1, 1909. His major league career as a pinch hitter and an outfielder began on September 2, 1929 and ended on September 12, 1930. In his 26 game career he had 14 hits including one double, one triple and one home run. He had a career batting average of .241. He passed away on November 29, 1980 in Reading ,Pennsylvania and was buried in the Charles Evans Cemetery in Reading, Pennsylvania.—1929-1930 Boston Braves NL

Bill "Hank" Karlon was a pinch hitter and a left fielder in the major leagues from April 28, 1930 until May 12, 1930. In two games he came to bat five times and did not get a hit. He was born in Palmer, Massachusetts on January 21, 1909 and passed away on December 7, 1964 in Ware, Massachusetts. He was buried in St. Ann's Cemetery in Palmer. –1930 New York Yankees AL

PEABODY

Matt Antonelli plays second base in the major leagues. His career began on September 1, 2008. So far he has appeared in only 21 games for the San Diego Padres and that was during the 2008 season. He does have 11 hits including two doubles and one home run and his batting average is .193. He was born April 8, 1985 in Peabody, Massachusetts.

Lloyd "Chick" Davies' major league career was from July 11, 1914 until September 13, 1926. During that time frame he played in parts of only four seasons, appearing in 117 games. He had 39 hits including eight doubles and four triples and his batting average was .193. He was an outfielder as well as a pitcher and in the 45 games that he was in as a pitcher he had a record of 4-6 and a career earned run average of 4.48. He was born in Peabody, Massachusetts on March 6, 1892 and passed away in Middletown, Connecticut on September 5, 1973. His remains were later cremated. –1914-1915 Philadelphia Athletics AL, 1925-1926 New York Giants NL

Sam King was born in Peabody, Massachusetts on May 17, 1852. His three week major league career went from May 1, 1884 until May 23, 1884. He was a first baseman who played in 12 games getting a total of eight hits including two doubles. His batting average was .178. He passed away on August 11, 1922 in Peabody and is buried in the King Cemetery in Peabody.—1884 Washington Nationals AA

John Leighton was born in Peabody, Massachusetts on October 4, 1861. He was a centerfielder whose career lasted from July 12, 1890 until July 20 1890 which is a total of seven games. He had eight hits in 27 at bats including two doubles and hit for a .296 batting average. Leighton passed away on October 31, 1956 in Lynn, Massachusetts and is buried in the Pine Grove Cemetery in Lynn. – 1890 Syracuse Stars AA

PITTSFIELD

Mark Belanger—SEE BERKSHIRE COUNTY PLAYERS

Jack Ferry—SEE BERKSHIRE COUNTY PLAYERS

Tom Grieve—SEE BERKSHIRE COUNTY PLAYERS

Gene Hermanski—SEE BERKSHIRE COUNTY PLAYERS

"Doc" Powers—SEE BERKSHIRE COUNTY PLAYERS

Howie Storie—SEE BERKSHIRE COUNTY PLAYERS

Earl Turner—SEE BERKSHIRE COUNTY PLAYERS

Matt White—SEE BERKSHIRE COUNTY PLAYERS

Walter Zink—SEE BERKSHIRE COUNTY PLAYERS

QUINCY

Designated hitter and pinch hitter were the positions of **Kevin Buckley** in the major leagues when he played from September 4,

1984 until September 25, 1984. He had two hits in seven at bats and a .286 batting average. He was born in Quincy, Massachusetts on January 16, 1959. – 1984 Texas Rangers AL

Ted Olsen was born in Quincy, Massachusetts on August 27, 1912. He was a pitcher in the major leagues from June 21, 1926 until September 13, 1938. In 18 games he had a record of one win and one loss and a 7.18 ERA. He passed away in Weymouth, Massachusetts on December 9, 1980 and is buried in the Church of St John the Evangelist Cemetery in Hingham, Massachusetts. –1936-1938 Boston Red Sox AL

Quincy, Massachusetts was the hometown of **John Rudderham**, who was a left fielder in the major leagues for only one game on September 18, 1884. He had one hit in four at bats for a .250 batting average in his only major league game. He was born in Quincy on August 30, 1863 and passed away in Randolph, Massachusetts on April 3, 1942. He is buried in St. Mary's Cemetery in Randolph. – 1884 Boston Reds UA

Marc Sullivan was born in Quincy, Massachusetts on July 25, 1958. He was a catcher in the major leagues from October 1, 1982 until October 3, 1987. In 137 games he had 67 hits including 11 doubles and five home runs and his lifetime batting average was .186. He is the son of Haywood Sullivan who played in the major leagues from 1955 to 1963 and later went on to become part owner and general manager of the Boston Red Sox. – 1982-1987 Boston Red Sox AL

RANDOLPH

Gene McAuliffe played in only one game in the major leagues and that was on August 17, 1904. He was a catcher who had one hit in two at bats for a lifetime batting average of .500. He was born in Randolph, Massachusetts on February 28, 1872 and passed away in Randolph on April 29, 1954. He is buried in Randolph's St. Mary's Cemetery. – 1904 Boston Beaneaters NL

RAYNHAM

Tim "Bridget" Donahue was born in Raynham, Massachusetts on June 8, 1870. He made his major league debut on July 28, 1891 and played in his final game on May 17, 1902. He was a catcher who appeared in 466 games. He had 354 hits in 1,500 at bats for a .236 batting average. Of those 354 hits 57 were doubles, 12 were triples and two were home runs. He had 163 runs batted in and also scored 196 runs himself. He passed away in Taunton, Massachusetts on June 12, 1902 and is buried in St. Joseph's Cemetery in Taunton. – 1891 Boston Reds AA, 1895-1897 Chicago Colts NL, 1898-1900 Chicago Orphans NL, 1902 Washington Senators AL

Ezra Lincoln was born in Raynham, Massachusetts on November 17, 1868, and he made his first appearance in a major league baseball game on May 2, 1890. He pitched in the major leagues until August 12, 1890 and compiled a record of three wins and 14 losses to go with a 5.28 ERA. He passed away on May 7, 1951 in Raynham and is buried in that city's Pleasant Street Cemetery. – 1890 Cleveland Spiders NL, 1890 Syracuse Stars AA

REVERE

Richie Barker was born in Revere, Massachusetts on October 29, 1972. He made his first major league appearance on April 25, 1999. He was in five games as a pitcher and did not have a win or a loss to go with his 7.20 earned run average. – 1999 Chicago Cubs NL

Billy Conigliaro was born in Revere, Massachusetts on August 15, 1947. He was an outfielder who played in the major leagues from April 11, 1969 until September 30, 1973. In 347 ballgames he had 289 hits including 56 doubles, 10 triples and 40 home runs. Billy C also had 128 runs batted in and scored 142 runs himself. His lifetime batting average is .256. Also he was a member of the 1973 World Champion Oakland Athletics. He is the younger brother of former major leaguer Tony Conigliaro. – 1969-1971 Boston Red Sox AL, 1972 Milwaukee Brewers AL, 1973 Oakland Athletics AL.

Tony (Tony C) Conigliaro was born in Revere, Massachusetts on January 7, 1945. His story is one of baseball's saddest. He was signed by the Boston Red Sox as an outfielder right out of St Mary's High School in Lynn, Massachusetts. He was a right fielder and he made his major league debut on April 16, 1964 and in his first at bat in the major leagues at Fenway Park, he hit a home run. All told that year 1964 he hit a total of 24 home runs which is the most ever by a teenager. The next year he hit 32 home runs and that was a record for the youngest player to ever lead the league in home runs. In the first game of a double header on July 23, 1967 he hit his 100th career home run and became the youngest player in the American League to reach that figure.

Tragically on August 18, 1967 in an at bat in the fourth inning against Angel's pitcher Jack Hamilton, Tony C had his world come apart. He was hit in the left eye and cheekbone by a Hamilton fastball. His season and maybe his career had just ended. He was unable to come back in 1968 and finally in 1969 he made a comeback and on Opening Day in Baltimore he hit a two run home run in the top of the 10th inning to put the Red Sox ahead in a game they eventually won in the 12th inning when Conigliaro scored the winning run after being walked to start the inning. In 1970 he had a career best 36 home runs and 116 runs batted in, but it was becoming more and more difficult for him to get up close to the plate and he finally ended up retiring on June 12, 1975. He was a member of the 1967 American League All Star team and in 1970 won the Major Leagues Hutch Award, which is given to the player who best exemplifies spirit and desire on the playing field. The award is given in memory of the late Cincinnati Reds manager Fred Hutchinson who fought a losing battle with lung cancer while managing the Reds in1964. Conigliaro suffered a heart attack in 1982 and as a result had irreversible brain damage. He lingered in that state until finally and tragically he passed away on February 24, 1990 in Salem, Massachusetts.

During his career he appeared in 876 games and had 849 hits including 139 doubles, 23 triples and 166 home runs. He scored 464 runs and also had 516 runs batted in. After passing away in Salem, he was buried in the

Holy Cross Cemetery in Malden, Massachusetts. –1964-1967, 1969-1970 Boston Red Sox AL, 1971 California Angels AL, 1975 Boston Red Sox Al

ROSLINDALE

Claude "Skip" Lockwood was born in Roslindale, Massachusetts on August 17, 1946 He pitched in the major leagues from April 23, 1965 until September 10, 1980. He had a record of 57 wins and 97 losses to go with a 3.55 ERA. He also had a total of 68 saves for his career. –1969 Seattle Pilots AL, 1970 -1973 Milwaukee Brewers AL, 1974 California Angels AL, 1975-1979 New York Mets NL, 1980 Boston Red Sox AL

ROXBURY

Art Corcoran was born in Roxbury, Massachusetts on November 23, 1894.On September 9, 1915 he played in his only major league ballgame when he appeared as a third baseman and went hitless in four plate appearances. He passed away on July 28, 1958 in Chelsea, Massachusetts and was later buried in St. Joseph's Cemetery in West Roxbury. – 1915 Philadelphia Athletics AL

Minot "Cap" Crowell was a pitcher in the major leagues from June 23, 1915 until June 10, 1916. In 19 games Cowell had a record of two wins and 11 losses and a 5.27 ERA for his career. He was born in Roxbury on September 5, 1892 and passed away in Central Falls, Rhode Island on September 30, 1962. He was buried in the Swan Point Cemetery in Providence, Rhode Island. –1915-1916 Philadelphia Athletics AL

Charlie Daniels had a career in the major leagues that lasted six days from April 18, 1884 until April 24, 1884. He was a pitcher and a right fielder and as a pitcher he played in two games and had a record of no wins and two losses and a 4.32 ERA. Batting he is credited with playing in three games and had three hits in 11 at bats and a batting average of .273. He was born July 1, 1861 in Roxbury, and passed away in Boston, Massachusetts on February 9, 1938. He is buried in the Mount Hope Cemetery in Boston, --1884 Boston Reds UA

John "Jiggs" Donahue was born in Roxbury on April 19, 1894. He played in the major leagues from September 25, 1923 until October 7, 1923 as a right fielder. In the 10 games he played in he had 10 hits including four doubles and a batting average of .278 for his career. He passed away on October 3, 1949 in Boston and is buried in St. Joseph's Cemetery in West Roxbury. – 1923 Boston Red Sox AL

Pitching, playing both right field and first base is what **John Fox** did in a major league career that lasted from June 2, 1881 until August 9, 1886. Fox had a pitching record of 13 wins and 28 losses in the 45 games he pitched and he also had a career ERA of 4.16. His batting line reads like this: he appeared in 62 games and had 42 hits in 238 at bats for a batting average of .176. 5 of the 42 hits were doubles and he also scored 24 runs. He was born on February 7, 1859 in Roxbury and passed away on April 16, 1893 in Boston. He is buried in the Mount Benedict Cemetery in West Roxbury. – 1881 Boston Red Stockings NL, 1883 Baltimore Orioles AA, 1884 Pittsburgh Alleghenies AA, 1886 Washington Senators NL

Major league left fielder **Gene Good** was born in Roxbury on December 13, 1882. His major league career ran from April 12, 1906 until September 4, 1906. After being in 34 games, he had a total of 18 hits and a batting average of .151. He passed away on August 6, 1947 in Boston and is buried in Boston's New Calvary Cemetery. – 1906 Boston Beaneaters NL

Alphonse "Ike" Kamp was a pitcher in the major leagues from September 16, 1924 until September 21, 1925. He had a record of two wins and five losses as well as a 5.10 ERA in the 25 games he pitched in. He was born in Roxbury, Massachusetts on September 5, 1900 and passed away on February 25, 1955 in Boston where he is buried in the Mount Calvary Cemetery in Boston, -- 1924-1925 Boston Braves NL

Second base was where **Freddie Maguire** played in a career that went from September 22, 1922 until September 27, 1931. He was in a total of 618 games and had 545 hits with 90 of the hits being doubles, 22 being triples and one home run. He had a .257 batting average. Maguire was born in Roxbury on May 10, 1899 and passed away on November 3, 1961 in Boston. He was buried in St. John's Cemetery in Worcester, Massachusetts. – 1922-1923 New York Giants NLO, 1928 Chicago Cubs NL, 1929-1931 Boston Braves NL

Harold Winthrop "Doc" Martin was born on September 23, 1887 in Roxbury, Massachusetts. He pitched in 14 games between October 7, 1908 and June 5, 1912. He had a record of one win and two losses and an earned run average of 5.48. He passed away in Milton, Massachusetts on April 14, 1935 and was buried in the Milton Cemetery in Milton, Massachusetts. – 1908/1911-1912 Philadelphia Athletics AL

Tom McNamara played in only one major league baseball game and that was on June 25, 1922. He pinch hit in his only big league at bat and did not get a hit. He was born in Roxbury, Massachusetts on November 5, 1885 and passed away in Danvers, Massachusetts on May 5, 1974 where he is buried in the Annunciation Cemetery in Danvers. – 1922 Pittsburgh Pirates NL

Andy O'Conner was born in Roxbury on September 14, 1884. In his only big league appearance on October 6, 1908 he was credited with a loss as a pitcher. He ended up after the game with an ERA of 10.13. He passed away on September 26, 1980 in Norwood, Massachusetts and is buried in St. Joseph's Cemetery in West Roxbury. – 1908 New York Highlanders

Paul "Shorty" Radford was a right fielder, shortstop and third baseman in a career that went from May 1, 1883 until September 29, 1894. In 1,361 games played he had 1,206 hits of which 176 were doubles, 57 were triples and 13 were home runs. He also had 462 runs batted in and scored another 945 runs by himself, and had a lifetime batting average of .242. He was born in Roxbury, Massachusetts on October 14, 1861 and passed away on February 21, 1945 in Boston. He is buried in the Brookdale Cemetery in Dedham, Massachusetts. – 1883 Boston Beaneaters NL, 1884-1885 Providence Grays NL, 1886 Kansas

City Cowboys NL, 1887 New York Metropolitans AA, 1888 Brooklyn Bridegrooms AA, 1889 Cleveland Spiders NL, 1890 Cleveland Infants PL, 1891 Boston Reds AA, 1892-1894 Washington Senators NL

Art Rico was born in Roxbury, Massachusetts on July 23, 1895. He caught and played the outfield in a career that began on July 31, 1916 and ended on September 3, 1917. In 17 games he had four hits including a double and his batting average for his career was .222. He passed away on January 3, 1919 in Boston and is buried in the Holyhood Cemetery in Brookline, Massachusetts. – 1916-1917 Boston Braves NL

Richard "Pete" Varney was born in Roxbury, Massachusetts on April 10, 1949. He was a catcher in the majors from August 26, 1973 until September 12, 1976. In 69 games he had 47 hits in 190 at bats for a .247 batting average. Of those hits, seven were doubles, one was a triple and five were home runs. –1973-1976 Chicago White Sox AL, 1976 Atlanta Braves NL

Jim Walsh pitched in the major leagues from August 25, 1921 until September 4, 1921. He was in three games and did not record either a win or a loss, but he did have a 2.25 earned run average for his career. He was born in Roxbury, Massachusetts on July 10, 1894 and passed away on May 13, 1967 in Boston where he was later buried in that city's New Calvary Cemetery.

SALEM

John "Handsome Jack" Carney was born in Salem, Massachusetts on November 10, 1866. His first appearance in a major league baseball game was on April 24, 1889. He played first base and right field in a career that ended on October 4, 1891. He played in 252 baseball games. Carney had 129 runs batted in, and scored 120 runs himself. He had 258 hits that included 30 doubles, 13 triples and seven home runs and his career batting average was .273. He passed away in Litchfield, New Hampshire on October 19, 1925 and is buried in the Pine Grove Cemetery in Manchester, New Hampshire. – 1889 Washington Nationals NL, 1890 Buffalo Bisons PL, 1890 Cleveland Infants PL, 1891 Cincinnati Kelly's Killers AA 1891 Milwaukee Brewers AA

Jeff Juden was born in Salem, Massachusetts on January 19, 1971. He was a pitcher in the major leagues from September 15, 1991 until October 3, 1999. In 147 games he had a record of 27 wins and 32 losses and a 4.81 earned run average for his career,-- 1991/1993 Houston Astros NL, 1994-1995 Philadelphia Phillies NL, 1996 San Francisco Giants NL, 1996-1997 Montreal Expos NL, 1997 Cleveland Indians AL, 1998 Milwaukee Brewers NL, 1998 Anaheim Angels AL, 1999 New York Yankees AL

Tom Darby O'Brien was born in Salem, Massachusetts on June 22, 1860. He debuted in the major leagues on June 14, 1882 and played until July 28, 1890. During the course of his career he played in 270 as a first and second baseman as well as an outfielder. He had a total of 257 hits including 50 doubles, 20 triples and four home runs. He had 61 runs batted in and scored 158 runs himself. He passed away in Worcester, Massachusetts on April 21, 1921 and is buried in St. John's Cemetery in Worcester. – 1882 Worcester Ruby Legs NL, 1883 Baltimore Orioles AA, 1884 Boston Reds UA, 1885 Baltimore Orioles AA, 1887 New York Metropolitans AA, 1890 Rochester Broncos AA

SANDWICH

Sandwich, Massachusetts is the hometown of **Ed Conley** who was born there on July 10, 1864. Conley's major league career was from July 20, 1884 until October 9, 1884. In the eight games he pitched in he had a record of four wins and four losses and a 2.15 ERA. He passed away in Cumberland, Rhode Island and is buried in the Mount Calvary Cemetery in Cumberland. -1884 Providence Grays NL

SAUGUS

Erasmus "Arlie" Pond was born in Saugus, Massachusetts on January 19, 1873. He pitched in the major leagues from July 4, 1895 until July 6,

1898. He had an ERA of 3.45 and a record of 35 wins and 19 losses in the 69 games he pitched in. Pond later became a surgeon in the United States Army serving in both the Spanish American War and World War I. He passed away in Cebu in the Philippines on September 19, 1930 and was later cremated.—1895-1898 Baltimore Orioles NL

SCITUATE

Paul "Bill" Otis played centerfield between July 4, 1912 and July 6, 1912. In the 4 games he played in he had one hit in 17 at bats for a .059 batting average. He was born in Scituate, Massachusetts on December 24, 1889 and passed away nine days short of his 101st birthday on December 15, 1990 in Duluth, Minnesota where he is buried in the Forest Hill Cemetery in Duluth.—1912 New York Highlanders AL

SHELBOURNE FALLS

Jim Andrews was born in Shelbourne Falls, Massachusetts on June 5, 1865. He was a right fielder who played in the major leagues from April 19, 1890 until July 4, 1890. In 53 games he had 38 hits including four doubles, two triples and three home runs. His career batting average was .188. He passed away on December 27, 1907 in Chicago, Illinois where he is buried in the Mount Oliver Cemetery. – 1890 Chicago Colts NL

SHIRLEY

Major league outfielder and pitcher **Mike Golden** was born in Shirley, Massachusetts on September 11, 1851. He played in the major leagues from May 4, 1875 until September 14, 1878. As a pitcher he was in a total of 49 games and had a record of 10 wins and 32 losses and a 2.79 ERA. When he was credited for batting, he appeared in 107 games and had 90 hits including nine doubles and three triples and a .217 batting average. He passed away on January 11, 1929 in

Rockford, Illinois and is buried in the St. Mary and James Cemetery in Rockford. – 1875 Keokuk Westerns NA, 1875 Chicago White Stockings NA, 1878 Milwaukee Grays NA

Jerry White was an outfielder in the major leagues as well as a pinch hitter and he had a career that went from September 16, 1974 until June 9, 1986. In 646 games he had 303 hits including 50 doubles, nine triples and 21 home runs. He also scored 155 runs and had 109 runs batted in. his lifetime batting average was .253. – 1974-1978 Montreal Expos NL, 1978 Chicago Cubs NL, 1979-1983 Montreal Expos NL, 1986 St Louis Cardinals NL

SOMERVILLE

Prosper "Al" Blanche pitched in the major leagues from August 23, 1935 until June 19, 1936. His 17 game career shows him with a record of zero wins and four losses and a 3.78 earned run average. He was born in Somerville, Massachusetts on September 21, 1909 and passed away on April 2, 1997 in Melrose, Massachusetts. He was later buried in the Woodlawn Cemetery in Everett, Massachusetts. –1935-1936 Boston Braves/Bees NL

Jim Galvin was born in Somerville, Massachusetts on August 11, 1907. He was a pinch hitter in his major league career which lasted only two games, September 27 and September 28, 1930. He had two at bats and did not record a hit. He passed away in Marietta, Georgia on September 30, 1969 and is buried in the Resthaven Garden of Memories in Decatur, Georgia. – 1930 Boston Red Sox AL

Ed Gill was a pitcher who played in the major leagues from July 5, 1919 until September 28, 1919. In the 16 games that he appeared in he had a record of one win and one loss and a 4.82 career earned run average. He was born in Somerville, Massachusetts on August 7, 1895 and passed away on October 10, 1995 in Brockton, Massachusetts. He is buried in the Mount Benedict Cemetery in West Roxbury, Massachusetts.—1919 Washington Senators AL

Arthur "Skinny" Graham was a right fielder who debuted in the
major leagues on September 14, 1934. He played in 21 games with his
last game being in September 29, 1935. He had 14 hits in 57 at bats
and three of the hits were doubles and one was a triple. His lifetime
batting average was .246. He was born in Somerville, Massachusetts
on August 12, 1909 and passed away on July 10, 1967 in Cambridge,
Massachusetts. He is buried in the Woodlawn Cemetery in the town
of Everett, Massachusetts. – 1934-1935 Boston Red Sox AL

Pitching was what **Leo Hafford** did in the major leagues in a career
that spanned nine days, April 25, 1906 to April 24, 1906. He was in a
total of three games and had a record of one win and one loss and a
0.95 ERA. He was born in Somerville, Massachusetts on September
17, 1883 and passed away on October 1, 1911 in Willimantic, Connecticut. He is buried in the Holy Cross Cemetery in Malden, Massachusetts. – 1906 Cincinnati Reds NL

James "Shanty" Hogan was born in Somerville, Massachusetts on
March 21, 1906. He made his first appearance in a major league baseball
game as a catcher on June 23, 1925 and was in the major leagues until
his last game in June 13, 1937. He appeared in 989 games and had 939
hits including 146 doubles, 12 triples and 61 home runs. He also scored
288 runs and had a total of 474 runs batted in. He was a fine defensive
catcher as he caught 58.1% of the runners trying to steal in 1927 and
75.0% in 1933, which both led the National League. He also led the
league in fielding percentage as a catcher in 1931 with a .996 and in 1937
with a .997. Five times he was in the top five in fielding percentage and
for his career he caught 46.2 % of the runners trying to steal which is
good enough for 65th best all time. He had a career batting average of
.295 as well. He passed away in Boston on April 7, 1967 and was later
buried in Oak Grove Cemetery in Medford, Massachusetts. –1925-1927
Boston Braves NL, 1928-1932 New York Giants NL, 1933-1935 Boston
Braves NL, 1936-1937 Washington Senators AL

Frank "Yucca" Kelliher pinch hit in his only major league appearance which was on September 19, 1919. He did not get a hit in his

only at bat. He was born in Somerville, Massachusetts on May 23, 1899 and passed away on March 4, 1956 in Somerville, Massachusetts and is buried in the Oak Grove Cemetery in Medford, Massachusetts. – 1919 Washington Senators AL

Somerville, Massachusetts is the home of **Art Mahan** who was born in that city on June 8, 1913. Mahan was first baseman who got into his first major league baseball game on April 30, 1940. His last game was on September 29, 1940 and in 146 games he had 133 hits in 544 at bats for a batting average of .244. Of his 133 hits, 24 were doubles, five were triples and two were home runs. He passed away in Rydal, Pennsylvania on December 7, 2010 and is buried in the Holy Sepulchre Cemetery in Philadelphia, Pennsylvania.—1940 Philadelphia Phillies NL

Charlie Osgood was a pitcher who got into the only game of his major league career on June 18, 1944. He did not register either a win or a loss in that game, but he had an ERA of 3.00 after giving up one run in the three innings he pitched. He was born on November 23, 1926 in Somerville, Massachusetts. – 1944 Brooklyn Dodgers NL

Clarence "Pat" Parker was a right fielder who played in two major league baseball games August 10th and August 11th 1915. He had one hit in six at bats for a .167 batting average. He was born in Somerville on May 22, 1893 and passed away on March 21, 1967 in Claremont, New Hampshire where he was later buried in Claremont's Mountain View Cemetery. – 1915 St Louis Browns AL

Left field and first base were the positions played by **Paul Sorrento** in the major leagues in a career that went from September 8, 1989 until October 2, 1999. In the 1,093 games that he appeared in he had 876 hits that included 176 doubles, 5 triples and 166 home runs. He also scored 454 runs and had 565 runs batted in. his lifetime batting average was .257. He was born in Somerville, Massachusetts on November 17, 1965, and also was a member of the 1991 World Champion Minnesota Twins. –1989-1991 Minnesota Twins AL, 1992-1995 Cleveland Indians AL, 1996-1997 Seattle Mariners AL, 1998-1999 Tampa Bay Devil Rays AL

Gil Whitehouse was born in Somerville, Massachusetts on October 15, 1893. He debited in the major leagues on June 20, 1912 and played in his final game on October 3, 1915. He was a right fielder and a catcher who in 37 games had 27 hits in 123 at bats for a batting average of .220. He also had six doubles and two triples. He passed away on February 14, 1926 in Brewer, Maine where he was buried in that town's Oak Hill Cemetery. –1912 Boston Braves NL, 1915 Newark Pepper FL

Art Williams was a right fielder and a first baseman in the major leagues from May 7, 1902 until September 1, 1902. In the 49 games he appeared in he had 38 hits in 168 at bats for a .228 batting average. Three of those 38 hits were doubles and he also scored 20 runs while having a total of 14 runs batted in. Williams was born in Somerville on August 26, 1877. He passed away in Arlington, Virginia on May 16, 1941. 1902 Chicago Orphans NL

SOUTH ACTON

Fred Robinson was born in South Acton, Massachusetts on July 6, 1856. His career in the major leagues was from April 17th to April 19th in 1884. He was a second baseman who got into three games and had three hits in 13 at bats for a .231 batting average. He passed away in Hudson, Massachusetts on December 18, 1933 and is buried in Hudson's Forestvale Cemetery. He is the brother of Wilbert Robinson who is enshrined in the Baseball Hall of Fame in Cooperstown, New York. –1884 Cincinnati Outlaw Reds UA

SOUTH BOSTON

John "Jack" Slattery was a catcher and a first baseman in the major leagues. He was born in South Boston, Massachusetts on January 6, 1878. He appeared in his first baseball game as a major leaguer on September 28, 1901 and played in his last game on September 29, 1909. In between he had a total of 62 hits in 288 at bats after playing in 103 baseball games. He had five doubles and two triples and a batting average of .212. He passed away Boston on July 17, 1949 and was later buried in St. Joseph's Cemetery in West Roxbury. He is also one of only 16 Boston natives to play for the city of Boston's American League franchise.—1901 Boston Americans AL, 1903 Cleveland Naps AL, 1903 Chicago White Sox AL, 1906 St Louis Cardinals NL, 1909 Washington Senators AL

SOUTH DEDHAM

John Kiley was born in South Dedham, Massachusetts on July 1, 1859. He was a pitcher and a left fielder that made his debut in the major leagues on May 1, 1884. He played in 14 games, but then did not play in the major leagues again until May 7, 1891 when he played in his final game. Batting he is credited with appearing in 15 games with 12 hits in 58 at bats for a .207 batting average. Two of those hits were doubles and two were triples. He pitched in only one game and was credited with a loss and a career ERA of 6.75. He passed away on December 18, 1940 in Norwood, Massachusetts and he is buried in that town's Highland Cemetery. – 1884 Washington Nationals AA, 1891 Boston Beaneaters NL

SOUTH NATICK

Jack Coveney was born in South Natick, Massachusetts on June 10, 1880. He was a catcher who first appeared in a major league baseball game on September 19, 1903 and played in his last game on September 27, 1903. In four games he had two hits and a .143 batting average. He passed away in Wayland, Massachusetts on March 28, 1961 and is buried in St. Patrick's Cemetery in Natick, Massachusetts. –1903 St Louis Cardinals NL

SOUTH WILLIAMSTOWN

Jack Mills—SEE BERKSHIRE COUNTY PLAYERS

SOUTHBOROUGH

William Murphy was born in Southborough, Massachusetts on October 11, 1869 and had the distinction of having three nicknames: Yale, Tot or Midget. He made his first major league appearance on April 19, 1894 and played in the outfield as well as shortstop and third base in a career that ended on July 26, 1897. He was in a total of 131 games and had 114 hits including 12 doubles and four triples and a .240 batting average. He passed away on February 14, 1906 in Westborough, Massachusetts and is buried in St. John's Cemetery in Westborough. –1894-1895, 1897 New York Giants NL

SPENCER

Frank "Dodo" Bird was born in Spencer, Massachusetts on March 10, 1869. He was a catcher who played in the major leagues from April 16, 1892 until June 10, 1892. He had 10 hits in 50 at bats and three of the hits were doubles, one was a triple and one was a home run. In the 17 games he played in, he ended up with a .200 batting average. He passed away in Worcester, Massachusetts on May 20, 1958 and is buried in St. Mary's Cemetery in Spencer, Massachusetts. –1892 St Louis Browns NL

Earle Mack was born in Spencer, Massachusetts on February 1, 1890. He made his major league debut on October 5, 1910 and played until October 1, 1914 appearing in only five games. He played first and third base and caught in the games he played in. He had two hits in 16 at bats for a .125 batting average. He passed away in Upper Darby, Pennsylvania on February 4, 1967 and is buried in the Forest Hill Cemetery in Morganton, North Carolina. He is the son of legendary Hall of Fame manager Connie Mack. –1910-1911/1914 Philadelphia Athletics AL

Jim McCormick was born in Spencer, Massachusetts on November 2, 1868. He played in only two ball games in the major leagues, September 9th and 10th 1892. He did not have a hit in 11 at bats. He passed away in Saco, Maine on February 1, 1948 and is buried in St. Mary's Cemetery in Biddeford, Maine. –1892 St Louis Browns NL

SPRINGFIELD

Chris Capuano was born in Springfield, Massachusetts on August 19, 1978. He made his major league pitching debut on May 4, 2003 and is still pitching in the major leagues today. So far he has recorded 69 wins and 76 losses in the 214 games he has pitched in. He also has a career ERA of 4.28 and has twice led the league in games started (2005-35 games, 2012-33 games). He also was a member of the 2006 National League All Star team.—2003 Arizona Diamondbacks NL, 2004-2010 Milwaukee Brewers NL, 2011 New York Mets NL, 2012 Los Angeles Dodgers NL

Pinch hitting and left field are where **Doug Clark** played in the major leagues from September 14, 2005 and in 2006. He has not retired but has not played in a major league game since 2006. In the 14 games he has appeared in, he has one hit in 11 at bats for a .091 batting average. He was born in Springfield, Massachusetts on March 5, 1976 –2005 San Francisco Giants NL, 2006 Oakland Athletics AL

Kevin Collins was born in Springfield, Massachusetts on August 4, 1946. He made his first appearance in a major league baseball game on September 1, 1965 and played second and third base as well as doing some pinch hitting until September 29, 1971 when he played in his final major league baseball game. In the 201 games he played in, he had 81 hits in 388 at bats good enough for a .245 batting average. Included in his 81 hit totals were 17 doubles, four triples and six home runs. 1965-1969 New York Mets NL, 1969 Montreal Expos NL, 1970-1971 Detroit Tigers AL

Sam Crane was born in Springfield, Massachusetts on January 2, 1854 and made his major league debut on May 1, 1880 playing in 373

games before his final big league appearance on June 28, 1890. He was a second baseman and a shortstop that had 276 hits in 1,359 at bats for a batting average of .203. Included in his 276 hits were 30 doubles, 18 triples and three home runs. He also had 45 runs batted in and scored 183 runs. He passed away on June 26 1925 in New York, New York and is buried in the Lutheran All Faith Cemetery in Queens, New York. – 1880 Buffalo Bisons NL, 1883 New York Metropolitans AA, 1884 Cincinnati Outlaw Reds UA, 1885-1886 Detroit Wolverines NL, 1887 Washington Nationals NL, 1890 New York Giants NL, 1890 Pittsburgh Alleghenys NL, 1890 New York Giants NL

Raymond "Snooks" Dowd was a second baseman, shortstop and a pinch runner in a major league career that began on April 27, 1919 and ended on April 17, 1926. He played in only the 1919 and 1926 seasons only appearing in a total of 16 games. He had three hits in 26 at bats for a .115 batting average. He was born December 20, 1897 in Springfield and passed away on April 4, 1962 in Northampton, Massachusetts. He is buried in St. Michael's Cemetery in Springfield, Massachusetts. –1919 Detroit Tigers AL, 1919 Philadelphia Athletics AL, 1926 Brooklyn Robins NL

Nick Gorneault was born in Springfield, Massachusetts on April 19, 1979. He played in the major leagues for two days, June 30th and July 1st 2007. He did not have a hit in four at bats. –2007 Los Angeles Angels AL

Wayne Granger was born in Springfield, Massachusetts on March 15, 1944. His major league career began on June 5, 1968 and ended on June 25, 1976. He was a pitcher who had a record of 35 wins and 35 losses with a 3.14 earned run average. He also had a total of 108 career saves and in fact led the National League in saves in 1970 with 35. –1968 St Louis Cardinals NL, 1969-1971 Cincinnati Reds NL, 1972 Minnesota Twins AL, 1973 St Louis Cardinals NL, 1973 New York Yankees AL, 1974 Chicago White Sox AL, 1975 Houston Astros NL, 1976 Montreal Expos NL

John Henry was born in Springfield, Massachusetts on September 2, 1863. In his major league career which began on August 13, 1884, he was both a pitcher and a left fielder. As a batter in 60 games he had 53 hits in 218 at bats with nine of the hits being doubles. His batting average was .243 for his career. When he was a pitcher he was in a total of 18 games and had a record of four wins and 14 losses. His ERA was 4.09 and his last major league baseball game was on August 7, 1890. He passed away in Hartford, Connecticut on June 11, 1939 and was buried in Bloomfield, Connecticut in the Mount St. Benedict Cemetery. –1884 Cleveland Blues NL, 1885 Baltimore Orioles AA, 1886 Washington Nationals NL, 1890 New York Giants NL

Bob Keating appeared in only one game in the major leagues. He was a pitcher and the game took place on August 27, 1888, and he was the losing pitcher in that contest that saw him end up with an 11.00 ERA. He was born in Springfield, Massachusetts on September 22, 1862 and passed away on January 19, 1922 in Springfield where he is buried in St. Michael's Cemetery. –1887 Baltimore Orioles AA

Paul "Lefty" Lapalme was born in Springfield, Massachusetts on December 14, 1923. He made his first appearance in a big league baseball game on May 28, 1951. He was a pitcher and in 253 games he had a record of 24 wins and 45 losses to go with a 4.42 earned run average. His final baseball game was on April 28, 1957. He passed away in Leominster, Massachusetts on February 7, 2010 and is buried in St. Leo's Cemetery in Leominster. – 1951-1954 Pittsburgh Pirates NL, 1955-1956 St Louis Cardinals NL, 1956 Cincinnati Red Legs NL, 1956-1957 Chicago White Sox AL

Dan Mahoney was a catcher and a first baseman in a career that went from August 20, 1892 until July 30, 1895. In 11 games he had six hits including one triple and ended up with a career batting average of .182. He was born in Springfield, Massachusetts on March 20, 1864 and passed away in Springfield on January 31, 1904. He is buried in St. Michael's Cemetery in Springfield. –1892 Cincinnati Reds NL, 1895 Washington Senators NL

Matt Mangini was born in Springfield, Massachusetts on December 21, 1985. He is a third baseman and designated hitter who so far has appeared in 11 games after debuting in the majors on September 23, 2010. He has eight hits in 38 at bats for a .211 batting average. –2010 Seattle Mariners AL

Walter James "Rabbit Maranville was a native of Springfield, Massachusetts having been born there on November 11, 1891. He played in his first major league baseball game on September 10, 1912. He was a second baseman and a shortstop that played in 2,670 baseball games and had a total of 2,605 hits in 10,078 at bats. He had 380 doubles, 177 triples and 28 home runs. He scored 1,255 runs himself and also had 884 runs batted in. He had a lifetime batting average of .258. He was a member of the 1914 World Champion Boston Braves that swept Connie Mack's Philadelphia Athletics team in one of baseball's greatest upsets. He was also regarded as a pretty good fielder as evidenced by him being the career leader in assists for shortstops with 8,967. He passed away in New York City on January 5, 1954, just a couple of weeks before he was elected to the Baseball Hall of Fame in Cooperstown. He was later buried in St. Michael's Cemetery in Springfield, Massachusetts. –1912-1920 Boston Braves NL, 1921-1924 Pittsburgh Pirates NL, 1925 Chicago Cubs NL, 1926 Brooklyn Dodgers NL, 1927-1928 St Louis Cardinals NL, 1929-1933/1935 Boston Braves NL

Joseph "Cyclone" Miller was a pitcher and a right fielder in a career in the major leagues that started on July 11, 1884 and went until October 14, 1886. His pitching record shows him having 14 wins and 11 losses as well as an ERA of 3.04 in 27 games. As a batter he was credited with appearing in 29 games with 11 hits. Of those 11 hits, two were doubles and his lifetime batting average was .113. He was born in Springfield, Massachusetts on September 24, 1859 and passed away in New London, Connecticut on October 13, 1916. He is buried in Comstock Cemetery in Montville, Connecticut. –1884Chicago/Pittsburgh NL, 1884, 1884 Providence Grays UA, 1884 Philadelphia Quakers NL, 1886 Philadelphia Athletics AA

Willie "Gentle Willie" Murphy was a left fielder in the major leagues from May 1, 1884 until August 2, 1884. In 47 games he had 48 hits in

189 times at bat for a batting average of .269. Of those 48 hits, there were three doubles, three triples and one home run. He was born in Springfield, Massachusetts on March 23, 1864.—1884 Cleveland Blues NL, 1884 Washington Nationals AA

Phil Page was born in Springfield, Massachusetts on August 23, 1905. He made his first major league appearance on September 18, 1928, with his final appearance coming on May 13, 1934. He was a pitcher who appeared in 31 ballgames and had a record of three wins and three losses and a 6.23 ERA. He passed away in Springfield on July 27, 1958 and is buried in Springfield's Hillcrest Park Cemetery. –1928-1930 Detroit Tigers AL, 1934 Brooklyn Dodgers NL

Steve Peek was a pitcher who made his big league debut on April 16, 1941 and played in a total of 17 games with his last appearance being on September 6, 1941. He had a record of four wins and two losses and a career earned run average of 5.06. He was born in Springfield, Massachusetts on July 30, 1914, and he passed away on September 20, 1991 in Syracuse, New York. He was buried in the Crown Hill Memorial Park in Kirkland, New York.—1941 New York Yankees AL

Frank Quinn was born in Springfield, Massachusetts on November 27, 1927. He made his major league debut on May 29, 1949 and was a pitcher in the major leagues until April 26, 1950. In the nine games that he pitched in he did not record a win or a loss and his career ERA was 3.38. He passed away in Boynton Beach, Florida on January 11, 1993 –1949-1950 Boston Red Sox AL

Vic Raschi was born in Springfield, Massachusetts on March 28, 1919 and had the nickname of the "Springfield Rifle." He was a pitcher who made his big league debut on September 23, 1946 and pitched in his last major league contest on September 13, 1955. He appeared in a total of 269 major league baseball games and had a record of 132 wins and 66 losses. He also had a career earned run average of 3.72. In 1949 and 1951 he led the American League in games started with 37 and 34 respectively. In 1950 Raschi had a record of 21 wins and eight losses for a .724 winning percentage which led the league. In 1951 he led

the American League in strikeouts with 164. Three times he had 20 or
more wins during the baseball season (1949-21, 1950-21 and 1951-21).
He was a member of the American League All Star team in 1948, 1949,
1950 and 1952. It would be him, Allie Reynolds and Eddie Lopat who
would be the Yankees big three pitchers during their dynasty years
of the late 1940's and early 1950's. Raschi was also a member of the
World Champion New York Yankees in 1947 and from 1949 through
1953 when they won an unprecedented five straight World Series
titles. He passed away on October 14, 1988 in Groveland, New York
and was later cremated. – 1946-1953 New York Yankees AL, 1954-1955
St Louis Cardinals AL, 1955 Kansas City Athletics AL

Bill Spanswick was a pitcher in the major leagues from April 18,
1964 until September 20, 1964. He pitched in a total of 29 ballgames
and had a record of two wins and three losses to go with his career
ERA of 6.89. He was born in Springfield, Massachusetts on July 8,
1938. –1964 Boston Red Sox AL

Al "Lefty" Stanek was born in Springfield, Massachusetts on
December 24, 1943. He pitched in the major leagues from April 26,
1953 until September 27, 1963. He did not record a win or a loss in
the 11 ballgames he pitched in and he ended up with a career ERA of
4.73.—1963 San Francisco Giants NL

Pat Strange was born in Springfield, Massachusetts on August 23,
1980. He made his major league debut on September 23, 2002 and
pitched in the majors until June 5, 2003. He did not record a win
or a loss and ended up with a 6.35 ERA after pitching in 11 games.
–2002-2003 New York Mets NL

Dick Teed made only one appearance in a major league baseball
game and it was on July 24, 1953 as a pinch hitter and he did not get
a hit in that at bat. He was born in Springfield, Massachusetts on
March 28, 1926. –1953 Brooklyn Dodgers NL

Mike Trombley was born in Springfield, Massachusetts on April
14, 1967. He debuted in the major leagues on August 19, 1992 and

pitched until his final game which was on May 27, 2002. He appeared in 509 baseball games and had a record of 37 wins and 47 losses to go with a 4.48 ERA. He also had a total of 44 saves for his career. –1992-1999 Minnesota Twins AL, 2000-2001 Baltimore Orioles AL, 2001 Los Angeles Dodgers NL, 2002 Minnesota Twins AL

STONEHAM

Bill Annis was born in Stoneham, Massachusetts on May 24, 1857 and had a major league career that lasted from May 1, 1884 until August 8, 1884. He was an outfielder who played in a total of 27 games. In those games he had a total of 17 hits including two doubles. His lifetime batting average was .177. He died in Kennebunkport, Maine on June 10, 1923 and is buried in Lindenwood Cemetery in Stoneham. – 1884 Boston Beaneaters NL

Marty McHale was born in Stoneham, Massachusetts on October 30, 1886. He made his major league debut as a pitcher on September 28, 1910. His final game was on May 8, 1916 and in his career he appeared in a total of 64 games and had a record of 11 wins and 30 losses and a 3.57 career earned run average. He passed away on May 7, 1979 in Hempstead, New York and is buried in the Cemetery of the Holy Rood in Westbury New York. –1910-1911 Boston Red Sox AL, 1913-1915 New York Yankees AL, 1916 Boston Red Sox AL, 1916 Cleveland Indians AL

STURBRIDGE

Bill Fox played in the major leagues as a shortstop and a second baseman from August 20, 1897 until September 12, 1901. He only got into a total of 47 games and had 32 hits in 173 at bats. Of those hits, 12 were doubles and one was a triple and he ended his career with a batting average of .185. He was born in Sturbridge, Massachusetts on January 15, 1872 and passed away in Minneapolis, Minnesota on May 7, 1946. He is buried in Minneapolis at St. Mary's Cemetery. –1897 Washington Senators NL, 1901 Cincinnati Reds NL

STOUGHTON

Bill Chamberlain pitched in the major leagues from August 2, 1932 until September 23, 1932. In the 12 games he pitched in he had a record of zero wins and five losses and a career ERA of 4.57. He passed away in Brockton, Massachusetts on February 6, 1994 and he is buried in the Milton Cemetery in Milton, Massachusetts. –1932 Chicago White Sox AL

Scott Stewart was born in Stoughton, Massachusetts on August 14, 1975. He made his major league debut on April 5, 2001 and pitched in the major leagues until October 3, 2004. He appeared in 214 games and had a record of 11 wins and six losses as well as a 3.99 earned run average for his career. –2001-2003 Montreal Expos NL, 2004 Cleveland Indians AL, 2004 Los Angeles Dodgers NL

TAUNTON

George Bignell was born in Taunton, Massachusetts on July 18, 1858 and played in the major leagues as a catcher from September 27, 1884 until October 5, 1884. In four games he had two hits in nine at bats and also scored four runs. He ended his career with a batting average of .222. What a lot of people do not know about Bignell is that on October 3, 1884 he set a record for catchers in the major leagues that still stands today. That record is that Bignell had 17 putouts and six assists in a nine inning game for a total of 23 chances, a record that has lasted for almost 120 years. He passed away on January 16, 1925 in Providence, Rhode Island and is buried in St. Joseph's Cemetery in Taunton, Massachusetts. –1884 Milwaukee Brewers UA

Scott Hemond was a catcher and a second and third baseman in a major league career that lasted from September 9, 1989 until September 29, 1995. In 298 games he scored 79 runs and had 58 runs batted in.

He had a total of 132 hits including 30 doubles and 12 home runs and his lifetime batting average was .217. –1989-1992 Oakland Athletics AL, 1992 Chicago White Sox AL, 1993-1994 Oakland Athletics AL, 1995 St Louis Cardinals NL

TEMPLETON

Mike Kelley was born in Templeton, Massachusetts on December 2, 1875. His major league debut was on July 15, 1899 and he played in the major leagues until October 14, 1899. He played in 76 games as a first baseman and had 68 hits in 282 at bats for a .241 batting average. Of those hits, 11 were doubles, two were triples and three were home runs. He passed away in Minneapolis, Minnesota on June 6, 1955 and is buried in the Lakewood Cemetery in Minneapolis. – 1899 Louisville Colonels NL

TURNERS FALLS

Rico Brogna was born in Turners Falls, Massachusetts on April 18, 1970. He was a first baseman in the major leagues from August 8, 1992 until July 16, 2001. In 848 games he had 458 runs batted in and he scored 379 runs. He had a total of 795 hits including 176 doubles, 13 triples and 106 home runs. He also had a lifetime batting average of .269. He was also a pretty good defensive player as he handled a total of 6,924 chances and only had 33 errors which figures out to a .995 fielding percentage which is good enough for 17th place all time. In fact, in 1998 he led the National League with a fielding percentage of .998 when he only made three errors in 1,208 chances. – 1992 Detroit Tigers AL, 1994-1996 New York Mets NL, 1997-2000 Philadelphia Phillies NL, 2000 Boston Red Sox AL, 2001 Atlanta Braves NL

Leroy "Chick" Maynard was born in Turners Falls, Massachusetts on November 2, 1896. His major league career, which went from June 27, 1922 until July 8, 1922, was spent as a shortstop. He appeared in 12 ballgames and had a total of three hits in 24 at bats for a .125 batting average. He passed away in Bangor, Maine on January 31, 1957 and is buried in the Millinocket Cemetery in Millinocket, Maine. – 1922 Boston Red Sox AL

UPTON

Walter "Doc" Curley was born in Upton, Massachusetts on March 12, 1874. His playing career lasted only from September 12th until September 22, 1899. In that period he appeared as a second baseman in 10 games. In those 10 games he had a total of four hits including a triple. He scored four runs and had two runs batted in and his career batting average was .108. He passed away in Worcester, Massachusetts on September 23, 1820 and is buried in St. Mary's Catholic Cemetery in Milford, Massachusetts. –1899 Chicago Orphans NL

WAKEFIELD

Andy Harrington was born in Wakefield, Massachusetts on November 13, 1888. He made his major league debut on September 8, 1913 which ended up being his only big league appearance. He was a pitcher and he did not record either a win or a loss in his only pitching performance. He did end up with a career earned run average of 9.00. He passed away on November 12, 1938 in Malden, Massachusetts and is buried in the Mount Calvary Cemetery in Roslindale, Massachusetts. – 1913 Cincinnati Reds NL

WALPOLE

William "Roscoe" Coughlin was born in Walpole, Massachusetts on March 15, 1868. He made his debut in the major leagues on April 22, 1890 as a pitcher and he pitched in his final game on October 2, 1891. After appearing in 19 games, he had a record of seven wins and 10 losses to go with a 4.10 ERA. He died in Chelsea, Massachusetts on March 20, 1951 and is buried in St. Patrick's Cemetery in Lowell, Massachusetts. – 1890 Chicago Colts NL, 1891 New York Giants NL

Joe Morgan was a third baseman, second baseman and pinch hitter in a career that began on April 14, 1959 and ended on October 3, 1964. In 88

games he had 36 hits including five doubles, three triples and two home runs. His lifetime batting average was .193 and he was born in Walpole, Massachusetts on November 19, 1930. – 1959 Milwaukee Braves NL, 1959- Kansas City Athletics AL, 1960 Philadelphia Phillies NL, 1960 -1961 Cleveland Indians AL, 1964 St Louis Cardinals NL

WALTHAM

Tom Cotter was born in Waltham, Massachusetts on September 30, 1866. He made his major league debut on September 3, 1891 and played until October 5, 1891. He was a catcher and a right fielder that got into a total of six games for his career. He had three hits in 12 at bats for a .250 batting average. He passed away on November 22, 1906 in Brookline, Massachusetts and is buried in the Calvary Cemetery in Waltham. –1891 Boston Reds AA

Frank "Runt" Cox was a shortstop in the major leagues from August 13, 1884 until September 29, 1884. He appeared in 27 games and had 13 hits in 102 at bats. Included in those hits were three doubles and one triple and a .127 batting average. He was born in Waltham, Massachusetts on August 29, 1957 and passed away on June 24, 1928 in Hartford, Massachusetts. He is buried in the St Bernard Cemetery in Rockville, Connecticut. – 1884 Detroit Wolverines NL

John "Cliff" Happenny was born in Waltham, Massachusetts on May 18, 1901. His major league career was from July 2, 1923 until October 6, 1923. He was a second and third baseman as well as a shortstop that appeared in 32 baseball games. In those games he had a total of 19 hits including five doubles in 86 at bats. He ended up his career with a batting average of .221. Happenny passed away on December 29, 1988 in Coral Springs, Florida and is buried in Our Lady Queen of Heaven Cemetery in Fort Lauderdale, Florida. – 1923 Chicago White Sox AL

Lee King played left field, shortstop and third base in a career in major league baseball that lasted from June 24, 1916 until April 28,

1919. In the 44 games that he appeared in, he had 27 hits including one double and three triples and a lifetime batting average of .188. He was born in Waltham, Massachusetts on March 28, 1894 and passed away on September 7, 1938 in Chelsea, Massachusetts. He is buried in the Mount Benedict Cemetery in West Roxbury, Massachusetts. – 1916 Philadelphia Athletics AL, 1919 Boston Braves NL

John "Jack" Leary was born in Waltham, Massachusetts on May 2, 1891. His career in the major leagues started on April 14, 1914 and ended on September 27, 1915. He appeared in 219 games as a catcher and a first baseman and had 196 hits including 38 doubles and three triples to go with a lifetime batting average of .258. He passed away on August 18, 1961 in Waltham and was buried in the Calvary Cemetery in Waltham. – 1914-1915 St Louis Browns AL

Tom Stankard played shortstop and third base during the course of his major league baseball career, which lasted for only two games, July 2, 1904 and July 26, 1904. He did not record a hit in two times at bat. He was born in Waltham, Massachusetts on March 20, 1882 and passed away in Waltham on June 13, 1958. He was later buried in the Calvary Cemetery in Waltham. – 1904 Pittsburgh Pirates NL

WARE

William "Candy" Cummings was born in Ware, Massachusetts on October 14, 1848. His major league debut was on April 23, 1872 and his final game was on August 18, 1877. He was a pitcher and an outfielder and as a batter he is credited with appearing in 247 games. He had 227 hits in 1,068 at bats which is a batting average of .213. Of the 227 hits he got, 29 were doubles and nine were triples. He scored 149 runs and had 107 runs batted in. He did not ever lead the league in any category as a hitter other than in 1872 when he led the league in striking out. As a pitcher he appeared in 242 games and had a record of 145 wins and 94 losses. His career ERA was 2.42 and in 1872, he was the league leader in games and games started with 55. He also led the league in complete games with 53 and shutouts with three as well as innings pitched with 497. In 1875 he led the league in shutouts with seven and he also struck out 82 batters which led the league. Strangely you may ask then why was he elected to the Baseball Hall of Fame in Cooperstown in 1939 as a Pioneer/Executive? Well, Cummings was credited with inventing what is known as the curveball. It is even more amazing given the fact that Cummings pitched according to the rules at the time which stipulated that the pitcher's arm must be perpendicular to the ground as he threw underhanded. Through much practice he found success with the curve and that is why he was elected to the Hall of Fame with the statistics he has. He passed away in Toledo, Ohio on May 16, 1924 and was later buried in the Aspen Grove Cemetery in Ware. – 1872 New York Mutuals NA, 1873 Baltimore Canaries NA, 1874 Philadelphia Whites NA, 1875 Hartford Dark Blues NA, 1876 Hartford Dark Blues NL, 1877 Cincinnati Reds NL

Joe "Peco" Giard was a pitcher in the major leagues from April 18, 1925 until September 25, 1927. He had a record of 13 wins and 15 losses and a 5.96 career earned run average. He was born in Ware, Massachusetts on October 7, 1898 and passed away in Worcester, Massachusetts on July 10, 1956. He was later buried in the Mount Carmel Cemetery in Ware. – 1925-1926 St Louis Browns AL, 1927 New York Yankees AL

John "Nig" Grabowski was born in Ware, Massachusetts on January 7, 1900. He made his major league debut on July 11, 1924 and played until September 21, 1931. He was a catcher who played in 296 games and had 206 hits. Of the hits he had, 25 were doubles, 8 were triples and 3 were home runs. He scored 84 runs and had 86 runs batted in. His lifetime batting average was. 252. He was also a member of the famed 1927 World Champion New York Yankees team, which is a team many people consider to be the greatest baseball team on all time. He passed away on May 23, 1946 in Albany, New York and is buried in the Park View Cemetery in Schenectady, New York. – 1924-1925 Chicago White Sox AL, 1927-1929 New York Yankees AL, 1931 Detroit Tigers AL

Pat McCauley was a catcher in the major leagues from September 5, 1893 until September 3, 1903. He was in a total of 37 games and had 23 hits including three doubles and three home runs and he had a lifetime batting average of .193. He was born in Ware, Massachusetts on June 10, 1870 and passed away on January 17, 1917 in Hoboken, New Jersey. He was buried in St. William's Cemetery in Ware, Massachusetts. – 1893 St Louis Browns NL, 1896 Washington Senators 1896, 1903 New York Highlanders AL

Billy Jo Robidoux was a first baseman and a left fielder in a career that started on September 11, 1985 and ended on September 17, 1990. He was in 173 games and had a total of 98 hits in 498 at bats for an average of .209. He also had 43 runs scored and 43 runs batted in. In his hit total of 98, he had 21 doubles and five home runs. He was born on January 13, 1964 in Ware, Massachusetts. – 1985-1988 Milwaukee Brewers AL, 1989 Chicago White Sox AL, 1990 Boston Red Sox AL

John "Nap" Shea was born in Ware, Massachusetts on May 23, 1874. He was a catcher who started in the major leagues on September 11, 1902. Then four days later on September 15, 1902 he played in his last ball game. He had one hit in eight at bats for a .125 average. He passed away in Bloomfield, Michigan on July 8, 1968 and is buried in St. Mary's Cemetery in Ware, Massachusetts. – 1902 Philadelphia Phillies NL

Patrick "Red" Shea was born in Ware, Massachusetts on November 29, 1898. He pitched in the major leagues from May 6, 1918 until June 9, 1922. In the 23 games he pitched in, he had a record of five wins and five losses and a 3.80 ERA. He passed away in Stafford, Connecticut on November 17, 1981 and is buried in St. Thomas's Cemetery in Palmer, Massachusetts. –1918 Philadelphia Athletics AL, 1921-1922 New York Giants NL

WATERTOWN

Edward "Dee" Cousineau was born in Watertown, Massachusetts on December 16, 1898. He was a catcher in the major leagues who played from October 6, 1923 until May 2, 1925. In the five games he played in he had a batting average of .500 with two hits in four at bats. He passed away in Watertown on July 14, 1951 and is buried in St. Patrick's Cemetery in Watertown. – 1923-1925 Boston Braves NL

John "Jack" Hoey was born in Watertown, Massachusetts on November 10, 1881. He played left field for his major league career which began on July 27, 1906 and ended on October 7, 1908. In 146 games he had 116 hits that included 10 doubles and five triples. His batting average for his career was .232. He passed away on November 14, 1947 in Waterbury, Connecticut and is buried in St. James's Cemetery in Naugatuck, Connecticut. – 1906-1908 Boston Americans/Red Sox AL

WAYLAND

Frank Leary was a major league pitcher from April 30th until May 5th 1907. In the two games he pitched in he had no wins and one loss and an ERA of 1.13. He was born February 26, 1881 in Wayland, Massachusetts and passed away on October 4, 1904. He is buried in St. Patrick's Cemetery in Natick, Massachusetts. – 1907 Cincinnati Reds NL

WEBSTER

George "Jonah" Derby was born in Webster, Massachusetts on July 6, 1857. He both pitched and played the outfield in a career that began on May 2, 1881 and ended on July 3, 1883. As a pitcher he had a record of 48 wins and 56 losses in a total of 110 games. He also had a career earned run average of 3.01. In 1881 when he had a record of 29 wins and 26 losses, he led the league in strikeouts with 212. As a batter he was credited with appearing in 115 games with 87 hits in 444 at bats. Of the hits he had, six were doubles and two were triples and his lifetime batting average was .196. He passed away in Philadelphia, Pennsylvania on July 4, 1925 and is buried in the Wellsboro Cemetery in Wellsboro, Pennsylvania. – 1881-1882 Detroit Wolverines NL, 1883 Buffalo Bisons NL

Frank "Shadow" Gilmore was a pitcher in the major leagues from September 11, 1886 until July 4, 1888. He appeared in 49 big league ballgames and had a record of 12 wins and 33 losses and a 4.26 earned run average for his career. He was born in Webster, Massachusetts on April 27, 1864 and passed away in Hartford, Connecticut on July 21, 1929. He is buried in the Mount St. Benedict Cemetery in Bloomfield, Connecticut. – 1886 – 1888 Washington Nationals NL

Mike Sullivan was born in Webster, Massachusetts on June 10, 1860. He was a left fielder and a third baseman who made his debut in the major leagues on April 26, 1888 and played in the majors for only a short time until June 20, 1888. In 28 games he had 31 hits in 112 at bats for a .277 batting average. Included in his hit total were five doubles, six triples and one home run. He passed away in Webster, Massachusetts on June 16, 1929 and is buried in the Calvary Cemetery in Dudley, Massachusetts.—1888 Philadelphia Athletics AA

WELLESEY HILLS

Jack Sanford was born in Wellesley Hills on May 18, 1929. He made his major league pitching debut on September 1, 1956 and then threw in his final game on August 6, 1967. He was in a total of 388 games and had a record of 137 wins and 101 losses to go with his 3.69ERA. In 1957 he led the National League in strikeouts with 188. He was a member of the 1957 National League All Star team and also was voted Rookie of the Year in the National League for the 1957 season. He passed away on March 7, 2000 and was later cremated. – 1956-1958 Philadelphia Phillies NL, 1959-1965 San Francisco Giants NL, 1965-1967 California Angels AL, 1967 Kansas City Athletics AL

WENHAM

Joe Batchelder was born in Wenham, Massachusetts on July 1, 1898. He made his pitching debut on September 29, 1923 and then he pitched in his final game on May 20, 1925. In 11 games he had a record of one win and zero losses and a 5.66 ERA. He died in Beverley, Massachusetts on May 5, 1989 and was buried in the Hamilton Cemetery in Hamilton, Massachusetts. – 1923-1925 Boston Braves NL

WEST BOLYSTON

Charlie Baker was born in West Boylston on January 15, 1856. His major league career began on August 1, 1884 and ended on August 27, 1884. During that career in the majors Baker played right field, shortstop and third base in a total of 15 games. In those games he had eight hits in 57 at bats for a .140 batting average. Those hits included two doubles and one home run. He passed away in Goffstown, New Hampshire on January 15, 1937 and is buried in the Forest Vale Cemetery in Hudson, New Hampshire. – 1884 Chicago Pittsburgh UA

WEST BRIDGEWATER

Wally "Doc" Snell was born in West Bridgewater, Massachusetts on May 19, 1889. He played in the major leagues from August 1, 1913 until October 4, 1913 as a catcher. In the six games he played in he had three hits in 12 at bats for a .250 batting average. He passed away in Providence, Rhode Island on July 23, 1980 after a distinguished career in science and teaching at Brown University. He was later cremated. – 1913 Boston Red Sox AL

WEST NEWTON

Bill "Crungy" Cronin was born in West Newton, Massachusetts on December 26, 1902. He made his major league debut on July 4, 1928 and played in the big leagues as a catcher until his final game on September 21, 1931. In 126 games he had 68 hits in 296 at bats for a .230 batting average. Included in his hit total were 15 doubles and two triples. He passed away on October 26, 1966 in Newton, Massachusetts and is buried in the Newton Cemetery. –1928-1931 Boston Braves NL

George "Chippy" Gaw was born in West Newton, Massachusetts on March 13, 1892 and made his major league debut on April 20, 1920 and in his career that ended on July 4, 1920, he pitched in a total of six games. He had a record of one win and one loss and a 4.85 earned run average. He passed away on May 26, 1968 in Boston and is buried in the Calvary Cemetery in Waltham, Massachusetts. – 1920 Chicago Cubs NL

Don Nottebart was born in West Newton, Massachusetts on January 23, 1936. He was a pitcher who played in the major leagues from July 1, 1960 until September 6, 1969. He had 36 wins and 51 losses in the major leagues after pitching in 296 baseball games. His career earned run average was 3.65. He passed away in Cypress, Texas on October 4, 2007 and was later cremated. – 1960-1962 Milwaukee Braves NL, 1963-1965 Houston Colt 45's / Astros, 1966-1967 Cincinnati Reds NL, 1969 New York Yankees AL, 1969 Chicago Cubs NL

WEST QUINCY

Bill Ferrazzzi was born in West Quincy, Massachusetts on April 19, 1907. His career in the major leagues was from September 7 to September 16, 1935. He was a pitcher in three games who had a record of one win and two losses as well as a 5.14 ERA. He died in Gainesville, Florida on August 10, 1993 and is buried in the Forest Meadow Memorial Park in Gainesville. – 1935 Philadelphia Athletics AL

Ralph McLeod was a pinch hitter and a left fielder that played in the major leagues from September 14, 1938 until October 1, 1938. In the six games he was in, he had two hits including a double for a batting average of .286. He passed away on April 27, 2007 in Weymouth, Massachusetts and is buried in the Pine Hill Cemetery in Quincy, Massachusetts. – 1938 Boston Bees NL

WEST SPRINGFIELD

Leo "Leo the Lip" Durocher was born in West Springfield, Massachusetts on July 27, 1905. He was a shortstop and a second baseman that played in the major leagues from October 2, 1925 until April 18, 1945. As a player he appeared in 1,637 games and had 1,320 hits in 5,350 at bats for a batting average of .247. He had 210 doubles, 56 triples and 24 home runs. He also had 567 runs batted in and scored another 575 runs himself. He was a member of the 1928 World Champion New York Yankees as well as the 1934 World Champion St Louis Cardinals. It was that Cardinals team with the Dean Brothers and Pepper Martin that became known as the "Gashouse Gang" for their hustling play. Durocher was also a member of the 1936, 1938 and 1940 National League All Star teams.

Durocher also was player manager of the Brooklyn Dodgers from 1939 to 1945, and then he went on to manage a number of different teams for the next 24 years. While he was a manager his teams won three pennants and in 1954 he was the manager of the 1954 World Champion New York Giants. His total of 2,008 wins as a manager place him 10th on the all-time list ahead of Casey Stengel and just behind Walter Alston and Joe McCarthy. Durocher died on October 7, 1991 in Palm Springs, California and is buried in the Forest Lawn-Hollywood Hill Cemetery. Three years after he passed away he was elected to the Baseball Hall of Fame as a manager by the Veterans' Committee. – 1925/1928-1929 New York Yankees AL, 1930-1933 Cincinnati Reds NL, 1933-1937 St Louis Cardinals NL, 1938-1945 Brooklyn Dodgers NL

WEST STOCKBRIDGE

Peter Noonan—SEE BERKSHIRE COUNTY PLAYERS

WESTFIELD

Al Hubbard was a catcher and a shortstop in his major league career which lasted from September 13th to September 15th 1883. In the two games he appeared in he had two hits in six at bats for a .333

batting average. Hubbard was born in Westfield, Massachusetts on December 9, 1860 and passed away on December 14, 1930 in Newton, Massachusetts. He is buried in the Newton Cemetery in Newton, Massachusetts. – 1883 Philadelphia Athletics AA

William "Adonis" Terry was born in Westfield, Massachusetts on August 7, 1864. He was a pitcher and an outfielder in his major league career which lasted from May 1, 1884 until April 27, 1897. As a pitcher he appeared in 440 games and had a record of 197 wins and 196 losses to go with a 3.74 ERA. During his pitching career 3 times he had 20 or more wins (1889-22 wins, 1890- 26 wins, 1895-21 wins). He had a total of 1553 strikeouts in his career as a pitcher and has 367 complete games. As for when Terry was batting, he was in 667 games and had 594 hits in 2,389 at bats which is a .249 batting average. He had included in his hit total, 76 doubles, 54 triples and 15 home runs. He also had 287 runs batted in and scored 314 runs himself. He passed away in Milwaukee, Wisconsin on February 24, 1915 and was later cremated. – 1884-1885 Brooklyn Atlantics AA , 1886-Brooklyn Grays AA , 1887-1889 Brooklyn Bridegrooms AA, 1890-1891 Brooklyn Grooms NL, 1892 Baltimore Orioles NL, 1892-1894 Pittsburgh Pirates NL, 1894-1897 Chicago Colts NL

WESTON

Ed McLane was born in Weston, Massachusetts on August 20, 1881. He was a right fielder whose only appearance in a major league baseball game came on October 5, 1907. He did not have a hit in two at bats. He passed away on August 21, 1975 in Baltimore, Maryland and he is buried in the New Cathedral Cemetery in Baltimore. – 1907 Brooklyn Superbas NL

WEYMOUTH

Frank "Buster" Burrell was born in Weymouth, Massachusetts on December 22, 1866. He was a catcher for his major league career which began on August 1, 1891 and ended on October 2, 1897. He appeared in 112 games and had 96 hits including 13 doubles, three triples and three home runs. His career batting average was .246. He passed away on May 8, 1962 in Weymouth and is buried in the Fairmount Cemetery in Weymouth. – 1891 New York Giants NL 1895-1897 Brooklyn Bridegrooms/Grooms NL

John Dowd (born John Leo O'Dowd) was a shortstop in the major leagues from July 3, 1912 until July 13, 1912. He appeared in 10 games and had six hits in 31 at bats including one1 double for a .194 batting average. He passed away in Fort Lauderdale, Florida on January 31, 1981. –1912 New York Highlanders AL

Dan "Howling Dan/Dapper Dan" Howley was born on October 16, 1885 in Weymouth Massachusetts. He played in the major leagues from May 15, 1913 until August 23, 1913. He was a catcher and he appeared in 26 games and had four hits including two doubles for a .125 batting average. He passed away on March 10, 1944 in Weymouth and is buried in St. Francis Xavier Cemetery in Weymouth. – 1913 Philadelphia Phillies NL

Leon "Doc" Martel was born in Weymouth, Massachusetts on June 29, 1883. He was a catcher and a first baseman when he played from July 6, 1909 until June 18, 1910. In 34 games he had 15 hits in 72 at bats for a .208 batting average. Those hits included three doubles and one triple and he later passed away in Washington DC, on October 11, 1947. He is buried in Arlington National Cemetery. – 1909 Philadelphia Phillies NL, 1910 Boston Doves NL

Joe "Big Joe" Mulligan was a pitcher in the major leagues from June 28, 1934 until September 30, 1934. In the 14 ballgames he pitched in he had a record of one win and zero losses and a 3.63 ERA. He was born in Weymouth, Massachusetts on July 31, 1913 and passed away in West Roxbury, Massachusetts on June 5, 1986. He was buried in St. Joseph's Cemetery in West Roxbury. – 1934 Boston Red Sox AL

Ken Nash was born in Weymouth, Massachusetts on July 14, 1888 and made his major league debut on July 4, 1912. During the course of his 35 game career he played second and third base as well as shortstop. He had a total of 18 hits in 74 at bats for a .243 batting average. Of those 18 hits that he had, three were doubles and one was a triple. He passed away in Epsom, New Hampshire on February 16, 1977 and is buried in the city of Weymouth's Highland Cemetery.—1912 Cleveland Naps AL, 1914 St Louis Cardinals

WHITMAN

Fred "Sugar" Kane was born March 9, 1895 in Whitman, Massachusetts. He was a left fielder in the major leagues from September 13, 1915 until April 28, 1919. His career was four games long and he had two hits including a triple in 10 at bats and his lifetime batting average was .182. He passed away in Brockton, Massachusetts on December 2, 1962. He was later buried in Brockton's Calvary Cemetery.—1915 Brooklyn Tip Tops FL, 1919 New York Yankees AL

WILBRAHAM

Ed Cassian was born on November 28, 1867 in Wilbraham, Massachusetts. He pitched in the major leagues from June 26, 1891 until September 20, 1891. After pitching in 13 games his record was three wins and seven losses with a 4.45 ERA. He passed away in Meriden, Connecticut on September 10, 1918 and is buried in that city's St John's Cemetery. –1891 Philadelphia Phillies NL, 1891 Washington Statesmen AA

WILLIAMSTOWN

Bob Petit—SEE BERKSHIRE COUNTY PLAYERS

WINCHENDON

Fred Woodcock was a pitcher in the major leagues from May 17, 1892

until June 17, 1892. He was in a total of five games for his career and had a record of one win and two losses and a 3.55 ERA. He was born in Winchendon, Massachusetts on May 17, 1868 and passed away on August 11, 1943 in Ashburnham, Massachusetts where he is buried in the New Cemetery in Ashburnham. – 1892 Pittsburgh Pirates NL

WINCHESTER

Art "Lefty" Johnson was born in Winchester, Massachusetts on July 16, 1919. He was a major league pitcher from September 22, 1940 until September 19, 1942. In the 49 ballgames that he pitched in, he had a record of seven wins and 16 losses and a 3.68 ERA. He later died in Holden, Massachusetts on April 27, 2008. He was buried in St. Mary's Cemetery in Holden. – 1940-1942 Boston Braves/Bees NL

Catching, first base and pinch hitting were where **Matt Merullo** played during the course of his major league career which ran from April 12, 1989 until September 29, 1995. He was in a total of 223 games and scored 37 runs while also having 59 runs batted in. Out of the 116 hits that he had in 496 at bats, 17 were doubles, two were triples and seven were home runs. He had a lifetime batting average of .234. Merullo was born in Winchester, Massachusetts on August 4, 1965 and is the grandson of Lennie Merullo who played in the major leagues from September of 1941 until August of 1947. – 1989/1991-1993 Chicago White Sox AL, 1994 Cleveland Indians AL, 1995 Minnesota Twins AL

WINTHROP

Art Ditmar was born in Suffolk County in the town of Winthrop, Massachusetts on April 3, 1929. He made his major league debut on April 19, 1954 and pitched in the major leagues until May 19, 1962 which was his final big league appearance. In 287 games he had a record of 72 wins and 77 losses to go with a career earned run average of 3.98. He was a member of the 1958 World Champion New York Yankees. He was the pitcher for the Philadelphia Athletics when the A's played their last game in Shibe Park before moving to Kansas City. His son Todd has coached soccer at Westfield State College in Westfield, Massachusetts for a number of years.—1954 Philadelphia Athletics AL, 1955-1956 Kansas City Athletics AL, 1957-1961 New York Yankees AL, 1961-1962 Kansas City Athletics AL

Bill Vinton was born in Winthrop, Massachusetts on April 27, 1865. In the major leagues he pitched and played the outfield from July 3, 1884 until September 16, 1885. As a pitcher he appeared in 37 games and had a record of 17 wins and 19 losses to go with a 2.46 career earned run average. When he was hitting he was credited with appearing in 37 games and had a total of 15 hits in 134 at bats for a .112 career batting average. He passed away on September 3, 1893 in Pawtucket, Rhode Island. –1884-1885 Philadelphia Athletics NL, 1885 Philadelphia Quakers AA

WOBURN

Arthur "Jocko" Conlon was born in Woburn, Massachusetts on December 10, 1897. During the course of his major league career which began on April 17, 1923 and ended on October 6, 1923 Conlon was a second and third baseman as well as a shortstop that appeared in 59 games. He had 32 hits in 147 at bats including three doubles. He had a career batting average of .218 and he later passed away on August 5, 1987 in Falmouth, Massachusetts. He is buried in the Massachusetts National Cemetery in Bourne. – 1923 Boston Braves NL

John Doherty was born in Woburn, Massachusetts on August 22, 1951. He made his major league debut on June 1, 1974 and was in the major leagues until July 30, 1975 when he played in his final game. His career was spent as a first baseman and he had a total of 76 hits in 317 at bats. Out of his total hits, 17 were doubles, one was a triple and four were home runs. He also had a lifetime batting average of .240. –1974-1975 California Angels AL

Henry "Doc" McMahon was born in Woburn, Massachusetts on December 19, 1886. His major league career consisted of only one game and that was on October 6, 1908. He was a pitcher and in that game he was credited for the win and ended up with a career ERA of 3.00. He died in Woburn on December 11, 1929 and is buried in the Calvary Cemetery in Woburn. – 1908 Boston Red Sox AL

Dominic Mulrenan was born in Woburn, Massachusetts on December 18, 1893 and went on to a career in the major leagues that lasted from April 24, 1921 until August 5, 1921. In the 12 major league ballgames that he appeared in as a pitcher he had a record of two wins and eight losses and a 7.23 ERA. He passed away in Melrose, Massachusetts on July 27, 1964 and is buried in the Wyoming Cemetery in Melrose, Massachusetts. – 1921 Chicago White Sox AL

Ken Weafer played in his only major league baseball game on May 29, 1936. He was a pitcher and in that game he did not get credit for the win or the loss and ended up with a 12.00 ERA. He was born February 6, 1913 in Woburn, Massachusetts and passed away in Guilderland, New York on June 4, 2005. He is buried in the St. Agnes Cemetery in Menands, New York. 1936 Boston Bees NL

WORCESTER

George Adams was born in Worcester, Massachusetts in January of 1855. He was a first baseman and a center fielder in a major league career that went for a total of one week from June 14, 1879 until June 21, 1879. In the four games he appeared in he had three hits in 13 at bats for a .231 batting average.—1879 Syracuse Stars NL

Pat Bourque was born in Worcester, Massachusetts on March 23, 1947. He was a first baseman and a pinch hitter in the major leagues for his career which was from September 6, 1971 until September 28, 1974. In 201 games he had a total of 87 hits including 17 doubles, three triples and 12 home runs. His lifetime batting average was .215 and he also scored 36 runs while having 61 runs batted in. Bourque was also a member of the 1973 World Champion Oakland Athletics. – 1971 Chicago Cubs NL, 1973- 1974 Oakland Athletics AL, 1974 Minnesota Twins AL

Steve Brady was a right fielder, as well as a first and second baseman during the course of his major league career which began on July 23, 1874 and ended on October 5, 1886. In the 490 games that he appeared in, he had 529 hits in 2,030 at bats. Included in the hits were 50 doubles, 20 triples and four home runs. He also scored 313 runs and had 114 runs batted in. He was born in Worcester, Massachusetts on July 14, 1851 and passed away on October 5, 1886 in Hartford, Connecticut. He was buried in Bloomfield, Connecticut at the Mount St Benedict Cemetery.—1874 Hartford Dark Blues NA, Washington Nationals NA, 1875 Hartford Dark Blues NA, New York Metropolitans AA

William "Kitty" Bransfied was born in Worcester, Massachusetts on January 7, 1875. He made his major league debut on August 22, 1898 and his final game was on September 14, 1911. He was a first baseman who appeared in 1330 games. He had a total of 1,351 hits including 225 doubles, 75 triples and 13 home runs. He scored 529 runs and also had 637 runs batted in and a batting average for his career of .270. He passed away in Worcester, Massachusetts on May 1, 1947 and was buried in St. John's Cemetery in Worcester. –1898 Boston Beaneaters NL, 1901-1904 Pittsburgh Pirates NL, 1905-1911 Philadelphia Phillies NL, 1911 Chicago Cubs NL

Hugh "Hugo" Canavan was born in Worcester, Massachusetts on May 13, 1897. He was a pitcher and outfielder in his career which lasted from April 23, 1918 until July 25, 1918. In 11 games as a pitcher he had a record of zero wins and four losses and a career ERA of 6.36. Batting stats showed he had two hits in 21 at bats for a .095 batting average. One of his two hits was a double and he managed to score two runs. He passed away on September 4, 1967 in Boston and is buried in St. John's Cemetery in Worcester. – 1918 Boston Braves NL

Ralph "Doc" Carroll was a catcher who played in the major leagues from July 27, 1916 until July 26, 1916. In 10 major league ballgames he had two hits in 22 at bats and scored one run. He ended up with a career batting average of .091. He was born in Worcester, Massachusetts on December 28, 1891, and he passed away in Worcester on June 27, 1983. He is buried in St. John's Cemetery in Worcester. –1916 Phialdelphia Athletics AL

Allan Collamore was born in Worcester, Massachusetts on June 5, 1887. He was a pitcher who got into his first major league game on April 15, 1911 and then threw in his last game on October 2, 1915. In between he was in a total of 40 games and he had a record of five wins and 13 losses with a 3.30 ERA. He passed away on August 8, 1980 in Battle Creek, Michigan and is buried in the Oak Hill Cemetery in Battle Creek. –1911 Philadelphia Athletics AL, 1914-1915 Cleveland Naps/Indians AL

Tim "Tiny" Collins was born in Worcester, Massachusetts on August 21, 1989. He is a pitcher in the major leagues who threw in his first contest on March 31, 2011 and so far has pitched in a total of 137 games for the Kansas City Royals in the American League. He had a record of nine wins and eight losses and a 3.49 ERA.

Gene "Red" Desautels was a catcher in the major leagues from June 22, 1930 until September 22, 1946. In 712 baseball games he had 469 hits in 2,012 at bats. Included in those hits are 73 doubles, 11 triples and three home runs, and his lifetime batting average is .233. He has 187 runs batted in and had scored 211 runs himself. He was born in Worcester, Massachusetts on June 13, 1907 and passed away on November 5 1994 in Flint, Michigan. He is buried in the New Calvary Catholic Cemetery in Flint. – 1930-1933 Detroit Tigers AL, 1937-1940 Boston Red Sox AL, 1941-1943/1945 Cleveland Indians AL, 1946 Philadelphia Athletics AL

Mark "The Bird" Fidrych was born on August 14, 1954 in Worcester, Massachusetts. He pitched in the major leagues from April 20, 1976 until October 1, 1980. During the course of his career he had gained a reputation for "dancing to the beat of his own drummer." He would do such things as talk to the ball as he was on the pitching mound, manicure the mound every inning when he pitched and thank his fielders for spectacular plays. He had created quite the sensation. He also was not a bad pitcher as he ended up with a record of 29 wins and 19 losses and a 3.10 ERA for his career. In his rookie season of 1976 Fidrych led the league with a 2.34 ERA. Also in that year he had a record of 19 wins and nine losses and he completed 24 of the 29 games he started. He was voted Rookie of the Year that year and was elected to the American League All Star team. He was also selected for the All Star team in 1977 as well. Tragically he passed away at home after an unfortunate accident in Northborough, Massachusetts on April 13, 2000 and he was later cremated. – 1976-1980 Detroit Tigers

Shaun Fitzmaurice was a center fielder and a pinch runner that played in the major leagues from September 9, 1966 until October 2, 1966. In the nine games he appeared in he had two hits in 13 at bats for a .154 batting average. He was born in Worcester, Massachusetts on August 25, 1942. – 1966 New York Mets NL

Martin Flaherty was born in Worcester, Massachusetts on September 24, 1853. He was a center fielder who played in his only major league baseball game on August 18, 1881. He did not have a hit in two at bats. He passed away on June 10, 1920 in Providence, Rhode Island and is buried in East Providence at St. Anne's Cemetery. – 1881 Worcester RubyLegs NL

Rich Gedman was born in Worcester, Massachusetts on September 26, 1959. He was a catcher who made his major league debut on September 7, 1980. He played in 1,033 games and had 795 hits including 176 doubles, 12 triples and 88 home runs. He had 382 runs batted in and scored 331 runs himself. He was selected to the 1985 and 1986 American League All Star teams. He played in his final major league baseball game on October 4, 1992. – 1980-1990 Boston Red Sox AL, 1990 Houston Astros NL, 1991-1992 St Louis Cardinals NL

Tom Grant was an outfielder and a pinch hitter in a major league career that went from June 17, 1983 until October 2, 1983. In 16 ballgames he had three hits in 20 at bats including a double. His lifetime batting average was .150 and he was born in Worcester, Massachusetts on May 28, 1957. – 1983 Chicago Cubs NL

Bruno "Boon" Haas was born in Worcester, Massachusetts on May 5, 1891. He began his major league career on June 23, 1915 and played both left field and pitched until his last game which was on September 18, 1915. His pitching record shows that he had zero wins and one loss and an 11.93 ERA. Batting, he had one hit in 18 at bats during the course of 12 games. His career batting average was .056. He passed away on June 5, 1952 in Sarasota, Florida and is buried in the Hope Cemetery in Worcester, Massachusetts. –1915 Philadelphia Athletics AL

Archibald "Al" Hall was a centerfielder in the major leagues from May 1, 1879 until May 13, 1880. In the 70 games he appeared in he had 80 hits in 314 at bats. Included in his hit total were seven doubles and three triples. His lifetime batting average was .255. He was born in Worcester, Massachusetts, and he passed away in Warren, Pennsylvania on February 10, 1885. –1879 Troy Trojans NL, 1880 Cleveland Blues NL

Alva "Beartracks" Javery was born in Worcester, Massachusetts on June 15, 1918. He pitched in the major leagues from April 23, 1940 until May 8, 1946. In 205 games he had a record of 53 wins and 74 losses as well as a 3.80 career earned run average. He was selected to the National League All Star team in both 1943 and 1944. He passed away on August 16, 1977 in Putnam, Connecticut and is buried in the St. Roch Cemetery in Oxford, Massachusetts. – 1940-1946 Boston Bees/Braves NL

Mark Johnson was a first baseman, outfielder and pinch hitter in a career that began on April 26, 1995 and ended on June 2, 2002. He appeared in 428 games and had 229 hits including 50 doubles, four triples and 38 home runs. He scored 142 runs and had another 137 runs batted in. His lifetime batting average was .232 and he was born in Worcester, Massachusetts on October 17, 1967. – 1995-1997 Pittsburgh Pirates NL, 1998 Anaheim Angels AL, 2000-2002 New York Mets NL

Bryan Lahair was born in Worcester, Massachusetts on November 5, 1982. He is a first baseman and a right fielder whose major league career began on July 18, 2008. As of now he had appeared in 195 games and has 139 hits in 535 at bats. Included in the hits total are 26 doubles, one triple and 21 home runs. He also has scored 66 runs and has 56 runs batted in. –2008 Seattle Mariners AL, 2011-2012 Chicago Cubs NL

Catcher and first baseman were the positions played by **Art LaVigne** in a career that began on April 24, 1914 and ended on October 5, 1914. In 51 games he had 14 hits in 90 at bats with two of the hits being doubles. He ended up with a batting average of .156. He was born in Worcester, Massachusetts on January 26, 1885, and he passed away on July 18, 1950 in Worcester. He is buried in the Hope Cemetery in Worcester. – 1914 Buffalo Buffeds FL

Henry Lynch was a right fielder in the major leagues from September 21, 1893 until September 25, 1893. In his four game career he had three hits with two of the hits being doubles. His career batting average was .214. He was born in Worcester, Massachusetts on January 26, 1885 and he passed away on July 18, 1950 in Worcester. He is buried in the Hope Cemetery on Worcester. – 1893 Chicago Colts NL

Keith McWhorter was a pitcher in the major leagues from May 10, 1980 until October 5, 1980. In 14 games he had a record of zero wins and three losses and a 5.53 ERA. He was born in Worcester, Massachusetts on December 30, 1955. –1980 Boston Red Sox AL

James "Chippy" McGarr was born in Worcester, Massachusetts on May 10, 1863. He played in the major leagues as a second and third baseman as well as a shortstop from July 11, 1884 until September 26, 1896. In 827 games he had 875 hits with 116 doubles, 28 triples and nine home runs. He had a batting average of .269 as well as having scored 538 runs and driving in 388 runs. He passed away in Worcester, Massachusetts on June 6, 1904 and he was later buried in St. John's Cemetery in Worcester, Massachusetts. – 1884 Chicago/Pittsburgh UA, 1886-1887 Phialdelphia Athletics AA, 1888 St Louis Browns AA, 1889 Kansas City Cowboys AA, 1889 Baltimore Orioles AA, 1890 Boston Beaneaters NL, 1893-1896 Cleveland Spiders NL

Paul Mitchell pitched in the major leagues from July 1, 1975 until September 21, 1980, and in 125 games he had a record of 32 wins and

39 losses and a 4.45 ERA. He was born in Worcester on August 19, 1949. –1975 Baltimore Orioles AL, 1976-1977 Oakland Athletics AL, 1977- 1979 Seattle Mariners AL, 1979-1980 Milwaukee Brewers AL

Con "Monk" Murphy was a pitcher and a right fielder in the major leagues from September 11, 1884 until September 6, 1890. Murphy was given credit for batting in 26 games and had 15 hits in 79 at bats with a .190 batting average with two of the hits being doubles. As a pitcher he had a record of four wins and 13 losses with a 5.07 ERA. He was born in Worcester, Massachusetts on October 15, 1863 and he passed away on August 1, 1914 in Worcester. He is buried in St. John's Cemetery in Worcester. – 1884 Philadelphia Quakers NL, 1890 Brooklyn Ward Wonders PL

Eddie Phillips was born in Worcester, Massachusetts on February 17, 1901. He was a catcher in the major leagues from May 4, 1924 until September 29, 1935. In 312 games he had 126 runs batted in and he scored 82 runs. He had 236 hits in 997 at bats for a .237 batting average with 54 of the hits being doubles, six being triples and 14 being home runs. He passed away in Buffalo, New York on January 26, 1968 and is buried in the Mount Calvary Cemetery in Cheektowaga which is in New York – 1924 Boston Braves NL, 1929 Detroit Tigers AL, 1931 Pittsburgh Pirates NL, 1932 New York Yankees AL, 1934 Washington Senators AL, 1935 Cleveland Indians AL

Walt Ripley was born in Worcester, Massachusetts on November 26, 1916 and made his major league debut on August 17, 1935. He pitched in the big leagues only until September 11, 1935. In the two games he appeared in he did not get credit for the win or the loss and ended up with a 9.00 ERA. He passed away in Attleboro, Massachusetts on October 7, 1990 and is buried in the Massachusetts National Cemetery in Bourne, Massachusetts. He is the father of Allen Ripley who pitched in the major leagues from 1978 until 1982. – 1935 Boston Red Sox AL

Wilfred "Rosy" Ryan was born in Worcester, Massachusetts on March 15, 1898. He pitched in the major leagues from September 7, 1919 until

September 17, 1933. In his career which totaled 248 games he had a record of 52 wins and 47 losses and a 4.14 ERA. He was a member of the World Champion New York Giants in 1922 and he passed away in Scottsdale, Arizona on December 10, 1980. He is buried in St. John's Cemetery in Worcester, Massachusetts.—1919-1924 New York Giants NL, 1925-1926 Boston Braves NL, 1928 New York Yankees AL, 1933 Brooklyn Dodgers NL

Steve Shea was born in Worcester, Massachusetts on December 5, 1942. He made his major league debut as a pitcher on July 14, 1968 and stayed in the majors until May 21, 1969. During his 40 game career he had a record of four wins and four losses and a 3.22 ERA. –1968 Houston Astros NL, 1969 Montreal Expos NL

Tanyon Sturtze was a pitcher in the major leagues from May 3, 1995 until August 25, 2008. Sturtze appeared in 272 games in his career and had a record of 40 wins and 44 losses to go with a 5.19 career earned run average. He was born in Worcester, Massachusetts on October 12, 1970. 1995-1996 Chicago Cubs NL, 1997 Texas Rangers AL, 1999-2000 Chicago White Sox AL, 2000-2002 Tampa Bay Devil Rays AL, 2003 Toronto Blue Jays AL, 2004-2006 New York Yankees AL, 2008 Los Angeles Dodgers NL

Charles "Pussy" Tebeau was a right fielder in the major leagues from July 22, 1895 until July 24, 1895. In the two games he appeared in he had three hits and scored three runs and ended up with a .500 batting average. He was born in Worcester, Massachusetts on February 22, 1870 and passed away in Pittsfield, Massachusetts on March 25, 1950. He was later buried in St. Joseph's Cemetery in Worcester. –1895 Cleveland Spiders NL

YARMOUTH

Joel Sherman was born in Yarmouth on November 4, 1890. He pitched in the major leagues for a one week period from September 24, 1915 until September 30, 1915. In the two games he pitched in he had a record of one win and no losses and a 2.40 career earned run average. He passed away on December 21, 1987 in Cape Coral, Florida and is buried in Westerly, Rhode Island at the River Bend Cemetery. –1915 Philadelphia Athletics AL

YARMOUTHPORT

Keith Reed was a right fielder and a pinch runner in the major leagues from May 11, 2005 until May 18, 2005. In six games he had one hit in five at bats for a .200 batting average. He was born in Yarmouthport, Massachusetts on October 8, 1978. –2005 Baltimore Orioles

Baseball In The Berkshires
Williams College

Nestled in the northwestern corner of Berkshire County in Massachusetts is Williams College which was founded in 1793 because of a bequest from Colonel Ephraim Williams. At one point faculty members and trustees wanted to move the college east because of the need to attract new students. The plans fell through in 1820 and Zephaniah Swift Moore, who was president of the college at the time, left the school. When he left, 15 students went with him and supposedly some of the school's library found its way to a new home with Moore as well.

One may wonder why Williams College is included in a book devoted to the history of baseball in Massachusetts. Well, first we have to go back just a bit and discuss when Mr. Moore left Williams College and founded a new school. The new school that Moore founded was to become Amherst College in Amherst Massachusetts. Throughout the years Amherst and Williams have had a heated rivalry in the fields of academics as well as athletics. In the spring of 1859 Williams College was challenged by Amherst College to a baseball game. Williams accepted the challenge and also requested that the two schools meet in a chess match as well and Amherst agreed to that. The schools then met and discussions ensued as to where the ball game should take place. The city of Pittsfield was chosen as it was a neutral site. However, that was not without a bit of controversy as Amherst complained that Pittsfield was not a neutral site given its close proximity to Williams College. Along with the chess match, this turned into a two day event which ended up being hosted by the Pittsfield Baseball and Chess Club. The baseball game was held on July 1, 1859 and the chess match occurred on the next day. So on the corner of North Street and Maplewood in the city of Pittsfield, the first ever intercollegiate baseball game was played, pitting Amherst College versus Williams College. Amherst was victorious in the contest which went 26 innings and ended with the final score being 73 to 32 in favor of Amherst.

When it came to 1859 and the rules, there were a set of New York rules and a set of Massachusetts rules. The two schools decided to use Massachusetts rules and they also agreed that there would be 13 players on a team. The first team to score 65 runs would be declared the winner. What is kind of funny is that neither Amherst nor Williams had an organized baseball team at the time, so democracy took over and the teams ended up being filled by players the students at the two schools had voted for. Fast forward to 150 years later on Sunday May 3, 2009 at Wahconah Park, Williams and Amherst met for another game in this long and historic rivalry. The game was televised on ESPNU and the nationally syndicated show "Talking Baseball" was broadcast from the park as well. For those of us who are statistically minded there have been 323 baseball games played between Williams and Amherst, and Amherst is ahead in the all-time series with 189 wins while Williams has 131 wins, with two ties in the series as well.

But that is not the only part of baseball history that Williams College is a part of although this next part ties two events together. On April 23, 1923 a young pitcher for the Columbia University baseball team set a record when he struck out 17 Williams College batters during a ballgame between the two schools. The pitcher later went on to play in the majors where he won six World Series titles and two American League MVP awards as well. This man was also voted to the All Star team for six consecutive years. That player from Columbia was Lou Gehrig, otherwise known as the "Iron Horse." However, that is not the only historical event that happened that day in baseball, for it was on the day, April 23, 1923 that Yankee Stadium opened its gates for the first time.

Williams College also has many well-known and famous alumni in all fields such as Elia Kazan who as a 1931 Williams College graduate later went on to direct such classic movies as Gentlemen's Agreement and On the Waterfront. Stephen Sondheim, composer and lyricist, and James Garfield, the 20th president of the United States, are some of these graduates. But this is about baseball, so let's see who in the field of baseball has an academic connection to Williams College.

When it comes to alumni from Williams College who later went into major league baseball, the man most closely associated with both Williams College and baseball is no one better known than George Michael Steinbrenner III aka"The Boss."

Steinbrenner was born on July 4, 1930 in Rocky River, Ohio the only son of Rita Haley and Henry George Steinbrenner II. He also has two sisters, Susan and Judy. His father Henry was a world class athlete in track and field as a hurdler and while he was at the Massachusetts Institute for Technology, he graduated number one in his engineering class. George II became a very wealthy man in the shipping industry by owning and operating the ships that hauled grain and ore across the Great Lakes.

George III went to the Culver Military Academy in Illinois and he graduated there in 1948. He then went on to Williams College where he obtained a Bachelor of Arts degree after graduating in 1952. He was an average student, but active in the classroom. He was also a hurdler like his father although not quite as good. He also was a halfback on the Williams College football team as a senior. He was on the staff of the Williams Record as a sports editor. He also played the piano in the band and was a member of the Delta Kappa Epsilon fraternity. He later joined the United States Air Force where he was commissioned as a second lieutenant. He got a Master's Degree in physical education while doing post graduate work at Ohio State University. Also while at Ohio State, he served as a graduate assistant to legendary Buckeye coach Woody Hayes. The year Steinbrenner was there Ohio State went undefeated and won the national collegiate football championship.

In 1960 Steinbrenner became involved with the Cleveland Pipers of the American Basketball League. The bad thing was that the league folded after the 1962 season just after his team had won the league title. Steinbrenner and his partners lost quite a lot of money, and it took him awhile to pay off all of the creditors. By 1972 he had purchased Kinsman Transport which was a family owned company, and he also helped to found the American Ship Building Company. So on January 3, 1973 George M Steinbrenner and Michael Burke led a group of investors who purchased the New York Yankees baseball team from CBS for around $10 million. After he became majority owner of the team, he became famous and very demanding as he changed management personnel at a rapid rate. In fact during the first 23 years of his ownership of the Yankees, Steinbrenner changed managers 20 times and also went through 11 general managers in the first 30 years of owning the Yankees. But this, like his other forays in the field of athletics, led to great success. He had been part of a team that won a national championship in college football, he had been part of an ownership group that won a title in the American Basketball League and in the 30 plus years of owning the New York Yankees his teams won World Series titles in 1977,1978, 1996, 1998,1999,2000 and 2009.

Even though he had a reputation as being overbearing and humorless, he did in fact have a sense of humor. Because of his military schooling and background, he was very adamant about players having neatly trimmed mustaches and short hair. One day Lou Pinella was in his office and was complaining because he (Pinella) had to get his hair cut to conform to the rules. Pinella told Steinbrenner that the Lord Jesus Christ had long hair and that seemed to make George think for a minute. He and Pinella then walked out of his office and stood looking over a pond. Steinbrenner turned to Pinella and said, "When you can walk across that pond like Christ, then you can have long hair like him. Until then you must cut your hair." He was also able to poke fun at himself as he had once gotten on Derek Jeter for his (Jeter) going out and partying all night in the city. He and Jeter were then in a commercial where they both ended up dancing in a conga line and paying for the night with a VISA card.

But for all his bravado he delivered what he said he would. He promised the Yankee fans he would bring the team back to prominence and bring the World Series Championship back to New York. He did winning the first of seven world titles in 1977. He also had the ability to make money as when he bought the Yankees , he and his investment group paid $10 million dollars for the team which is now valued at $1.2 billion dollars. After he passed away in 2010, many things came out about him and it had many people rethinking that maybe he wasn't such a bad guy after all. He had many philanthropic gestures like giving $1 million dollars to help set up a fund for the victims of the Virginia Tech massacre. He also set up a charity to pay for the college tuition for the children of police officers killed in the line of duty. He also had a favorite restaurant in Tampa that fell behind on the mortgage payments and he paid off the mortgage. In fact some of his friends and up and coming athletes were on the Yankee payroll for no other reason other than sentiment.

In closing, this part it would be impossible to describe the life of this man in only a couple of pages, but if it had to be done, the best way to describe him would be by the inscription that is on his headstone. It is short and simple but definitely to the point. It says, "He never stopped trying."

George Steinbrenner was not the only member of his family to attend Williams College. His youngest son Harold Z. (Hal) Steinbrenner is also an alumnus of Williams College having graduated from there in 1991. He also had an MBA from the University of Florida and like his father also attended Culver Military Academy.

It is very hard to follow in the footsteps of someone who casts a shadow like George Steinbrenner, but Hal appears to be up to the task of running the Yankee Empire. He has been involved in the Yankees and the Steinbrenner business empire since he was 21 years old. In addition to being co-chairperson and managing general partner of the Yankees, Hal oversees the baseball and business operations of the ball club as well as directing the finances of the organization and the Yankee Global Enterprises and its affiliates. He is on the board of directors of Legends Hospitality LLC, which is a combination of merchandising and concessions that was developed with the Dallas Cowboys. That is not all for Hal is also the chairman and CEO of Steinbrenner Hotel Properties and sits on the Board of Directors for both the Boys and Girls Clubs of Tampa Bay and the Special Operations Warrior Foundation.

He has inherited his father's desire to win which bodes well for Yankee fans everywhere. He is a fiscally responsible person who still manages to put the best team possible on the playing field. At first it did not seem as though Hal had a desire to run the club, but he has managed to accomplish a lot of great things that help to keep the Yankees at the top of the baseball world and it surely can be said that both men represent Williams College quite well.

In the history of baseball there have been nine commissioners: Kennesaw Mountain Landis, Albert "Happy" Chandler, Ford C. Frick, William D. Eckert, Bowie Kuhn, Peter V. Ueberroth, A. Barlett Giamatti, Francis T. "Fay" Vincent and Allen H. "Bud" Selig. These men helped to shape baseball through some rough times with Solomon- like decisions, and one of them is a graduate of Williams College.

Francis "Fay" Vincent was born in Waterbury, Connecticut on May 29, 1938 and he was the eighth baseball commissioner. He served from September 13, 1989 until September 7, 1992. Besides being the commissioner of baseball, Vincent was also a partner in the Washington DC law firm of Caplin and Drysdale, and he was an Associate Director of the Division of Corporate Finance of the United States Securities and Exchange Commission. He was also the chairman of Columbia Pictures and vice chairman of Coca Cola starting in 1982. In 1986 he was promoted to Executive Vice President of Coca Cola which put him in charge of the company's entertainment activities.

Vincent is a graduate of the Hotchkiss School in Lakeville, Connecticut and a member of the class of 1960 at Williams College, which he attended on a full academic scholarship. He was an honors graduate at Williams and also graduated from Yale Law School in 1963. As a youngster he was a good athlete who displayed talents in track and field as well as football. One day, however, his life changed after a prank was pulled on him while a student at Williams. He was locked in his dorm room at Williams and he climbed out on to the roof to escape. Unfortunately he slipped off the roof which was four stories off of the ground. He suffered a crushing injury to his legs as well as his spine and ended up with his legs being paralyzed. He was in traction of some form for three months and was told by doctors he would never walk again. He did not fully recover, but was able to walk again with the help of a cane.

The seventh commissioner of baseball Bart Giamatti appointed Vincent as Deputy Commissioner. After Giamatti died September 1, 1989 Vincent was named as his successor. Om October 17, 1989 while seated behind the San Francisco Giants' dugout during the World Series Game 3, he was forced to make the decision to postpone the game due to the devastating earthquake which struck the Bay Area. It would be 10 days before the World Series resumed. After the earthquake perhaps there could have been nothing that would have an impact on the game of baseball as the earthquake did, but in February of 1990 the baseball owners made a startling announcement that spring training would not start on schedule. The Major League Baseball Players Association Executive Director Donald Fehr was afraid the owners were going to institute a salary cap which would restrict the free agent choices of the players. The lockout lasted 33 days and all of spring training was wiped out. Vincent was able to work with the MLBPA and the owners and on March 19, 1990 the lockout was ended.

Now Vincent would be forced to deal with fellow Williams College alumni George Steinbrenner. On July 30, 1990 Vincent banned Steinbrenner from baseball for life because Steinbrenner had paid a gambler by the name of Howard Spira $40,000 to dig up some dirt on Yankee outfielder Dave Winfield who had sued Steinbrenner because of alleged missed payments to Winfield's foundation. The ban was lifted though after Vincent left office in 1993. Two years later in 1992, Vincent had pitcher Steve Howe suspended for life for repeated drug offenses. He threatened to have Gene Michael, Buck Showalter and Jack Lamb expelled from the game because they were going to testify on behalf of Howe. The three men did ultimately testify and remained in baseball keeping the jobs they held in the Yankee organization.

Throughout his term in office as commissioner, Vincent had a rocky relationship with the baseball owners that culminated with him resigning after the owners took a no- confidence vote in him with the voting margin being 18-9. The owners were upset because Vincent had intervened during the 1990 lockout and also because of dwindling TV ratings. After resigning Vincent was replaced by Bud Selig and he (Vincent) became involved in the New England Collegiate Baseball League as its president from 1998 through 2003. He became a private investor and an author as he wrote some books on baseball. He also returned to Williams College in 2007 with sportscaster Bob Costas for a discussion called "A Conversation About Sports."

Jim Duquette was a member of the Williams College class of 1988 where he was a standout baseball player. He has been in an executive position in baseball, most notably with the New York Mets where he was a General Manager. He remained with the Mets and then moved to the Baltimore Orioles where he worked with General Manager Mike Flanagan. He is now the co-host of a show called "Power Alley" on Sirus XM Radio's Major League Baseball Network.

QUIZ ANSWERS

1. TRUE

2. TRUE

3. Lou Gehrig struck out 17 Williams College batters while pitching for Columbia and Yankee Stadium opened up

4. True

5. Pittsfield Colts of the New York State League

6. Jack Chesbro of Adams and Frank Grant of Pittsfield

7. TRUE

8. Carlton Fisk

9. Len Barker (perfect game) AJ Burnett(no hitter)

10. FALSE Massachusetts ranks seventh all time

11. South End Grounds Boston Braves 1876-1914, Fenway Park Boston Red Sox 1912 to present, Braves Field Boston Braves 1915-1952, Dartmouth Grounds Boston Reds 1884, Congress Street Grounds Boston Reds 1890 and Huntington Avenue Grounds Boston Americans/Red Sox

1901-1911

12. Berkshire Pleasure Park

13. Lee Raymond

14. D. Carlton Fisk

15. Harold "Pie" Traynor

16. John Clarkson, Tim Keefe and Tom Glavine

17. Greg Maddox

18. Walter "Rabbit" Maranville

19. Jack Chesbro, John Clarkson, Mickey Cochrane, Candy Cummings, Leo Durocher, Tom Glavine, Frank Grant, Tim Keefe, Joe Kelly, Connie Mack, Rabbit Maranville, Tommy McCarthy, Wilbert Robinson, Pie Traynor

20. Williams College and Amherst, it was at the corner of North Street and Maplewood in Pittsfield, final score was 73-32

Baseball in the Bay State Bibliography

Pittsfield's place in Baseball History www.berkshireeagle.com/artofthegame

History of Baseball-www.bugabooa/pine.com/article/early-history-of-baseball-in-america

History of Baseball-www.buzzle.com/article/history-of-baseball.html

Some history of Baseball-whoinventedbaseball.com/some-history-of-baseball

Early history of Baseball in America-ezinearticle.com/Early history of Baseball in America

Early References in Baseball: Baseball Chronology-www.baseball-chronology.com

www.greatdreams.com

Origin of Baseball---www.sports-facts.com

Stoolball and Stowball www.tradegames.org.uk

Stoolball: a medieval game http://slumberland.org

Prisoners base www.britannica.com

Prisoners base www.databaseof games.com

Prisoners base www.inquiry.net

Stoolball, Rounders, Townball, Lapta, Oina, Pesapallo, Brannboll, Cricket en.wikipedia.org

What is the history of baseball www.stevepinto.com

Origins of baseball en.wikipedia.org

Major League Baseball Rules Changes Throughout History www.majorleagueblogging.com

Knickerbocker Baseball Rules www.baseball-almanac.com

The Massachusetts Game en.wikipedi.org

Pittsfield's 1791 baseball Bylaw pittsfieldlibrary.org

Pittsfield: Small city big time baseball boston.redsox.mlb.com

City of Pittsfield honored for role in baseball history www.boston-herald.com

Pittsfield Electrics (Eastern Association), Pittsfield Hillies, Pittsfield Cubs, Pittsfield Red Sox, Pittsfield Senators, en.wikipedia.org

Pittsfield Colts www.baseball-reference.com

1894 Pittsfield Colts sabrpedia.org

Pittsfield Colonials www.baseballdigest.com

Wahconah Park www.leagueoffans.org

History Pittsfield 250 pittsfield250.com

Wahconah Park en.wikiopedia.org

Wahconah Park www.davidpetrusza.com

Wahconah Park www.charliesballparks.com

New baseball team readies move to Pittsfield www.berkshireeagle.com

Elysian Fields Quarterly www.efq.com

1st collegiate baseball game athletics.williams.edu

Amherst Athletics www.amherst.edu

150th anniversary of 1st collegiate baseball game Williams.presto-sports.com

Jim Duquette, George Steinbrenner, Hal Steinbrenner, Fay Vincent, Dan Duquette en.wikipedia.org

George Steinbrenner's place in Amherst/Williams Rivalry www.nytimes.com

Post Mortem-The little known George Steinbrenner voices.washingtonpost.com

Hal Steinbrenner remains in charge of the New York Yankees sports.espn.go.com

What everyone should know about the sons of George Steinbrenner voices.yahoo.com

Biographical Encyclopedia of the Negro baseball Leagues by James A Riley

Encyclopedia of Minor League Baseball 3rd edition Baseball America

Fenway 1912 The Birth of a Ballpark and Championship Year and Fenway's Remarkable 1st Year by Glenn Stout

George: The Poor Little Rich Boy Who Built the Yankee Empire by Peter Golenbock

Steinbrenner: The Last Lion of Baseball by Bill Madden

Baseball in the Garden of Eden by John Thorn

www.baseball-reference.com/minors/teams

http://projectballpark.org

http://www.baseball-reference.com/bio/MA_born

http://baseballhall.org

http://www.baseball-almanac.com

http://sabr.org

http://negroleaguebaseball.com

http://www.coe.ksu.edu/nlbemuseum/history

The New England League of Baseball History by Charlie Bevis

Black baseball in Boston: recovering a lost legacy http://www.baystate.banner.com/archives

Cape Cod League Baseball, Bourne Braves, Hyannis Harbor Hawks, Cotuit Kettlers, Brewster Whitecaps, Wareham Gatemen, Harwich Mariners, http://en.wikipedia.org

Cotuit Kettlers www.kettlers.org/history

SABR biography page for the following ballplayers: Bob Adams, Harry Agganis, Mike Balas, Mark Belanger, Marty Bergen, Peter Bergeron, George Bignell, Hugh Bradley, Kitty Bransfield, Jack Chesbro, John Clarkson, Walter Clarkson, Mickey Cochrane, Tony Conigliaro, Bill Conway, Dick Conway, Ed Crane, Same Crane, Jim Cudworth, Candy Cummings, Claude Davidson, Fred Doe, Tim Donahue, Denny Driscoll, Leo Durocher, Turk Farrell, Mark Fidrych, Ed Gallagher, Jim Galvin, Daff Gammons, Doc Gautreau, Russ Gibson, Haddie Gill, Barney Gilligan, Skinny Graham, Eddie Grant, Gene Hermanski, Tom Hernon, Paul Howard, Hal Janvrin, John Keefe, Skip Lockwood, Walter Lonergan, Joe Lucey, Lou Lucier, Tony Lupien, Danny MacFayden, Connie Mack, Bunny Madden, Frank Mahar, Chris Mahoney, Rabbit Maranville, Bill Mareshall, Ray Martin, Chick Maynard, Tommy McCarthy, Marty McHale, Stuffy McInnis, Jud McLaughlin, Ralph McLeod, Doc McMahon, Jack Mills, Fred Mitchell, Freddie Moncewicz, Pat Moran, Cy Morgan, Allie Moulton, Hugh Mulcahy, Joe Mulligan, Danny Murphy, Alex Mustaikis, Buck O'Brien, Mike Palm, Arlie Pond, Art Rico, Wilbert Robinson, Sy Rosenthal, Mike Ryan, Dick Siebert, Jack Slattery, Doug Smith, Wally Snell, Andy Spognardi, Denny Sullivan, Carl Sumner, Pussy Tebeau, Pie Traynor, Wilbur Wood

About the Author

Kevin Larkin has been an avid baseball fan for most of his life. Like all boys growing up he harbored a dream of playing baseball but unfortunately he could not hit a curveball so he spent his time reading and collecting baseball books. He is a retired police officer living in his hometown of Great Barrington Massachusetts nestled in the heart of the Berkshires in Massachusetts. He has two children, a daughter Ashley and a son Steven and he has passed his love for baseball onto them. He now works as a security guard at Fairview Hospital in Great Barrington Massachusetts. Baseball in the Baystate is his first attempt at writing.

....

About the Cover Painting

Massachusetts artist Tom Warner was born and raised in Great Barrington where he paints and has his studio. Many of his paintings are in private collections and his work is also in the James Weldon Johnson collection at Emory University and Fisk University honoring Civil Rights leader James Weldon Johnson. Others who have his work include President Bill Clinton and famed Boston Marathon runner Bill Rodgers. He is also listed in Berkshire View: Exhibiting Some of America's Finest US Treasures and American Art Gallery, Greatest American Painters.

"As the late artist Norman Rockwell said to me when I was a young artist, if you are going to paint a picture have it tell a story, otherwise don't bother painting." "I am pleased to be painting the cover for Kevin Larkin's book. His appreciation and passion of baseball is unmatched by anyone I have met and so my painting for the cover to his book is to honor that enthusiasm".

In encompassing the spirit of baseball in Massachusetts the cover shows a bat, a glove and a baseball all with special meaning.

The glove is a Wilco Model made in Woburn Massachusetts where at a time they had 26 leather tanneries. Oh to have a Wilco Model glove today. The bat is a 1924 Wright and Ditson, not just any bat but the first bat the Red Sox used with their team name on the bat. Founder George Wright was named to the Baseball Hall of Fame in 1937 after a career with the Cincinnati Red Stockings and after that team folded, the Boston Red Stockings. A Massachusetts Spalding Model ball would be my choice for the sun in my painting for where there is baseball the sun shines in our hearts.

Finally with great thought a baseball diamond on the state map of Massachusetts. First base towards Boston is where our state capital holds so much baseball history. On to second base where the base represents the town city of Amherst the city which had one of the first participants in a collegiate baseball game. Heading towards third base is Pittsfield where the earliest known reference of playing baseball was discovered. The 1791 bylaw prohibited anyone from playing baseball within the area of a meeting house. Finally home plate is the Springfield area. In the earliest days of baseball home plate was made of wood or stone tile. Springfield native and former major leaguer Robert M Keating changed that and in 1887 patented his invention, the two part home plate made of rubber.